Running: The Consequences

Running:
The Consequences

by
Richard C. Crandall

McFarland & Company, Inc., Publishers
Jefferson, North Carolina, and London

Library of Congress Cataloguing-in-Publication Data

Crandall, Richard C.
  Running: The consequences.

  Bibliography: p. 225
  Includes index.
  1. Running—Physiological aspects.   2. Running—
Psychological aspects.   I. Title.
RC1220.R8C73   1986   617'.1027   85-43574

ISBN 0-89950-201-6 (acid-free natural paper)

Printed in the United States of America.

McFarland   Box 611   Jefferson NC 28640

To my father
whose love and wisdom provided me
with the freedom and guidance to grow

Contents

Bibliography

Preface

Like most exercises, sports or other vigorous activities, running has undergone numerous changes in recent decades, both in the physical dimensions and in the perceptions of men and women. Each stage can be characterized, for the runners' needs were different in each. For convenience, let us say there are five stages. While elements of the first four stages are clearly still present, the emphasis has shifted to the fifth stage.

The first stage consisted primarily of "how to." As many who were reading the running literature of the fifties and sixties remember, hundreds of articles and books appeared containing anecdotal or common sense reports of how to run. Later they branched off into "how to run your first 10-kilometer" or "your first marathon."

The second stage was marked by biographies and autobiographies. At times it seemed as though anyone who had ever run, from world class runners to "average" citizens, wrote an account of their running life.

The third was the "philosophy" stage. Here running became more than just a sport or exercise, it became an existential experience. Although I do not believe that the writings of this stage were intended to justify participation in a grueling, sweaty, physical sport in a hedonistic, clean, cerebral society, it was nonetheless interpreted by many to provide an apology for running.

The fourth stage is the one currently in vogue, the injury stage. Most everyone is aware that there can be these unfortunate consequences to running. As I write in early 1986, books and articles on how to prevent or heal injuries abound. This new interest of runners has occurred at a good time, and provides an excellent base for a fifth stage in the recent evolution of runners' concerns, namely thorough, comprehensive, and scientific analyses of all aspects of running.

Currently, runners have two choices if they want to find out about the medical, that is, physiological, consequences of running: professional journals and popular magazines. The professional journals are often too technical for the layperson and furthermore there are literally hundreds of them in English alone. Although the popular running magazines have frequently included articles on the scientific basis of running, they often have had a bias toward the more positive aspects. This is understandable since their circulation and advertising are dependent upon runners continuing to run. Many have a tendency, however, to report only certain portions of professional articles or to "stretch" the conclusions of a scientific report. Most also try to bring closure to an issue, even if closure is not warranted.

The present book was written because there was clearly a need. Although millions of Americans run, most do so under the assumption that running is strictly beneficial. I have heard runners recite clichés like, "Anything that hurts that much must be good for you." This book will allow runners to decide for themselves, from scientific research, if running is good for them.

I have certain expectations about this book. First, nearly every reader is likely to discover that some well known "fact" about running is a myth. Second, some will claim that the book is too technical. Third, some will complain that I have not been technical enough. I have tried to write in a way that both the lay reader and the exercise physiologist or physician can understand what I have said, even if both are unhappy to some degree with the way I have said it. (And those desiring more information have the bibliography to consult; it is arranged by chapter and is at the back of the book.)

Fourth, I am almost certain that someone will be unhappy because there are many issues left unresolved. Too often answers have been given for "runners," when they really only apply to certain runners. Each runner or would-be runner needs to satisfy him- or herself through more reading and more talking with exercise experts, and doctors. This book is an especially good place to begin.

Fifth, some will point out that the book is not "complete," a charge I will readily admit to. I have not covered all of the systems of the body, all possible age groups, or a number of other areas that I could have. I have addressed the major issues in running and the major concerns of runners.

In writing the book I have tried to concentrate mostly on recent literature. To find my sources I conducted a computer search of relevant data banks. With only one or two exceptions, I have reported only on studies conducted on human beings. I will let a rat write the definitive book on the consequences of treadmill running for rats.

There are several people I would like to acknowledge. First, my parents who even though things didn't always turn out as they had expected, never stopped trusting, believing, supporting, encouraging, or loving me. Second, Sue, who has twice had to put up with my absence while I have gone to the office to "work on the book." I sincerely hope that by reading this book she will acquire the knowledge that will allow her to "pick up her pace" on our runs through Lakeshore. Third, to Amanda the swimmer. There will now be more time to talk and take bike rides in the country. Fourth, to Jordan who will be happy to know that there will now be time for fishing, but unhappy to find out he is going to have to bait his own hook.

Thanks to Shirley for bringing happiness, and for arranging great surprise parties.

1
Running and the Heart

Introduction

There are few areas in running that have been written about as frequently or about which as many claims have been made as the heart. Over the last decade there have been numerous claims and counter-claims about the impact of running on the heart.

On the positive side writers have claimed that in comparison to those who do not exercise runners are: immune from or have a lower rate of coronary heart disease, have greater longevity and better health, and have fewer coronary heart disease risk factors such as high blood pressure or obesity. It has also been claimed that running will stop or reverse the progression of coronary heart disease, and that for those who have had a heart attack running is an excellent form of heart rehabilitation.

However, not all writers have written positively of the benefits of running on the heart. In fact, some writers have claimed that running damages the heart. Some of those who are pessimistic about the benefits of running on the heart have pointed to the large number of runners who have died from "heart attacks." Many of these dead runners were found to have had severe heart disease, something from which running was supposed to protect them. Many of these writers also believe that in the near future there will be a significant increase in the number of deaths from heart disease for those who ran for several years and then stopped. The belief is that the heart muscle, which became enlarged through exercise, will turn to fat from non-use and that this enlarged mass of fat will predispose these individuals to heart disease.

A third group has taken a more neutral position. They claim that it is not running per se that contributes to the better health and greater longevity of runners. Some individuals in this group claim that it is the runners' life style, not running, that protects them. These individuals contend that the health benefits of running can be obtained without sweating, periodic shin splints, and a closet full of sweaty clothing; one simply has to avoid smoking and smokers, maintain a normal weight to height ratio, and eat a sensible diet. Others in this group contend that it is not running *or* life style that offers protection. Rather, they claim, it is simply that runners are initially an elite group in terms of health. This, they believe, is easily demonstrated by the fact that runners' bodies manage to survive horrific abuse from

1

running on a regular basis. Thus, it is not running that is beneficial but rather a select group in terms of health that is running.

The proponents of all three positions have made their claims well-known to anyone who reads or listens to the mass media. The question is, of course, "which position is correct?"

In an attempt to answer the above question this chapter is broken into five sections. The first section will examine the extent of heart disease in contemporary American society. In the second section the development of the belief that exercise is beneficial in preventing heart disease will be presented. The third section will investigate the impact of running on the coronary heart disease risk factors of high blood pressure, cholesterol level, smoking, and obesity. The fourth section will evaluate one of the most widely known and frequently quoted hypotheses in running, namely that running a marathon will provide the runner with immunity from coronary heart disease. The fifth and last section will concern itself with a review of the effectiveness of running as a form of rehabilitation for victims of heart attacks.

Much of the literature is best understood if we define some of the terms that are used.

Heart disease is a very broad term that can refer to a large number of pathological conditions affecting the heart. For this book we will separate heart disease into two types. The first is heart disease that affects the vessels that supply blood to the heart muscle, and the second is heart disease that affects the heart muscle. As we will see shortly, one type of heart disease often causes the other.

A number of terms are used to describe the first type of heart disease noted above, namely that which affects the vessels that supply blood to the heart. Some of the terms are *cardiovascular disease, coronary heart disease, ischemic heart disease,* and *coronary artery disease.* These are all generic designations for some of the numerous conditions that may affect the coronary arteries. This book will use the term coronary heart disease when discussing the first type.

The most frequently mentioned type of coronary heart disease is *arteriosclerosis.*It refers to a disease of the arteries that is characterized by either a loss of elasticity or by a thickening of the internal walls of an artery, both of which restrict the flow of blood to critical organs such as the heart or the brain. There are three types of arteriosclerosis. For this book we are only concerned with one, *atherosclerosis. Athero* means mass of fat and this disease refers to the formation of fatty masses, sometimes called *atheromas,* on the inner lining of coronary arteries. After gradually enlarging over a period of years the atheroma can either severely or completely restrict the flow of blood to the heart muscle.

The reduction in the flow of blood to the heart can bring about the second type of heart disease, namely that which affects the heart muscle. This is commonly called a "heart attack." Where heart disease refers to a condition, "heart attack" refers to an event. Again, "heart attack" is a very general term and can refer to a variety of medical conditions. When someone has suffered a heart attack it generally means that part of the heart muscle has died. The reduction in the flow of blood to the heart, from a disease such as atherosclerosis, is called *myocardial ischemia*. The term *myocardial* refers to the heart muscle, or *myocardium*. *Myo* means muscle and *cardium* refers to the heart. *Ischemia* refers to an inadequate blood/oxygen supply to maintain the life of the affected area. When this occurs a "heart attack," or *myocardial infarction*, occurs. An *infarction* means that tissue has died because of a lack of blood/oxygen. Thus atherosclerosis can cause myocardial ischemia which can bring about a myocardial infarction.

With this limited but necessary vocabulary we are now ready to examine the extent of heart disease in contemporary American society.

Cardiovascular Disease in American Society

Cardiovascular disease is currently the major cause of death in the United States. In 1980 almost one million Americans died from cardiovascular disease; 38.3 percent of all deaths that year were from cardiovascular disorders. The second leading cause of death was cancer, which accounted for 21.1 percent of all deaths.

Cardiovascular disease is a major cause of death for almost every age group. For the age group 15–24 cardiovascular disease is outranked by accidents, suicide, homicide, and cancer. In the age category 25–44 only accidents rank higher than cardiovascular disease as a cause of death. For the age group 45–64 cardiovascular disease is the number one cause of death for men; for women, cancer is number one and cardiovascular disease number two. For the age group 65 and over, cardiovascular disease is the leading cause of death for both sexes (U.S. Bureau of Census, 1984).

From the above figures it can be seen why cardiovascular disease has been described as the "Achilles tendon" of contemporary American society. Not only is it an all too prevalent disease but a very deadly one. This can be clearly seen not only in the death rate but also by the fact that one-third to one-half of first "heart attacks" are fatal. Cardiovascular disease also produces long periods of disability. In fact, cardiovascular disease is the major cause of hospitalization and disability for those under 65 years of age.

The good news is that the death rate from cardiovascular disease has been declining since 1950. In fact, between 1950 and 1970 the death rate from cardiovascular disease decreased by 18 percent. During the 1970s it declined at a rate of about 1 percent a year. Some of the explanations for the decrease are the increase in the quantity and quality of emergency medical services and of coronary care units, a decrease in the percentage of the population that smokes, improved management of high blood pressure, a decrease in the dietary intake of saturated fats, and an increase in the percentage of the population engaging in physical exercise (see Thom and Kannel, 1981).

Exercise is widely believed to be one of the factors involved in the reduction of the death rate from cardiovascular disease. One of the questions that we might naturally ask is, "How did the belief that exercise is beneficial in the prevention of cardiovascular disease develop?"

The Belief That Exercise Is Beneficial

As we have seen above, cardiovascular disease is "epidemic" in contemporary American society. As most readers are aware, there are many other countries where cardiovascular disease is virtually unknown. For example, Sula Benet's book *Abkhasians: The Long-Living People of the Caucasus*, says that signs of arteriosclerosis are found infrequently among the Abkhasians and when they are found it is in "extreme" old age. Similar studies have appeared on societies in South America, Central America, and Africa. Thus, heart disease is not concomitant with growing older. Nor is it an inevitable consequence of living in an industrial society. For example, in the United States in 1979 the death rate for men from ischemic heart disease was 261.1 per 100,000. It was 39.6 in Japan. For women the corresponding figures were 132.8 and 22.6 (U.S. Bureau of the Census, 1982). Thus, we have two progressive, industrial societies with very different rates of heart disease. The question thus becomes, "What can be done to prevent or at least reduce the development of heart disease?"

The first step is, of course, to find the cause. Researchers have implicated many factors that contribute to coronary heart disease: hypertension, blood lipid abnormalities, cigarette smoking, physical inactivity, obesity, diet, heredity, personality, electrocardiogram abnormalities, and stress. Researchers have generally found that as the number of risk factors increases, the risk of a "coronary event" (i.e., heart attack) increases exponentially. Although the above factors have been associated with the development of coronary heart disease for over two decades, many researchers are still hesitant to state unequivocally that they are "causal" factors.

To find out the causes of coronary heart disease many epidemiological studies have been conducted. Epidemiology is the branch of medicine that deals with the patterns of health and illness in a society. Epidemiologists try to ascertain the causes of diseases as well as ways to eliminate the causes. Very often, rather than using the laboratory, epidemiologists study large groups of individuals living in society to discover if those manifesting certain illnesses were exposed to risk factors to which those without the disease were not exposed. Epidemiologists also study the consequences of selected life styles on the development of certain illnesses and diseases. Thus, society becomes the laboratory and the variables that affect health are not introduced artificially but are generally simply a result of life style.

The first epidemiological studies of the impact of physical activity on coronary heart disease started to appear in the early 1950s. These studies did not examine exercise or running per se but the amount of energy expended at work, or the amount of energy expended during leisure activities.

To put this research in context, the reader must remember that although the benefits of physical activity are widely publicized in contemporary society, in the past physical activity was believed by many to damage the heart. This belief was held because many individuals believed in the "mechanical concept" of the body. This belief compared the body to a machine and stated that the more the body was used the sooner it would break down and wear out.

One example of how differently a consequence of physical exercise was perceived of in the past can be seen by examining beliefs about heart rate. While in contemporary society a low heart rate is generally believed to be symptomatic of good health, the reverse was true in the not too distant past. For example, during World War II, several runners were "rejected" for military service because of their low heart rates. One specific example of this was Leslie MacMitchell. Although a forgotten name to most individuals, during his track career at New York University MacMitchell was heralded as the first man who would break the four minute barrier in the mile. After graduation from college in 1942 MacMitchell was twice rejected for military service because of his low, 38–43 beats per minute, heart rate (Mattingly, 1976). It should also be noted that until very recently the enlargement of the heart, which is now seen as a normal consequence of continued strenuous exercise, was considered to be representative of a pathological condition.

The trend away from thinking of exercise as something bad for health started to emerge in the late 1940s and then developed in the 1950s, 1960s, and especially the 1970s and 1980s. As noted above, the early studies did not examine exercise per se but rather the amount of heart disease in men with active and sedentary occupations.

One of the first studies that examined the extent of coronary heart disease in men with active and sedentary occupations was published in 1953 by Morris and his associates (1953a) on employees of the London Transport Authority. The researchers examined 31,000 bus drivers, who had sedentary jobs, and conductors, who had to do a considerable amount of walking and climbing on double-decker buses. In comparison to the conductors it was found that the drivers had significantly more coronary heart disease, that the disease manifested itself earlier clinically, and that those having a "heart attack" had a higher fatality rate. For example, the rate of the first clinical episode of coronary heart disease for drivers was 2.7 per 1000. It was 1.9 for conductors. In terms of the age at which the first clinical symptoms appeared, the rates for the drivers per 1000 for the age categories 35–44, 45–54, and 55–64 were .7, 2.5 and 6.5. For the conductors the corresponding figures were 0, 2.0 and 5.0. More significant, however, was the type and severity of the first clinical manifestation of the disease. Among the conductors, heart disease was more likely to manifest itself as angina pectoris, or chest pain. Among the drivers it was much more likely to appear as a "heart attack" and result in death. The mortality rates following the first clinical manifestation of coronary heart disease were twice as high for the drivers as the conductors.

Although the results appeared to be unequivocal, Morris recognized that the differences might be due to factors other than the amount of physical activity. For example, the differences could be accounted for if men

with different physiological constitutions selected different types of occupations, or if different types or levels of mental strain were associated with
different occupations. To further investigate this Morris and his associates
published a parallel study (1953a) on workers in the post office and civil service. Morris reasoned that his conclusions on bus drivers and conductors
would have greater credibility if he could find other occupational categories
that exhibited similar results. That is, perhaps the differences in the transit
workers were not due to physical activity but factors such as mental strain.
However, if other occupational groups with both sedentary and active jobs
were also found to have heart disease rates similar to the London Transit
workers, then the probability that it was that occupational physical activity, and not other coronary risk factors, would be increased.

In this second study Morris compared seven grades of civil service
workers. The only physically active occupation was that of postman. Some
of the sedentary occupations examined were postal and telegraph officers,
supervisors, and telephone operators. Although conclusions in this study
were limited because of greater job mobility and transfer, the study still
found that coronary heart disease was lower in postmen than in those with
sedentary occupations. The analysis indicated that the disease pattern was
similar in postal workers and civil servants as it was in the transit workers.

On the basis of these two studies, Morris and his associates (1953b) concluded that "men in physically active jobs had a lower incidence of coronary
heart disease in middle age than have men in physically inactive jobs." Morris also noted that those with physically active jobs had the disease manifest
itself in a less severe form, and that they had a lower death rate from the
disease.

To extend the testing of the hypothesis, Morris and his associates
studied the occupational mortality data from three social classes. Although
the researchers postulated the existence of five social classes (Social Class
I — professionals, managers, and owners; II — lesser professionals,
managers, and owners; III — skilled workers; IV — semi-skilled workers; and
V — unskilled workers), for a variety of reasons, only classes III–V were
studied.

The three classes were then subdivided into the type of work that was
involved (heavy, intermediate, or light). Essentially, the study found that
workers involved in physically heavy work had half the coronary mortality
of those in the physically light work group. They also found that the mortality of the light workers was about the same in all three social classes. Because
the differences were found in all of the social classes, Morris claimed that
there was not a psychological factor that appeared to be involved that could
account for the excessive mortality of workers who had jobs involving little
physical energy. That is, although Morris recognized that psychological
variables, such as work satisfaction, could affect the development of coronary heart disease, he also postulated that it was "unlikely" that
psychological variables could explain the consistency of findings among the
different social classes, and different occupations.

Although the results of the research by Morris and his associates again seemed clear and unequivocal, Morris recognized that methodologically the study could be criticized and that further studies were needed on one potentially confounding variable. The weakness was that perhaps different types of men selected different types of occupations, and perhaps one "type"was more likely to have conditions that predisposed them to coronary heart disease. To investigate this factor, Morris and his associates (1956) examined one potential coronary risk factor in the bus drivers and conductors, namely physique. Since physique had been related to the likelihood of developing coronary heart disease in other studies, Morris studied the uniform sizes of conductors and bus drivers. He found that the waist and chest sizes of the drivers were larger than those of the conductors, and that this was true for even the youngest age groups. For example, the drivers were more likely to have waist sizes of 38 inches and over while the conductors were more likely to have an average waist size of 32 or less inches. This difference was found even in the 25–29 age group. Although claiming that the available data were not sufficient for a "clear judgment," this indicated that at least part of the difference in coronary heart disease rates may be due to physique rather than amount of physical activity and that different "types" of men may select different types of occupations.

Recognizing the limitations the above study imposed on his data, Morris published another study in 1958 (Morris et al., 1958) stating that, "It is a principle of epidemiological research of this type to seek evidence from as many, as various, and as independent sources as possible." He again asked the question, "Can the hearts of men be seen to vary with the kind of work they have done?"

To examine this question Morris collected 5,000 autopsy reports from 206 hospitals. Morris wanted to find out the relationship between the amount of physical activity required in the autopsied men's occupations and the frequency of ischemic myocardial heart disease. Morris was interested in men who had died from causes of death other than coronary heart disease; he wanted to find out the amount of heart disease in men who had had occupations that required different levels of energy expenditure. The occupations of the men were evaluated in terms of the amount of physical activity required as light, active, or heavy. This study allowed Morris to examine the extent of coronary heart disease among a wide age-range of men who had been killed or died from a variety of causes, and to then compare the extent of coronary heart disease development with the amount of physical activity exerted at work. By excluding men who had died from coronary heart disease, Morris eliminated men who might have been assigned light physical activity jobs because of existing heart disease and who might have therefore distorted the results.

Morris again confirmed his earlier findings. He found, for example, that heart scarring, from heart attacks, was more common in the light than the heavy occupational group. While coronary heart disease was prevalent in all the occupational categories, actual occlusion or blockage of coronary vessels was more common in the light workers than in the active or heavy workers. Morris concluded that occupations that involve physical activity protect the worker from coronary heart disease, and that men in physically active occupations have less coronary heart disease than those who are less active and what disease they have is less severe.

In 1959, after he had gathered more data, Morris published an article called "Occupation and Coronary Heart Disease." Morris made no pretense about his interpretation of the data when he said that an alternative title for the paper might have been "The Pathology of Inactivity" or "The Occupational Hazards of Sedentary and Light Work." In this study Morris repeated his earlier findings that bus drivers had a sudden death rate that was three to four times greater than that of bus conductors. He also reported that the differences in coronary heart disease rates were especially profound in the younger age groups. Morris then went on and noted the high rate of coronary heart disease among sedentary government workers. Basing his conclusions on a national study, Morris said that government workers whose jobs involved light work were more likely to develop coronary heart disease than those whose jobs involved moderate to heavy physical activity.

This study was an important extension of his study on uniform size in that Morris went on to examine other coronary risk factors. Although still believing in the importance of physical activity in the prevention of coronary heart disease, Morris started to expand his analysis to include differences in coronary risk factors between men whose occupations required them to be physically active and those whose occupations required them to be physically inactive. Although at this point Morris did not know if physical activity produced different levels of coronary risk factors or if people with different levels of coronary risk factors selected different occupations, this study was an important first step in attempting to find the answer. This was one of the first studies not just to note the differences in the rates of coronary heart disease in relationship to the amount of physical activity required in certain occupations, but to note that there were distinctions between the coronary risk factors of active and sedentary workers. For example, this study found that the workers whose occupations required light physical activity were more likely to have a higher incidence of coronary risk factors, such as high blood pressure and high cholesterol levels, and that they were more likely to be overweight than were their colleagues in more physically active occupations.

Although based on this study Morris did not diminish the importance of physical activity in the prevention of coronary heart disease, he did admit that part of the difference may be explainable by the fact that workers select certain types of occupations within governmental service based on certain characteristics. That is, obese men were more likely to select sedentary jobs than were slim men. Therefore, it may not be level of physical activity in and of itself that was the determining variable. Rather, other variables, such as blood pressure or cholesterol levels, may also be significant variables.

Thus, although Morris' studies were important and appeared to demonstrate the importance of physical exertion, the studies also found that other variables may account for the different rates of coronary heart disease. Because Morris had raised many important questions, because for the first time the American public was being made aware of the epidemic nature of heart disease, and because many individuals were starting to look for more significant ways of preventing heart disease, a host of studies started to appear which tried to clarify the questions Morris had raised.

Most of the early studies did nothing but replicate Morris' earlier findings on the relationship between coronary heart disease rates and the amount of physical activity required by an individual's occupation. In a study published in 1959 Zukel and his colleagues found a large difference in coronary heart disease rates between individuals who performed "heavy" work and those who did little physical work. A further analysis of Zukel's data revealed that individuals who did one to two hours of heavy physical work a day had a rate of coronary heart disease that was only 18 percent that of their more sedentary counterparts who performed less than an hour of heavy physical work per day (see Fox and Hyskell, 1968).

In another study published in 1960 on Chicago utility workers it was found that physically active workers had a slightly lower incidence of coronary heart disease than their less active colleagues (Stamler, 1960). And, in a retrospective study on the elderly in Birmingham, England, it was found that individuals who had been active when younger had less coronary heart disease than those who had been sedentary (Brown, 1957).

Further evidence of the protective factor of a physically demanding occupation on the prevention of coronary heart disease was added with a study on lumberjacks (Karvonen et al., 1961). Lumberjacks were studied since it was widely believed that they have one of the most physically demanding occupations in the world. The study found that the lumberjacks had less heart disease than other men living in the area with whom they were compared. This study had an important component in that it tried to discover if the differences in the rates of coronary heart disease were due to physical activity or coronary risk factors. The study examined several coronary risk factors in the two groups and concluded that the difference in coronary heart disease rates was not explainable by level of serum cholesterol, blood pressure, or smoking habits since these were similar in both groups. The authors did admit, however, that the differences may be explainable by the "type" of individual who was or who could remain a lumberjack. That is, lumberjacks are a physically elite group from which most individuals are prevented entry because of the demanding work. Additionally, those who develop physical problems must find a less physically demanding occupation.

A study similar to that of Morris was published on railway employees in the United States (Taylor et al., 1962). This particular industry was chosen because of the accuracy of the records that were available to the researchers as well as the fact that labor contracts between management and labor unions made it so that there was little mobility between the occupational categories. Thus, once an employee was assigned to one of the occupational categories, because of seniority regulations, men seldom changed to another occupational category, especially since income and privileges were associated with seniority. In this study the researchers examined three groups: clerks who had sedentary jobs, switchmen whose jobs were "moderately" active, and "section men" who replaced track and thus had very active jobs. The study found that the more energy expended on the job the lower the rate of coronary heart disease.

In 1963 Harold Kahn published a study in the *American Journal of Public Health* on postal clerks and postal letter carriers. Although this study was difficult to conduct, in part because of the amount of transfer from one job category to another, the conclusion supported the inverse relationship between physical activity and coronary heart disease.

By the middle to late 1960s most studies were becoming more complex in their analysis of data. For example, in 1966 the data supporting vigorous physical leisure-time activity were published in the *American Journal of Epidemiology*. The study examined 40,000 former University of Pennsylvania and Harvard University students. This study is important since there were student health and medical records available from when the students attended college (circa 1926–1950) as well as when the study was conducted. This provided sources of medical information at two points in time. The study found several "precursors" of death from coronary heart disease: high blood pressure, obesity, heavy cigarette smoking, shortness in stature, nonparticipation in precollege and college athletics, early parental death, and only-child status (Paffenbarger et al., 1966).

The above study was important not only in the number of variables that it examined but because it was one of the first to examine athletics. Although limited in its examination of precollege and college athletics and because it did not distinguish aerobic and nonaerobic athletics or the duration of participation in athletics, it indicated the possible importance of athletics as a factor in coronary heart disease rates.

In 1969 the authors of a study on Italian railroad workers (Menotti et al., 1969) reported that those workers in sedentary occupations had a higher incidence of coronary heart disease than those engaged in physically demanding work. This study confirmed the findings of several other studies. It was also found, however, that the men who had sedentary occupations had coronary risk factors that were higher than the men engaged in phsyically demanding occupations. The authors concluded that although level of physical activity was probably an important factor in the prevention of coronary heart disease, on the basis of this study it was impossible to formulate any conclusions.

In 1970 another set of studies on an occupational group began to emerge. These came from Dr. Ralph Paffenbarger and his associates based on their research on 3,263 longshoremen. This research is unique in that the initial research was done in 1953 and the men were then re-examined several times for more than 20 years. In a 16 year follow-up study it was found that longshoremen who had physically demanding jobs had a lower death rate from coronary heart disease than their colleagues who had jobs that were less physically demanding. In fact, the sedentary workers had a death rate from coronary heart disease that was 34 percent higher than their more active counterparts. It was interesting to note that the differences in death rates were the greatest in the younger age groups, 35–44, and then steadily decreased with increasing age. There were two possible explanations offered for this "equalizing" of death rates from coronary heart disease with increasing age. The first was that many of the sedentary workers may have been at high risk and thus died off earlier. Thus, the equalization occurred because in the less active group only the healthier longshoremen were left. The second reason may have been that with increasing age many of the longshoremen who were in the active group at the start of the study were shifted to sedentary positions through promotions or mechanization, and thus became sedentary and experienced a delayed but similar death rate from coronary heart disease as did the men who were in the nonactive group at the beginning of the study.

Unlike most studies, Paffenbarger examined several coronary risk factors such as smoking habits, blood pressure levels, and height to weight ratios. Again the results were as expected. Heavy smokers had a death rate from coronary heart disease that was double that of those who did not smoke or those who were light smokers. Those with high systolic blood pressure had a risk factor 89 percent higher than those with normal blood pressure. Finally, those who had a height to weight ratio indicating obesity had a death rate 35 percent higher than those who had a normal height to weight ratio.

In an attempt to expand scientific knowledge about coronary risk factors, Paffenbarger and his associates examined the data from a perspective that had not frequently been used in the past. Where several studies had found that sedentary workers had a higher death rate from coronary heart disease than physically active workers, these studies had also noted that the less active group also generally had more coronary risk factors. Thus, it was difficult to say if the higher death rate in the less active group was caused by a lower rate of physical activity or a higher rate of coronary risk factors. What Paffenbarger and his associates did was to compare men with the *same* coronary risk factors but who had jobs that involved different amounts of physical activity. This allowed them to ascertain if it was physical activity that was having an impact on the coronary heart disease death rate or other coronary risk factors.

They found that among longshoremen who were heavy smokers the active men had a lower death rate from coronary heart disease than those who were less active. The same trend was true for light smokers. When they examined blood pressure they found that for those who had high blood pressure, the active men had a much lower death rate from coronary heart disease than less active men with similar blood pressure readings. The same trend was found when the researchers examined height to weight ratios. That is, obese men who were active had a lower death rate from coronary heart disease than obese men who were less active. When they further examined the four risk factors (low level of occupational physical activity, high blood pressure, obesity, and smoking) it was found that the risk of death from coronary heart disease increased exponentially as the number of risk factors increased. This suggested a cumulative effect of these risk factors on the development of coronary heart disease.

In 1971 a study confirmed earlier findings on occupational activity and heart disease. This study was conducted on workers in Evans County, Georgia. The study reported that physical activity, as measured by type of work performed, appeared to protect workers from coronary heart disease. The researchers noted, however, that there appeared to be a critical physical activity threshold above which protection occurred, although they could not document the exact threshold (Cassel et al., 1971).

Some research in the early 1970s tried to discover if the different death rates from coronary heart disease were due to physical activity or coronary risk factors. One study examined the blood pressure levels of almost all of the male residents over the age of 16 in a small Michigan community. Specifically, this study wanted to see what the relationship was between physical activity and the coronary risk factors of obesity and high blood pressure. The authors found that men who expended more energy in occupational and recreational activities had lower blood pressure than their less active counterparts. However, the more active men were also leaner than the less active males. Thus, the question became, "Is it activity or leanness that protects the men from high blood pressure?" The researcher then found that regardless of body size, there was a tendency for active individuals to have lower blood pressure. Thus, an obese active individual had lower blood pressure than an obese nonactive person, and a light active individual had lower blood pressure than a light nonactive individual. (See Montoye et al., 1972).

By the early 1970s the research findings were consistent. They demonstrated that individuals who had occupations that demanded vigorous physical activity had lower death rates from coronary heart disease than those whose occupations required little or no physical activity. Although these studies were important, their results were being published at a time most individuals had occupations that did not require vigorous physical activity. The industrial age had eliminated most of it. A new trend began to emerge in the literature, the examination of leisure-time activities. The question now became, "Do those who engage in vigorous leisure-time activities have a lower death rate from coronary heart disease than those who do not?"

One of the first studies to appear that addressed this question was published by Morris (et al., 1973), the man who had investigated the relationship between occupational physical activity and coronary heart disease in the 1950s. Morris and his associates examined 16,882 executive-grade male civil servants aged 40 to 64 who were office workers in Britain. All of the workers had occupations that involved low physical activity. Since most workers could not achieve protection from coronary heart disease through their occupations, Morris wanted to find out if protection could be achieved through leisure-time activities. The men were questioned about their leisure-time activities and then classified according to the physical intensity of these activities. The study found that for men who engaged in vigorous exercise during their leisure time, the risk of developing coronary heart disease was one-third that of similar men who had nonvigorous leisure-time activities. The study concluded that habitual, vigorous exercise during leisure time for middle-aged men with sedentary occupations reduced the incidence of coronary heart disease (see also Hennekens et al., 1977).

In an extension of the 1973 study, Morris and his associates (Epstein et al., 1976) published an article in the *British Heart Journal* in which they tried to eliminate some of the limitations of previous studies. Many researchers criticized some of the early studies that demonstrated an inverse relationship between the level of physical activity and coronary heart disease by noting that samples with different risk factors had been studied and that the differences were not due to physical activity but different risk factors in the groups examined. That is, critics claimed that many researchers had failed to demonstrate that it was physical activity that was the important variable rather than life style or coronary risk factors. It may be that those who exercised were not encumbered with coronary risk factors such as obesity or high blood pressure.

To eliminate the criticisms, Morris and his associates constructed a study that involved extensive medical testing of the subjects. In this study, electrocardiographic evidence on middle-aged, male, civil servants with similar occupations and socioeconomic standing were examined. Since the occupations of the men were all sedentary, their leisure-time activities were examined and the men were classified as reporting vigorous activities or not reporting them. To further eliminate some of the criticisms of previous studies, the extensive medical testing of the men indicated that there were no significant differences between the groups in coronary risk factors such as age, height, weight, skinfold measurements, cholesterol levels, blood pressure, or smoking habits. The study found significantly fewer electrocardiogram abnormalities in the group reporting vigorous exercise in their leisure time than in the group not reporting vigorous leisure time activity. This study concluded that the differences in electrocardiograms were unlikely to be due to the effects of other variables and were probably related to the patterns of physical activity in which the men engaged.

Another study sought to eliminate one of the major criticisms of other studies, namely that there were unmeasured factors in the life style of the exercise participants that accounted for the differences reported. This study was conducted at a kibbutz in Israel and was similar to the others in that it studied workers who had jobs consuming high levels of energy and workers whose jobs required low levels. In this study, however, the men were more comparable than in some of the other studies because they had similar life styles. The kibbutz was socialistic and the men all ate in a communal dining area, had similar food, and were all at a similar socioeconomic level. The study also stated that the two categories of workers were similar in factors that may contribute to the development of coronary heart disease such as leisure-time activities, serum cholesterol, and body type. The study found that angina, myocardial infarction, and death from coronary heart disease was two to four times higher in the workers who had occupations that required a low energy output (Brunner et al., 1974).

Even though the early studies overwhelmingly reported that vigorous physical activity was inversely related to coronary heart disease, this conclusion was still being challenged by those who claimed that the studies only demonstrated that certain types of individuals chose certain types of occupations or that certain types of individuals chose to engage in vigorous leisure time activity. The critics went on and pointed out that the researchers were comparing two very different groups: men who were sedentary and probably overweight with high cholesterol and blood pressure, and men who were probably much leaner and who had lower cholesterol and blood pressure readings. The critics suggested that it was not energy output that was the causal factor in the development of coronary heart disease but rather the differences in the groups being studied.

To examine this criticism Paffenbarger (Paffenbarger et al., 1977) reported on a 21 yearlong study on longshoremen. The study found that longshoremen who were engaged in low energy work were at an 80 percent greater risk of having a fatal heart attack than longshoremen engaged in high energy work. The study also found that exercise was a cause of the reduction in fatal heart attacks, rather than simply an indication that a selection process has gone on in assigning specific occupations. Specifically, Paffenbarger noted that in 1951 the risk factors of the high and low energy workers were similar. That is, the low energy workers did not have a higher incidence of high blood pressure or cholesterol, or diagnosed heart disease. The high activity workers did weigh and smoke less, although this could not account for the 80 percent difference. The study demonstrated that physical activity is strongly associated with a lowered risk of a coronary event. The conclusion of the authors was that the importance of exercise in the prevention of coronary heart disease was no longer in question (see Thomas et al., 1961).

Further support was given the above conclusion when Kenneth H. Cooper, author of *Aerobics*, and his associates published an article in 1976 that quantified levels of fitness. Where the others generally used self-reports of leisure activities and then projected the amount of energy expended, Cooper and his associates examined cardiovascular fitness in nearly 3,000 men whose average age was 44.6 years. The men had a number of medical tests performed to assess coronary risk factors and ascertain level of fitness. The major purpose of the study was to ascertain if the level of cardiovascular fitness correlated with coronary heart disease risk factors. Cooper used his now famous cardiorespiratory fitness levels to categorize the men (very poor, poor, fair, good, excellent). He also recorded a number of medical/physiological variables such as blood pressure, heart rate, cholesterol levels, and body fat. Cooper and his associates then compared known cardiovascular risk factors, such as high blood pressure, with cardiovascular fitness levels. The authors concluded that their data showed "a direct inverse relationship between levels of cardio-respiratory fitness and variables related to a higher CHD risk. The differences in CHD risk were minimal for adjacent levels of fitness groups, but became more marked among the groups with greater differences in levels of fitness." The authors concluded by saying their data supported those of others who had found that higher levels of physical fitness appeared to protect individuals from coronary heart disease (Cooper et al., 1976).

In 1978 Paffenbarger and his associates extended their 1966 study on college alumni to include data on postgraduate physical activity patterns. This was to ascertain the association between physical activity patterns and heart disease. Based on several indices of physical energy exerted, the respondents were classified as light or vigorous, and the amount of energy expended per week was also assessed. The study found that those who expended the most energy had a 50 percent lower risk of heart attack. The study also found that men with characteristics associated with coronary heart disease reported in the 1966 study had a higher incidence of heart attacks than men without the characteristics. In a favorable light, the men with coronary risk factors who were in the high energy expenditure group had a much lower rate of heart attacks than similar but less physically active classmates (Paffenbarger et al., 1978).

In 1980 Morris and his colleagues published another study on the effects of vigorous leisure-time exercise on the prevention of coronary heart disease. This study was a follow-up of a study started in 1968 on 17,944 middle-aged male Civil Service office workers. The results of this study were consistent with previous studies. From the start of the study in 1968 to the end of the study in 1976, the men reporting vigorous leisure-time exercise had an incidence of coronary heart disease that was less than half that of their sedentary counterparts. The incidence was lower both in terms of the clinical manifestation of coronary heart disease and in terms of death from coronary heart disease.

Morris also examined several coronary risk factors for those who engaged in vigorous exercise and those who were sedentary. Although it is well known that coronary risk is greater for those whose families have a history of coronary heart disease, this study reported that for men who had similar family histories, those reporting vigorous physical activity had an incidence of heart disease about half that of men who were sedentary. It is also known that short men have a higher incidence of coronary heart disease than taller men. Again, it was found that short men engaging in vigorous exercise had an incidence rate of coronary heart disease that was about half that of their counterparts in size. The same trend was found concerning smoking, which has consistently been found to be related to the development of coronary heart disease. Again, smokers who engaged in vigorous exercise had about half the incidence of coronary heart disease as did sedentary smokers. Although there were no significant differences in blood pressure or cholesterol levels between those who engaged in vigorous exercise and those who were sedentary, the study revealed that for men reporting similar blood pressure readings those who engaged in vigorous exercise had fewer abnormal electrocardiographic readings. The same was true for cholesterol levels. The authors concluded that for those who engaged in vigorous exercise the risk of developing coronary heart disease was only 40 percent that of their sedentary counterparts.

Although the vast majority of studies were consistent in their finding that exercise was beneficial, one nagging methodological limitation was present — namely, that healthy individuals are more likely to engage in exercise than unhealthy ones. Thus, exercise may not offer protection; rather, unhealthy individuals do not exercise because of a prior illness or condition. The existing illness or condition may also predispose them to death.

A study published in the *Journal of the American Medical Association* addressed this issue in 1982 (Siscovick et al., 1982). The researchers examined all reports of out-of-hospital primary cardiac arrest cases filled out by trained paramedics for a period of more than a year. Only cases in which the cause was believed to be heart disease were considered; cases where cardiac arrest was induced by drug overdose or trauma were excluded. Detailed information was obtained on each victim of cardiac arrest, and only those who were healthy and capable of engaging in physical activity were included in the study. By only including individuals who were known to be healthy, and capable of engaging in exercise, the study sought to eliminate those with illnesses and conditions that prevented them from exercising and predisposed them to a cardiac event. Each victim of cardiac arrest was then matched with an individual in the community. Information on leisure-time activity of both the cardiac arrest and controls was gathered using a detailed questionnaire through which the researchers were able to estimate energy expenditure. The results demonstrated that the risk of a primary cardiac arrest in those who engaged in high intensity leisure-time activities was 55 to 65 percent less than for those who engaged in low intensity leisure-time activities (see Kannel, 1982).

In 1983 another study appeared, similar to that of Cooper and his associates, which relied on objective measures of physical fitness rather than self-reports to determine the effects of exercise on heart disease. The study examined the physical work capacity of 2,779 men. Coronary risk factors such as blood pressure and smoking were also noted. The men were followed for approximately five years. During the study there were 36 myocardial infarctions. The less physically fit men were twice as likely to have heart attacks as were the physically fit men. The higher rate of myocardial infarctions in the less physically fit men was not explainable by the other risk factors. Men with low physical work capacity and two risk factors were six times more likely to have heart attacks. The authors concluded that "poor physical fitness is an important risk factor" in the development of myocardial infarctions (Peters et al., 1983).

In 1984 Paffenbarger and his associates published further evidence on the benefits of physical activity. Based on self-reports of Harvard alumni on the amount of calories expended in physical activity per week the researchers reported:

   1. There is an inverse relationship between amount of post-college physical activity and likelihood of developing cardiovascular disease.

College athletes who became sedentary after graduation had a risk factor 49 percent higher than college athletes who remained active after graduation. Sedentary students who became active after graduation had less than one half the risk factor of their sedentary peers. In fact, sedentary students who became physically active after graduation had approximately the same likelihood of developing cardiovascular disease as athletes who remained active.

2. As expected, smoking and exercise have an opposite effect on the probability of developing cardiovascular disease. Smokers were 30 percent more likely to develop cardiovascular disease than nonsmokers. Smokers who become nonsmokers had a substantially reduced risk factor.

3. Exercise had a significant influence on the hereditary influence involved in cardiovascular disease; those with a family history of cardiovascular disease who exercised had a risk factor significantly less than those with a family history who did not exercise.

4. The risk factor that had the greatest success in predicting a cardiovascular accident was high blood pressure. Those who exercised were more likely to have normal blood pressure levels.

5. In examining cause of death the researchers found that there was a strong inverse relationship between the amount of physical activity and certain causes of death: those who engaged in the most physical activity had significantly lower rates of death from cardiovascular disease and respiratory disease. Interestingly enough, the same relationship was not found for cancer, or for death from suicide or accidents.

Still, however, many believe that there is no "firm" evidence that demonstrates the relationship between physical activity/inactivity and the development of coronary heart disease (see Caldwell, 1985). Perhaps one of the best methods of assessing the impact of physical activity on the development of heart disease is to examine some of the factors that are believed to be involved in the development of heart disease and then assess the impact that running had on them. The factors mentioned the most frequently are high blood pressure, abnormal cholesterol levels, cigarette smoking, obesity, and physical inactivity.

The Influence of Running on Coronary Risk Factors

We have seen epidemiological evidence that vigorous physical activity is associated with a lower risk of coronary heart disease. It was noted, however, that it was difficult for these studies to single out physical activity as the single or even the most important factor in reducing coronary risk factors. Other factors such as physique, blood pressure, smoking, and stress may also have been contributing factors.

How important is physical activity, specifically running, in the prevention of coronary heart disease? Before answering this question, we need to briefly review the assumed causes of heart disease, which can be placed into two categories, those that can be altered and those that cannot. Those risk factors that cannot be altered include gender, race, age, and family history of coronary heart disease. Studies indicate that women have a much lower rate of coronary heart disease than men until after menopause, that blacks have a higher rate of coronary heart disease than whites, that with increasing age the propensity for coronary heart disease increases, and that those whose families have a history of coronary heart disease are at a greater risk of developing the disease. All of these factors are assumed to be related to the risk of developing coronary heart disease. Obviously running will not cause any of these factors to change.

There are a number of other risk factors that are believed to contribute to heart disease that can be altered. Some of them are high blood pressure, high blood lipids (cholesterol), smoking, physical inactivity, obesity, diet, personality, and stress. It is widely believed that running has an excellent chance to change all of the above either through the effects of running per se or through changes in the life style that frequently accompany running.

To find out if running reduces any of the risk factors believed to cause coronary heart disease, we will examine four coronary risk factors that can be altered: blood pressure, cholesterol level, smoking, and obesity. Physical activity does not need to be examined per se since it is addressed both directly and indirectly in the investigation of the other factors. Diet, personality, and stress will not be examined. This section of the chapter will be somewhat different from the last section in that rather than reporting on epidemiological studies, this section will examine primarily experimental studies.

Blood Pressure

High blood pressure (HBP) or hypertension is very prevalent in the United States. Although researchers and clinicians do not agree on one set of figures as representing "normal" or "abnormal" blood pressure levels, one widely used source has established the following levels for consistent readings (Miller et al., 1978): *Mild* = systolic 140–159mm, diastolic 90–95mm; *Moderate/severe* = systolic 160 + mm, diastolic 95 + mm. Another way of defining HBP is to say that it is the blood consistently placing high pressure on the arterial walls.

As noted above, HBP is epidemic in American society. Depending on the figures used to define HBP, it is estimated that from 23 million to 60 million Americans have the disorder (U.S. Department of Health, Education, and Welfare, 1980). In fact, HBP is the most common pathological condition in contemporary adults (HEW, 1979). It is especially dangerous because its symptoms go undetected while it harms various parts of the body. Unfortunately, HBP is often only detected after it has caused damage and the symptoms for which individuals finally seek treatment are not those of HBP per se but those of an organ or system irreversibly damaged by HBP.

For example, HBP is a major contributor to strokes, as well as to kidney and eye damage.

High blood pressure can also accelerate the development of atherosclerosis and hence coronary heart disease. One study found that the probability of developing coronary heart disease was increased four to six times for those with high blood pressure (see Phibbs, 1971).

There are many variables that affect blood pressure levels. One of them is increasing age: blood pressure generally goes up with increasing age. In fact, what would be considered high blood pressure for a 20-year-old male, 160mm systolic, is considered normal by many physicians for a 70-year-old male (Shaver, 1981). Gender also influences blood pressure. Until menopause women tend to have blood pressure levels lower than men's. After menopause, the levels become more equal and may surpass those of men after age 65 (U.S. Bureau of the Census, 1984). Emotions also influence blood pressure levels. It is well known that emotions such as fear, excitement, anger, or anxiety can cause blood pressure levels to vary. Physical exertion also has an impact on blood pressure levels. As cardiac output increases so do both the systolic and diastolic levels.

Thus, individuals are subjected to a number of variables that cause their blood pressure levels to change frequently throughout a given time period. A conditioned athlete may have "high" blood pressure during a strenuous exercise period; however, it will return to "normal" levels shortly after exercise. In contrast, someone with high blood pressure will have readings that are continually high.

Given the serious consequences of HBP, there are sound medical reasons to try to lower it. There are a variety of ways to do this. For example, weight loss, changes in diet — especially in reducing salt intake — and certain drugs have all been proven effective. Although given relatively little attention in comparison to the other methods of lowering HBP mentioned above, exercise is also effective (see Storer and Ruhling, 1981).

Generally, studies have supported the hypothesis that exercise will reduce blood pressure levels. For example, a six month jogging program for 23 hypertensive men found that systolic blood pressure was lowered by an average of 12mm and diastolic by 13mm (Boyer and Kasch, 1970). Numerous additional studies have found that a significant lowering of blood pressure takes place with physical exercise (see McArdle et al., 1981; Boyer and Kasch, 1970; Wilmore et al., 1970; Hanson and Nedde, 1970).

A personal self-report by a 44-year-old male with HBP said that after jogging his blood pressure returned to normal levels for several hours (Fitzgerald, 1982). Experimental investigation of this was confirmed in a treadmill experiment with ten hypertensive men. In this experiment it was found that blood pressure readings dropped significantly for four to ten hours after "vigorous" exercise. The authors concluded that a "good walk" twice a day might be an effective course of treatment for many individuals with HBP (Wilcox et al., 1982).

It must be mentioned that not all studies have yielded positive results. For example, Tzankoff and his colleagues (1972) exercised 15 sedentary men

46–66 years of age 2.3 times per week for 55 minutes each session. Although there were many other changes, such as loss of weight, their blood pressure remained constant. Another study on 16 sedentary men who participated in a 20 week walking program found that while no decrease took place in systolic blood pressure there was a small decrease in diastolic (Pollock et al., 1971). The conclusions of both of these studies, and several similar studies, need to be treated with caution since the men were not noted as having high blood pressure at the beginning of the study. Thus, the men may have had "normal" blood pressures at the beginning of the study and therefore there was "little room" for decline to take place. It has been previously noted that individuals with "normal" blood pressure experience little or no change as a result of exercise programs (Pollock et al., 1978). Another interpretation of the studies that found no decrease in blood pressure after vigorous exercise may be that the intensity and duration of the exercise programs were not sufficient to bring about change.

Although runners do not generally have high blood pressure they are not immune from it. That is, running by itself is not enough to keep blood pressure at "normal" levels. This was made clear in a study on 50 members of the San Diego Track Club. The study examined the "best" runners from five male and three female age groups. The participants all ran from 35 to 100 or more miles per week and participated in road races on a regular basis. None of the participants smoked and alcohol intake was modest. The study found that 40 percent of those examined had a resting systolic blood pressure of 130 + or a resting diastolic blood pressure of 85 + . Although these readings are not considered "high" (the study does not provide information on how many of those examined were above systolic 140 and diastolic 90), it did conclude that although exercise was important in helping to lower blood pressure, diet was more important and even after many years of intensive physical exercise those who ate the "standard American diet" were not immune to HBP (Elrick, 1982).

Cholesterol

Few medical terms generate as much emotionality as the term cholesterol. Singled out by the mass media in the early 1960s as the primary cause of coronary heart disease, and conveniently labeled "fat," Americans for more than two decades have been fat/cholesterol conscious. Foods high in fat/cholesterol have been assiduously avoided by concerned shoppers, which has caused manufacturers to produce a variety of formerly high fat foods in low fat forms.

Although given a negative label, cholesterol is present in all human cells and is essential for life. For example, cholesterol is essential for the production of certain hormones. The greater part of cholesterol in our bodies by a large measure is endogenous (manufactured by the body). Only a small percentage is exogenous, meaning that it came from outside the body, primarily from food.

Generally, Americans believe that a high cholesterol reading is a death sentence. There is a large body of data, which started with animal studies in the early 1900s, which clearly demonstrate that individuals with high cholesterol readings have a disproportionate chance of developing coronary heart disease, although how and why it occurs cannot be answered (McArdle et al., 1981). For example, individuals aged 35 to 44 who have serum cholesterol levels above 265 mg/dL are five times more likely to have heart attacks than individuals who have cholesterol levels of 220 mg/dL or below (U.S. Department of Health, Education, and Welfare, 1980).

More recently it has been learned that it is the "type" of cholesterol that an individual has, rather than the total amount, which is the important variable in the development of coronary heart disease. There are three types of cholesterol we are concerned with. They are very low-density lipoproteins (VLDL), low-density lipoproteins (LDL) and high-density lipoproteins (HDL). Before distinguishing between the three terms it should be noted that cholesterol is either a lipid or fat, and that to circulate in the body it combines with a protein. Thus, the term lipoprotein refers to a fat that has combined with a protein.

Although essential for life, VLDL and LDL are seen as "bad" types of cholesterol. This is because they are responsible for depositing fat in the arterial walls. It appears that the VLDL and LDL function to transport fat to the cells and artery walls for use by the body. In doing this the VLDL and LDL also contribute to a fat or plaque buildup in the arteries. The HDL, in contrast, is seen as a "good" type of cholesterol. It is believed that HDL cholesterol transports the fat away from the arteries and to the liver where it is either excreted or broken down into other substances. Thus, the HDL does not cause atherosclerosis and may prevent its occurrence by preventing a buildup of fat in the arterial walls (see Miller and Miller, 1975). The beneficial effects of HDL have been known since the early 1950s. Its importance was especially noted in the Framingham study (see Gordon et al., 1977). Here it was found that those individuals studied with HDL levels below 35 ml/dL had a rate of coronary heart disease eight times higher than those with levels of 65 ml/dL or higher.

Thus, what people are now striving to achieve is to lower their VLDL and LDL levels while raising their HDL levels. The question is, "Does running produce this effect?"

Although this is a relatively recently asked and researched question, the answer appears to be yes. Wood and his associates (1976) found that it did. They examined 41 male runners between the ages of 35 and 59. The men had been running at least 15 miles a week for a year. They were matched with a control group of 743 nonrunning men. The study found that there were significant differences between the plasma lipoprotein levels of the runners and the nonrunners. The differences for the runners and nonrunners were (mg/100 ml): total cholesterol 200 versus 210; LDL 125 versus 139, and HDL 64 versus 43. There were two major differences between the runners and the nonrunners—the runners were leaner and did not smoke. However, further analysis found that the leanness of the runners accounted for only part of the difference in cholesterol levels. The authors concluded that although they did not demonstrate that "running per se" was the cause of the lipoprotein profile difference, it was clear that the "running package" (i.e., exercise and life style) was associated with a lipoprotein profile that was beneficial in terms of preventing heart disease.

Two additional studies appeared in 1977 that supported this conclusion. The first study compared 41 male and 43 female runners with 747 male and 932 female nonrunners. The male runners averaged 45 years of age, female runners averaged 42 years of age. The corresponding figure for the nonrunners was 47 for both sexes. The male runners ran an average of 37 miles a week. The corresponding figure for the female runners was 31. The study found that total cholesterol levels were lower in the runners than the nonrunners. These differences were modest between the running and nonrunning men, and substantial between the running and nonrunning women. The total cholesterol values (mg/100 ml) for male runners were 200 ± 22. The corresponding value for women was 193 ± 33. The value for male nonrunners was 212 ± 38, and for female nonrunners it was 209 ± 38. The differences between the two groups were more pronounced when different types of cholesterol were analyzed. The LDL and VLDL were significantly lower and the HDL levels significantly higher in runners than nonrunners. The LDL values for male and female runners were 125 ± 21, and 113 ± 33. The corresponding values for male and female nonrunners were 139 ± 32 and 124 ± 34. The readings for the VLDL for male and female runners were 11 and 7. For male and female nonrunners the readings were both 28. The HDL levels for male and female runners were 64 ± 13 and 75 ± 14. For male and female nonrunners the values were 43 ± 10 and 56 ± 14. In conclusion the authors noted that total cholesterol, VLDL, and LDL were significantly lower and HDL significantly higher in the runners. They went on to note that only part of the differences could be attributed to life style and that a significant percentage of the differences were due to exercise. They concluded by saying that the runners were remarkable in that they had a low probability of developing cardiovascular disease (Wood et al., 1977).

In the second study 20 elite runners (average mileage per week was 85) were compared to eight "good" runners (average mileage per week was 60). Also, ten young sedentary males were examined. The average age of the participants was 28.6 years. The total plasma cholesterol levels did not differ significantly among the three groups. The authors noted that this finding was in concurrence with other studies that had shown that physical activity did not result in a decrease in total plasma cholesterol. For example, the total average cholesterol levels (ml/100 ml) were 175 ± 26.3 for elite runners, 185 ± 35.5 for good runners, and 189 ± 36.4 for nonrunners. Most studies showing a drop in total plasma cholesterol have noted that the decrease resulted from dietary changes and weight loss rather than running. This study did find, however, that LDL and VLDL levels were significantly lower in the runners than the controls. The LDL levels for the elite, good, and nonrunners were: 108 ± 24.5, 121 ± 29.5, and 124 ± 35.6. The VLDL levels for the three groups were 11 ± 5.2, 12 ± 11.8, and 15 ± 7.5. The authors then went on to report that there was a "striking" difference in the HDL levels, with higher levels being found in the runners. The figures for the three groups were 56 ± 12.1, 52 ± 10.9, and 49 ± 10.5. This study also noted that the HDL levels seemed to increase with age in the runners and either decline or remain at constant levels in the nonrunners (Martin et al., 1977).

The same trend was shown in a study of 50 runners and 43 nonrunners in 1980. The runners were physicians who participated in the 1977 Boston Marathon. The runners were matched with a group of nonrunners in terms of age (average age for physicians was 40.19, average age for nonrunners was 43.60), and sex (one female in each group). The study found that the total cholesterol profiles did not differ significantly for the two groups (mg/dL): runners 194.5 ± 31.2, nonrunners 199.6 ± 37.0. Also, the LDL profiles did not differ significantly: runners 110.8 ± 24.6, nonrunners 121 ± 28.2. There was, however, a significant difference in their HDL levels: runners 54.8 ± 14.1, nonrunners 45 ± 9.4. Since the study also found that the relative weight of the runners was significantly lower than that of the nonrunners and because several studies have indicated that there is an inverse relationship between weight and HDL levels, the study did a separate analysis to ascertain if difference in weight accounted for the difference in HDL levels. The study found that weight did not necessarily account for the difference in HDL levels. Although offering additional support to the hypothesis that long-distance running increases levels of HDL, which in turn decrease the likelihood of coronary heart disease, the authors cautiously said that the hypothesis remained "unproved" and that further studies were needed (Adner et al., 1980).

Another study published in 1980 supported the hypothesis that jogging/running elevates HDL levels. This study examined 85 joggers, 59 marathon runners and 74 inactive men. The joggers ran an average of 11 miles per week and averaged 46.78 years of age. The marathoners ran an average of 40+ miles per week and averaged 44.41 years of age. The inactive men averaged 46.07 years of age. It was found that each group differed significantly from the other two in terms of total cholesterol, LDL, and HDL levels. The total cholesterol levels were: joggers 204 ± 44 mg/dL, marathoners 187 ± 28 mg/dL, and inactive 211 ± 40 mg/dL. Thus, the marathoners had a significantly lower level of total cholesterol than the joggers who had a significantly lower level of total cholesterol than the inactive men. The same trend persisted for LDL (joggers 125.00 ± 39, marathoners 107.05 ± 27, and inactive 136.55 ± 36 mg/dL) and HDL levels (joggers 58.04 ± 18, marathoners 64.76 ± 14, and inactive 43.31 ± 14 mg/dL).

The above study was unique in that one of the variables examined was diet. Because several studies have suggested that it may be dietary differences that account for the LDL and HDL differences, rather than running, one of the purposes of this study was to examine diet. It found that the dietary habits of the inactive men differed from the runners/joggers only in that the inactive men ate more meat than the active men. After a detailed

analysis the researchers concluded that it was not diet but running and jogging that elevated the HDL to levels "associated with a significant reduction
of coronary risk" (Hartung et al., 1980; see Thompson et al., 1983).

Although most of the changes so far have been in HDL levels, a study
was done to assess if a six-week jogging program would lower LDL
cholesterol levels. In this study 16 males (average age 31 years) jogged an
average of 5.8 miles per week for six weeks. By the end of the study it was
found that HDL levels had not significantly changed. However, significant
declines in both LDL and total cholesterol levels were found in those who
jogged as little as 8 or 9 miles per week (Kaufman et al., 1980).

A more recent study has confirmed the above. This study examined 48
healthy men between the ages of 30 and 55 who had been sedentary for more
than a year. The men were then placed in a jogging program. Their motivation to jog was enhanced by the presence of "young, attractive female runners who ran with them." The joggers were then studied over the course of
a year. This study found that it took nine months with a minimum of ten
miles per week to raise HDL levels. The study also ruled out other factors
that might have accounted for the changes such as weight loss, dietary
changes, or changes in smoking habits (Williams et al., 1982; see Dunn,
1981).

There is another variable that has recently been found to be associated
with increased HDL levels: alcohol consumption. In 1980 a study was
published that tried to ascertain if it was alcohol or physical activity that
was increasing the HDL levels of runners. The study examined 99 male
physicians (average age 42) who were running in the 83rd Boston Marathon.
Two of the variables examined were alcohol intake and HDL levels. Alcohol
intake was evaluated using the Framingham formula:

$$\text{ounces of alcohol} =$$
$$(\text{12-oz. cans of beer} \times 0.6) + (\text{4-oz. glasses of wine} \times 0.67) +$$
$$(\text{2-oz. drinks of liquor} \times 1.0)$$

The study found that physicians who drank no alcohol had an average
HDL reading of 51.7 (mg/100 ml). Those who drank up to six ounces of
alcohol weekly had an average HDL reading of 53.9. Those who drank 6
to 18 ounces of alcohol per week had an average HDL reading of 61.5. All
of the differences were statistically significant. Since all of the men were
marathoners, further analysis was done to find out if miles run per week or
best marathon times correlated with HDL level, but neither did. The
authors speculated that "moderate" alcohol consumption may "enhance the
production of HDL." Nonetheless, they did not believe that the results of
their study were sufficient to recommend that nondrinkers start drinking to
increase HDL production. Rather, they suggested that more studies were
needed (Willett et al., 1980).

Three other studies appeared 1982 through 1984 that explored the influence of alcohol on HDL levels in runners.

The first was on the HDL levels of 12 men entered in the Great

Hawaiian Foot Race (a 28-day, 500km road race). The men ran an average of 28km per day for the first ten days of the race; they then rested for three days and then ran 28km a day for another eight days. The researchers found that after one week of running HDL levels increased 18 percent in the runners. During the three-day rest the HDL levels decreased to prerace levels. When the race resumed, the HDL levels again increased. The researchers mentioned that the runners engaged in a great deal of beer drinking, to replace fluids and carbohydrates, and noted that alcohol has been associated with increased HDL levels. However, the researchers also believed that part of the increase in HDL levels was due to the intensity of the exercise (Dressendorfer et al., 1982).

The second study dealt with the influence of alcohol abstinence or consumption on 16 marathon runners, 15 joggers, and 13 inactive men (Hartung et al., 1983). The study found that three weeks of alcohol abstinence brought about a significant decrease in HDL levels in the inactive men (from 50 to 42 mg/dL), but did not result in any significant change for the marathon runners (58 to 60 mg/dL), or for the joggers (49 and 49 mg/dL). Three weeks of drinking three cans of beer a day elevated the HDL levels of the inactive men to 51 mg/dL. There was not a significant change for the marathon runners (61 mg/dL) or the joggers (49 mg/dL). The authors did not recommend that alcohol be used to increase HDL levels.

A more recent study sought to ascertain the "type" of HDL cholesterol that was increased with alcohol consumption. Essentially, HDL consists of HDL_2 and HDL_3: HDL_2 is the type of cholesterol associated with a reduction in cardiovascular disease; HDL_3 does not appear to have an impact on heart disease. Does alcohol consumption affect HDL_2 or HDL_3? To answer this question, the researchers designed a study involving two groups. The first, abstention, group consisted of "moderate drinkers" who stopped drinking for six weeks. The second, control, group consisted of individuals who were instructed to drink "moderate" amounts of alcohol during the study.

The abstinence group had a significant decline in total HDL and HDL_3; HDL_2 remained unchanged. Resumption of alcohol consumption brought total HDL and HDL_3 levels back to pretest levels. The HDL levels in the control group did not change during the study. The researchers concluded that alcohol consumption does not play a role in increasing HDL_2 levels (Haskell et al., 1984; see Arends, 1985).

Two recent studies have indicated that a common practice of many athletes may have a significant negative influence on HDL levels. Essentially the studies have reported that anabolic steroid use decreases HDL levels (Costill et al., 1984; Peterson and Fahey, 1984).

Smoking

Smoking is different from cholesterol or blood pressure: where most individuals do not have the ability to rapidly raise or lower cholesterol or blood pressure levels, they do have the ability to start or stop smoking. Since smoking is a somewhat different matter, this section will take a slightly different approach, examining first the coronary risk, then why smoking is damaging to runners, and finally the impact of running on smoking.

The dangers of smoking have been widely publicized. As a result the percentage of the total population over the age of 20 that smokes has dropped. For example, in 1965, 34.4 percent of the population smoked but by 1979 that figure had dropped to 30.7.

The risks of smoking are certain: for the age group 25–64, cigarette smokers have a death rate from heart disease almost twice that of nonsmokers; for the same age group, cigarette smoking is responsible for more cases of cancer and for more deaths than any other known factor (HEW, 1980). The question that naturally comes to mind is, why does smoking increase the risk of developing coronary heart disease?

The first element is nicotine. The nicotine that is inhaled in the smoke causes the release of adrenalin. Adrenalin causes the blood vessels to constrict and the heart rate to increase. The constricted blood vessels cause the blood pressure to rise and the heart to work harder to circulate the blood and its oxygen and nutrients. Nicotine also has an impact on the ability of the blood to clot. Heparin normally circulates in the blood to prevent blood clots from forming in the arteries. Nicotine combines with heparin and causes it to disappear for 10–15 minutes in the circulating blood of someone who had smoked two cigarettes. This greatly enhances the risk of a blood clot forming which may precipitate a heart attack.

Another risk of smokers is due to carbon monoxide inhalation. This has been proven to have a negative impact in two ways. First, the rate of atherosclerosis in increased. Second, the amount of oxygen carried by the blood is reduced by about 10 percent for a pack-a-day smoker. This means that the heart will have to work 10 percent more to supply the body with the oxygen that individuals would have if they were nonsmokers.

Lastly, several studies have shown that smoking reduces the amount of HDL cholesterol in the body. For smokers of one pack a day the amount of HDL is reduced 12–15 percent (Weltman and Stamford, 1982b; Phibbs, 1971).

The dangers of smoking are real and have been demonstrated repeatedly. The last question to be examined is what impact does running have on smoking? The point is not to ascertain if running will offset the damaging consequences of smoking and thus allow smokers to rationalize their addiction. Rather, it is to demonstrate the impact of running on smoking habits. That is, does running bring about a change in life style?

Although there have been several studies on this topic, the most recent and the most methodologically correct was done by Koplan and his associates (1982), who examined a random sample of runners from the 1980 Peachtree Road Race. The study found that among current runners who had smoked, 81 percent of the men and 75 percent of the women stopped smoking when they began running. Fewer than 1 percent of the men and 2 percent of the women had started smoking after they began to run. The study also found that for men, but not for women, the probability of smoking cessation increased as did weekly mileage. An interesting finding was that the number of years the smoker had been running did not have an impact on smoking cessation.

Koplan's study also examined individuals who had run in the 1980 Peachtree Road Race but who had stopped running by the time the data was gathered. As expected, the cessation of smoking was more common among current runners than for "retired" runners. As pointed out above, for current runners 81 percent of the men and 75 percent of the women who had been smokers stopped after starting to run. The figures for the retired runners were 46 percent and 41 percent. After starting to run most individuals quit smoking. The percentage of individuals who start smoking after starting to run is very small.

Obesity

Obesity in this section is in some ways similar to smoking as a topic, in that unlike cholesterol or blood pressure level (over which most individuals have no conscious control), obesity is something over which the individual generally has conscious control. This section will examine the extent of obesity in contemporary American society, the coronary risk factor of obesity, and the impact of running on obesity.

There is little doubt that American society is weight-conscious. Low calorie foods and drinks are a booming fad. Weight consciousness even prompted Congress temporarily to suspend the Delaney Act for saccharin. (The Act was passed in 1959 and says that ingredients that have been proven to cause cancer in test animals cannot be added to foods intended for human consumption.)

Unfortunately, diet soft drinks, beers, wines, and foods have not made the American population thin. Between the ages of 20 and 74, 14 percent of men and 24 percent of women are "significantly" overweight (HEW, 1980).

Obesity has been linked with the development of coronary heart disease both as a factor in and of itself and because it is associated with high blood pressure and undesirable cholesterol levels. Obesity also places a much greater load on the heart since one pound of fat creates approximately one additional mile in the vascular system for the heart to pump blood through. This can place a much greater load on the heart. The impact of obesity can be seen when the death rate is examined. For example, between the ages of 40 and 50 the death rate increases substantially for every ten pounds the individual is overweight. The chance that someone who is ten pounds overweight will die increases by 8 percent. The same percentages for those 20 pounds, 30 pounds and 50 pounds overweight are 18, 28, and 56 percent. The obese person is more prone to the development of coronary heart disease, kidney disease, diabetes, and gallbladder disease (Miller, 1976).

What impact does running have on obesity? The study by Koplan and his associates (1982) on runners in the Peachtree Road Race is important.

For those over the age of 22 the studies found that after starting to run, 38 percent of the men and 16 percent of the women reported a weight loss of a little over 5 kg (about 11 pounds). Weight loss was more common for those who were heavier to begin with and for those who started running to lose weight. Also, weight loss correlated positively with number of miles run per week.

In summary then, it appears that running does bring about a loss of weight, especially for those who are overweight when they start running.

Research has unequivocally demonstrated, in a large number of studies, that running can lower coronary risk factors; it has also shown that generally the more one runs the more beneficial it is. Is there a threshold distance that would provide immunity from coronary heart disease?

Immunity from Coronary Heart Disease

"Marathon runners have immunity from coronary heart disease!"

Certainly almost anyone involved in running during the last few years has read or heard the above hypothesis, or one of its many variations. It is a hypothesis almost certain to gain attention, given the fact that heart disease is the major cause of death in contemporary American society, but can it be supported scientifically?

Let us examine the origins of the hypothesis (relatively simple to find) and trace its development to the present (complicated by the many forms it has taken and its intrinsic ambiguity, as well as the fact that data, both supporting and not supporting the hypothesis, have been discredited, retracted, and presented again in new forms). In trying to understand literally hundreds of articles and letters that have defended or attacked the hypothesis, the best approach appears to be to examine its chronological development.

An article was published in the *New England Journal of Medicine* in 1961 on the autopsy results of Clarence DeMar, a man also called "Mr. Marathon" because of his 49 years of marathon running and more than 1,000 long-distance races (Currens and White, 1961). When DeMar died from cancer at the age of 70, one of the long-standing questions researchers wanted to answer was whether long-continued physical exercise has an adverse effect on the heart. While the autopsy did find "mild" atherosclerosis, it also found that DeMar's coronary arteries were two to three times larger than normal. The authors of the article could not say if he was born with arteries this size, and if it was thus heredity that gave him the ability to perform at the level he did, or if the enlarged arteries developed as a result of intensive and prolonged physical exercise. Others, however, were not so timid in offering the explanation that it was exercise that enlarged DeMar's coronary arteries.

From the DeMar autopsy results the hypothesis developed. The most tenacious, vocal, prolific, and skillful defender of the hypothesis that running a marathon protects the individual from coronary heart disease has been Dr. Thomas J. Bassler, a pathologist at Centinella Hospital in Los Angeles (see Ullyot, 1980, for a short biography, and Olsen, 1982, for an interview).

One of the first articles by Bassler on this subject appeared in the *New England Journal of Medicine* in 1972. In it he said, "a search of the literature has failed to document a single death due to coronary atherosclerosis among marathoners of any age." He added that to be considered in his analysis runners had to have completed a marathon in under four hours, and that only autopsied cases had been considered. Bassler repeated this claim in letters to numerous scientific and medical journals over the next few years. For example, in 1973 in *Science* magazine he said that he had been "unable to document a single death resulting from coronary heart disease among marathon finishers of any age" (1973a) and in the *Journal of the American Medical Association* he repeated, "there has never been a documented fatal myocardial infarct among marathon finishers of any age" (1973b). In 1974 he said, "The life style of a marathon runner has few risk factors and there has never been a documented CHD [coronary heart disease] death among finishers" (1974b), we have been "unable to document a fatal myocardial infarction among marathon runners" (1974a), we have been "unable to document a fatal C.H.D. in a marathon finisher of any age" (1974d), and we have "never seen a death ... of fatal coronary heart disease in an individual who had finished a 42km marathon run at any time in his life" (Bassler and Schaff, 1974).

In 1975 Bassler wrote in *Physician and Sportsmedicine* that "no marathon finisher has died of coronary heart disease" (1975a), "To date there have been no documented CHD deaths among marathon finishers of any age," "No marathon finisher has died of coronary heart disease," immunity from coronary heart disease "co-exists with the ability to cover the 42km on foot, either walking, running, or cross-country skiing," and "for a non-smoker who trains at distances over six miles for a total of 1,000 miles, protection starts here and continues as long as he continues running" (1975a), "we have been unable to document a single death from ischemic heart disease among marathon finishers of any age" (Bassler and Schaff, 1975a), "we advocate the vigorous exercise and teetotaling life-style of the Olympic marathon runner" (Bassler and Cardello, 1975), and we have been "unable to document a single death from ischemic heart disease among marathon finishers of any age" (Bassler and Schaff, 1975b).

As is perhaps apparent, the "Bassler Hypothesis" has taken many different forms. Marathoning appears to offer protection from coronary heart disease, ischemic heart disease, myocardial infarction, and coronary atherosclerosis. At one time a marathoner was defined as someone who had run a marathon in under four hours, or as someone who could walk or ski the distance in an unspecified period of time, or as someone who trained at a distance of over six miles (it was not specified if this was per day, week or month) and had accumulated at least 1,000 miles. In at least two letters he wrote of the desirability of the "teetotaler" way of life and then in a recent interview he advocated beer drinking (Olsen, 1982). Starting about 1976 Bassler added four "new components" to his "hypothesis." The first was that running a marathon could cause regression of atherosclerosis or the resorption of plaques (Bassler, 1978b; 1978d; 1980c; see Crawford et al., 1979; Hall et al., 1982; Nolewajke et al., 1979; Ferguson et al., 1973). The second was that runners who had low body fat, intensive training schedules, high weekly mileage, and certain dietary restrictions were at a greatly increased risk of death from "nutritional arrhythmia" (1980b; 1984a; 1984b). The third was that fiber played an important role in the prevention of atherosclerosis (1976c). The last was that it was "impossible for atherosclerosis to progress in anyone capable of ... walking ... 42 km" (1978c).

Amidst the many forms of the hypothesis and its new components, it was not completely clear what was providing the "immunity." It appears that Bassler was *not* saying that marathon running was necessarily the factor that was providing protection. Rather, it was the "marathoner's life style" (Bassler, 1974c). This point was emphasized when Bassler "restated" his hypothesis in 1980. In the restatement he said, "the marathon runner's life style will protect against the aging process" (1980a).

Although the hypothesis has taken several different forms, been modified frequently, and had new components added, because the original hypothesis attracted so much attention and has been frequently referred to in running books and magazines, when referring to the Bassler Hypothesis this section of the book defines the hypothesis as: "Runners who complete a marathon are immune from coronary artery disease." Since Bassler never placed a time limit on how long from the completion of a marathon a runner would be protected, I will not add new components to the hypothesis.

Bassler's hypothesis initially attracted relatively little attention, other than polite letters suggesting that the hypothesis was being presented as a proven and scientifically accepted fact rather than as a hypothesis, which is nothing more than an educated guess. It was suggested that the hypothesis was premature and that more research was needed before any such definitive statement could be made. However, rather than responding to the concerns of his critics, Bassler made his hypothesis into an almost regular feature in several scientific and medical magazines and journals. Initially, this feature consisted primarily of Bassler's letters restating the hypothesis in one of its many versions, his critics' rebuttals offering data to show that Bassler was incorrect or premature, and then Bassler's rejoinders demonstrating weaknesses in his critics' arguments and data. Although Bassler's hypothesis seemed logical, given recent studies on the positive impact of exercise in reducing coronary risk factors such as high blood pressure and high cholesterol levels, it appears that many of his critics were upset by certain components of the hypothesis. While an occasional letter could be ignored, it became more and more difficult to ignore the number of letters Bassler was writing and the attention the hypothesis was receiving. Although there were challenges to the hypothesis, its vagueness and chameleon-like nature made it difficult to discredit, and generally only contributed to more publicity.

One of the most frequent criticisms of Bassler during this time period was that he had not published the results of the research that supported the hypothesis. For example, in 1974 Dr. Frederich H. Epstein said that Bassler had failed to provide "acceptable evidence" and that there was "no factual support for his thesis" (Epstein, 1974). In 1975 Dr. Seymour Dayton repeated the same accusation in a letter to the editor of the *New England Journal of Medicine* expressing concern for the fact that Bassler's hypothesis was being repeated so frequently in letters to the editors of various medical magazines and journals that it was becoming widely accepted as fact without scientific support.

This sentiment was repeated in 1975 when Dr. H.D. McIntosh wrote a reply to a letter Bassler had sent to an editorial McIntosh had written in the *American Journal of Cardiology* on life expectancy. Bassler (1975b) complimented McIntosh in calling for a change in life style and then said that heart disease was absent among marathon runners and that their life style was under investigation by the American Medical Joggers Association as one that would prevent heart disease. McIntosh (1975) replied that he hoped that in the future the data would be examined by pathologists without preconceived ideas.

Dr. Paul Milvy (1978a) of the Mount Sinai School of Medicine echoed the same sentiments in 1978. In his article he said that Bassler was prone to making statements without offering any empirical evidence. Milvy noted, for example, that Bassler did not inform the reader how many death certificates he had examined, or how many marathoner deaths would be expected per year (Milvy, 1978b). Milvy estimated that based on the number of male marathoners in 1975 — 10,000 by Milvy's estimate — and taking into account their ages and life styles, there should be only one to two deaths per year from heart disease. Thus, the fact that Bassler had failed to document a death was not surprising.

Bassler replied that the number of marathoners was closer to one million and that if marathoning offered no protection, there would be one to two deaths per day from heart disease (Bassler, 1978a). Milvy responded that he did not know where Bassler obtained the figure of one million. He pointed out that in 1977 the New York Marathon had 3,701 finishers and that in 1978 the Boston Marathon had 3,826 finishers. He then noted that if there were in fact one million marathoners that surely there must have been more deaths than the 200 reports that Bassler had collected, which by Bassler's admission consisted of many duplicates and nonmarathoners (Milvy, 1978b).

Bassler's claim of one million marathoners is interesting since in 1974 he said that there were only 5,000 marathon finishers in the United States (Bassler and Schaff, 1974).

It appears that Bassler believed that he had provided adequate "scientific" evidence to support his hypothesis. For example, in 1978 he said, "Nothing is more precise than a 42km run or a forensic autopsy" (Bassler, 1978c). However, there were many others who believed that Bassler's hypothesis had not been adequately supported by empirical evidence and because of the ambiguity of the hypothesis several writers again called for Bassler to stop publicizing the hypothesis until he could offer acceptable scientific evidence (Noakes and Opie, 1977; Dayton, 1975; Siegel, 1978).

One writer who requested that Bassler stop publicizing the hypothesis noted that until there was more evidence it was just as possible that while marathon runners are at a decreased risk of cardiovascular death when at rest they may be at an increased risk when running (Pickering, 1979). This possibility was repeated by two of Bassler's most frequent critics, Dr. Lionel H. Opie and Dr. Tim Noakes of Cape Town, South Africa. In a 1974 issue of the *American Heart Journal* Dr. Opie wrote cautiously about both the benefits and protections offered by exercise (Opie, 1974). In 1975 he wrote letters to the *New England Journal of Medicine* and *Lancet* which said that while exercise may prevent heart attacks, it may also "precipitate heart attacks" (Opie, 1975c) and that "exercise is believed to precipitate arrhythmia and myocardial infarction in certain individuals" (Opie, 1975a). Opie then went on to report on three sudden deaths in long-distance runners. In a subsequent letter Opie later "corrected" his report on two of the three deaths, noting that he had collected the autopsy evidence by "telephonic report" and letter but found upon further investigation that one of the individuals had not had an autopsy performed and that for the other individual there were no written records available (Opie, 1976). Bassler said, concerning Opie's initial challenge to his hypothesis and Opie's correction, that a "fabricated autopsy can be very misleading" (Bassler, 1978b).

Although Opie had to correct his data, he did, nonetheless, bring up important questions concerning Bassler's hypothesis. Opie pointed out that serious readers and researchers were uncertain as to what exactly the hypothesis was and that they were unclear as to what provided the marathoner with "immunity": having run a marathon or the marathoner's life style?

In support of his hypothesis Bassler repeated his claim that he had collected over 200 reports of dead marathoners, most of whom had allegedly died from heart attacks (Bassler, 1978). He claimed that none of the reports disproved his theory and that most of the deaths fell into the categories of no autopsy, death from causes other than cardiac disease, or death from cardiac disease other than atherosclerosis (Bassler, 1976a).

By 1976 Bassler's hypothesis had received a great deal of attention. However, Bassler had been able easily to dismiss the evidence of his critics challenging his hypothesis, generally by pointing out that no autopsy had been performed or that the individual had not been a marathon runner. That came to a halt in 1976 with an article published in the *Annals of Internal Medicine*. The authors started the article by saying they had "the first documentation of a myocardial infarction in a trained athlete while running a marathon" (Green et al., 1976). The runner examined was a 44-year-old male who collapsed while running in the 1973 Boston Marathon and died shortly thereafter. The man was a vegetarian and abstained from alcohol and cigarettes. At autopsy the diagnosis was "myocardial infarction." The coronary artery system was described as "large in diameter and 'widely

patent' through...." Also, there was only "mild" atherosclerosis in one of the
coronary arteries. One other possible cause given for death by the authors
was the high heat and humidity the day of the race. The authors concluded
that "the role of heat stress must be considered in the pathogenesis of the infarct.... It is well-documented that heat stroke can cause significant cardiovascular damage, usually manifested by congestive heart failure."

As would be expected, this article attracted a great deal of attention.
In fact, in response to the article the *Annals of Internal Medicine* published
15 letters. One of the "lighter" letters, in a serious area, was written by Dr.
Joseph Stokes III who said that Green and his associates were actually reporting on the second death from myocardial infarction during marathon
running, Pheidippides being the first. He went on to say, "I suppose that one
can anticipate that the third case may be reported before the year 3000
A.D."

Most of the letters, given the emotionality this area had attracted, were
not so light-hearted. The letters generally centered on two issues. First that
this was not the "first" reported case, and second that the "actual" cause of
death was from "heat stroke" not heart attack.

Concerning the first issue, namely that this was not the first reported
incidence, several writers mentioned that two articles by Opie (1975a;
1975b) superseded Green and his colleagues. Opie's earlier evidence and the
fact that it did not meet Bassler's criteria in terms of an autopsy have already
been discussed. The second issue, namely heat stroke, needs to be examined.
One of the letters written in response to Green's article was by Dr. George
Sheehan, a well-known physician, runner, and writer. Sheehan said, "I can
attest to the enormous heat stress that day...." He went on and said that the
heat was particularly stressful because it came so early in the year and
presumably most runners had not had time to acclimate to it. To empirically
demonstrate the impact of the heat, Sheehan mentioned that a 150-pound
friend had lost 12 pounds in the first 13 miles of the race.

Based on the evidence presented by Green and his colleagues, several
other physicians suggested that the cause of death should have been listed
as "dehydration, and hyperpyrexia" (Kostrubala, 1976), "acute brain death
due to heat stroke" (Orselli, 1976), "heat stroke" (Bassler, 1976b; 1979b),
and "fatal heat stroke precipitated by marathon running" (Schaff, 1976a).

Green responded to the "heat stroke" criticisms by noting that although
the heat was a factor which had been considered, heat had been dismissed
as the cause of death because among other factors, the runner did not have
"the temperature elevation ... that typifies heat stroke" (Green, 1976).

Thus, there is considerable controversy involved in this particular case
and because of the confounding variables involved, it did not satisfy either
Bassler or his critics as being "solid evidence." Some have noted, however,
that this points out that marathon running, even in the presence of normal
coronary arteries, may precipitate a myocardial infarction (Noakes, Rose,
and Opie, 1979).

The article by Green and his colleagues and the response it triggered
did little to settle the issue. In 1977 both Bassler (1977) and Opie (Noakes,

Opie, and Beck, 1977) were given the opportunity to present their "evidence" at the 1977 meeting of the New York Academy of Sciences. The results of the conference were published in a 1000-plus page book, *The Marathon: Physiological, Medical, Epidemiological, and Psychological Studies* (formally: *Annals of the New York Academy of Sciences*, 301, October 1977). Bassler started his article by saying that, "To date, there have been no reports of fatal ASCVD (atherosclerosis) histologically proven among 42km men." Early in the report he emphasized the need for confirmation by autopsy. He also pointed out that other causes of cardiac death are similar to ASCVD upon gross autopsy and that because of this, microscopic slides are essential.

As noted above, Bassler claimed to have examined over 200 reports of marathoners who had died, allegedly from a form of heart disease, that would disprove his theory. Bassler claimed to have discredited all of the reports. According to Bassler, the majority of the reports examined did not disprove his hypothesis because: the runners were in fact low-mileage runners who were mistaken for marathon runners; or there was no autopsy performed or no histological studies; or ASCVD was mistakenly diagnosed.

In the article Bassler did take a conservative stance by saying that simply because ASCVD had not been found in marathoners this could not be used as evidence that exercise in and of itself was providing the protection. Rather, Bassler noted that tobacco avoidance and dietary factors were also important (Bassler, 1977).

The article that followed Bassler's was called "Coronary Heart Disease in Runners," and was by Noakes, Opie and Beck (1977). They started their article by criticizing 27 of Bassler's published letters, claiming that each was simply a repetitive statement and that to date there had been no empirical evidence presented to support the hypothesis. They also noted the ambiguities in the hypothesis, and then went on to report on six cases of "myocardial infarction in highly-trained marathon runners."

Of the six marathon runners studied by Noakes, Opie, and Beck, only one had died and no autopsy had been performed. Although Bassler's "standards" required an autopsy (Bassler, 1978b), those surviving had had a variety of tests performed which indicated myocardial infarction (electrocardiogram, heart catherization, angiography). Bassler dismissed the article by saying, "Autopsy material is needed to identify the 44 different diseases that may cause myocardial infarction" (Bassler, 1978b).

Although Bassler dismissed Noakes, Opie, and Beck's "evidence," the number of articles challenging the hypothesis started to increase. For example, Cantwell and Fletcher (1978) examined two physicians who had died while jogging. The first was a 52-year-old active male who although not a regular jogger was in excellent physical condition. This individual died while jogging. The authors pointed out that his death was explainable due to the extent of heart disease found. The second case, however, was more difficult to explain. Here a 28-year-old active male who regularly jogged 3.5 miles per day and who had normal coronary arteries was found dead along his jogging path. It was suggested that he died from a fatal rhythm disturbance. The authors noted that a change in the rhythm, or neural activity of the heart, may cause a fatal cardiac arrhythmia to occur and more research is needed to determine if medical tests can detect potential jogging victims.

These reports could be dismissed by Bassler since he made no claim of immunity for "low mileage" joggers, especially those who trained at distances of under six miles a day (Bassler, 1975a).

Much of the controversy concerning Bassler's original hypothesis appeared to reach a head in 1979 when Noakes, Opie and their associates published an article in the *New England Journal of Medicine* called "Autopsy-Proved Coronary Atherosclerosis in Marathon Runners." In the article the authors reported on five deceased, autopsied, marathon runners, four of whom had advanced atherosclerosis. The first case presented was that of a 44-year-old man who had been running for 14 months. He had completed several marathons and did not smoke or drink. This man had complained of "lack of energy" prior to his death. Shortly thereafter he collapsed and died during an 18 mile road race. The autopsy found a healed infarction (i.e., an area of the heart that had died from a myocardial infarction and had healed into scar tissue) that was three to six months old and extensive coronary atherosclerosis.

The second runner was a 41-year-old male who had been running marathons for two years when he had a myocardial infarction. Coronary angiography showed severe atherosclerosis of the coronary arteries. For rehabilitation he was advised to continue jogging but told not to run marathons. He increased his mileage and during the 28 months after his heart attack he ran in several marathons. His training log, made available by his widow, made numerous references to chest pains during his training runs, for which he did not seek medical treatment. Twenty-nine months after his heart attack another angiography showed that his atherosclerosis *had progressed* and that a coronary by-pass operation was needed. The runner died while awaiting such an operation. The autopsy confirmed severe coronary atherosclerosis. The authors also argued that data from this runner argued against Bassler's statement (1978c) that "it is biologically impossible for atherosclerosis to progress in anyone capable of even walking the 42km distance." They noted that in 1976 angiography showed a 50 percent narrowing of the right coronary artery and in 1978 angiography showed that the narrowing had increased to total occlusion.

The last three cases examined were all marathoners who were killed in an automobile accident. Two of the individuals smoked; one was a 38-year-old male who had been running for three years. He had normal coronary arteries. The other was a 27-year-old male who had been physically active all of his life but had only been running for about one year. He showed advanced heart disease. The third individual was a 36-year-old male who had been running for seven years. Before his death he had been running 50 miles per week. He had run several marathons. An autopsy found mild to advanced coronary atherosclerosis.

The authors concluded that there was now "firm" evidence to disprove

"Bassler's Hypothesis." They did mention, however, that marathon running might offer partial protection or delay the development of coronary atherosclerosis. However, they continued by saying that marathon running may also "hasten" the deaths of runners.

The editorial response to the Noakes, Opie, and colleagues article was clear and concise. First it said that until the publication of their research the debate had consisted more of "repetition than documentation." It then went on to say that the research had "unequivocally" destroyed Bassler's hypothesis (Rennie and Hollenberg, 1979).

As expected, Bassler did not consider his hypothesis destroyed. In a letter Bassler responded (1980a) by noting that the 44-year-old runner had died from ventricular fibrillation caused by a low ion ratio. He went on and said that this runner's atherosclerosis was "stable" and the fatal arrhythmia "had a nonischemic cause, probably due to a potassium deficiency." Bassler then noted the hazards of a potassium deficiency in runners and wrote that this runner's lack of energy and his high "dietary risks," as imposed by his intense training/racing schedule, had contributed to the deficiency and subsequent death. Bassler said that there was evidence of recanalization of coronary arteries. Bassler also said the individual did not have the HDL rating that would have been expected, which suggested a form of dyslipoprotein-emia.

Bassler dismissed the 41-year-old runner because Bassler incorrectly assumed that he smoked. This was an error Noakes and Opie (1980) corrected. The 27- and 38-year-old runners were also dismissed by Bassler because they smoked. Bassler made no attempt to discredit the information provided on the 36-year-old runner, although the individual had only been running for seven years and his coronary atherosclerosis may have developed prior to his starting to run.

In a response to Bassler's criticism of their research and interpretation Noakes and Opie (1980) noted that they were not trying to demonstrate that running was not beneficial in the prevention of coronary heart disease. Rather, they went on to say, the major purpose of their report was "to show that persons who have previously completed marathon races can subsequently die from coronary heart disease."

They were also "thankful" to Bassler for restating his hypothesis in language they "found more reasonable than his previous statement." Bassler's revised hypothesis was that "the marathon runner's life style will protect against the aging process." Bassler also said, "no serious research should ever say that marathon running provides complete immunity from CHD" (Bassler, 1980a).

Noakes and Opie (1979) published another article in 1979 that attempted to further discredit Bassler's hypothesis. They again pointed out the results of their research on the four autopsied marathon runners with coronary heart disease and on five living marathon runners who had suffered heart attacks and who had angiography confirming myocardial infarction. They concluded that although their data disproved Bassler's hypothesis, his work and writing was important because he had "beneficially publicized the role of exercise and life style modifications in the prevention of, and rehabilitation from, coronary heart disease." They went on to point out that marathon running and the life style it encourages do probably help prevent the development of and spread of CHD, but that the "protection is not absolute."

They then said it was important that the record be set straight since runners who believed in the hypothesis might be harming themselves. They pointed out that several athletes with advanced coronary heart disease who had been told by physicians to stop training and racing in marathons had ignored the advice, perhaps in the belief that running a marathon would grant them immunity from the spread of their disease or bring about the regression of their disease. They noted that at least one runner attributed his chest pain to "unfitness."

Thompson and his associates (1979) found the same trend. For example, they mentioned in their article that several of the dead runners they included in their study had exhibited physical conditions symptomatic of coronary heart disease but that none of them had decreased their training as a result of the symptoms. Thompson asked if the "exaggerated claims for the benefits of physical exercise may have contributed to the denial" of the symptoms and thus resulted in the joggers' either ignoring or postponing an evaluation of their symptoms. Thompson and his associates reported that of the 13 joggers they studied who died from coronary heart disease, six had warning symptoms and yet continued to jog.

The tendency for athletes to ignore warning symptoms had been noted earlier by Opie (1975a) in his study of sudden death among athletes. Of the 19 deaths from coronary heart disease that he examined, 13 of the men had physical symptoms preceding their deaths such as chest pain. Yet, in almost every case the men did not alter their physical training as a result of the symptoms.

Noakes, Opie, and Beck (1977) found this same trend. In the six runners reported on previously, they said that shortly before each had his heart attack, all had clear warning signs of CHD that they ignored. The first had chest pains he attributed to "unfitness." The second ignored his chest pain until it became severe. The third had severe pain and nausea during a marathon but finished the race, after which it was diagnosed he had suffered a myocardial infarction. He was subsequently hospitalized for eight days. After a medical examination he was told to stop running, a prescription he did not follow. The fourth runner had chest discomfort during a marathon but ignored the pain and completed the marathon. When the pain returned two days later he saw a physician and it was diagnosed that he had suffered an acute myocardial infarction. The runner was hospitalized for nine days. The day after his discharge, and against medical advice, he resumed running. The fifth runner was in a 50 mile race when he became extremely tired and nauseated and started sweating profusely. He finished the race and went to a hospital, where it was diagnosed that he had had a myocardial infarction. The last runner had a pain in his chest while running but continued to run. He consulted a physician about the pain four days afterwards, having run several times between the onset of the pain and the medical consultation, including a ten mile time trial. A myocardial infarction was diagnosed. The man refused hospitalization and temporarily stopped jogging, although he did mow his lawn for five hours while suffering severe chest pain. Although advised against it, he subsequently ran a three-day, 93 mile race.

Colt (1980) added to the literature when he said that he knew of two runners who had denied warning symptoms and subsequently suffered myocardial infarctions. The first occurred in a 49-year-old male runner who had chest pains shortly after the start of the New York City Marathon. The man had continued to run for several miles before he collapsed. The second runner, also a 49-year-old male, had observed and ignored physical symptoms. He died while training for a marathon. He had recently worn a T-shirt that said, "You haven't really run a good marathon until you drop dead at the finish line—Pheidippides." Colt said that both men could be characterized by a "marathon mania" and that both exhibited a "remarkable reluctance to stop running" even though both had clear CHD warning symptoms.

In defense of Bassler it must be mentioned that his hypothesis has been widely "misinterpreted and misquoted." He has reported an instance where a widely-read book gave a "simplistic" version of his hypothesis (Bassler, 1980a). In reading Bassler's letters and articles one cannot help but be struck by the "cautiousness" of many of his statements: "appear immune" (1976c), "the protection appears to be absolute" (1973; 1974), "our forensic surveillance of marathon runners suggests that their life style is very favorable" (1978c), "the marathoner's life style appears" (1975), "absence of fatal ASCVD ... cannot be construed as evidence for the protective role of exercise alone" (1977), and "until there is autopsy evidence of fatal atherosclerosis among marathon runners it seems prudent to advise this life style for the prevention of the disease" (1976b).

As can be seen from the above quotes, Bassler was *generally* very conservative in his statements. He limited most controversial statements with terms such as "appears" or "suggests." As with any hypothesis, when conflicting evidence is found it is natural for those who believe in the hypothesis to question the evidence. If the evidence is found to be valid, then it is logical to examine ways the hypothesis can be modified. It "appears" that Bassler did this.

Since the Noakes and Opie article came out there have been several other articles all indicating that running, either at marathon or lesser distances, does not provide immunity from heart disease. These articles will be examined below.

Thompson and his associates (1979) studied 18 individuals who had died while jogging or shortly thereafter who were autopsied. They concluded that 13 of the individuals died from CHD. Although Thompson's study is important, there was a great deal of information missing and the data were, even by the author's standards, not what Bassler or even his critics would accept as firm evidence. For example, Thompson did not provide a case by case analysis but rather collectively summarized the data on all 18 runners. Furthermore, Thompson did not provide information on factors such as mileage, or length of time running. Additionally, the study was retrospective in design. That is, Thompson and his colleagues gathered the information by obtaining copies of autopsy reports. The autopsies were often not performed to ascertain the type of information needed for Thompson's study, and thus there was no standard autopsy protocol used.

In 1979 Noakes, Rose, and Opie published an article on a 42-year-old male marathoner who collapsed and died while running a marathon. An autopsy showed the man had normal coronary arteries even though he had been warned at the age of seven to avoid strenuous physical exercise because of a heart murmur. The man ignored the advice and was an excellent athlete throughout his life. At age 39 he started long-distance running. In a race one year before his fatal race the man experienced a number of symptoms such as chest pain and labored breathing, symptoms he chose to ignore and to conceal from his physician. The authors noted that although his coronary arteries were normal he did have heart disease; in this case the heart muscle was diseased and the heart was enlarged. The authors stated that even marathoners are not immune from cardiac death.

In 1980 more evidence appeared to challenge Bassler's original hypothesis. Waller and Roberts (1980) provided information on five men who died while running. Autopsies were performed. The men ranged in age from 40 to 53 and had been running from one to ten years. Two of the men had run marathons and all died from "severe coronary atherosclerosis." They said that the "Bassler hypothesis was incorrect," although they pointed out that the only two marathoners in the study started running "late" in life and probably had "severe coronary atherosclerosis by the time they started to run" as well as other coronary risk factors. They went on and said that if marathon running is going to provide immunity to atherosclerosis, "the running must start before the fifth decade of life."

Waller and his colleagues presented another case in 1981. This was a 51-year-old man who died from coronary heart disease after a 5km run. The man had been running five years, and had high blood pressure and cholesterol, and was undergoing diuretic therapy. The man had never run a marathon and was running 12 miles per week at the time of his death. The authors admit that the man probably had considerable coronary atherosclerosis by the time he started running, but offered the study to demonstrate that running per se does not provide immunity from coronary heart disease.

Bassler, of course, took exception (Bassler, 1982). In a retrospective examination of the dead runner's diet, coupled with his diuretic therapy, Bassler concluded, based on the man's symptoms such as "arm tiredness," that the runner was in a potassium deficient state which produced death.

Asay and Vieweg (1981) presented the case of a 54-year-old male runner, physically active all of his life, who had "angiographically documented coronary artery disease." The man had been running for 20 years and his only known coronary risk factor was a family history of coronary heart disease. The authors concluded that this study "negates the contention that exercise absolutely protects from coronary atherosclerosis."

The Bassler hypothesis took a more severe beating from three articles that appeared in 1982. The first article was on a highly trained, life-long active, 48-year-old marathoner who had been running 50–70 miles per week for eight years and who had no risk factors (the man had relatively low blood pressure and cholesterol levels, high HDL, low family risk, and a 50 beats per minute pulse) other than he had smoked until he started running. Cardiac catherization showed severe CHD. Although atherosclerosis may have been present prior to age 40 and the onset of running, according to the authors since the man did not have any symptoms before he started to run at age 40 it was demonstrated that the disease had progressed and that running does not prevent the progression of coronary atherosclerosis.

The authors went on to reiterate a comment made previously, that claims of immunity from heart disease give the illusion of invincibility and contributed to runners' ignoring symptoms. They concluded that although running does not offer protection from the development of CHD, it may lead to the manifestation of symptoms earlier when the disease is "more amenable to therapy" (Handler et al., 1982).

It should be mentioned that three letters responded negatively to some of the conclusions made by the authors. The first letter said that the runner had a significant coronary risk factor, namely an elevated VLDL level (Gurewich and Lapinska, 1983). The second and third letters pointed out that the runner had started exercising at age 40 and that the disease may have been present prior to his starting to run (Pierach, 1983; Coverman, 1983).

The second article in 1982 described 12 men aged 28–74 who died while jogging in Rhode Island (Thompson et al., 1982). Eleven of the 12 died from coronary heart disease and eight of the 11 were autopsied. Many of the men had one or more CHD risk factors in that they smoked, had high cholesterol levels, or a family history of heart disease. Furthermore, most had not jogged for very many years and only one ran more than 12 miles per week. Thompson did not mention if any had run a marathon.

The article concluded that the death rate from coronary heart disease is seven times higher during jogging than during sedentary activity. The article went on to say that this "suggested" that "exercise contributes to sudden death in susceptible persons."

An editorial that appeared in the same issue noted that although the death rate during jogging was higher than "would be expected by chance," it was not known what percentage of the runners had known coronary heart disease and ran as a form of rehabilitation. The editorial also said that running may precipitate the symptoms of coronary heart disease which would allow the individual to seek earlier medical treatment (Jones, 1982).

Bassler responded (1983) by saying that at autopsy the term coronary heart disease is used as an euphemism for "sudden unexpected death." He also said that there was an inverse relationship between death during jogging and age, with younger joggers having a higher death rate than older joggers, which Bassler claimed was the reverse of what one would expect given the expectation that the older group would have the more advanced disease and thus be more affected by vigorous exercise.

Thompson (1983) replied that he "appreciated" Bassler's "provocative" comments, but that the risk of death from coronary heart disease increased with increasing age. He also said that he felt that there was ample evidence at autopsy to indicate that the men had died from coronary heart disease. Thompson concluded by saying that he "eagerly" awaited the "presentation of Bassler's data."

The third article appeared in 1982 and was written by Virmani and his associates (1982). They studied 30 runners who had died and been autopsied. Only three of the men were marathon runners. Of the three marathoners, one was a 38-year-old man who ran 105 miles per week and who had a 23 year history of running. This means that he should have started exercising at an age that should have provided him with protection, if his early exercise was at an intensive enough level; he did have a history of transient ischemic attacks. He died from coronary heart disease. His only known risk factor was a family history of coronary heart disease. The second marathoner was a 42-year-old man who had been running for three years. He had several coronary risk factors such as a family history of coronary heart disease and high blood pressure and cholesterol. The degree of atherosclerosis was described as "severe." The third marathoner was only 27 when he died. He died from a "floppy mitral valve."

Although the 27-year-old who died from a defective valve and the 42-year-old who had only just started running and who had several coronary risk factors can be dismissed in terms of not contradicting Bassler's hypothesis, the 38-year-old marathoner stands as a glaring and damaging contradiction.

Virmani and his associates found that the cause of death was very clear for most: 73 percent had severe coronary atherosclerosis. However, the cause of death could not be determined in seven of the runners. Six of the seven had a condition known as myocytolysis, a condition where the cells in the muscles die or decompose: *myo* (muscle) + *cyto* (cells) + *lysis* (destruction of red blood cells). The authors hypothesized that an inadequate oxygen supply was reponsible for this condition.

Does *running* prevent coronary heart disease? The answer is no! Even the ability to run a marathon does not imply the absence of serious coronary heart disease.

Bassler has continued to modify his views. In a recent interview in *The Runner* (see Olsen, 1982) it is apparent that he has not lost the ability to be both thought-provoking and controversial.

Bassler's new concern is runner deaths. He has collected the autopsy reports on male runners who were very physically fit, lean, and running many miles a week. They died for reasons medical examiners have difficulty explaining. Bassler believes that their leanness, high mileage, and diets are the cause. He noted that individuals such as these generally have PVB — premature ventricular beats, or extra heart beats. He claims that these occur prior to fatal arrhythmia. Specifically he said that runners lose the fat they need to sustain life. When they run out of fat because of their high mileage and restricted diets, they die (Bassler 1984a; 1984b).

He also talked about "nutritional arrhythmia." This is when a runner has an irregular heart beat because he lacks something in his diet. He said that runners often sweat out minerals such as copper, zinc, and potassium, all of which are important in maintaining a regular heart beat (see Barnes, 1979).

Although Bassler originally advocated "teetotaling" (Bassler and Cardello, 1975) he now "advocates" beer drinking. He is also very much against running in competition, in part because of the high rate of injury and in part because of the Type A personality it appears to create. He also says that it is all right to eat junk food.

The Bassler hypothesis appears to be that many of the disorders and diseases associated with aging can be prevented by running three one-hour runs per week and by being able to walk a marathon.

The Bassler hypothesis brings up one other issue that needs to be briefly addressed: dead runners. Many runners were shocked when Jim Fixx, well-known runner and author of two best-selling books on running, died while on a ten mile run. Although Fixx's death may be explained by his history that included obesity, smoking, a family history of heart disease, and his ignoring classic warning symptoms of CHD, there are other examples of dead runners that are more difficult to ignore.

Two studies have addressed this issue. The first was by Siscovick and his associates (1984). This was a community-based study of individuals who had suffered an out-of-hospital primary cardiac arrest from suspected heart disease. The study only included individuals who were apparently healthy until their cardiac arrest.

The study was attempting to resolve the discrepancy between studies demonstrating that exercise is associated with a reduction in heart-related disease and deaths, and studies demonstrating that a disproportionately large number of cardiac events occur during exercise. Thus, which is greater during exercise, risk or benefit?

The study found that the likelihood of primary cardiac arrest *was* greater during exercise. However, among those who exercised, the overall likelihood of cardiac arrest was only 40 percent of that of sedentary individuals. In an editorial response to the article, Thompson and Mitchell (1984) said that "any short-term risk of exercise is outweighed by the long-term beneficial effects of physical activity."

The second study was by Noakes, Opie, and Rose (1984). Although written to apply a final *coup de grâce* to the Bassler hypothesis, the article provided valuable information on marathon runners who died suddenly or developed symptoms of CHD. The article pointed out that the runners generally had a high incidence of CHD risk factors: HBP, family history of CHD, lipid abnormalities, smoking. The study also reported that several runners ignored classic warning symptoms of CHD. It also observed that an abnormally high number of cardiac events occurred during or shortly after competitive races. The authors reiterated that running, even long distances, does not provide immunity from CHD or death. They also emphasized that runners need to seek medical advice when symptoms develop, and that physicians needed to investigate the symptoms to ascertain the cause.

It is clear that many individuals develop heart disease. The question thus becomes, is running a good form of cardiac rehabilitation?

Cardiac Rehabilitation Through Running

Today cardiac rehabilitation through running seems almost commonplace. This is partly because of the widespread publicity on such programs whose patients "graduate" after they have run a marathon. It is only relatively recently, however, that exercise has been used as a form of cardiac rehabilitation. In the past, physical exertion for cardiac patients, even to the extent of sitting in a chair, was considered life-threatening.

The Belief in Rehabilitative Exercise

The treatment of heart disease has obviously varied according to the dominant medical belief of the time. In this country prior to the 1870s, there were few medical men who recognized the value of bed rest for a diseased heart. The dominant belief was that a diseased heart needed to be strengthened through exercise (see Pratt, 1920).

However, in the 1870s exercise fell into disfavor and a "cardinal principle in the treatment of injury and disease," namely that of rest, became the standard mode of treatment (Levine, 1951).

Rest is well known, respected, and widely used in the treatment of injury and disease. For conditions such as broken bones, sprains, or infections there are few who would argue with rest as a therapeutic principle. Although it is relatively easy to immobilize most injured body parts, the heart presents a problem since it cannot be immobilized. In the early part of this century, physicians used the next "best" procedure for cardiac patients; they demanded bed rest for at least six weeks after a cardiac event such as a myocardial infarction.

In 1920 Dr. Joseph Pratt summarized the dominant medical belief about exercise in the treatment of heart disease when he said that rest "acts beneficially and that it does so by increasing the reserve force of the enfeebled heart" (see Barker, 1920).

The belief in bed rest for cardiac patients was not without scientific support. In 1939 a study was published in which it was determined that at least six weeks were needed for heart muscle that had died as the result of a myocardial infarction to be transformed into "firm scar tissue." It was believed that if physical activity was started before the scar tissue had formed, that an aneurysm might form or that the myocardium (heart muscle) might rupture. Several defects in this study have now been recognized, the most important one being that the researchers examined only *very* ill heart patients, all of whom died shortly after their heart attacks. Thus, the individuals examined for this study were not necessarily comparable to most cardiac patients (Mallory et al., 1939; see Pratt, 1920; Barker, 1920).

In fact, in challenging the wide-spread belief and practice of bed rest for cardiac patients, the chairman of the American Medical Association said, in his 1944 address to that organization, that "Within the last three decades there has developed a tendency to regard prolonged rest in bed ... as the *sine qua non* of the proper management of the more serious forms of heart disease" (Harrison, 1944). To demonstrate just how ingrained bed rest was as *the* form of treatment for cardiac patients, Harrison related that when he visited European cardiac clinics in 1927 and saw cardiac patients sitting in chairs and walking, he thought of it as a "shocking practice." He went on with the observation that allowing patients mobility within the limits of their disease had beneficial effects both medically and psychologically.

Harrison was not the first to claim that "complete" bed rest was probably more damaging than beneficial to many cardiac patients. One of the first significant challenges to the "traditional" American method of treating cardiac patients was an article written by Samuel A. Levine in 1940. While Levine acknowledged the importance of rest, he also pointed out that complete bed rest can introduce new symptoms, such as pulmonary distress. In other words, Levine saw supine bed rest placing a greater work load on the heart than would be placed on the heart in a normal sitting position. Although Levine did not recommend marathon running, he broke from the traditional method of treatment and recommended that cardiac patients be allowed to rest in chairs.

In 1944 Levine wrote another article for the *Journal of the American Medical Association* called "Some Harmful Effects of Recumbency in the Treatment of Heart Disease." In the article he said, "we see gross evidence of the deleterious results that are produced by bed rest," and that "Rest in bed, which has been the backbone of our treatment of heart failure, needs reconsideration in light of some possible harmful effects" (see Dock, 1944).

Harrison and Levine's articles did not bring about a rapid revolution in the medical care and treatment of cardiac patients. In 1950 Dr. C. Warren Irvin and Dr. Alexander M. Burgess wrote a scathing article for the *New England Journal of Medicine* in which they severely criticized the traditional method of treating cardiac patients. They spoke of medicine's "ritualistic following of unproved traditional procedures," and of widely accepted medical practices conflicting with the "natural, perhaps instinctive tendencies of patients." They went on and said that there was no "statistical evidence" that the traditional method of treating cardiac patients through bed rest was of positive benefit, or of more benefit, than other courses of treatment (Irvin and Burgess, 1950).

Additionally, Levine was not through with his criticism of the traditional form of treatment for cardiac patients. In 1951 he wrote an article for the *American Heart Journal* in which he again challenged the almost "universal practice" of enforcing 24 hour bed rest for cardiac patients. Levine was very critical of the medical establishment for not recognizing what cardiac patients "must have known from time immemorial," namely that they could obtain relief from their breathing difficulties by sitting up in a chair.

Levine mentioned that he had personally observed several patients undergo a remarkable recovery by using this process, and said that as a result he had "gradually developed enough courage to treat patients with congestive heart failure ... by keeping them in a chair." In reporting the case of a man who seemed on the verge of death Levine said that after sitting in a chair he made "amazing" improvements. Levine reported that the nurses and physicians described the change as a "miracle."

Levine continued by saying that after three to four weeks of rest in a chair, if the patient had made "satisfactory" progress, the patient could be allowed to walk. Thereafter, the patient's activities could be gradually increased.

Both Levine and Harrison reported not only the positive medical consequences of deviating from the traditional form of treatment, but also of the positive psychological benefits. It was mentioned, for example, that as a result of complete, absolute, and prolonged bed rest, many patients exaggerated the extent of their illness and this created a "post infarctional anxiety state."

In 1952 Levine and his colleague presented the first "scientific" evidence that sitting in a chair was *not* harmful to patients and that this treatment reduced cardiac output by 23 percent and thus accelerated the rehabilitation process while eliminating some of the negative consequences of prolonged bed rest such as constipation, pneumonia, prostate problems, pulmonary edema, and exhaustion. Among other developments they concluded that their patients had a "continued sense of well-being and high morale." They also wrote that when their patients were allowed to walk, the dizziness or weakness commonly associated with those who had undergone bed rest was absent (see Coe, 1954).

The major point to be made is that even coming into the 1950s, exercise for cardiac patients — in fact, sitting in a chair — was considered an inappropriate and perhaps even dangerous method of treatment. However, Levine, Harrison, and others had started the slow process of change in the way cardiac patients would be treated in the future.

Although the process was slow, significant change had been made by 1970. For example, after World War II most patients stayed in bed four to eight weeks, and returned to work after four to six months. A survey of physicians conducted in 1970 to assess practice with patients who had suffered a myocardial infarction found that the hospital stay for cardiac patients had been reduced to three weeks and that most patients returned to work within two to four months (Wenger et al., 1973).

The authors of the above study did not examine which type of cardiac program physicians placed their patients in. They did ask, however, if they used "exercise testing" to better assess their cardiac patients' functioning. It was found that exercise testing was used by 12 percent of internists, 20 percent of general practitioners, and 24 percent of cardiologists. Of those who did not use exercise testing, 36 percent of the internists, 27 percent of the general practitioners, and 30 percent of the cardiologists did not use it primarily because they feared for the safety of their patients. The actual percentage of physicians who believed that exercise testing was "dangerous" was probably much higher than the figures noted above. This is because many physicians may have listed their "primary" reason for not using exercise testing as the lack of equipment; they did not have equipment because they believed exercise testing to be dangerous. The authors concluded that these physicians had "unwarranted misconceptions" concerning the safety of exercise testing on cardiac patients (see Vaisrub, 1980b; Theroux et al., 1979).

It is apparent that as late as 1970 a significant percentage of physicians believed exercise testing was "dangerous" for their patients. It is unlikely that these physicians would place their patients in a cardiac rehabilitation exercise program.

One of the factors that helped to change the way cardiac patients were treated was the results of studies on early mobilization and discharge for those who had suffered a myocardial infarction. A number of studies demonstrated that patients with uncomplicated myocardial infarctions could be safely mobilized and discharged much earlier than previously believed (see Lamers et al., 1973; Harpur et al., 1971; Hayes et al., 1974; Ross, 1978).

One of the most nearly definitive studies on early discharge was conducted at the Duke University Medical Center (McNeer et al., 1978). Here the researchers studied 67 patients who had not had any serious complications after their fourth day of hospitalization and who were considered candidates for early release. Thirty-three of the 67 were discharged after one week. Those who were not discharged early stayed primarily because their private physicians preferred a more "traditional" form of treatment. Most of these individuals were discharged by their eleventh day of hospitalization. Those discharged early were supplied with portable cardiac monitors, and for the next two weeks were visited about every other day by a nurse.

After six months those who were released early and those who were recommended for early release but stayed an additional period of time were compared. There were no significant differences in the number of deaths, the incidence of recurrent myocardial infarction, the frequency of angina attacks, or heart failure. The authors concluded that "it is feasible and ethically justified to discharge such uncomplicated patients at one week after an acute myocardial infarction." The authors also found that early release could save each patient an average of $2,032.

The current trend appears to be a shift away from hospitalization for uncomplicated myocardial infarction patients. A recent commentary in the *Journal of the American Medical Association* was titled, "Is It Good Practice to Treat Patients with Uncomplicated Myocardial Infarction at Home?" The article said available research had not demonstrated that mortality rates were different for those who received home care versus those who were placed in coronary care units. The commentary concluded by saying that "forcing all patients into the same kind of high-technology expensive care is hardly defensible" (Eggertgen and Berg, 1984).

Cardiac Rehabilitation Through Running

A number of studies were conducted between the 1950s and the early 1970s to further evaluate the impact of physical activity on cardiac rehabilitation. The results were generally favorable and indicated that those whose rehabilitation involved physical activity were discharged from the hospital earlier, had better self concepts, returned to work earlier, and could engage in more self-care than those treated by the traditional method. Additionally, these studies did not find a higher death rate or a higher rate of complications for those cardiac patients who participated in cardiac rehabilitation exercise programs.

Although a variety of studies appeared on cardiac patients demonstrating that exercise could increase physiological indicators such as physical work capacity, most cardiac rehabilitation units still waited for more research to appear before implementing exercise programs. Slowly the results of cardiac rehabilitation exercise programs started to appear.

In 1968 Daniel Brunner published an article about a three year cardiac rehabilitation exercise program for coronary patients. Brunner had collected and analyzed research in the early 1960s on coronary heart disease in an Israeli kibbutz. He found that sedentary workers had an incidence of coronary heart disease two to three times higher than those engaged in physically active occupations. He also found that after a heart attack the sedentary workers had a death rate that was four times higher than those in physically active occupations. Brunner and his associates used these observations in establishing a rehabilitation program for coronary patients that included physical reconditioning.

The program was cautious in its implementation of physical reconditioning and did not introduce physical conditioning until three months after the heart attack. The program involved gradually increasing the physical workload. For example, during the first stage patients were limited to 30 minutes of exercise two to three times per week. During the second stage the intensity and duration of the exercise was increased. Brunner mentioned that as a result of this program much of the psychological stress of having had a heart attack was eliminated since the patients could demonstrate to themselves that they were not permanently incapacitated, and that in time they would be able to lead "normal" lives.

The preliminary data were very positive. After one year, of the 64 patients, two had died and four had suffered recurrent heart attacks. In a group matched by age and extent of coronary heart disease but who did not exercise, there were seven deaths and nine recurrent attacks.

While other studies started to appear on exercise programs for postcardiac patients, most of them stressed mild exercise and noncompetitive sports. However, in 1968 one study appeared that reported on a vigorous exercise program for cardiac patients that emphasized competitive sports. Again, it was a study done in Israel (Gottheiner, 1968). The author reported that vigorous exercise was used for four reasons. First, because the dangers of vigorous exercise for postcoronary patients had been exaggerated, second because the program was undertaken in a gradual manner and the patients were closely monitored, which reduced the risk factor, third that vigorous exercise was needed to produce the results needed, and fourth, that vigorous competitive exercise provided a wider range of more interesting and stimulating sports which would enhance the participants' self-concepts and motivation and thus the participants were more likely to continue in the program.

Over a five year span 1,103 individuals participated in the program. All of the sports had a rhythm to them, such as swimming, running, walking, cycling, or rowing. Sports that included irregular bursts of energy were considered unsuitable. Ten to 12 weeks after their heart attacks the participants were started in a seven stage program. The first three stages were "preparatory" stages and started off with breathing exercises and a slow walking program. After approximately nine months the individuals could "graduate" to the last four stages that were called the sports stages. Again, progression through these stages was a gradual process.

After five years 55 percent of the participants had progressed through all seven stages and an additional 25 percent had obtained either stage five or six. Of the 1,103 original participants, 49 died during the five year study period, which represented 3.6 percent of the total. Nine of these deaths were from noncardiac causes (i.e., automobile accident, cancer, etc.). In terms of death and stage in the program, 17 were in stage one, 17 were in stage two, seven were in stage three, two were in stage four, three were in stage five, one was in stage six, and two were in stage seven. Thus, there was a higher incidence of death for those who had not progressed very far in the program. This may have been because they did not achieve the level of fitness necessary to provide them any protection, or that their disease was too advanced to allow them to progress. It should be noted that the 3.6 percent death figure was low in comparison to the national figure of 12 percent for coronary patients in general. At least part of the difference is attributable to the fact that not everyone had equal access to this program. Thus, there was a selection process in the participants for this program that explains part of the differences in death rate, but it is unlikely that it can explain all of the difference.

Overall the study found that the participants' heart rates were reduced, they had more normal electrocardiographic readings, and their blood pressure levels were lowered.

By the late 1960s research in the United States on cardiac rehabilitation through exercise was primarily limited to studies on research animals. However, there were a few experimental research programs underway. The results of one such program were published in 1968 in the *Bulletin of the New York Academy of Medicine* (Hellerstein, 1968). The author reported that "physical training has not as yet found acceptance in this country as an integral part of the management of the patient with a myocardial infarct." He went on to explain that experimental research programs on animals had found that exercise induced greater "collateral circulation."

The author reasoned that the findings on animals were applicable to humans with atherosclerosis and developed a study to test his hypothesis. Hellerstein wanted to find out if "sedentary, lazy, hypokinetic, sloppy, endomesomorphic, overweight males," who had atherosclerosis, could become interested in participating in an exercise program. The author also wanted to ascertain if life expectancy and the quality of life could be increased through an exercise program. The study included individuals who had suffered heart attacks. The study also sought to change the diets and life styles of the participants, although the primary emphasis was on exercise. The research examined 254 white, middle to upper class males with arteriosclerotic heart disease whose average age was 49.

The exercise program started with exercises tailored to the individuals' abilities and then gradually increased in intensity. The initial levels of physical fitness were very low for the men.

The results were very positive. The study found that 75 percent of the men stayed in the program, and that there was a significant increase in their physical fitness as measured by heart rate, blood pressure, and oxygen consumption. The researcher also found that the electrocardiographic readings of the men became more normal. There were additional benefits in that the men slept and thought better, felt less tense, and had more "zest for life."

The mortality rate was lower for the exercise group than for subjects treated in the "traditional" manner. This study reported a mortality rate of 1.95 per 100 patient-years. The normal mortality rate for men in a traditional program would have been from 4.5 to 6 per 100 patient-years. Part of the difference may have been because the study was somewhat selective of its participants in that it did not take those with congestive heart failure, or others who were extremely ill. Although the author admitted that the study was still in the "experimental stage," he concluded that an exercise program for patients with coronary heart disease was both a safe and effective mode of treatment.

Although numerous "experimental" exercise cardiac rehabilitation programs published the results of their research in the late 1960s and early 1970s, most had one major defect: those who participated in the exercise programs were different from those who participated in traditional programs. That is, the researchers in the exercise programs selected cardiac patients who had less disease, whose myocardial infarction had been less extensive, or who had the greatest chance of survival. The traditional programs did not have this option. Thus, many claimed the differences between the cardiac rehabilitation programs that used exercise and those that used traditional methods were not a result of the impact of the programs but of different types of patients.

This criticism was addressed in a study published in 1972 (Rechnitzer et al., 1972). Over a seven year period this study examined 68 males who had suffered myocardial infarctions and who participated in a cardiac rehabilitation program that included exercise. These men were then matched with controls similar in age and extent of disease but who chose not to participate in an exercise program. The findings were startling. After seven years 3 percent of those in the exercise program had a recurrent non-fatal myocardial infarction. The same figure for the control group was 13 percent. In terms of cardiac death the study found that 8 percent of those in the exercise group had died in comparison to 14 percent of the controls.

In addition to the benefits of a lower myocardial infarction recurrence rate and a lower death rate, the researchers also pointed out the possible physiological/medical benefits that those in the exercise group obtained: increased collateral blood supply, lowered heart rate, increased heart efficiency. They also found that generally those in a cardiac rehabilitation exercise program lost weight and stopped smoking, and that these variables may help to explain the differences in the myocardial infarction recurrence and death rates. The researchers did recognize that those willing to participate in an exercise program may be very different in terms of personality and that this might also explain part of the difference.

In 1973 and 1974 the *Journal of the American Medical Association* published two articles on marathon running after a myocardial infarction. Both of the articles were studies conducted at the Toronto Rehabilitation Center. The first was published in the "Medical News" section (Anonymous, 1973) and said that seven men, all of them recovering from myocardial infarctions, had run in and completed the Boston Marathon. The director of the program, Dr. Terrence Kavanagh, said that this demonstrated that with proper conditioning, those who have had a myocardial infarction could withstand physical stress as much, "if not more," than a normal individual. Kavanagh added that this viewpoint would have been considered highly "dangerous" only ten years previously.

Kavanagh and his colleagues, Roy Shephard and Veena Pandit, published the results of the Boston Marathon run in an article in 1974. They said that the men completed the race in from four and one half to slightly over five hours and that the medical examinations carried out immediately after the race found no serious physical problems. The men ran at an average of 81 percent of their maximum oxygen consumption. The authors did report that a substantial weight loss occurred but that the temperature was relatively high and the men did not consume the necessary amount of fluids.

In 1974 Dr. William Haskell of the Cardiac Rehabilitation Program at Stanford University Medical School published an article that summarized the research to date on physical activity for myocardial infarction patients.

Haskell said that although the results from the studies of cardiac rehabilitation programs that had used physical activity had been positive, "definitive evidence" was not yet available. Haskell pointed out that the benefits of such programs seemed obvious: less physical deconditioning and less psychological trauma. He also mentioned some of the possible complications of exercise for cardiac patients, such as precipitation of another infarction, the formation of an aneurysm, or cardiac rupture. Haskell summarized that those in the physical rehabilitation programs may have more positive results not because of the exercise but because they were a select group, or because the exercise programs brings about a psychological change that enhances well-being and self-confidence.

The problems mentioned by Haskell in adequately evaluating a cardiac rehabilitation program were emphasized by Bruce and his colleagues (1974) that same year. They published a study on the first 603 individuals who enrolled in the Cardiopulmonary Research Institute rehabilitation program at Washington University in Seattle. The study reported that 58.4 percent of the participants had dropped out of the program after slightly more than a year. After three years fewer than 30 percent of the original participants were still active in the program. The study found several differences between the dropouts and those who remained active. For example, the mortality rate of the dropouts was 4.9 per 100 person-years and for the active participants, 2.6; the authors found that the two groups were not comparable, however. 38 percent of the dropout participants were working in comparison to 67 percent of the active participants. This indicated that those in the dropout group had more extensive disease than those in the active group. This study repeated the frequently stated concern with studies of this type, namely that researchers may be comparing an exercise group with a nonexercise group but that the two groups are not comparable.

The above study also pointed out one other frequently mentioned problem in exercise cardiac rehabilitation programs, namely that of safety. That is, how safe is it for an individual who has had a myocardial infarction to engage in a vigorous exercise program without medical supervision? It might be mentioned that when Kavanagh's patients ran the Boston Marathon they were followed by two cars with emergency medical equipment and medical personnel. Although most studies have stressed the safety of their programs, during the first three years of the program mentioned above by Bruce and his associates (1976) there were 11 instances of heart arrest during exercise. Defibrillation was successful in all 11 cases but it pointed out the potential dangers involved.

Another study published in 1982 also addressed the issue of the safety of exercise for cardiac patients (Faraday et al., 1982). The study pointed out that too often cardiac patients are given subjective exercise guildelines to follow such as "don't exercise too hard" or "exercise until you have discomfort." The study reported that the "subjective" guildelines were not enough — 15 percent of the cardiac patients who were taking a treadmill test prior to entry into a cardiac rehabilitation exercise program had "life-threatening events" occur which resulted in the cancellation of the tests. It is interesting that those who had their tests terminated generally perceived their level of effort as "light" and were unaware of any problems. Thus, according to the authors, the cardiac patients "probably would have continued to exercise even though they were experiencing possible life-threatening cardiac abnormalities."

Based on three years of research the authors of the above article formulated three recommendations. First, that during the exercise testing of cardiac patients, ECG monitoring is necessary to ascertain the appropriate "exercise prescription." Second, that upper and lower extremity exercise require the same amount of monitoring. Third, that cardiac patients entering a rehabilitation exercise program should be monitored for 12 weeks.

Although there have been many studies demonstrating the value of exercise for cardiac patients, studies that have helped change the way cardiac patients are treated, it must also be pointed out that not all of the studies conducted on rehabilitation exercise programs for cardiac patients have found positive results.

For example, a frequently made claim is that the program will increase coronary collateral circulation. This result had been found in several animal studies (see Eckstein, 1957; Stevenson et al., 1964) and although some studies have reported an apparent increase in coronary collaterals in humans (see Ferguson et al., 1973), most have not and the current belief is that cardiac rehabilitation exercise programs will probably not increase coronary collaterals (see Rechnitzer, 1982; Nolewajka et al., 1979).

Another study published in the *New England Journal of Medicine* in 1981 questioned the need for "in-hospital" exercise for myocardial infarction patients. This study addressed a trend that came into existence during the early 1970s, shortly after early mobilization for cardiac patients, namely in-hospital exercise for cardiac patients. In-hospital exercise came about as a result of the studies indicating that extensive physical deconditioning and psychological disturbances occurred as a result of prolonged hospitalization. The in-hospital exercise was to prevent these problems. This study was not being critical of exercise programs for those who had been discharged from the hospital but was questioning the need for them while the cardiac patient was hospitalized.

The study said that one of the reasons for the establishment of exercise programs for coronary patients was to prevent a decrease in physical conditioning and to prevent the psychological depression that occurred from prolonged incapacitation. However, the authors pointed out, the average length of in-hospital stay for myocardial infarction was now so short that the negative consequences of prolonged incapacitation were not likely to take place to any significant degree.

To find out if in-hospital exercise programs were beneficial for myocardial infarction patients, the researchers devised a study in which patients were randomly assigned to either an exercise or nonexercise group. Those in the exercise group engaged twice daily in a very mild regime of exercises. At the end of their hospitalization, about 10 days for each group, exercise testing was done on a treadmill to ascertain if the exercise group had a better treadmill performance. The study found that there were no significant differences between the two groups. The authors concluded that their study did not demonstrate that an in-hospital cardiac exercise program was beneficial in preventing deconditioning. The study described the safety procedures of the program and also stressed that the program may have helped identify individuals who needed surgery (see Jennings et al., 1984). The study pointed out that the intensity of the exercise the patients participated in was very light and that there were only about ten exercise sessions. It also said that both groups were ambulatory after only three to four days and that this, coupled with the shortened time period, may have been responsible for the results.

Sivarajan and her colleagues (1981) also found little value in an in-hospital exercise program for myocardial patients. The researchers pointed out that although there was a growing trend toward starting exercise much earlier than previously, the risks and benefits of these programs had not been studied. To assess the impact of an in-hospital program the researchers randomly assigned myocardial infarction patients to either a nonexercise or exercise group. The exercise group started exercising twice a day four to five days after admission. The exercises were primarily arm and leg exercises with weights and pulleys. There was also a walking program. Patients in both groups were discharged after an average of 10 days. Before discharge both groups had a low-level treadmill exercise test conducted. The researchers did not find any differences between the two groups and concluded that there were no "beneficial or deleterious effects of an early, in-hospital program." The researchers did say that starting an exercise program shortly after the myocardial infarction, when the patient's motivation was usually highest, may help to establish a regular pattern of exercise.

In 1981 the results of the National Exercise and Heart Disease Project on the effects of exercise on the morbidity and mortality rates of myocardial infarct patients were presented. In total, 651 men who had suffered a myocardial infarction were studied for three years. The men were separated into two groups: exercise and nonexercise. Three times a week the exercise group jogged for 15 minutes and played 25 minutes of games. At the end of three years 7 percent of the nonexercise group and 4.6 percent of the exercise group had died, a nonsignificant difference. Approximately 18 percent of each group experienced a recurrent nonfatal myocardial infarction during the study. The study concluded by saying that a prescribed "supervised" exercise program for individuals who have had a myocardial infarction "may be beneficial in reducing subsequent cardiac mortality, but the evidence is not convincing" (Shaw, 1981).

A study published in 1981 in the British medical journal *The Lancet* also concluded that "early" exercise training was of little value to cardiac functioning. This study examined 129 men admitted to a hospital for treatment of myocardial infarction. The men were randomly assigned to one of three groups. The first was the control group in which the patients received "standard medical care." The second, the exercise group, started in a twice-weekly (for four weeks) program approximately four weeks after they were admitted to the hospital. The third group was the "advice" group. This group received "normal treatment" and they and their wives met with a therapist for "discussion and advice."

The three groups were examined at three months and 18 months after their myocardial infarctions. The study found that in terms of psychological factors, and amount of physical activity, that there were no differences among the three groups. After three months the exercise group did differ from the other two in that its participants were more "enthusiastic" about their treatment. In exercise testing they also achieved a higher work load level than the other two groups. The only significant findings after 18 months were that the advice group had a better adjustment in satisfaction and frequency of sexual intercourse. The researchers found no differences among the groups in terms of compliance with dietary or smoking guidelines. Also, after 18 months there were no differences in cardiac symptoms. The authors concluded that exercise training shortly after myocardial infarction was of little value in physiological or psychological rehabilitation (Mayou et al., 1981).

An article that appeared in the *American Journal of Cardiology* reported the results of a four year study on 733 myocardial patients over four years to ascertain the impact of both a low- and high-intensity exercise program. This study eliminated several of the methodological criticisms of other studies by placing men in both groups who had other coronary risk factors such as high blood pressure. The dropout rate in both groups was, however, very high, about 45 percent. The study concluded that a high-intensity exercise program for postmyocardial patients is no more effective in reducing the risk of a recurrent myocardial infarction than a low-intensity exercise program. In defense of the program, however, the rate of myocardial infarction recurrence in both groups was about half of what would have normally been found. This may have been because of the effects of the program, the high dropout rate, or the extensive medical supervision (Rechnitzer et al., 1983; see Goldberg and McMahon, 1983).

The above studies are important in that they show that not all research on cardiac rehabilitation programs using exercise have found the expected positive results. Although the studies on in-hospital exercise were not a criticism of exercise rehabilitation programs per se, they did note that little deconditioning takes place in most cardiac patients because of the shortened hospitalization period, and that the expense of exercise programs may not be justified. Some of these studies can be criticized because they did not report the intensity of the exercise in which the patients engaged.

We have also seen that there have been studies indicating that cardiac rehabilitation exercise programs have not always found significant differences between exercise groups and normal treatment groups (see Kavanagh et al., 1970; Kavanagh et al, 1973). Some studies also have indicated that exercise programs may be dangerous for certain patients. Additionally, the results of exercise programs that have found significant results have been criticized because of the high dropout rate and the way participants were selected.

Additionally, these studies have also pointed out that cardiac rehabilitation programs may cause a coronary event (a myocardial infarction). Because of this it has also been suggested that cardiac rehabilitation exercise programs may exacerbate existing coronary conditions. For example, a recent article in *The Physician and Sportsmedicine* was titled "Can an Exercise Program Worsen Heart Disease?" The study reported on five individuals whose heart disease became more severe during their participation in an exercise cardiac rehabilitation program at the University of California at San Diego. The authors said that they were not trying to discredit the research showing that exercise can be beneficial to cardiac patients, but rather to "balance" the literature. That is, they saw the studies showing positive exercise-induced benefits generating much attention while the opposing research received very little. They also saw "broad conclusions" often being drawn from "unusual patients" (Gamble and Froelicher, 1982).

As a result, they published five case histories of individuals who had been participating in an exercise cardiac rehabilitation program and whose heart disease grew worse during the program. The men participated in the program varying lengths of time, from five months to about two years. Most of them showed significant increases in physical performance, yet all of them had their conditions grow worse. One man, for example, had very rapid atherosclerosis occur in a coronary artery bypass graft.

The authors admitted that there were many benefits from exercise programs and that a variety of factors could explain the deterioration of the men's condition. However, they also stated their belief that more research was needed. The authors mentioned that even though the men's heart disease grew worse, it was not known if the deterioration process would have been more rapid without the exercise program.

In 1981 Dr. Victor Froelicher of the Department of Cardiology at University Hospital in San Diego remarked (see Hage, 1981) at the American College of Sports Medicine that exercise had been oversold for cardiac patients. One of his concerns was that cardiac patients were believing that exercise in and of itself would be sufficient to nullify other coronary risk factors. As a result they were not taking medication or modifying their life style in needed areas. He also said that although exercise may help an individual live longer, "the time they spend living longer will be spent exercising."

Because the increasing awareness of physical fitness had led to the increase in the number of cardiac rehabilitation programs employing exercise and because no definitive studies existed, the Council on Scientific Affairs of the American Medical Association called for a study of "the state of the art of exercise rehabilitation in ... heart disease" (Council on Scientific Affairs, 1981). The results of the study were published in the *Journal of the American Medical Association*. The Council described the "potential" benefits of an exercise program as both psychological — an increase in self concept, less mental depression — and medical — an increase in oxygen uptake, better muscle utilization of oxygen, lower heart rate and blood pressure, faster return to premyocardial infarction state, decrease in fatty tissue, increase in HDL.

The Council said that cardiac rehabilitation exercise programs were safe, but concluded, "To our knowledge, there has been no study that shows the superiority of exercise rehabilitation over a less closely supervised home program." They pointed out that many of the conclusions of the researchers in these programs have been subjective. They also concluded that there was no firm evidence to demonstrate that an exercise cardiac rehabilitation program had a lower mortality or morbidity rate than those programs employing traditional methods.

The Council was not against exercise in cardiac rehabilitation programs. It simply pointed out that because of the variety of exercise programs that had been used and the differences in subject selection, to date no definitive conclusions could be drawn. The Council recommended that further studies be done to examine the long-term consequences of exercise programs (see Rigotti et al., 1983).

In contrast to the American Medical Association's position, an editorial in the *British Journal of Medicine* on cardiac rehabilitation exercise programs for myocardial infarction patients said that "the evidence does show very clearly that progressive exercise is safe, good for morale, and makes people feel better." The author went on and said that he was surprised at how "reluctant" the medical profession was in accepting exercise as a form of treatment for coronary disease given the fact that it was inexpensive, did not produce significant negative side-effects other than temporary muscle soreness, and "makes people feel better" (Carson, 1984).

The debate on cardiac rehabilitation exercise programs will continue until researchers address some of the concerns that have been presented. The major areas that researchers need to concern themselves with are subject selection and the intensity and duration of the program. It is also important for researchers to examine life style changes that occur as a result of an exercise program. For example, some of the exercise programs have reported that participants have stopped smoking and changed to healthier diets. It needs to be ascertained if it is exercise or other life style modifications that are bringing about the differences in myocardial recurrence rates, and death rates.

Although the articles in this section have discussed cardiac rehabilitation exercise programs for myocardial infarction patients, a recent report appeared on exercise for a heart transplant patient. The report was on a 48-year-old man who had undergone a heart transplant in August, 1982. In June, 1983, he jogged in a 12 mile race, beating both his physical therapist and his surgeon (DeSmet et al., 1983; Niset et al., 1985).

2
Women and Running

Introduction

Until recently, sports in American society have been dominated by men. Women were generally restricted to spectators. The extent of women's participation in sports was restricted by three factors. First, by the coverage of the mass media. Stories about women athletes were relegated to seldom-read sections of newspapers and magazines because editors perceived women's sporting events to be dull and uninteresting, and because they saw women athletes as unfeminine and, perhaps even, "unnatural." Because of this, the role models to which women were exposed were generally not sports figures. Second, women were largely ignored by exercise physiologists; when they were studied, the studies were often slanted in that untrained women were compared to highly trained men. The results of these studies confirmed the belief that males were physically superior to females, and that for physiological and biological reasons, women should not participate in athletics. Third, there were a myriad of rules and laws that prohibited women's participation in certain sports and certain events.

In the past, information about women in sports came largely from sexist, superstitious, and unsubstantiated beliefs, selective observations, and inaccurate information. Women were for instance told that if they participated in sports they would lose their "femininity" and the ability to bear children, they would have frequent injuries, they would become "muscle bound," and their breasts would hang down. Given these as the consequences of engaging in sports, most women elected to engage in nonsporting activities.

Even though women were repeatedly told inaccurate stories of what would happen to them if they became athletic, many ignored the warnings. They found that even after years of intensive training they did not become muscle-bound or crippled with injuries, they were capable of having children, they maintained their "femininity," and their breasts stayed firmly in place. Furthermore, the women found they enjoyed not only the athletic activity but also its physiological and psychological benefits.

Fortunately, there has recently been a good deal more interest and research conducted on women and the consequences of their participation in sports. This new research, though often inconclusive, is a needed first step in providing accurate answers for many important questions.

Although women have made gains in the area of running, the gains have been slow and it must be remembered that 1973 was the first year women were officially admitted to the Boston Marathon and 1984 was the first time the marathon event for women was allowed in the Olympics. Ideally, new research will eliminate the remaining barriers (see Andrews, 1979; Kuscsik, 1977).

Gynecological Considerations in Running

As both the number of women participating in running and the intensity of their training increase, so does the demand for and the frequency of gynecological studies. The major concerns appear to be:

1. Will running prevent or delay menarche (an individual's first menstrual period)?
2. In women with normal menstrual cycles, will running cause menstrual disorders? If the answer is yes, why do the disorders occur?
3. For women who have running-induced menstrual disorders, are the disorders harmful, and will reducing weekly mileage bring about a "normal" menstrual cycle?
4. For runners who continue to menstruate, does running have an impact on the length, duration, amount of flow, or amount of discomfort experienced?
5. Does menstruation have an influence on running performance?
6. Once pregnant, should a woman who has been running continue to do so, and if she does, what are the consequences for the fetus and the delivery?
7. Does running have an impact on women who take birth control pills?

The menstrual cycle is a 28-day one (average) in which the uterus of an adult female prepares for the fertilization and growth of an egg by developing a mucous membrane, and if fertilization does not occur, discharges the mucous membrane as blood, dead cell debris, and secretions through the vagina and then starts the cycle over again, unless interrupted by pregnancy, menopause, or a pathological condition. The period of time the discharge takes place is generally four to five days during each cycle. The onset of *menstruation* (the word for the process of the discharge itself) is often considered the first day of the menstrual cycle but technically it is the end of a cycle. *Menarche* is the first occurrence in a young woman of the menstrual cycle.

The term *amenorrhea* refers to the absence of menstruation. There are two types, primary and secondary. Primary amenorrhea refers to a condition where menstruation did not start at puberty. Secondary amenorrhea refers to a condition where menstruation had started but then stopped. Other terms are *oligomenorrhea*, a condition where menstruation is infrequent, *eumenorrhea*, a normally functioning menstrual cycle, and *dysmenorrhea*, which is painful menstruation, such as cramps.

Age at Menarche

The first question is, does running delay the onset of the first menstrual cycle?

Two studies in the 1960s came up with conflicting results on the impact of vigorous exercise on menarche. A study on Hungarian female athletes found that age at menarche was not affected by participation in athletic events (Erdelyi, 1962), but a study on Swedish swimmers found that menarche appeared to occur slightly earlier in athletic than in nonathletic girls (Astrand et al., 1963).

Both of these studies conflict with more recent research which has consistently shown that menarche occurs later in athletes. Additionally, generally the more competitive the athlete, the more delayed the menarche. This has been found in runners, swimmers, ballet dancers, gymnasts, divers, volleyball players, and figure skaters (Malina, 1983; Malina et al., 1978).

A related question is, why does the delay occur? The influence of early training, diet, intensive exercise, and body composition have all been implicated as factors that delay the onset of menarche. It is difficult to separate out the influence of any one single factor since they generally occur in combination with each other. That is, an athlete may start an intensive exercise program early in life that involves a special diet; the results are a body composition more lean than fat. Thus, a study that would single out and implicate just one of these factors is difficult to construct and conduct. This section will examine premenarcheal training, intensive physical activity, body composition, and "other" factors as possible causes of the delay in menarche.

Premenarcheal Training

Athletes who start their training before menarche generally have a significantly delayed menarche. For example, a study of college runners and swimmers found that the average age at menarche for premenarcheal-trained athletes was 15.1. This was significantly later than for athletes who started training after menarche, 12.8, or for nonathletes, 12.7 (Frisch et al., 1981; Frisch, 1982). In fact, one researcher found that every year of training before menarche resulted in a five month delay in menarche (Frisch et al., 1981).

The impact of premenarcheal training on the onset of menarche has been reported in other sports. For ballet dancers who started their training at an average age of 7.4, it was demonstrated that the girls reached menarche at age 13.7, significantly later than for American girls in general (Frisch, et al., 1980). Similar results were found for girls on high school, college, or the 1976 United States Olympic Volleyball team (Malina et al., 1978).

Intensive Physical Activity

Studies are now also implicating intensive physical activity as a causal factor in the delay of menarche. A recent study in the *British Medical*

Journal found that both thinness and intensive physical activity had an impact on the onset of menarche; when the two variables occurred together the results were more significant. The researchers studied 648 girls between the ages of 10 and 14. The percentage who had reached menarche was 15 percent for girls who were thin and engaged in intensive physical activity; 37 for girls who were thin but did not engage in intensive physical activity; and 75 percent for girls who were not thin who did not engage in intensive physical activity. This study thus found that both thinness and intensive physical activity were separately and jointly associated with a delay in menarche (VanDenbroucke et al., 1982).

Body Composition

Studies indicate that for menstruation to occur girls need about 17–22 percent body fat. Young women generally have between 21.9 and 34.4 percent body fat (mature women have between 28.9 and 34.4 percent body fat) (McArdle, et al., 1981). Body fat in women is a factor in menstruation since it converts androgens to estrogens. Estrogen is one hormone that is important for triggering menarche. The percentage of body fat also has an outcome on how estrogen is metabolized by the body. Low body fat can result in a metabolism of estrogen in its least potent form (Frisch et al., 1981; Frisch, 1982).

Although early research examined body weight as the important variable, it should be noted that it is not body weight of itself that is the significant factor, as many have speculated; rather, it is the ratio of lean mass to body fat. It was found, for example, that women athletes who were amenorrheic or oligomenorrheic may have average or above average weight for their height. However, their body weights were more muscle mass and less fat than those of nonathletic women (Frisch et al., 1981).

Other Factors

There are other possible causes for the delay in menarche for many athletically active girls. One possible factor was presented by Malina (1983), who after a thorough analysis of many existing studies as well as his own research, presented a theory with two components.

The first is physique. The basic concept is that most athletes are not selected randomly but on the basis of certain characteristics, such as physique, coordination, and motor skills. Thus, athletes are unique in certain physical characteristics. In his research Malina found that girls who reached menarche later than average tended to have body builds that were more suited for athletic participation. He called the physique "lineal" because the girls with this physique had long legs, narrow hips, and less body fat. Girls who reached menarche at the average age tended to have a different physique which was characterized by short legs, broad hips, and significantly more body weight. His conclusion was that it is not necessarily participation in athletics that is causing the delay in menarche; rather, the physique that assists girls in becoming good athletes is also a type of physique that is associated with a delay in menarche.

The second component deals with socialization. Malina found that age at menarche was also a good indicator of other forms of development, such as pubic hair and breast development. He speculated that girls who are more likely to have been excluded from athletic participation because of body type, are also more likely to develop earlier physiologically. As a result, these girls were socialized away from athletics and toward other social activities. This is for two reasons. First, these girls "appeared" more physiologically mature and were seen as "ready" for other types of socialization. Second, traditionally in American society menstruation and athletics have not "mixed." That is, women have been told that participation in athletics during menstruation was harmful. Although this is a myth, its prevalence removed many young women from athletic activity.

In summary, according to Malina, girls with physiques which reduced their likelihood of athletic participation also develop earlier physiologically. As a result they are socialized away from athletic activity and into other areas where they can find "success." Girls who have physiques that make their selection and participation in athletic activity more likely, also have physiques that develop slower physiologically. These girls are socialized into athletic activity where they find "success."

Besides the above explanations, some researchers believe that the delay in menarche is overstated and merely an indication of small, biased samples. These researchers claim there is no problem, and that studies emphasizing that athletic activity causes a delay in menarche will only have a negative impact on women and sports since the results confirm the expectations and allegations of those who believe that women should not engage in vigorous physical activity (see Malina, 1982).

Menstrual Disorders

Not only can most female athletes expect menarche to be delayed but, after the onset of menstruation, can expect a higher incidence of menstrual disorders than nonathletes (see Loucks and Horvath, 1985).

It should be pointed out, again, that recent studies conflict with earlier findings. For example, in the study conducted on Hungarian female athletes in the 1960s, the author concluded that only 11.3 percent of the women surveyed had menstrual disorders (Erdelyi, 1962). Similar results were found in a study of women athletes at the Tokyo Olympics, where 7.6 percent stated they had menstrual disorders (Zaharieva, 1965).

Although the figures have varied, generally because of differences in the definition of menstrual disorder, more recent studies have almost always found a much higher incidence than the earlier studies, with some reporting rates as high as 90 percent. This is not to say that the earlier studies were incorrect; rather, they examined many different kinds of athletes. It appears that some sports, such as running, are more conducive to producing menstrual disorders than others. Another possible explanation is that women are now training at more intensive levels than in the past, and this is producing the difference in results.

One example of the increase in the reporting of menstrual disorders can be seen by examining the figures reported by American women participating in the 1976 Montreal Olympic games. In this study 59 percent of the women surveyed said that they experienced changes in their menstrual cycles during the competitive season of their sport (Webb et al., 1979).

The prevalence of menstrual disorders in women runners has been well documented. One recent study examined the menstrual histories of women marathoners, distance runners, athletes in other sports, and nonathletes. The study found that the number of menstrual cycles each had experienced during the last year was: marathoners 7.8, distance runners 8.5, other athletes 11.2, and nonathletes 11.5 (Dale et al., 1979b).

A study on 174 female college runners found that 90 percent of them said they experienced changes in their menstrual cycles during the competitive season (Webb and Proctor, 1983).

In a study of runners and swimmers it was found that 61 percent of premenarcheal-trained athletes had irregular cycles and 22 percent were amenorrheic. Seventeen percent had regular cycles. Even for female athletes who started training after menarche, 40 percent had irregular cycles while 60 percent had regular (Frisch et al., 1981). This finding has been replicated several times (see Feicht et al., 1978; Schwartz et al., 1981; Baker et al., 1981).

The above figures are meaningless without a base with which to compare them. That is, the reader does not know what percentage of women in the general population have menstrual disorders. Although exact figures are difficult to obtain, one prominent gynecology textbook has estimated that menstrual irregularity (amenorrhea/oligomenorrhea) is present in fewer than 5 percent of gynecology patients (Novak et al., 1970; see also Shangold and Levine, 1982; Shangold, 1985). Another recent study has noted that about 2 percent of sedentary women are amenorrheic (Sanborn et al., 1982). Thus, it appears that athletes have a much higher incidence of menstrual disturbances than the "normal" population.

It is now well documented that a high percentage of female runners have secondary amenorrhea; the question is why. As with the delay in menarche, a variety of explanations have been offered; again the explanation does not appear to be a simple one. Some of the variables that have been listed as causal factors in menstrual disorders are: premenarcheal training, prior pregnancy, stress, nutrition, previous menstrual history, distance run per week, weight loss, amount of body fat, and hormone changes. Each of these factors, as well as a section on "other" factors, will be examined below.

Premenarcheal Training

As noted above, a study on college swimmers and runners found that only 17 percent of the premenarcheal-trained swimmers had regular cycles while 83 percent had irregular or absent cycles. However, 60 percent of the postmenarcheal-trained swimmers had regular cycles and 40 percent had irregular.

One explanation for this is that the premenarcheal-trained athletes reached menarche approximately two years later than their postmenarcheal-trained teammates and that irregular cycles may be expected for one to three years after menarche (Frisch et al., 1981). Thus, the higher incidence of menstrual disorders in premenarcheal-trained athletes may be explainable because these athletes reached menarche later than postmenarcheal-trained athletes and the regulatory devices involved in the menstrual cycle are still not fully developed. To an extent, this hypothesis is supported by the next variable, prior pregnancy.

Prior Pregnancy

Relatively few studies have examined the importance of prior pregnancy on menstrual disturbances in female runners. Those which have examined this variable have noted that women runners who had been pregnant had a lower incidence of menstrual disorders than those who had not been pregnant. One study found that 21 percent of runners who had been pregnant had either oligomenorrhea or amenorrhea, in contrast to 51 percent of those who had not been pregnant (Dale et al., 1979a; 1979b). Two additional studies have found similar results, 25 versus 47 percent (Baker et al., 1981), and 27 versus 34 percent (Galle et al., 1983).

Although more research on this needs to be conducted, it is a likely hypothesis that prior pregnancy indicates a maturity of the reproductive system, and hence a decreased likelihood of other variables disrupting the menstrual cycle.

In the future, researchers need to find out if the differences noted are merely a function of age. That is, it may not be pregnancy itself which is the important factor, but rather the runners who have been pregnant are generally older than those who have not been pregnant. In support of this belief, one study found that the incidence of amenorrhea was significantly higher in younger runners (less than 30 years of age) where 66 percent had amenorrhea, than in older runners (over 30) where the incidence was 9 percent (Baker et al., 1981).

Stress

Stress has been found to be a major causal variable in producing physiological changes in the body. For example, it has been found that stress can produce peptic ulcers, cardiovascular disease, and arthritis (see Crandall, 1980). Thus, stress can produce a variety of disorders, including menstrual.

One study found that women runners who viewed running as a recreational form of activity had fewer menstrual disturbances than women who viewed it as a competitive activity (*Physician and Sportsmedicine*, 1981). In a study of women on 15 collegiate track and field teams it was found that amenorrheic runners considered their training to be of a higher intensity for a greater part of the year than did runners with normal menstrual cycles (Feicht et al., 1978).

A study by Galle and his associates (1983) found that runners with amenorrhea had higher levels of emotional distress than runners with regular cycles. This suggested, according to the authors, that emotional distress may be related to the development of amenorrhea in some runners.

However, even though stress is unquestionably an important variable, it may not be the primary explanation. In a study of women ballet dancers and women musicians, both of whom had similar stressful career-oriented life styles, it was found that the ballet dancers experienced a higher rate of amenorrhea than the musicians (Warren, 1980). Thus, it may not be stress alone that is the causal factor. Rather, it may be that stress, when combined with other factors, will produce menstrual disorders.

Nutrition

One possible cause of menstrual disturbances that has not been widely investigated is nutrition. One study of 34 high-level ballet dancers found both a high percentage of menstrual disturbances (50 percent), of diets low in nutritional quality, and little knowledge of nutrition. Although the authors could not attribute the high rate of menstrual disturbances to nutrition, they did suggest that this area receive further investigation as a possible causal variable (Calabrese et al., 1983; see Dale and Goldberg, 1982; Norval, 1980). "Pathogenic weight control" in female college athletes (e.g., self-induced vomiting, diuretics, laxatives) has also been examined as a cause of nutritional deficiencies (Rosen et al., 1986). Pressure to reduce body fat caused 32 percent of the athletes and 47 percent of distance runners to use pathogenic weight-control behavior. This often resulted in nutritional deficiencies.

A strong association has been found between amenorrhea and a vegetarian diet, defined as a diet of fewer than 200 grams of meat per week. In investigating this association, the researchers found that 82 percent of the amenorrheic runners were vegetarian, while only 13 percent of the eumenorrheic runners were. The researchers also found that both groups were similar in chronological age, age at menarche, weekly mileage, and percentage of body fat. Although the researchers could not show that a vegetarian diet caused amenorrhea, they stated that the relationship needs further study (Brooks et al., 1984).

Previous Menstrual History

Although not much research exists on this topic, it may be that many of the menstrual disorders reported are nothing more than extensions of existing conditions. For example, in a survey of women who ran in the 1979 New York City Marathon it was found that generally those who had regular menstrual cycles before starting to run had regular menstrual cycles afterwards; those who had irregular menstrual cycles before starting to run had irregular menstrual cycles afterwards (*Physician and Sportsmedicine*, 1981).

In support of this, a paper presented at the International Congress on Women and Sport reported that after starting to train more women marathoners went from irregular to regular cycles than from regular to irregular cycles (Anonymous, 1980). Of the women who had regular cycles before training, 7 percent experienced menstrual disturbances after starting to train. Of the women with irregular cycles before training, 26 percent achieved "normal" cycles after starting to train (see Galle et al., 1983).

Distance Run per Week

The factor that has been examined the most frequently as the suspected cause of menstrual disturbances is distance run per week. Although few studies have examined only this one variable, many have found a correlation between distance run per week and incidence of menstrual disorders; an increased distance has a high positive correlation with menstrual disorders. One study of 128 women collegiate track and cross-country athletes found that 6 percent of those running the shorter distances and 43 percent of those running the longer distances had amenorrhea (Feicht et al., 1978). Another study also found a positive correlation between physical exertion, as judged by miles per week, and the degree of menstrual disorders (Dale, Gerlach et al., 1979). Additionally, a study of women cross-country runners found that women with regular menstrual cycles ran an average of 63.8 miles per week versus an average of 79.6 miles for those with menstrual disorders (Bloomberg, 1977). Also, a study of women who had normal menstrual cycles before running found that the percentage experiencing amenorrhea increased as did weekly mileage: 36 percent of those running 40 or more miles per week had amenorrhea as compared to 27 percent of those running under 40 miles per week (Baker et al., 1981).

Another study titled "Is Athletic Amenorrhea Specific to Runners?" examined distance as a factor and tried to ascertain if it was the level of exertion, as represented by the distance run, that was responsible for amenorrhea. The study also wanted to find if women exerting similar levels of physical energy in different sports had similar rates of amenorrhea. To answer this question the researchers examined female distance runners, swimmers, and cyclists. The study found that as the distance increased for runners so did the incidence of amenorrhea; 40–50 percent of those running 80 or more miles a week were amenorrheic. For swimmers the percentage having amenorrhea was almost constant, about 10 percent, regardless of weekly distance. There was a small variation in the percent of cyclists who had amenorrhea, varying from about 10 to 12 percent (Sanborn et al., 1982).

It has also been reported that menstrual disorders do *not* correlate with miles run per week. A study on 900 women in Portland, Oregon, reported that women who had been running the longest period of time had a higher incidence of amenorrhea than women running a shorter period of time; there was, however, no correlation between amenorrhea and distance run per week. This study also noted that amenorrhea was more prevalent among younger, shorter women (Speroff et al., 1980). That it is distance per se that is the causal variable has also been dismissed by Baker and her associates (1981). They found little correlation between distance run per week and likelihood of amenorrhea. In fact, their "older" runners (30 and up) ran farther — 52 miles per week — than their "younger" runners (18–29 years old) — 38 miles per week — but experienced a lower rate of amenorrhea.

A study on 105 female runners, 15 percent of whom had amenorrhea, found that distance run per week was not related to amenorrhea. This study found that amenorrhea was not significantly different for females running fewer than or more than 30 miles per week. They obtained the same results when they repeated the analysis using either fewer than or more than 40 miles per week as the standard (Galle et al., 1983).

Although many studies have examined distance as a causal variable, it is interesting to note that the distance that "triggers" amenorrhea varied dramatically from study to study. In some studies running as few as 20 miles per week appears to be sufficient; in other studies, women running 60 miles a week did not experience any problems. In other words, there is not one threshold distance above which all or most women appear to experience menstrual disorders. Because of the large differences noted, researchers have turned their attention away from distance per se as the causal variable in menstrual disorders, and are now focusing on the consequence of running longer distances, namely loss of weight and body fat.

Weight Loss

Anorexia nervosa, a condition where individuals restrict their food intake and hence lose large amounts of weight, has often been associated with amenorrhea. Because of this, the weight loss most runners experience has been targeted as the cause of amenorrhea.

Weight loss as a consequence of running has been well-documented. A study of 168 women found that joggers (5–30 miles per week) averaged a loss of 6.58 pounds while runners (30 or more miles per week plus interval training) averaged a loss of 7.66 pounds (Dale et al., 1979).

A study found that women who weighed 115 pounds or less when they started running, and who lost 10 pounds or more, were the most likely to develop amenorrhea or other menstrual disorders (Speroff et al., 1980). It has also been found that women runners who lost 5 percent of their weight since starting their training, and who were 13 pounds below their weight for their height, were significantly more likely to develop menstrual disorders than sedentary women (Dale et al., 1979). Galle and his associates (1983) found that low body weight was an important predictor of amenorrhea. This study found that runners with amenorrhea were significantly more likely to weigh under 115 pounds. Additionally, a study by Lutter and

Cushman (1982) found that low body weight was associated with having fewer menstrual periods.

However, the research indicating it was weight loss that was the causal variable in producing menstrual disorders is contradicted by a study conducted at the University of Arizona on 14 women who were monitored while they trained for a marathon. At the beginning of the study all the women had normal menstrual cycles. As they increased their mileage their weight did not change, yet 13 of the women experienced changes, primarily oligomenorrhea, in their menstrual cycles (Boyden et al., 1982).

As we will see below, other researchers have also concluded that it is not weight loss nor miles per week that are the causal factors in menstrual disorders; these factors are simply correlates. Since high distance running generally leads to weight loss, and since distance and weight loss are two readily observable and measurable variables, they have mistakenly been assumed to be causal variables.

Amount of Body Fat

Running not only generally leads to weight loss but also to a change in the composition of the body. Specifically, a decrease in fat and an increase in muscle or lean mass occurs. It has frequently been reported that women runners have a lower percentage of body fat than nonrunning women. In examining body fat, one study found that women marathoners and distance runners had 18 percent body fat, versus 22 percent for sedentary controls (Dale et al., 1979).

Women runners lose a considerable part of their body fat after they start to run. One study found 30 percent to be an average (Wentz, 1980).

As with menarche, the amount of body fat in women is believed by many to be an important device regulating and producing hormones that control the menstrual cycle. Specifically, body fat is considered important for making estrogen, a hormone needed for a normal menstrual cycle. (Note: fat as an important source of estrogen has been questioned by some researchers — see Shangold, 1985.)

Although much of the current evidence points to body fat as the major causal variable in menstrual disorders, this explanation has also been challenged (see Caldwell, 1982). For example, the study conducted at the University of Arizona reported that menstrual changes occurred in 13 of the 14 participants before their fat levels had dropped below the 17–22 percent level, which is above the level believed critical for normal menstruation to take place (Boydon et al., 1982). Thus, at least in this study, the fat hypothesis was not supported (see Elliot et al., 1983).

There have been numerous other criticisms directed at the "critical fat" hypothesis. Some have dealt with the fact that there is no one acceptable method to measure body fat. Others have noted the numerous exceptions to the hypothesis.

Hormone Changes

The menstrual cycle is controlled by hormones. Although much more complex than described here, the basic menstrual cycle works as follows. A hormone called FSH (follicle-stimulating hormone) is secreted from the pituitary gland. This leads to the growth of a follicle, an immature sac containing an egg. Each ovary contains thousands of follicles. The growth of the follicle brings about an estrogen secretion. The increase in estrogen brings about a decline in FSH and a rise in LH (luteinizing hormone). The LH brings about a rupturing of the mature follicle and the release of an egg (ovulation). The luteinizing hormone also supports the transformation of the ruptured follicle into the corpus luteum. The corpus luteum (the ruptured follicle) secretes both estrogen and progesterone. Both of these cause the lining of the uterus (endometrium) to change in preparation for the implantation of a fertilized egg. The progesterone secretion brings about a decline in LH. The decline in LH means that the corpus luteum can no longer be supported and it ceases functioning. Thus, the levels of estrogen and progesterone drop rapidly and a degeneration of the uterine lining occurs. The decline in estrogen and progesterone also brings about a rise in FSH and the cycle repeats itself, unless interrupted by pregnancy or menopause (or disease or injury).

Several studies have shown that female athletes who engage in vigorous aerobic exercise have hormonal profiles that are very different from those of "normal" control groups. One study on four teenage swimmers found that FSH and progesterone failed to increase after the LH surge, suggesting anovulatory (or nonovulatory) menstrual cycles (Bonen et al., 1981). Jurkowski and her associates (1978), in a study of nine college students examined at different stages of their menstrual cycles and at different levels of exercise, found that exercise brought about the elevation of certain hormones, and that the hormones increased more in one stage than another of the cycle. Baker and her associates (1981) studied 23 women runners and found that those with amenorrhea had lower levels of certain hormones, such as LH, than runners who were not experiencing any menstrual difficulties. In another study of 168 women, hormonal levels were again found to vary between runners, joggers, and controls. FSH and LH hormone levels were found to be lower in the runners than the controls. Also, a decrease in progesterone was noted during the luteal phase of the menstrual cycle (6–9 days after ovulation) in the runners.

Shangold and her associates (1981) studied six women runners before and after 30 minutes of running at different stages of their cycles. The researchers wanted to examine prolactin and testosterone levels, both important in regulating the menstrual cycle before and after exercise. They found significant increases in both after exercise. They also found that the increased hormone level varied by the stage of the menstrual cycle, with large increases being seen in one, less in another. Although it contributes to knowledge about the impact of exercise on menstruation, the authors admitted that the study did little but establish the complexity of menstrual disorders.

Another study analyzed hormones in women before and after running a marathon and the members of the U.S. Women's Water Polo Team before and after a strenuous practice. The results demonstrated that after a marathon significant changes in certain hormone levels were present. For example, LH decreased 36 percent, prolactin increased 327, testosterone increased 195, and cortisol increased 211 percent. In comparison, the women on the water polo team had an increase of 70 percent in prolactin. The conclusion of the researchers was that the type of sport and level of conditioning appear to affect the changes in hormones, but that more research is needed before definitive conclusions can be made (Hale et al., 1983).

More recently it has been speculated that beta-endorphins, believed responsible for the "runners' high," may be responsible for exercise amenorrhea (see Ziporyn, 1984; Howlett et al., 1984; McArthur, 1985), although other studies have not supported this conclusion (see Dixon et al., 1984).

Without going into tremendous depth, and the myriad of other hormones that influence the menstrual cycle, it can be stated that exercise influences hormone levels (see Bonen et al., 1983). It appears that hormones are the answer to the question of what causes menstrual disorders. What has not yet been answered is whether the change in hormones causes changes in the menstrual cycle alone or in combination with factors such as diet, stress, training, amount of body fat, or some combination of the latter. What all this means for the reader is that more research is needed before a definitive answer can be given.

Other Explanations and Summary

A variety of other explanations exist for the high rate of menstrual disorders in runners. For example, some believe that runners have a propensity to consume low fat diets which do not provide enough cholesterol for the production of estrogen. Others claim that the hypothalamus, which is important in regulating the menstrual cycle, is not provided adequate insulation from the internal body temperatures generated while running and as a result sends incorrect information to the pituitary gland which then does not correctly regulate the menstrual cycle.

Confusion in this area has arisen because researchers have generally been looking for a single condition caused by a single factor; it may instead be several conditions caused by several factors.

Although menstrual disorders may occur more frequently among runners than nonrunners, the cause of the disorder should not automatically be assumed to be exercise related. The menstrual disorder may be caused by factors such as hypothyroidism, premature failure of the ovaries, pregnancy, or a tumor in the pituitary gland or ovaries (see Shangold, 1982).

Pathological conditions obviously need to be quickly corrected. For example, a pathological condition interfering with the production of estrogen will cause premature osteoporosis, a condition where calcium is removed from the bones. This causes the bones to become weak, to fracture easily, and to heal slowly (Rosenzweig, 1982).

Dr. Mona Shangold has stated that women who do not menstruate or who do so irregularly for unknown reasons, need a medical examination to determine the cause. She has detailed some of the conditions physicians should investigate when confronted by a runner complaining of menstrual disorders. She also listed several tests that can be performed to determine the exact cause of the disorder (Shangold, 1982; 1985; 1986).

Dr. Shangold has also detailed some of the treatments for amenorrheic runners (Shangold, 1985; 1986). She believes that a "normal hormone milieu" needs to be restored. This can be done through nonmedical intervention such as reducing training, increasing body fat, or increasing body weight. If one or more of these do not restore "normal" menstrual functioning, then she believes "medical therapy" is warranted.

Return of Menstruation

The next question that naturally comes to mind is even if only a small percentage of runners experience menstrual disturbances, are these changes harmful, and are they temporary or permanent? That is, does amenorrhea or oligomenorrhea cause any type of permanent damage, and will a reduction in running or the cessation of running cause the menstrual cycle to return to "normal"?

The first part of the question can be answered "perhaps" harmful. Until recently the answer would have been "no." However, recent research studies suggest that amenorrhea in runners may lead to premature bone loss. This finding was unexpected in that researchers had believed that exercise would increase bone density. Dr. Christopher E. Cann of the University of California Medical School has said that "women with amenorrhea due to exercise are at risk for bone loss" (see Gonzalez, 1982; see Anonymous, 1982). Since a number of the women in Cann's study had hypothalamic amenorrhea, (see Gunby, 1981), a "commentary" in *The Physician and Sportsmedicine* noted that none of the experts contacted saw the study as being a "cause for alarm" since the sample was small and there were "other" documented factors that could be causing the bone loss (Lutter, 1983a).

Evidence now suggests that there *may* be cause for alarm. The first study examined 28 female athletes; 14 were amenorrheic and 14 eumenorrheic. The two groups did not differ in age, height, body fat, weight, age at menarche, length of time in sports, amount of training, or best time in a 10 kilometer race. They did differ in miles run per week, with the amenorrheic runners averaging 42 miles and the eumenorrheic runners averaging 25 miles. Bone mass was measured at the distal radius and lumbar vertebrae. Bone mass did not differ at the radius but amenorrheic runners had significantly lower vertebrae bone mass. According to a three day dietary analysis, the eumenorrheic runners met their daily calcium requirements while the amenorrheic runners did not (Drinkwater, Nilson et al., 1984; see Drinkwater, Chestnut et al., 1984; Paty, 1984; Widmann, 1984).

The second study, by Marcus and his associates (1985) on elite female runners, found similar results. They again noted that dietary intake of calcium was low and recommended 1,500mg per day as a dietary supplement. They concluded by saying that women should not exercise to the point where normal menstrual functioning is altered. Estrogen replacement was mentioned as a way to maintain bone mass; they noted, however, that evidence was lacking as to its effectiveness and safety.

The third study again found similar results (Lindbert et al., 1984). This study examined 11 amenorrheic, five oligomenorrheic, and 15 eumenorrheic runners. Fourteen nonrunning eumenorrheic women and 10 postmenopausal women were also examined. The first four groups were similar in age, height, age at menarche, and use of birth control pills. The amenorrheic runners did have lower body weight than the other groups. Amenorrheic runners had significantly less bone mineral content than eumenorrheic runners or nonrunners. The consequence of the lower bone density was that 49 percent of the amenorrheic runners had suffered a stress fracture within the previous year; there were no stress fractures among the eumenorrheic runners. The researchers concluded that while exercise can be beneficial in maintaining bone mineral content, that this benefit can be negated by "other factors."

To decrease the possibility of bone loss, or other possible disorders, some physicians recommend a regime of estrogen-progesterone if amenorrhea persists for more than one year. It is believed that this will prevent bone loss and a decline in the functioning of the ovaries (see Diddle, 1983).

The answer to the second part of the question — will reducing running cause the menstrual cycle to return to normal? — is yes.

Generally, studies indicate that as training is reduced or stopped, the menstrual cycle will return to normal. One study of ballet dancers noted a high (37 percent) incidence of amenorrhea when the dancers were compared to controls. However, the researchers also noted that these symptoms disappeared when training was stopped or interrupted because of an injury. Of course, the cessation of training was associated with a weight gain and a fat gain, as well as less physical exertion, all of which are the variables previously associated with menstrual disturbance (Cohen et al., 1982; Frisch et al., 1980).

Another study, designed to determine the reversibility of athletic amenorrhea, was conducted with current and former female college long-distance runners, and a group of matched nonrunners. The study found that the runners had fewer menstrual cycles per year than the nonrunners (9.5 vs. 10). Eighty-three percent of the former runners reported that training had altered their menstrual cycles, but that normal cycles had returned 1.7 months after stopping or reducing training. The longest report of amenorrhea continuing after the cessation of training was six months. The study did not find a correlation between the amount of time the athlete had been amenorrheic and the length of amenorrhea after discontinuing training (Stager et al., 1984).

After a woman stops or reduces her running and the resumption of the menstrual cycle has occurred, has ovulation and hence the likelihood of pregnancy been irreparably damaged?

The answer appears to be no. One study reported on a woman long-distance runner who did not become pregnant while continuing to run high weekly mileage, but who became pregnant almost immediately after she stopped running (Bloomberg, 1977). In a recent letter to the *New England Journal of Medicine*, Dr. Colm O'Herlihy (1982) reported the case histories of two women joggers in their mid-twenties who ran 20 miles a week. Neither had menstruated since they had stopped taking birth control pills one year previously. Both had been given high dosages of a fertility drug which did not change their condition. When it was suggested that they reduce their weekly mileage both did, both began menstruating, and both became pregnant on half the dosage of the fertility drug previously given.

In a study of 319 women runners, Estok and Rudy (1984) found a low incidence of infertility, 4 percent, overall (N = 13). Eight of the 13 were infertile before starting to run. The infertility rate for the general population is 10–15 percent.

Another researcher reported on two women runners who had not menstruated for seven years; after reducing the intensity of their training both became pregnant, one with a fertility drug, and each subsequently had two children (*Physician and Sportsmedicine*, 1981).

Before leaving this section it should be mentioned that the cessation of menstruation does not necessarily mean that a woman cannot become pregnant (see *Physician and Sportsmedicine*, 1981; Shangold, 1982). It does, however, reduce the likelihood. Dr. Joan Ullyot, a physician, marathon runner, and frequent writer on women runners, says in her book *Running Free* that she has known several amenorrheic runners who became pregnant (1980).

Impact of Running on Menstruation

Does running have an impact on the length, duration, discomfort, or amount of menstrual flow? There have been several reports on this question, most more or less informal surveys and subjective reports rather than scientific studies. In one study of 168 women, it was found that runners had a significantly lighter flow, fewer and less intensive cramps than nonrunning women (Dale et al., 1979). Another study noted that women runners had fewer premenstrual symptoms, a shorter menstruation, and a reduced flow (Schwartz et al., 1981). In the study conducted at the University of Arizona on 14 women who gradually increased their distance while training for a marathon, of the 13 who experienced changes in their menstrual cycles, 11 reported a decrease in both flow and the number of days of blood loss. In this study menstrual cramps and other forms of dysmenorrhea improved in seven of the 14 but grew worse in three (Boyden et al., 1982). A study of 56 female athletes at the Montreal Olympics found that 33 believed that changes in their menstrual cycle occurred when they were training. Of these

33 women, about one-third noted a heavier flow, and one-third a lighter flow during training. Concerning length of menstruation, about one-third claimed that the duration was reduced and one-third said it increased during training (Webb et al., 1979). In contrast to other studies, a study of 105 women runners found that women running more than 30 miles a week were more likely to have "mild dysmenorrhea' than those running fewer than 30 miles a week (Galle et al., 1983). Although the impact of racing on menstruation has not been scientifically studied, at least one elite middle-distance runner has reported that her menstrual cramps become worse after a hard race (Anonymous, 1980b).

A study on 319 women runners by Estok and Rudy (1984) did not find a relationship between the intensity of running and dysmenorrhea. This study also reported that after starting to run, 63 percent of those studied reported no change in the amount of discomfort, 32 percent reported a decrease, and 5 percent reported an increase.

It has been reported by several sports physiologists that active women have fewer menstrual complaints, such as headaches, fatigue, or discomfort when compared with nonactive women (see *Physician and Sportsmedicine*, 1981). However, it may be that physically active women are more used to and accepting of discomfort than nonactive women. According to some researchers, athletic women may also experience less discomfort because their periods are shorter than those of nonathletes.

A study of 174 female college runners reported that 46 percent of them reported less discomfort during their menstrual cycles during the competitive season (Webb and Proctor, 1983).

Although studies are limited, it has been reported that women experiencing PMS (premenstrual syndrome) can significantly reduce the symptoms through low-intensity running (see Caldwell, 1984).

Although related only in a cursory manner to this section, it does appear that women who exercise have a lower rate of toxic shock than women who do not exercise. In an examination of toxic shock victims, the Minnesota Health Department found that toxic shock victims engaged in less exercise than those who did not contract toxic shock. Although not able to explain why exercise protected them, the researchers reported that other factors which might be suspected, such as method of contraception, frequency of pelvic examination, method used to insert tampons, or the number of tampons used during menstruation, were found to be irrelevant (Dunn, 1982).

Impact of Menstruation on Running Performance

The common folklore is that menstruation has a negative impact on athletic performance. In fact, until recently many coaches would not allow women athletes to train or engage in competition during menstruation.

In some ways the above beliefs seem to have a firm biological basis. After all, since each part of the menstrual cycle is associated with different levels of hormones, such as estrogen and progesterone, and these in turn have consequences on the body, it appears logical that physical performance may be affected. For example, blood pressure, blood volume, heart rate, and body temperature can all be influenced by hormone levels. A high estrogen level can cause the retention of salt which leads to water retention and hence a weight gain. It has been found that menstruating women start increasing in weight in the premenstrual phase, reaching the maximum on about the second day of menstruation, after which a decrease in weight will take place until the eighth day of the cycle (Albohm, 1976).

There have been many studies describing the impact of the different stages of the menstrual cycle on variables such as reaction time, motor performance, and cardiovascular efficiency. The studies are either contradictory or indicate that the stages of the menstrual cycle do not affect performance (see Gerber et al., 1974). In a study of women at the Tokyo Olympics, 36.9 percent of those surveyed said that menstruation had no impact on their performance while 16.9 percent said that their performance was always bad during menstruation. Another 27.7 percent said that their performance varied with each cycle. Only 3.1 percent said that their performance was always bad before menstruation (Zaharieva, 1965; see Albohm, 1976).

Estok and Rudy's (1984) study on 319 women runners found that 46 percent claimed that their running performance was not affected by their menstrual cycle. Of those who reported a change, 82 percent said that their running was better between or after menstruation, 15 percent felt that their premenstruation performance was best and 3 percent said that their best performance came during menstruation.

A recent study examined VO_2max, the key performance factor in most athletic events, during all phases of the menstrual cycle in ten female college athletes. The study concluded that VO_2max did not differ significantly during any of the phases of the menstrual cycle (Allsen et al., 1977).

At a conference held at Simon Fraser University in British Columbia, Dr. Sue Higgs reported on her tests on physical performance of women during four phases of the menstrual cycle (premenstrual, postmenstrual, first day of menstruation, and midcycle). Although she found no significant differences in level of physical performance during any of the four phases, she did find that during the premenstrual and during the first day of menstruation the women perceived that they were working harder than during the other phases (see Bloomberg, 1980).

Another study supported the above conclusion. Although not a study on running per se, 16 college women who engaged in four physical performance tests during different stages of their menstrual cycles demonstrated that the various stages did not produce any difference in performance (Doolittle and Engebretsen, 1972).

Based on the results of the studies examined, it appears that running is not dramatically affected by the menstrual cycle. Although the different stages of the menstrual cycle may cause slight physiological variations in women (e.g., weight gain), the most important variable is probably mental attitude. If the woman believes that her performance will be affected because of the stage of her menstrual cycle she is in, the likelihood is that her performance will be affected. Often however, the effect on performance can be positive. For example, a woman who believes that her performance will be negatively affected by the stage of the cycle she is going to be in during an important competition, may train harder or try harder during the competition to compensate for the perceived handicap.

More research in this area is needed since the evidence is less than concrete and because women use existing "knowledge" to try to maximize their performance. That is, women may believe certain "inaccurate information" about the menstrual cycle and its impact on athletic performance to be accurate. Thus, they may try to alter their menstrual cycles with birth control pills, follicular hormones, progesterone, or through menstrual extraction (*Physician and Sportsmedicine*, 1976). Since the consequences of some of these menstrual altering methods have not been fully investigated and since women may be altering their menstrual cycles on the basis of incorrect information and using untested and perhaps dangerous methods without medical supervision, it is important that more studies be done in this area soon.

Pregnancy and Running

The issue of pregnancy and running is one that involves many questions but few definitive answers. Further, the answers are not supported by much research.

As most of us are aware, for most runners, running is more than a sport or a form of exercise, it is a way of life. As such, most runners do not want to discontinue running for any length of time. This especially applies to women runners who do not want to discontinue running during pregnancy if it is not necessary. Traditionally, perhaps because of the lack of research or clear-cut answers, when asked by a pregnant runner if it was safe to continue running, most obstetricians answered to stop running but to engage in other forms of exercise. However, just as women have been critical of other practices of the medical establishment concerning childbirth, they have also questioned this practice. It appears that exercise in and of itself is not the issue; after all, most physicians recommend that their patients engage in an exercise program. The issue is whether running is an acceptable form of exercise.

Some of the questions that most individuals ask when they think about pregnancy and running are:

1. Does running damage the fetus?
2. Does running increase the likelihood of a miscarriage?
3. How does pregnancy affect running comfort?
4. How does pregnancy affect a woman's performance?
5. Does running have an impact on the duration of the pregnancy or does it contribute to potential complications during childbirth?
6. How long should a woman wait after childbirth before resuming running?

7. Does running have an impact on breast feeding?
8. Does a prior pregnancy have an impact on subsequent running performance?

Each of these questions will be considered separately below.

Damage to Fetus

The question of damage to the fetus has generally involved three issues. First, will the fetus be "bounced" around so much during running that it will be irreparably damaged? Second, will the mother's muscles' demand for oxygen cause the body to direct the blood and oxygen away from the fetus and thus cause it damage, perhaps to the brain? Third, will the increase in the core temperature of the mother, maternal hyperthermia, increase the likelihood of a birth defect?

It appears that for most women the first fear noted above is unfounded. The fetus is well-protected by the mother's body, as well as by its internal environment, from the bouncing induced by running (see Ullyot, 1980).

The second question, that an exercising pregnant woman may deprive the fetus of needed blood and oxygen, has yet to be clearly answered. Several studies have indicated that if a pregnant woman engages in vigorous exercise, the fetus may exhibit an abnormally slow or fast heart rate (see Dressendorfer et al., 1980; Anonymous, 1982a; Dale et al., 1982). The change in heart rate was assumed to be caused by a reduced blood flow to the fetus. A normal or stable fetal heart rate is between 120 and 160 beats per minute. A rate above or below this could indicate fetal distress. Fetal distress could be caused by the diversion of blood and oxygen from the fetus to the muscles of the exercising woman.

To test the impact of exercise on fetal heart rate, one study used five pregnant trained swimmers who exercised on stationary cycling equipment in which maternal heart rate was gradually increased. Maternal heart beats averaged 76 beats per minute at the beginning of the experiment and were raised to approximately 150 beats per minute by progressively increasing the intensity of the task. It was found that by increasing the maternal heart rate to 80 percent of its maximum, the fetal heart rate only increased from 142 to 149 beats per minute. The researchers concluded that fetal heart rates were within normal limits with non-weight bearing, submaximal aerobic exercise (Anonymous, 1981; Dressendorfer and Goodlin, 1980).

A second study at Emory University examined pregnant women running on a treadmill with a fetal heart monitor attached. Three of the four women tested in this manner had fetal heart tracings that were acceptable in that although the tracings showed an initial increase in fetal heart rate, the rate returned to normal within three minutes (Anonymous, 1982a).

Another recent study on seven pregnant women who jogged an average of 1.5 miles three times a week before and after becoming pregnant did not yield such positive results. The women were all studied during the third trimester of their pregnancies. They were evaluated before and after they jogged. It was found that fetal heart rates averaged from 140 to 150 beats per minute before the jogging but had increased to 180 to 204 beats per minute after jogging. The fetal heart rates returned to normal 12 to 30 minutes after the completion of jogging (Hauth et al., 1982).

Dale and his colleagues (1982) found in their study, of four pregnant women, that in three of the women the fetal heart rates declined during exercise from approximately 125–140 beats per minute to 90–115 beats per minute. The declines were all transitory and went back to "normal" within three minutes of the start of the exercise.

Thus, while some studies have indicated that aerobic exercise appears safe for the fetus, other studies have indicated that the fetus may be in cardiac distress during, and shortly after, exercise.

The third concern, maternal hyperthermia caused by running, has not been adequately investigated. A letter to the *Journal of the American Medical Association* (Schaefer, 1979) suggested that marathon running by pregnant runners "may pose a teratogenic [defect-causing] risk during early pregnancy." The author pointed out that several recent studies had shown an association between birth defects and maternal hyperthermia.

A response to the above said that qualifications need to be added so that women marathoners did not feel "unnecessary anxiety" (Orselli, 1980). The letter continued that research indicating an association between maternal hyperthermia and birth defects was all on disease-induced hyperthermia, and that no studies existed which indicated that exercise-induced hyperthermia caused birth defects. This author also noted that the marathoner's life style was almost certain to have a positive impact on the development of the fetus.

What does this mean for the pregnant runner? Because the American College of Obstetricians and Gynecologists believes that each pregnancy is unique, it does not have an official position statement (Jopke, 1983). Dr. Mona Shangold, a runner and "sports gynecologist" believes that pregnant women should only exercise with the approval of their obstetrician, and that there are symptoms that clearly indicate when exercise should be terminated and a physician notified. She noted, for example, that a pregnant woman should be careful not to raise her body temperature above 101°F. This could cause a birth defect to occur, especially if it happened early in the pregnancy. Overheating could also cause the woman to go into premature labor in the later stage of pregnancy. However, Dr. Shangold believes it "reasonable " for pregnant women to continue to exercise at the same level as before their pregnancy. The same level may mean that because of the effect of the pregnancy a "similar level" of exertion will be achieved by running a shorter distance. (Shangold, 1981b; see Morton et al., 1985). Shangold strongly advises pregnant runners to closely monitor their bodies, avoid exhaustion, and immediately report any unusual symptoms such as pain or bleeding.

Two physicians who conducted a study on 67 pregnant experienced joggers said that their study "suggested" that "jogging during pregnancy by healthy women accustomed to such activity is not harmful to the infant" (Jarrett et al., 1983a).

It might be noted that most studies on the newborn babies of running mothers indicate that the babies born are as healthy as those of nonrunning mothers. These studies have generally reported no difference between the weight of the newborn babies of running and nonrunning mothers. Most have also found no difference in the number or type of complications in newborn babies between running and nonrunning women (see Jarrett et al., 1983a). Only one study has indicated that the newborn babies of running mothers may have fewer complications than those of nonrunning mothers (Dale et al., 1982). Given the health-consciousness of runners, a difference such as this is not unexpected.

However, another study has noted that the babies of running mothers had a slightly higher rate of fetal anomalies than expected. The study found that 6 percent of the running women had babies with fetal anomalies. The figure for the general population is 2–4 percent. The authors noted that the anomalies were not "classic" anomalies and were not life-threatening (Jarrett et al., 1983a).

Running and Miscarriage

The literature is almost without material on the issue of whether running while pregnant increases the likelihood of a miscarriage. Data on this subject would be difficult to gather. Generally, we would expect to see a lower incidence of miscarriages in running women, not because of running per se but because of the characteristics of runners, such as better health, health consciousness, and higher incomes, which allow more access to health services.

In 1980 a survey of 24 women who ran while pregnant noted that two had miscarriages. Whether these miscarriages were running related is not known. Another study on Hungarian athletes indicated a 6.5 percent spontaneous abortion rate (*Physician and Sportsmedicine*, 1976). Another study found a 1.5 percent spontaneous abortion rate (Jarrett et al., 1983a). These figures should be compared with a 10–12 percent (Miller and Keanes, 1978) miscarriage rate in the general population (Estok and Rudy, 1984).

Another study on 67 pregnant joggers found that the prematurity rate of the joggers was only one-half that of nonjoggers (Jarrett et al., 1983). However, another study found a 20 percent miscarriage rate (Estok and Rudy, 1984).

A recent study found that runners had a higher incidence of "major" obstetrical complications than a control group of nonrunners. The major complications were "threatened abortion" and "premature rupture of membranes/premature labor" not associated with running (Dale et al., 1982).

Pregnancy and Running Comfort

Pregnancy unquestionably produces many changes in the pregnant woman. Again, in the study noted above several facts came out. First, the women became less apprehensive about running as their pregnancies advanced, and second, physical discomfort was experienced by 57 percent of the women (backaches, breast soreness, fatigue, and urinary frequency). It should be noted that the women did not blame running for their discomfort but their pregnancy.

In another study conducted at the University of Minnesota on 195 women who ran while pregnant, it was found that 76 percent had pregnancy-associated discomfort while running. Some of the complaints noted were: pain in the lower back, abdomen, and pelvic region; urge to urinate frequently; sore legs; and contractions and cramps. However, many of the women did not experience any of the typical pregnancy-associated discomforts such as those noted above or backaches, constipation, water retention, varicose veins, or an excessive weight gain. In this study, there were four miscarriages. The average weight of the babies who were born was seven pounds six ounces. For the first six months after birth, follow-up studies indicated that the babies were all in excellent health (Hage, 1982).

A study of a 32-year-old pregnant runner reported that she had no unusual discomfort from running. She did, however, start a walking program during her ninth month because running had become too strenuous (Hutchinson et al., 1981).

Another study on a 36-year-old pregnant runner, who ran four miles per day up to the day before she delivered her seventh child, has also been reported (Korcok, 1981). This report did not note that the woman experienced any unusual physical discomfort from her running.

Last, another study was conducted over a four year period and two pregnancies on a woman who was 27 years old at the beginning of the study to ascertain the effects of a strenuous running program on pregnancy and lactation (Dressendorfer, 1978). The woman did not suffer from any unusual physical discomfort as a result of running up to 15 miles per week before delivery; she did, however, have to reduce her training during the first three months of her pregnancies because of nausea.

The studies do note a commonality. Running will become much more strenuous as the pregnancy progresses, which results in a decrease in mileage and intensity. The study at Emory University found that before becoming pregnant the women in the study averaged 18.7 miles per week. This distance decreased to 14.2 miles per week in the first three months, to 10.9 miles per week in the middle three months, and to 6.6 miles per week during the last three months (Anonymous, 1982). A study on 67 pregnant runners found that weekly mileage during the first trimester was 16.5. By the third trimester it had decreased to six (Jarrett and Spellacy, 1983a). It has also been found that pregnant women tend to reduce their pace as their pregnancies progress (Anonymous, 1981).

Pregnancy and Running Performance

As we have seen, running while pregnant can be associated with many discomforts. This will cause most pregnant runners to reduce the amount and intensity of their training.

There are several articles that mention pregnant women competing in athletic events in the early stages of their pregnancies and even one mention of a pregnant woman winning an Olympic medal in diving while pregnant.

Also, one popular running magazine recently had an article about a 2:45 marathoner with Olympic aspirations who decided to keep running and competing while pregnant. She continued to run 60–80 miles per week up until the ninth month of her pregnancy. One month before delivery the woman completed a 10k race in 40 minutes. Shortly thereafter her physician suggested that she stop running since tests indicated that the baby was still small, perhaps, it was suggested, because she was burning too many calories running. The woman did stop running but exercised, without the consent of her physician, on a stationary bicycle. Shortly thereafter she gave birth to a healthy seven and a half pound baby (Higdon, 1981).

The above story elicited a positive response from a woman who also ran while pregnant, with the encouragement of her obstetrician. She delivered within 90 minutes of the onset of labor and was back racing five weeks after the birth (Rush-Morrow, 1982). However, a negative response came from a woman who regretted that the pregnant runner had "deceived" her obstetrician, who had "sound medical reasons for limiting her activity during" her later stage of pregnancy (Droel, 1982).

Impact of Running on Labor/Delivery

The belief among most runners is that a physically fit woman, especially one who runs, should have a labor shorter in duration and with less discomfort than a nonphysically fit woman. Others, however, believe that the muscles of the pelvic region become larger and stronger with running, which leads to a more difficult and protracted labor and to delivery problems (see Mathews et al., 1976; Zaharieva, 1972).

Although some recent studies will be reported below, unfortunately, again, the studies are too few, contradictory in results, or unscientific in design to warrant any firm conclusions. Also, as we will see, the majority of women either stopped, or greatly reduced their mileage during their pregnancies, especially during the last trimester, thus negating or certainly substantially reducing the possible beneficial effects of running on labor/delivery because of deconditioning.

Olympic athletes were the subject of a study which found that the first stage of the delivery was comparable to that of nonathletes, but the expulsion stage was significantly shorter. This made the overall birth process shorter. The study also noted that delivery was normal (Zaharieva, 1972).

One researcher studied a woman for four years and through two pregnancies and found that labor was 19 hours in the first pregnancy and three hours in the second (Dressendorfer, 1978). A 36-year-old jogger, pregnant with her seventh child, ran 4.8 kilometers throughout her pregnancy and walked the distance the day she delivered. She checked into the hospital at 2:15 p.m., and gave birth at 3:30 p.m. (Korcok, 1981). A study presented at the 14th Annual Northwest Sports Medicine and Conditioning Conference found that pregnant women who exercised appeared to have shorter labors than those who did not exercise (Leaf, 1981). Additionally, a survey of 24 women who ran while pregnant reported that the amount of time in labor for these women was two hours for 33 percent and from three to nine hours for 61 percent (Anonymous, 1981a).

Other studies have not always found that physical fitness shortens the length of labor. A study at Balboa Naval Hospital found that physically fit women had shorter labors only after their first pregnancy (Pomerance et al., 1974). Also, the study at Emory University on pregnant runners found that there was no difference in length of labor between runners and a group of pregnant nonrunners (Anonymous, 1982).

The study by Dale and his colleagues (1982) found that length of labor did not differ between runners and nonrunners. Dale's study did find a slight tendency for runners to fail to progress in labor which resulted in a higher percentage of cesarean births. The reasons for this are still being examined.

Resumption of Running After Pregnancy

Although pregnancy may not stop most women runners from running, childbirth will. When is it safe to resume running? Again, there are few clearcut answers. The ultimate answer of course depends on the woman and the physiological impact on her of the delivery.

The study of the 36-year-old runner and mother of seven indicated that she was running 6.4 kilometers a day, swimming, and playing tennis four weeks after her delivery (Korcok, 1981). The 32-year-old pregnant runner described previously was running six weeks after delivery (Hutchinson et al., 1981). The study on 24 women runners who raced while pregnant indicated that within three weeks after delivery more than half were running again (Anonymous, 1981). Last, the woman who was studied over four years and two pregnancies started running again two weeks after childbirth (Dressendorfer, 1978).

Although the number of studies and participants is not very large, the results appear to indicate that a return to running, in a well conditioned, highly motivated athlete, who had an uncomplicated delivery, does not have to be very long.

Running and Breast Feeding

Milk production in running women has been a source of concern for two reasons. First, running burns up many calories that might be needed as nutrients in milk. Second, in running, especially at longer distances, there is a fluid loss which may mean that the amount of milk produced will not be sufficient to sustain the nursing child.

Although studies are again limited, and must be treated with caution, those that have noted breast milk production have said that it is not affected

82 Women and Running

by running. The study on the 24 women who raced while pregnant reported that 93 percent were breast-feeding their children (Anonymous, 1981).

Postpregnancy Performance

Again, more studies are needed in this area before any definitive statements can be made.

It was found in the study of women at the Tokyo Olympics that after childbirth 46 percent increased their performance within one year after giving birth, and an additional 30.8 percent increased their performance between the first and second year after giving birth. The study was unable to obtain data on the remaining athletes (Zaharieva, 1965).

It has been suggested that many female athletes feel stronger after having children, and perhaps more confident of their own abilities having gone through the pregnancy. The major limiting factor to a woman's performance after childbirth appears to be that her child or children may not allow her the necessary time for the intense training necessary to be an elite runner (see *Physician and Sportsmedicine*, 1976).

Running and the Pill

There are few issues on women that have received as much debate as oral contraceptives. The negative and positive effects of the pill have been well documented in other sources. The question is, does running have an impact on any of the negative consequences of the pill?

It should be noted first, however, that running women have very different contraceptive practices than the general public. While approximately 50 percent of women 15–29 use oral contraceptives, studies on runners who use contraceptives found that 14 to 24 percent of them use oral contraceptives. Most runners use a barrier method of contraception, such as a diaphragm. While only 4 percent of women in the general public use diaphragms, studies have found that 48 to 60 percent of women runners use diaphragms. The reasons for the difference in contraceptive practices have not been investigated (U.S. Bureau of the Census, 1983; Jarrett et al., 1983; Galle et al., 1983; Lutter, 1983).

One negative consequence often associated with the pill is the increase in serum triglyceride levels and the decrease in HDL levels. As has already been pointed out elsewhere in this book, coronary heart disease risk increases as HDL levels decrease. Previous studies have indicated that exercise increases HDL levels. The question is, can running offset this particular negative consequence of the pill?

A study of 100 women ages 21–35 noted that aerobic exercise did increase HDL levels, although exercise did not completely offset the effects of taking the pill (Evenson, 1982).

Women and Injuries

Almost all books and research to date have noted the increased likelihood and incidence of athletic injuries in women. For example, Miller (1974) said women have a "proclivity to injury." Klaus (1964) pointed out that women have a rate of athletic injury double that of men. Paglino (1978) has noted that "women suffer a higher percentage of certain injuries as compared to men." According to Besson (1978), "women have more injuries than men." Quoting Heinonen (1974), "The overall incidence of injuries to women is double that of men." An article by Conniff (1981) said, "The probabilities are that, if female runners overindulge in long distance or speed running, they will have more risk of injury." The list could go on for some length. The point is that most writers have believed that female athletes are more injury prone than male athletes. In fact, the propensity of women to be injured in sports has been given as a primary reason for refraining from physically strenuous athletic events, and especially competition.

Although traditionally women have been excluded from running, and competition, this has now ended. For example, in 1970 there were 2,992 track teams for girls in the United States; by 1980 the figure had increased to 13,935 (Kissin, 1980).

The reported increased likelihood of injury in women seems logical given some basic anatomical differences. For example, it has been frequently noted that the bones, muscles, tendons, and ligaments of men compose a greater proportion of the male body. Studies indicate that bones compose 14.9 percent of the body weight of men, as compared to 12 percent in women. As for muscles, tendons, and ligaments the corresponding figures are 44.8 and 36 percent (McArdle et al., 1981).

According to deVris (1980), not only do women have less bone and muscle matter, but the bones and muscles are more "delicately constructed" than in men, and hence more prone to injury. This is supported by Shaver (1981) who says that the bones of women are less dense than those of men.

There have been numerous observational reports about women having a higher injury rate than men, especially by individuals in "sports medicine." This may indicate that women do actually have a higher rate of injury. Two alternative explanations are that women do not have the conditioning or the training of men, or that women are more likely than men to seek out medical attention when they are sick or injured. There have been few documented studies comparing injury rate for trained male and female runners participating in training programs of similar intensity. Furthermore, almost all the studies that have noted the increasing risk of injury for women have cited as their source one 1964 study. Thus, it appears that the bulk, if not all, of the references to the increased risk of injury in women are based either on selected firsthand accounts or one old study.

As is to be reported in the chapter on injuries, it does not appear that female runners have a higher rate of injury than male runners. Additionally, it also appears that the location of injuries do not differ by gender.

In a study of 361 colleges covering 19 major sports, it was found that well-trained women athletes were no more injury prone than men. In this same study 125 trainers were surveyed about women's injuries. Only four thought that women athletes had a higher rate of injury than male athletes.

This study and others (see Conniff, 1981; Gillette, 1975) found three areas of injury unique to women. First, because of the broader pelvis of women, and the propensity for the legs to turn in more (or, to be slightly "knock-kneed") and thus increase the angle between the tibia and femur, women have a higher incidence of knee problems than men since the patella, or knee cap, can move to the side more when the leg is bent. Also, because of the broader pelvis, women's hips move more when they walk or run, allegedly causing pain around the hip joints and in the lower back. Second, because the joints of women are not supported by muscles, tendons, and ligaments as firmly as those of men, they have a higher incidence of sprains. Third, there are certain "unique" injuries to women because of anatomical and sports differences. For example, injuries to the vagina from balance beams, or from IUDs perforating the uterus after severe blows from field games or martial arts have been noted (see Haycock and Gillette, 1976).

One major area of concern has been women's breasts. In the past it was assumed that women frequently had sports-related breast injuries. One study on 319 dedicated female runners found that while low intensity runners (1–10 miles per week) had breast pain, moderate and high intensity runners did not (more than 10 miles per week). It was speculated that the low intensity runners may have had more body fat, especially in the breasts, which caused more bouncing and pain. Another explanation is that they were novice runners who were not wearing a comfortable brassiere (Rudy and Estok, 1983; Estok and Rudy, 1984). One study found that 72 percent of women athletes had breast soreness or tenderness after exercise. Another study at the University of Nevada noted that 31 percent of female athletes experienced breast soreness as a result of exercise. This study also reported that many minor breast injuries had occurred, although none of them were serious. The most frequent injuries resulted from the metal or plastic portion of bras. Perhaps more important, however, was the observation that few of the women were satisfied with the bras they wore for athletics (Anonymous, 1977). A letter to a medical magazine recently noted that better bras are needed since many women who enter exercise programs are not slim and small-breasted but may be heavier and large-breasted. The letter said these women are more likely to find that the breast movement caused by exercise can be painful and may even cause skin abrasions. The writer went on to note that "unresolved breast discomfort" may cause many women to stop exercising, not only because of the immediate discomfort but also because of possible long-term damage (Lunn, 1983).

As a result of these studies and concerns several "sport" or "jogging" bras" have been manufactured. In fact, articles in *The Physician and Sportsmedicine* have evaluated several different sports bras to determine the extent to which they reduced breast movement during exercise (see Gehlsen and Albohm, 1980; Schuster, 1979).

Two recent studies have not supported the belief that exercise is traumatizing for women's breasts. The first was a two year investigation of four girls' high school athletic programs. Nine sports were examined, including cross-country and field and track; no injuries to the breasts of any of the athletes were reported (Garrick and Requa, 1978). The second study reviewed the injury records for intercollegiate sports at the University of Washington from 1976 to 1981. The study found that not one woman athlete had complained of breast pain to either a trainer or team physician during the study. Some women did note breast pain associated with cold weather or the beginning of menstruation (Hunter and Torgan, 1982).

A frequent claim is that running will result in sagging breasts. There are no studies that separate the impact of aging from running. The proponents of this belief say that the bouncing will cause the tissue that supports the breasts to stretch. Those who dispute this claim say that running generally results in a smaller breast size, and stronger breast-supporting tissue, essentially reducing the impact of gravity and age.

Another area of concern for women runners has been that the constant jarring will cause the uterus to "fall." It is believed that this will subsequently cause a variety of problems that will have to be surgically corrected. This is supported by the observation that some women runners do "leak a small amount of urine when they run" (Shangold, 1982c) and it has been assumed that running has caused uterine prolapse to occur, thus placing pressure on the bladder causing urine leakage. According to Dr. Mona Shangold, running does not cause or increase the likelihood of the uterine prolapse. Shangold has noted that urine leakage can be caused by a variety of problems, such as a bladder infection or by a uterus that has dropped as a result of childbirth (Shangold, 1982c; see also Haycock, 1981).

Uterine prolapse was the subject of a study on 319 women runners. The study found that 19 had uterine prolapse before starting a running program and 11 after starting to run. The number of females who had uterine prolapse after starting to run is too small to warrant any type of conclusion (Rudy and Estok, 1983; Estok and Rudy, 1984).

Overall, however, trainers believe that if women experience a higher rate of injury than men it is because of a lack of training and conditioning, inadequate facilities, poor coaching techniques, and inadequate equipment (Haycock et al., 1976; see Lewis and Strickland, 1983).

Women and Men Compared

This chapter will only examine the physiological differences between men and women; it must be remembered, however, that there are other factors that could be taken into account, for example, training, nutrition or psychological factors. That these other factors are important is obvious when one considers that women are now overtaking and surpassing the previous running records of men. For example, women's marathon times have now surpassed the 1947 men's world record and the pre–1952 men's

Olympic record. Since it is doubtful if the changes in marathon times since 1947 can be accounted for by evolutionary physiological changes, we must assume that some of these other factors account for them.

Although these other factors are unquestionably important, they are difficult to measure scientifically, and this book concentrates on only those aspects which can be empirically measured.

It should be reiterated that studies on women runners have not been as frequent as those on male runners. Also, studies that have included women have too frequently used women who did not equate to the men in the study in exercise background or level of physical conditioning. Thus, the studies often found large differences between the sexes, which were assumed to be a consequence of gender rather than a consequence of exercise background or level of conditioning (see Pate et al., 1985).

In this section of the chapter we will examine some of the physiological differences between men and women in areas important for running such as the ability to tolerate heat, the skeletal system, blood, the cardiovascular system, VO_2max, the amount of body fat, stride, and muscles.

Heat Tolerance

The ability of the body to regulate its temperature is important. After all, the body can only tolerate a core temperature drop of $10°C$ or an increase of $5°C$; the consequence of failure to regulate body temperature within these boundaries is death.

Body heat is generated from body metabolism, muscle activity, as well as from external sources such as the sun or heat radiating off the pavement. During vigorous exercise, the basal metabolic rate can increase 20–25 times and thus raise the core temperature of the body about $1°C$ every five minutes if the heat is not eliminated.

The more capable the body is of eliminating heat, the greater the probability of superior performance. This is because the body is facing a demand for blood to be directed to both the exercising muscles and to the skin to eliminate heat. As a result, each suffers (Morehouse et al., 1976). Even though the number of heat-related injuries and deaths in runners has increased dramatically in recent years, it is still apparent from the number of runners and the intensity of training many engage in, that the heat regulatory mechanisms of most individuals are capable of handling the level of activity in which the individual is participating.

The question for this section of the chapter is, do men and women differ in the ability to regulate heat?

The body has several different ways of eliminating heat. They are radiation, conduction, convection and evaporation. Since evaporation is the major method used by the body it will be the only method discussed in this book (see McArdle, 1981).

The average adult body has over three million sweat glands on its surface. Furthermore, the body is capable of producing up to one liter of sweat per hour. Sweat is a major factor in cooling the body since when it comes into contact with the skin it evaporates which causes a cooling effect.

Early studies indicated that although women had more sweat glands than men, they required a higher threshold to induce sweating (see Shaver, 1981).

Studies are now appearing that are challenging the above assumption. These studies claim that the earlier studies compared trained male athletes with untrained female athletes; thus the differences noted were not because of gender but training. Recent studies on women marathon runners supports this conclusion. One study that compared female marathon runners with nonrunners found, during elaborate exercise testing, that the runners had lower skin and rectal temperatures and a lower heart rate than the nonrunners. It was also found that sweating started earlier for the runners than for the nonrunners. Although this study did not examine men, it noted several similar studies on men and their results. The authors concluded on the basis of the available data that women marathon runners performed as well or better in terms of heat tolerance than the males (Drinkwater et al., 1977; see American College of Sports Medicine, 1980).

Recent studies have suggested that although women sweat less than men, and thus lose less water, they are still efficient regulators of body temperature. It appears that the thermoregulatory systems of women are less "wasteful" of sweat than those of men. It has also been found that the thermoregulatory systems of women "appear" to be unaffected by different phases of the menstrual cycle (see Wells, 1977).

Skeletal

Bones provide support, structure, and protection for the body. The bones in the lower part of the body are also important for running and a frequent source of injury.

Generally, it appears that males have an advantage over females in some respects. Their bones are larger and more dense; their joints tend to be broader, thus presenting a greater surface area for shock absorption. Although these differences exist, it does not appear that women suffer from a higher rate of injuries, such as stress fractures.

Blood

Blood is obviously important in aerobic exercise since it carries oxygen to the muscles. Studies have indicated that for aerobic exercise there are important gender differences in the composition of blood. For example, men have a hemoglobin count 15 percent higher than women. Since the hemoglobin in blood is the major oxygen carrier from the lungs to the skeletal muscles, this means that men have a significantly greater oxygen-carrying capability (Shaver, 1981; deVries, 1980; Wells and Plowman, 1983).

It has also been found that females are more likely to have an iron deficiency. The importance of iron can be seen by the fact that an athlete who has a hemoglobin count of 12mg/100ml only has an oxygen carrying capacity of 75 percent that of someone with a count of 16mg/100ml. About 25 percent of menstruating women are iron deficient. This is because of a low dietary intake of iron (less than 12 milligrams a day), because only about 10 percent of the iron consumed is absorbed, and because of the loss of iron through menstruation (1.5 to 2.0 milligrams per day)(Pate et al., 1979).

It should be noted that the iron found in meat is the type most easily absorbed by the body. However, many runners have diets low in meat and high in grains, fruits and vegetables. Where the body can absorb about 40–50 percent of the iron from meat, it only absorbs 5–10 percent of that in other foods (see Sheehan, 1983).

One study found that 25 percent of the female athletes examined, in comparison to 8 to 9 percent of the male athletes examined, were deficient in iron (Plowman, 1974). Other studies have found that up to 50 percent of female runners have an iron deficiency (Nickerson and Tripp, 1983; see Federickson et al., 1983). Clement and his associates (1982) found, in their study of women endurance runners, that 91 percent of them had an iron intake 10 percent or more below the recommended daily intake. The study also noted that iron absorption was lower in the runners than in a control group, suggesting that women runners may need a greater intake of iron because they absorb less of the iron they consume (see Shangold, 1982e). An iron deficiency has been shown to negatively affect VO_{2max} (see Cooter and Mowbray, 1978).

Iron is important in eliminating the lactic acid that accumulates and causes the muscles to become tired and sore. Although too much iron can cause serious problems, such as heart failure, Dr. Gabe Mirkin recommends that menstruating women take an iron supplement (Mirkin, 1982). A commonly recommended dosage is 18 milligrams per day (Pate et al., 1979), although one article recently recommended up to 50 milligrams of an iron supplement (ferrous sulfate) per day (Horner, 1984).

The consequences of iron supplements on iron status have varied. Cooter and Mowbray (1978) found, for example, that 18 milligrams of iron per day had no impact on the iron status of the female athletes they studied (see Parr et al., 1984; Frederickson et al., 1983).

Cardiovascular

As discussed earlier, the heart is a major factor contributing to an athlete's performance. A well-trained heart can pump blood much more efficiently than an untrained heart. The question becomes twofold: Is the cardiovascular system of women as amenable to training as that of men? Is the cardiovascular system of trained women as large and efficient, proportionally, as that of equally trained men?

In answering the first question it should be noted that relatively little research has been conducted in this area on women. The research that is available indicates that women can expect to experience many of the same changes as men and at the same levels. For example, it has been found that with training, increases take place in the hemoglobin count, blood volume, and heart volume of women, although the figures do not approach those of men who participate in the same duration or intensity of training. It was also found that after an identical training program, both males and females had a similar percentage increase in their VO_2max (Mathews and Fox, 1976).

Considering the second question it appears that between the ages of 10 and 60, in the ratio of heart size to body weight women have a value of 85–90 percent that of males (Shaver, 1981; Wells and Plowman, 1983). Thus, proportional to body weight, males have larger hearts and hearts that are capable of pumping more blood proportional to body weight. What all this means is that the hearts of women have to work harder than those of men to achieve the same effects.

VO_2max

Essentially, the VO_2max refers to oxygen consumption. As the intensity of the exercise increases so does the amount of oxygen consumed. When the amount of oxygen consumed does not continue to increase with an increasing workload, one has reached maximum oxygen consumption (also maximal oxygen uptake, or maximum aerobic power). The higher the VO_2max, the greater the potential for better performance in prolonged, aerobic exercises, other factors being equal.

The VO_2max is considered the single most important physiological measurement of potential physical performance in aerobic sports because the level attained requires the integration of several important physiological functions such as the cardiovascular, pulmonary, and neuromuscular systems.

To date, elite women runners do not obtain nearly the VO_2max levels found in elite male runners. The levels for trained athletes generally differ by sex, with men having scores 15–20 percent higher than those of women (McArdle et al., 1981). These values hold if the score is expressed as an absolute value or if it is computed for body weight. The difference appears to be for two reasons.

First, body fat. As mentioned previously, women generally have more body fat than men. Thus, since men have more muscle mass they are able to generate more aerobic energy (McArdle et al, 1981). In contrast, most women have approximately 10 percent more body fat, which is "dead weight" since it does not enhance athletic performance (Wells and Plowman, 1983).

Second, the blood composition of women differs from that of men. The hemoglobin levels of men are 10–14 percent higher than in women. Hemoglobin is, of course, the oxygen carrying component of the blood.

Thus, during aerobic exercise males have access to more oxygen than women.

The general way of reporting VO_2max scores is in milliliters of oxygen consumed per kilogram of body weight. While the maximum VO_2max measured in women is about 75, it has been reported as high as 89 in men.

Although the VO_2max in men is higher than in women, according to one study, women may use a larger percentage of the VO_2max. It is estimated that during a marathon, elite male runners use about 75 percent of their potential VO_2max. In a study of women training for the Fiesta Bowl Marathon, it was estimated that the women used on the average 81.9 percent of their VO_2max. Although some males also had a utilization rate as high as the women, most did not. Thus, women may be able to use their potential VO_2max more efficiently than men (Wells et al., 1981).

Related to the above, it is important to remember that the greater the percentage of VO_2max utilized, the greater the increase in blood lactate levels (see Daniels et al., 1977).

Fat

American society is a fat conscious society. Generally, fat is perceived of negatively. The positive features are seldom mentioned. For example, fat plays an important role in providing the body with energy, it serves as a cushion to protect the internal organs of the body from outside blows, and it serves as insulation against the cold.

Even though the percentage of body fat differs by age, the bodies of young women generally are 21.9 to 34.4 percent fat. The figure for young men is about 15 percent. Runners tend to have considerably lower body fat levels than nonrunners. Women long-distance runners often have fat levels in the 12–13 percent range, with some reporting levels as low as 6 percent. Male runners often have 8 to 10 percent body fat; at least one male Olympic gold medalist was reported as having 2.2 percent body fat (see Costill and Higdon, 1979). About 3 percent of the total body fat in both men and women is essential, or necessary to sustain life. In general, women accumulate fat in their hips, thighs, and breasts. Males accumulate fat in the upper and abdominal parts of their bodies (Shaver, 1981).

Although a greater percentage of body fat may be disadvantageous in most running events, it is a benefit in sports such as swimming where women will have greater buoyancy and lose less body heat than men.

Although body fat is one variable contributing to the poorer performance of women athletes, it is only a partial explanation. In a study designed to determine how much the fat differences in men and women contributed to the differences in performance times in events such as pull-ups, vertical jump, 50 yard dash, and 12 minute run, the authors concluded that body fat accounted for 19 percent of the difference in the vertical jump, 38 percent of the time difference in the 50 yard dash, 19 percent of the difference in the pull-ups, and 25 percent of the distance difference in the 12 minute run (Cureton et al., 1979). The authors of this article concluded that while percentage of body fat is a factor contributing to differences in performance, other factors also have to be considered.

Thus far the greater percentage of body fat in women has been examined primarily as a negative characteristic; it may, however, be of benefit in certain types of exercise. Specifically, it is speculated that women may have an advantage over men in sports requiring prolonged aerobic activity such as the marathon and the ultramarathon. This is because while at shorter distances the body relies equally for energy on carbohydrates and fat, after approximately an hour of exercise there is an increase in the percentage of fat utilized for energy. Studies have shown that in the first hour of exercise 50 percent of the energy comes from fat; by the start of the third hour as much as 70 percent of the energy comes from fat; and after prolonged exercise as much as 80 percent of the energy of the body comes from fat (McArdle et al., 1981).

Thus, fat is an important source of fuel. As noted elsewhere, fat is broken down into glucose for the brain. Glycogen, a form of sugar, is simply glucose in storage waiting to be used. The muscles and liver both store glycogen. While the brain needs pure glucose, the heart muscles use any type of fuel available, including fat. The skeletal muscles, however, work best with glucose.

One important question for longer running events is, then, do women burn fat more efficiently than men? If this is the case, they may be at an advantage over men. Many believe that because women have a greater percentage of body fat and because fat is a source of energy, they are at an advantage (see Besson, 1979; Ullyot, 1980). However, it is not body fat per se but the ability of the body to use the fat that is the important question.

Studies at the Human Performance Laboratory at Ball State University have found that trained males have an advantage in burning fat over trained females. It seems likely that those who have hypothesized that women will have an advantage over men because they have more fat to burn have not realized that women have more fat because their bodies burn fat less effectively. It appears that estrogen blocks the use of fat as a fuel (Costill and Higdon, 1979; see Powers et al., 1980; see Wells and Plowman, 1983).

In summary, currently researchers have found that body fat appears to be a detriment to the performance of women. Not only is it more mass to carry and less muscle but they appear to be less able to use body fat for fuel than males. However, this may change soon as many women lower their body fat percentages to figures approaching those of males and as they increase the level and intensity of their training (see Wilmore et al., 1977).

Stride

Although obviously important, relatively little research has been conducted on the differences in stride between men and women. One study on elite female runners did find that women, because they are shorter in total height and leg length, had shorter strides than males. However, when comparing their stride length to their height it was found that proportionally, women had longer strides than men, and thus may be overstriding. Females also tended to "be in flight" longer than men (Nelson et al., 1977). The above study found that women definitely have different running patterns than men. Through more advanced and intensive training over longer periods of time, men may have developed more efficient running patterns.

There are other physiological differences that influence stride. Because women have a wider pelvis, they have to shift the pelvis more than men to keep their center of gravity above the foot bearing their weight. Because of the greater pelvic movement and hip muscle use women generally have a decrease in running efficiency (Mathews and Fox, 1976).

Muscle

Muscles are again an obviously important component in running. Four questions arise. Are the muscles structually the same in men and women, do women have as much muscles as men, are women as strong as men, and are the muscles of women as trainable as those of men?

In the first question, there do not appear to be any structural differences between the muscles of men and women. That is, microscopically they are identical. Although males have more muscle mass than women, there are no differences in the percentage of fast-twitch (muscle used for short, fast running), and slow-twitch fibers (muscle used for slow, steady, distance running)(Besson, 1979).

Concerning the second question, however, we find that men have proportionally more muscle than women. In the average man, 44.9 percent of the body weight is muscle. In women the corresponding figure is 36 percent (McArdle et al., 1981).

Are women as strong as men? Generally, the absolute strength of males is higher than that of women (in both weight lifted and pulled). Although women only have about two-thirds the strength of men in the chest, arms, and shoulders, they approach the strength of men in their leg muscles. The reasons for this are obvious. In our society women are frequently discouraged from activities that would involve considerable utilization of the muscles in the upper part of the body. However, in everyday activity they have to use the muscles in their legs. Strength can be expressed as an absolute value, as above, or in relationship to body size. In this second approach, women approach the strength of males and surpass them in leg strength (Mathews and Fox, 1977).

The last question concerns the trainability of the muscles of women. Most of the early studies indicated that the muscles of women were less trainable than those of men. More recent studies have found, however, that the muscles of women are as trainable, if not more so. For example, one study of college students found that over a ten week period women had larger increases in strength than men did in grip, shoulder and chest muscles, and leg muscles (see Mathews and Fox, 1976).

One interesting feature, perhaps important for women who have been told they will become muscle-bound if they engage in sports, are the studies indicating that although an increase in strength is accompanied by an increase in muscle size, this is much more pronounced in men than in women. This is probably because of the hormone testosterone. Testosterone, which regulates muscle growth, is found in much higher levels in men than in women. This is why women are not likely to become "muscle-bound."

Running Records

Those of us who have been running and racing for some time have noted how races have changed in the awarding of prizes. In the distant past, only the first two or three finishers across the finish line were awarded any type of prize. That was it! As more and more runners started participating in races, various subdivisions were created, first by sex and then by age.

The divisions were inevitable and welcomed by almost all runners. The divisions were a way of recognizing that although a 65-year-old woman would probably not ever win a race where there were highly motivated and trained high school and college runners participating, she could still be recognized for her accomplishment.

The divisions by age and sex reflect a fact of life: generally, highly conditioned male runners run faster than highly conditioned female runners, and that, generally, highly conditioned runners in their twenties run faster than highly conditioned runners in their seventies. The important point is that individuals be allowed to compete within their own age or sex categories.

Even though the value of comparing different "categories" is dubious, there are some interesting observations to be made while examining the world record times of men and women.

Table I examines the current world records for men and women and notes by what percentage have men run faster than women (column A) and by what percentage longer it takes women to run an event than men (column B). Although no clear pattern emerges, generally the percentage difference appears to increase with the longer running events.

Table II presents the world record running times for 1972 and the current record and indicates the percentage improvement since 1972. As can be seen, for most events males made modest improvements while women made substantial gains, especially in the marathon.

The reasons for the percentage differences are obvious. Men have been training at more intensive levels, with better coaching, for a longer period of time. Thus, they approached their "maximum" performance far earlier than women. As more women start training with the same intensity, duration, and quality of coaching, we will see the records change dramatically for several years. Then, as with men the amount of change will "level off."

Table I
Current World Records

	Men (date)		Women (date)		Percentage difference	
					A	B
100m	0:09.93	(3/83)	0:10.79	(7/83)	8.64	7.95
200m	0:19.72	(9/79)	0:21.71	(6/79)	10.09	9.16
400m	0:43.86	(10/68)	0:47.99	(7/83)	9.41	8.61
800m	1:41.72	(7/79)	1:53.28	(7/83)	11.88	10.60
1500m	3:30.77	(8/80)	3:53.47	(8/80)	10.77	9.72
1 mile	3:47.33	(8/81)	4:17.44	(9/82)	13.21	11.67
10,000m	27:22.47	(4/82)	31:35.30	(7/82)	15.40	13.35
Marathon	2:07:11.00	(4/85)	2:21:06.00	(4/85)	10.94	9.86

A— men run faster than women by these percentages; **B**— it takes women longer to run the distance than men by these percentages.

Table II
Percent Improvement in Running Times Since 1972
(based on Table I)

	Women		Men		A	B
	1972	Current Record	1972	Current Record		
100m	11.00	10.79	9.93	9.93	1.90%	.02%
200m	22.40	21.71	19.80	19.72	3.08%	.40%
400m	51.00	47.99	43.86	43.86	3.94%	.59%
800m	1:58.50	1:53.28	1:44.30	1:41.72	4.23%	2.88%
1500m	4:01.00	3:53.47	3:33.00	3:30.77	3.33%	1.05%
1 mile	4:35.00	4:17.44	3:51.00	3:47.33	4.13%	1.73%
10,000m	34:51.00	31:35.30	27:39.40	27:22.47	9.37%	1.02%
Marathon	2:49:40.00	2:21:06.00	2:08:33.00	2:07:11.00	16.84%	1.06%

A— percentage of change in women; **B**— percentage of change in men.

3
Young Athletes and Running

Introduction

Exercise for children and adolescents? Only a few decades ago the idea of a planned vigorous exercise program for children and adolescents would have been thought of as ridiculous for two reasons. First, it was believed that children and adolescents received enough exercise through play and work, and second, as will be mentioned in the chapter on longevity, many believed that strenuous physical activity for children and adolescents was harmful, especially for hearts and lungs.

Nonetheless, in the 1950s physical fitness for children and adolescents became a national crusade when Americans were simultaneously made aware of the growing power of the Soviets and that their first line of defense, members of the young generation, were in poor physical condition. As a result of this awareness, fitness guidelines were established and exercise programs flourished.

Today vigorous physical exercise is still considered important for America's young, although social forces have changed the primary reason for fitness from military preparedness to health, recreation, appearance, and competition in athletic events.

Because the United States is a society with a tradition of doing few things in moderation, and because early training is essential since world-class athletes in many sports are now preadolescents, thousands of children and adolescents are now training and competing in athletic programs using equipment, rules, and procedures developed for adults. This has created many questions about the impact of vigorous physical exercise on youth.

There are a number of questions dealing with the safety of vigorous physical exercise for children and adolescents. For example, Will the growth plates in the leg bones be damaged because of repeated stress? Will heat injuries or death occur because of an immature thermoregulatory system? Will psychological trauma occur because of "pushy parents" or over-zealous coaches? Will growth be permanently stunted as a direct result of the training, or factors associated with the training such as weight loss or diet? Are their hearts capable of withstanding the stress of training and competition?

A second set of questions have been raised concerning the trainability of children and adolescents. For example, many have wondered if vigorous

physical exercise can produce a significant training effect before the hormone changes that accompany adolescence.

Another set of questions have dealt with requests for guidelines. Parents
ask questions such as, at what age should my child start running? and, at
her age, how many miles should my child be allowed to run?

All these are important questions that require answers. However,
many readers will be frustrated if they are looking for definitive answers —
information on the above questions are based, unfortunately, on a limited
amount of research and on anecdotal reports.

There is a lack of research for several reasons. Until recently there were
few young runners and the few who did run did not attract much attention
or cause for concern. There are many more ethical problems involved in
studying youths than there are with adults; as a result, researchers have
generally focused their attention on adults. Many of the answers to the questions being asked can only be obtained through research projects that span
several years. For example, to determine the effects of running on a variable
such as growth takes several years and most researchers prefer studies whose
results are more immediate.

Also, the questions being asked are complex and present the researcher
with both an expensive and difficult research project. For example, simply
demonstrating that one group of athletic children is shorter or taller than
"normal" does not demonstrate that the differential in growth was caused
by exercise. The difference may have been caused by diet, heredity, or selection. Designing and conducting a study that will control for all the "confounding" variables is both difficult and expensive.

Because of the lack of research, the American Academy of Pediatrics
has not established any guidelines for young runners (1982). The position of
the Academy is that before physical maturity, long-distance running events
that are designed primarily for adults "are not recommended for children"
(1982).

While we wait for research with more definitive answers to appear,
two distinct groups have emerged. The first group perceives running as a
natural and enjoyable activity for children and adolescents. This group
claims that in normal play children run 10 kilometers or half-marathons on
a daily basis and thus there is no need for concern. Individuals in this group
view running as an intrinsically enjoyable activity for children and
adolescents and support their position by offering anecdotal observations,
such as a child's looking up during the middle of a race and innocently asking why none of the adult runners look like they are enjoying themselves.

The second group perceives running as dangerous and damaging for
children and adolescents. Members in this group support their position by
taking note of sports such as wrestling or ballet, in which maintenance of
a low body weight may permanently stunt growth, gymnastics, in which
jarring dismounts or body contortions cause damage to the spine, or
baseball, in which the arms of Little League (or other child) pitchers have
been permanently damaged by repeated microtrauma. They also see

children as running in competitive events primarily because of bribes and verbal and physical threats rather than in a spontaneous reaction to a starting gun. One editorial even referred to children in competitive running events as exhibiting a new form of "child abuse" (O'Connell, 1979). In support of this position, some running magazines refuse to publish the marathon running times and records of children under the age of 12. These magazines take this position because they believe that the physical and mental stresses young runners are subjected to, both in training for and in racing a marathon, are "extreme" (see O'Connell, 1979). Another editor has noted that more needs to be learned so that an attempt to instill the habits of good health through running do not have "deleterious effects" (Hirsch, 1982). Some races, such as the New York and the Boston marathons, have established age minimums, generally around 16 to 18.

Potential or Alleged Dangers

Bones

A major tenet of those who believe it is physiologically damaging for children and adolescents to run is the belief that the growing long bones in the leg will be damaged (see Shaffer, 1966). There is good evidence indicating that permanent bone damage can occur in young athletes as a result of their participation in sports. The two most frequently cited examples where damage to bones has been found are the arms of Little League pitchers and the feet of ballet dancers.

As mentioned above, the primary area of concern for young runners is the long leg bones. The bones in the leg have a shaft called the diaphysis and ends which are called the epiphyses. In children and adolescents there is a growth plate of ossifying cartilage between the diaphysis and the epiphysis which is called the metaphysis, or epiphyseal disk. This growth plate is the major growth area in the long bones of the legs and is softer and more prone to damage than the other parts of the bone. Thus, while stress in an adult may result in a ligament injury, stress in a young athlete, because the ligaments are often three times stronger than the growth plate, may result in an injury to the growth plate (Kozar and Lord, 1983; Cage and Ivey, 1983).

If the damaged growth plate is not repaired or treated correctly, there is the potential for permanent damage, the most frequent consequence being a leg length discrepancy. The extent of the discrepancy depends, of course, on the severity of the injury, on the area of injury (the distal end of the femur is responsible for 70 percent of the total growth of the bone, the proximal end for 30 percent), and on the individual's age at injury. About 10 percent of skeletal injuries in childhood are injuries to the metaphysis and about 5 percent of these result in growth disturbances (see Pappas, 1983).

Injuries to the growth plate are especially problematic since they are difficult to diagnose. Radiographs of an injured area often appear normal and thus the injuries are treated as sprains. The extent of an injury to the growth plate may not be noticed for several months, until obvious growth variations are observed and the treatment of the injury then becomes more difficult, if not impossible.

While there have been several reports of sports-caused growth plate injuries in young athletes, there has not been a report published indicating the probability of injury for specific sports, for specific training levels in specific sports, or for specific age levels (see Speer and Braun, 1985). Because of the lack of long-term studies, Dr. Lyle J. Micheli, director of the Division of Sports Medicine at the Children's Hospital Medical Center and the Institute of Orthopedic Surgery at Harvard Medical School, believes that children in organized sports are part of a 40-year-long experiment with the conclusions and recommendations still in the future. Dr. Micheli has recommended that the training runs of children under 14 years of age not be any longer than six miles a day (*Physician and Sportsmedicine*, 1982; Anonymous, 1982).

The above conclusion agrees with the authors of an article on growth plate injuries in young distance runners. The authors stated that even though there were no empirical studies demonstrating that young long-distance runners have a higher than expected rate of growth plate injuries, based on existing knowledge caution was the best approach (Caine and Linder, 1984).

Besides bone damage, it has been hypothesized that when young athletes grow older they will be more prone to hip joint degeneration. The rationale for this speculation is that immature joints subjected to repeated stress during childhood and adolescence become damaged, and the damage will manifest itself during adulthood. While this has been investigated, the results are inconclusive. A study by Murray and Duncan (1971) supported the belief that "excessive" early vigorous exercise contributed to degenerative hip disease, while a study by Oka and Hatanpaa (1976) found that it did not.

In support of the belief that running does not contribute to hip degeneration is the research which demonstrates that physical activity increases skeletal mineralization. That is, as bones are stressed they become stronger, more dense, and wider. It is believed that this is simply the adaptation of the bone to repeated stress (see Malina et al., 1982; Bailey, 1976).

While intensive physical exercise may increase bone mineralization, it has also been postulated that in young athletes vigorous exercise may delay skeletal maturity, specifically skeletal ossification and the elimination of the growth plate. This is because skeletal maturity is dependent on certain hormones. As noted in Chapter 2, female runners appear to have a delayed menarche, presumably because many female runners have a different hormonal profile than nonrunners. If intense physical activity does in fact influence certain hormones, this could affect the maturation of the skeleton. To date, insufficient data on girls are available to indicate if skeletal maturity is delayed as a result of intensive physical exercise. Limited studies on boys have indicated that their skeletal maturity is not affected by intensive physical exercise (see Malina et al., 1982).

Heat Injury

Every year we are reminded of the possibility of heat-related injury and death to young athletes with the start of the high school football season. This is because every year ignorant, misinformed coaches cause thousands of needless heat-related injuries, as well as some deaths. This naturally brings to the minds of many the possibility that young runners are especially vulnerable to heat-related injuries (see Knochel, 1975).

Several studies have found that the thermoregulatory systems of children and adolescents are not as efficient as those of adults, and have thus concluded that children are more susceptible to heat-related injuries. This conclusion has been reached for six reasons. First, the young have a lower capacity than adults to transfer heat by blood from the body core to the skin. Second, exercising young athletes produce more metabolic heat than adults. Third, children do not have as great a sweating capacity as adults (adult sweating capacity is generally achieved by age 13). Fourth, although children and adolescents have a larger surface area to mass ratio than adults and this should allow for the dissipation of more heat, their lower sweating capacity nullifies this potential advantage and allows a greater heat gain from the environment. Fifth, children and adolescents need a longer period of time to acclimatize to exercise in the heat. Sixth, the young are more likely to become dehydrated because of inadequate fluid intake (see American Academy of Pediatrics 1983; Bar-Or et al., 1980; Wagner et al., 1972; Haymes et al., 1975; Drinkwater et al., 1977; Haymes et al., 1974; Bar-Or, 1980).

Because of the risks young athletes face when exercising in a hot environment, the American Academy of Pediatrics recommends:

1. A reduction in duration and intensity of physical activity during a period of elevated temperature and humidity.
2. An acclimatization period, either at the start of a vigorous exercise program or upon moving to a warmer climate, in which both the intensity and duration of exercise are restricted for 10–14 days.
3. Fully hydrating young athletes before prolonged, vigorous exercise, and monitoring them to make certain they have an adequate fluid intake during the exercise period.
4. Closely monitoring the clothing young athletes wear to reduce the risk of heat injury. In hot weather this generally means one layer of an absorbent lightweight cloth. Clothing that has become saturated with sweat needs to be replaced. Clothing that is rubberized and designed to produce a weight loss should *not* be used.
5. Making young athletes knowledgeable about heat-related injuries. Specifically, they need to know how to prevent heat injuries by learning what causes them. They should also know how to prevent heat injuries through adequate fluid intake, heat acclimatization, proper clothing, and sound exercise rules (for instance, exercise only when the temperature and humidity are below a certain level). Additionally, young athletes need to learn how to help one of their peers if he or she is affected by a heat-related injury, such as heat stroke.

It needs to be stressed that heat injuries are preventable! Additionally, parents, coaches, and young athletes must know the potential dangers and the allowable limits of exercise. This may require that someone, either the coach, the parent, or the athlete, will have to limit or even cancel practice or competition on a potentially dangerous day.

Psychological

The psychological consequences of children and adolescents' engaging in vigorous physical exercise have been frequently discussed, but without any definitive conclusions.

The alleged psychological consequences of exercise that have been postulated are diametrically opposed. There are those who list the positive consequences of early participation in athletics, such as character building, self-discipline, and enhanced self-concept. And there are those who list the negative consequences, such as premature emotional stress, forced entry into adulthood, and development of a competitive personality.

The negative psychological aspects have been reported frequently in anecdotal form for over two decades. The reports have ranged from the stereotypic Little League mother hurling threats and insults at her son, to a father riding a bicycle alongside his marathon-running daughter, screaming at her to fun faster.

The "psychological abuse" inflicted on young athletes has probably increased in recent years as the level of competition and expectations have increased. Although the psychological abuse is there, and there will undoubtedly someday soon be a plethora of books titled something like *Coach Dearest*, empirical studies are lacking. Thus, while it exists, the extent and the long-range consequences of such abuse are unknown.

There have been a few empirical studies that have demonstrated positive consequences of running for children and adolescents. One study of fifth and sixth graders wanted to find out the impact on self-concept of running one mile three times a week for seven weeks. The study found that the runners' self concepts improved while those of the nonrunners stayed the same (Percy et al., 1981).

A second study on children with behavioral disorders at the San Diego Center for Children found that by running 40 minutes a day, four times a week, the need for psychotropic medication was reduced. Although such a regimen is not effective for all disorders, the Center is conducting further studies to find out which psychological disorders benefit from running, and the amount of running necessary to produce positive changes (see Barnes, 1981).

A third study has also yielded positive results. This study examined both normal high school students and emotionally disturbed adolescents. All the participants started running a mile a day, five times a week. The study found that significant differences between the joggers and nonjoggers occurred, with the joggers perceiving themselves as more intelligent and assertive. The emotionally disturbed joggers became more outgoing and saw themselves as less excitable and impatient. The staff also saw them as more self-confident, less timid, less withdrawn, and less emotionally disturbed. The study did not state how long the changes lasted (Dulberg and Bennett, 1980).

Growth

With the trend toward prepubescent and adolescent world-class athletes in many sports, one question naturally arises: Does vigorous physical exercise have an influence on body growth?

There are two positions on this question. Some believe that vigorous physical exercise accelerates the growth of young athletes. They point to athletes in selected sports, generally football and basketball, as demonstrating the impact of sports on growth. Others believe that vigorous physical exercise has the potential to permanently retard growth. Those who support this position also point to athletes in selected sports, generally dancers and gymnasts, and as if their small size is a consequence of their participation in their sport.

The literature has addressed this question but without definitive answers. Obviously, experimentation into this area would have to be done on animals, since human experimentation would be unethical and immoral. Even comparing the heights of athletes and nonathletes would not yield any firm answers since different sports may select individuals of different heights. For example, while football might attract taller or heavier players than average, gymnastics would probably attract the smaller than average. The height differences seen in athletes in certain sports are not necessarily a result of the sport but more a reflection of selection by coaches for the sport. The differences in the average heights of athletes in different sports may also be a consequence of the life style imposed by the sport rather than the sport itself. For example, to be an elite athlete in several sports may mean a restricted diet. Studies indicate that a diet deficient in essential nutrients and calories will permanently retard growth. Studies on the effects of a restricted diet on children and adolescents during wartime have indicated that as a result of this diet, full height will not be reached.

There have been several short-term studies indicating that sports may accelerate the growth of athletes (see Andrew et al., 1972; Ekblom, 1969). This may be because exercise triggers the release of a growth hormone and thus potential height is achieved earlier (Astrand, 1976). Others believe, however, that early maturers are more likely to be selected for athletic teams. It has also been postulated that the difference in height between athletes and nonathletes is cosmetic, and is caused by the fact that athletes simply have better muscle tone and thus stand straighter than their less athletic peers (see Malina, 1969).

There have also been studies that have found that young athletes have a slower rate of growth than young nonathletes. One recent study found that children involved in high intensity training had a slower rate of growth than their nonathletic peers (Delmas, 1982). As noted previously, it may not be athletic participation per se that is producing the slower rate of growth. It may be that the sport is selecting individuals who have a strong probability of being average or below average in height. Additionally, growth may also be affected by diet. That is, it may not be the sport that affects growth but the life style and diet associated with it. Young athletes in certain sports who have a strong desire to "make the team" may restrict their diets, which may have an impact on their growth.

Studies have also found that exercise has no impact on growth (see Malina et al., 1982). One recent study of a girls' cross country team, where the average age was 16, and the average distance per week had been 50 miles for the last two years, found that the girls were of average height for their age (Burke et al., 1979). Another study of 34 male Finnish elite runners 12 to 16 years of age found that the runners did not differ in height from their nonrunning peers (Sundberg and Elovainio, 1982). A study of 14 boys between the ages of 10 and 15 at the start of the study found that after 22 months of running their heights were normal for their ages (Daniels and Oldridge, 1971).

The studies to date are too limited for any conclusions to be drawn. In the future, studies that will examine factors such as genetic potential and diet are needed.

The Heart

Although the risk is small, for certain young athletes vigorous exercise is a dangerous activity. Although we generally associate exercise-induced cardiac problems, such as a heart attack, with older individuals, cardiac events, often resulting in death, can also be precipitated in young athletes. This generally occurs in those who have an *undiagnosed* heart condition. Unfortunately, these conditions are often not diagnosed until the condition manifests itself through a cardiac event. While many heart pathologies in young athletes may be easily diagnosed, others can be found only if the physician suspects they exist; some conditions cannot be clinically diagnosed (Strong and Steed, 1982).

Several articles have been written on death in young athletes (see Thiene et al., 1983; Gunby, 1979; Maron et al., 1980; Luckstead, 1982). To prevent a fatal cardiac event some writers have suggested that a family history be completed on each athlete, with special emphasis being paid to questions dealing with family heart disease; that an investigation of any symptoms, such as chest pain and especially fainting during exercise, be made (symptoms should not be ignored); and that a cardiac exam should be completed on those with a family history of heart disease or possible symptoms of heart disease.

The Consequences of Training

There have been relatively few "good" studies on exercise and training effects in young athletes. Most studies in this area have not provided a nonathletic group to compare to the athletic group, thus making it impossible to separate the effects of training from those of maturation. Additionally, most of the existing studies have used young athletes of different ages and different sexes, who were engaging in different sports or in the same sport but at different levels of intensity and duration. The studies have not tried to focus on the consequences of exercise for a specific age group engaging in a specific sport at a specific level of intensity for a specific time period. Thus, the results are a hodgepodge of articles on the effects of exercise on young athletes in different age groups, of different sexes, who are participating in different sports at different levels of intensity and for different lengths of time.

The Heart

In the past, physicians and exercise physiologists believed that vigorous physical exercise was dangerous for young athletes, primarily because of its effect on the heart. This was because it was widely believed that the blood vessels of the heart developed at a slower rate than the heart muscle. Because of this, it was reasoned, the young athlete was at an increased risk of rupturing a blood vessel during vigorous exercise, or of causing other heart damage, such as an aneurysm, that would result in serious problems, including death, later in life.

It was also believed that vigorous exercise would lead to an enlarged heart, which in the past was considered symptomatic of a diseased heart.

These beliefs have now been largely dispelled. Researchers have found that there is a parallel growth rate for the heart muscle and blood vessels. Also, enlarged hearts are no longer automatically considered to be diseased.

In studying the heart there are two consequences of exercise that need to be examined. The first relates to the question of whether exercise will prevent coronary heart disease, which was addressed in Chapter 1 and will be again in Chapter 7, and has significance given the fact that heart disease is the number one cause of death in contemporary American society. Additionally, studies have indicated that there is a high prevalence of coronary heart disease risk factors in children and adolescents, and coronary heart disease is believed to start developing early in life (Linder and DuRant, 1982; see Siegel and Manfredi, 1984). Furthermore, although children appear to be active, studies have reported that most do not engage in the high-intensity activity necessary for cardiovascular fitness (Gilliam et al., 1982). In fact, a recent study by University of Michigan researchers of active children between the ages of 7 and 12 found that 62 percent of them had at least one risk factor for coronary heart disease (high blood pressure, high serum cholesterol level, smoking, obesity, diabetes mellitus, stress, sedentary life style, or a family history of coronary heart disease), and 36 percent had two or more risk factors (Gilliam et al., 1977). Other studies have found similar results (Berg et al., 1983; Blumenthal et al., 1975; Lauer et al., 1975; Kannel and Dawber, 1972; Wilmore and McNamara, 1974).

The second consequence of exercise as related to the heart deals with the training effect. To examine if an effect occurs in the hearts of young athletes as the result of vigorous physical exercise, both heart rate and heart volume will be examined.

Heart Rate

As is well known, the heart rate at birth is about 130 beats per minute. This becomes progressively slower until adolescence, when it stabilizes in the mid-70s and generally remains at that level through adulthood.

To determine the impact of exercise on heart rate one study compared a group of nonathletic boys with 34 elite Finnish endurance runners, 12–16 years of age, who had been running two to five years and who ran 40–100km per week. At age 12 the nonrunners' average resting heart rate was 83 beats per minute. The runners' average heart rate was 76 beats per minute. At age 14 the figures were 83 and 75. For both of these age categories the differences were not significant. At age 16, however, the nonrunners had an average heart rate of 85 while that of the runners was 62 beats per minute, a statistically significant difference (Sundberg and Elovainio, 1982). The difference may demonstrate a training effect; it may also demonstrate that the older runners had a more intensive training schedule, or that the older runners were a more highly select group.

A study of girls 8–13 years of age, who engaged in a 12-week cross-country training program, found that the average heart rate decreased by 5.2 beats per minute by the end of the program (Brown et al., 1972).

There are several other similar studies which indicate that a training effect can be achieved in the heart rates of young athletes. The exact age at which it will occur or the level of training necessary to produce the effect are not known.

Heart Volume

The study on the Finnish endurance runners also found that there was little difference between the heart volumes of the first two age groups (12 and 14 years of age) but that there was a significant difference between the heart volumes of the older groups (16 years). For example, at age 12 the nonrunners had an average heart volume of 495ml while those of the runners averaged 468ml; at age 14 the figures were 614ml and 585ml. At age 16 the differences were significant with the nonrunners having a volume of 664ml and the runners a volume of 792ml, an 11 percent greater volume.

In a 32 month study of boys who were 11 years old at the start of the study, the researchers found that those who exercised had a 43 percent increase in heart volume while those who were sedentary had only a 29 percent increase (Ekblom, 1969). Studies again indicate that a training effect can be achieved in heart volume in young athletes. However, again the studies are too few for the age and intensity to be specified.

VO_2max

Since VO_2max is an important determinant of performance, there has been a controversy over the impact training can have on its increase. Although several studies have found that young athletes have a higher VO_2max than their peers, the question of whether this is caused by training, heredity, or selection is still being investigated. (It is well known that from age four to 18 there is a steady increase in VO_2max; this occurs faster in boys than in girls [Astrand, 1976].) Thus, there have been several studies designed to differentiate the impact of maturation from training on VO_2max. One study on an elite cross-country team of girls, whose average age was 16 and who had been running about 50 miles a week for two years, found an average VO_2max of 63, a level almost double that of sedentary girls of the same age (Burke et al., 1979).

A study of girls 8–13 years of age found that after 12 weeks of cross-country training their VO_2max increased by 26 percent. A similar group of girls who were not trained showed no increase (Brown et al., 1972).

Another study on 127 girls whose average age was 15.6 and who were participating in a summer cross-country training program found that the average VO_2max was 50.8. The average for girls in this age group is 35.9 (Butts, 1982).

In a 32 month study on 14 boys it was found that the average increase in VO_2max for boys who exercised was 55 percent; boys who did not exercise had an increase of 37 percent (Ekblom, 1969).

A study on 34 competitive male athletes 12–16 years of age who had been training from two to five years and who ran from 40 to 100 kilometers per week was done in Finland. The boys who were 12–14 years of age were compared to nonathletic boys. The study found that the athletic boys had VO_2max levels 14 to 18 percent higher than the nonathletic boys. The athletic boys who were 16 years of age had VO_2max levels that were 20 percent higher than the nonathletic boys (Sundberg and Elovainio, 1982).

Another study of 11 male runners started when the boys were 12 or 13 years of age and continued until they were 18 years of age. The boys were involved in an intensive running program, up to two hours per day. Approximately one-half discontinued running after age 17, most, presumably, because they were not as good as those who continued to run. For those who continued to run, their VO_2max levels increased to an average of 65.4 at age 15, and to 76 by age 18. For those who discontinued training, their VO_2max within one year after the discontinuation of training had fallen to "normal" limits (Murase et al., 1981).

Thus, many studies have found that a significant training effect in VO_{2max} can occur in young athletes.

Fat

As would be expected, the fat levels measured in most young athletes are far below that of their nonathletic peers. One study of female cross-country runners whose average age was 15.6 and who ran 25 miles per week found an average fat composition of 15.4 percent, compared to 26.7 percent for nonathletes in the same age group (Butts, 1982).

A study of male runners and male nonrunners found similar amounts of body fat at age 14, but by age 19 the percentage of body fat in the runners had remained the same, 13 percent, but had increased to 19 percent in the nonrunners (Elovainio and Sundberg, 1983).

Muscle

Traditionally, it was believed that children would not add much bulk or strength to their muscles through training. It was thought that only after puberty and the release of testosterone and other androgens that bulk or strength could be gained (see Legwold, 1982c; Moore, 1982b).

A recent study by Dr. Lyle Micheli, director of the Division of Sports Medicine at the Children's Hospital Medical Center in Boston, refuted this belief. Dr. Micheli's study involved an analysis of strength gains in 30 children age 9 to 11. The children participated in a 12 week program of exercise involving weight training. The children had an average strength gain of 52 percent, compared to 2 percent for a similar group that did not participate in the program. Dr. Micheli concluded that it is a myth that children will not gain strength, based on "old ideas, not facts." An editor of the magazine *The Physician and Sportsmedicine* has suggested that Micheli's results need to be treated cautiously until other research supports his findings (see Legwold, 1983c; see Duda, 1986).

Recommendations

As is evident from the previous sections, definitive research that will answer the questions parents and coaches have concerning the consequences of running for children and adolescents has not been published. While there is a great deal of valuable information, there are still far more questions than answers. In lieu of definitive answers, several organizations and researchers have suggested guidelines based on what is known — or believed to be — safe at this time. The guidelines (from American Academy of Pediatrics, 1981a; 1981b; 1981c; 1983; Strong and Steed, 1982; Garrick,

1977; Ryan, 1986; Stackpole and Murray, 1982; Kozar and Lord, 1983; Rosegrant, 1981) follow.

1. Young athletes should be treated first and foremost as children and adolescents and only second as young *athletes*. Parents and coaches need to remember that because of their lack of muscular strength, VO_2max, and cardiac output, young athletes cannot and should not be expected to perform at adult levels.

2. Training programs that are developed should be based upon the physical, social, and psychological maturity of the young athlete. Again, the age of the youth must be considered. Too often programs of progressive intensity lead to an adult training program, or a program designed for a mature or exceptional young athlete.

The following schedule has been recommended for young athletes. Between the ages of 6 and 10 the primary emphasis of sports should be to create an interest in sports in general, to have fun, and to learn basic skills. Those 11 to 14 years of age should develop greater versatility and techniques as well as increase their training. Young adults between the ages of 15 and 18 can increase the intensity of their training, compete extensively and become more specialized.

3. Coaches need to be more knowledgeable in areas such as exercise physiology, the prevention and care of injuries, instructional methods, and even child and adolescent psychology.

A frequent cause of injury in young athletes is the training methods and philosophies of coaches. Many coaches have training schedules that place the athletes in their charge in potentially dangerous situations. Too often coaches overemphasize winning. It has been recommended that coaches be required to pass a written examination to ensure that they do have the knowledge needed to develop and manage a safe sports program. Although the specifics of the examination have not been developed, ideally the examination would cover more than the current requirements to be a coach — which appear to be owning a baseball cap with "coach" on it, a whistle, and a clipboard. Many organizations are hesitant to have an examination system. Passing the examination would certify that the individual was competent to coach. This could lead to liability suits against the organization that "certified" the individual to coach (Murphy, 1985).

4. Detailed medical records need to be kept of an athlete's injuries. Too often injuries are overlooked or conveniently forgotten, either by the coach or the athlete. A chronology of injuries would allow both the athlete as he or she matures, and future coaches, to develop a training program that would strengthen and protect weak areas.

5. The young athlete's perception of his or her limits must be respected.

6. Strength and flexibility training should be closely monitored. Many exercise physiologists believe that young athletes should not work with weights to develop strength. Rather, strength training should be developed by using chin-ups, pull-ups, push-ups, the rope climb, and other techniques that involve the athlete's body as the source of resistance. Additionally, it is

believed that many injuries could be prevented if warm-ups stressed stretching exercises that would enhance flexibility.

7. Different rates of physical and psychological maturity must be taken into account. Although it is easier and simpler to categorize individuals by chronological age, six-year-olds may vary in physical maturity by as much as four years and 12-year-olds by as much as six years. Thus, one 12-year-old may be ready to train and compete at an 18-year-old level while another is at a six-year-old level and definitely not ready for high-intensity training and competition. Thus, maturity and skill level are more important indicators than chronological age.

8. The season length for a sport should be appropriate for the age and maturity of the young athlete. Generally, the older and more mature the young athlete, the longer the season.

9. Medical care should be instituted, to include a thorough medical examinations for all athletes (which would allow undiagnosed and potentially dangerous or fatal congenital or other conditions to be diagnosed and treated), comprehensive health histories, periodic health checkups, the availability of a competent medical trainer, and established policies and procedures to deal with the referral of injured athletes and when they can return to training after their illness/injury.

10. Protective equipment that is safe, maintained, and properly fitted, and a safe, and well-maintained training facility should be provided.

11. A clearly specified line of authority involving the team physician, family physician, coach, parents, school, and the athlete should be established and proper supervision, competent teaching, and knowledgeable training provided.

Recommendations for road races for those 12 or under were given recently in *The Physician and Sportsmedicine* (see Rowland and Hoontis, 1985). They are:

> The course should be a flat two miles.
> The race should be run only during cool weather. Additionally, there should be ample water before, during, and after the race.
> The course should be "safe"; this means vehicles should be prevented from entering the course and dangerous obstacles removed. Spotters should also be placed along the course so that the runners can be seen the entire time they are racing.
> Preparation should be made for accidents and injuries.
> The race should be used as a learning experience for the runners. They can learn aspects of the sport such as exercise physiology, racing strategy, and its history.
> Emphasis should be on individual performance. Everyone should be a winner in terms of enjoyment and challenge. This does not mean that the competitive aspects have to be overlooked. It simply means that those who are physically or psychologically immature, should not be discouraged from running or racing because they continually "lose."

4
Running After 40

Introduction

For most runners, running is not a casual or temporary form of activity, it is a daily, lifelong activity. Runners are, as a result, generally interested in three issues, or questions about running and growing old. They ask, will running stop or delay the aging process? Will running over decades cause irreparable damage to joints or other parts of the body? And most important, will running be possible at age 90? A question asked by nonrunners is, if I am fat and 65, and have not exercised since high school will running do me any good?

Although most runners personally know runners over the age of 40, masters runners, there has not been much published on them in either the scientific journals or the running magazines. Although most runners have heard of Larry Lewis who was still running six miles a day when he was 106 (?) years of age, or Johnny Kelley who in 1981 at 73 years of age ran his 50th Boston Marathon, or even Jack Foster who at 44 years of age placed seventeenth out of 67 in the 1976 Olympic Marathon, still relatively little attention has been focused on older runners.

The articles that have been published have probably been beneficial to runners by showing them that athletically men and women do not "hit the wall" at 40. Many of the articles on masters runners have been on individuals who had been sedentary for more than half a century before starting to run. This has indicated to many that older runners are not anomalies but individuals whose life styles can be duplicated.

Before starting this chapter it should be noted that the terms "aging" and "aged" are difficult to define. For some researchers aging starts at birth. For others, the first 20–25 years are a period of growth and development, after which aging begins. Defining when someone is aged is even more difficult. Obviously chronological age is not a good measurement since many individuals who are 30 years of age are in "worse" physical condition than many individuals who are 60 years of age. Even social indicators, such as retirement, are inadequate since a football player may retire at 30. The United States Government has defined old age as occurring at age 65. This age was established in 1935 when the Social Security Act was created and a definite age was needed for payment eligibility. In 1935, 65 years of age seemed like a good idea since life expectancy at birth was 55 years of age.

While researchers argue endlessly over the definitions of "aging" and "aged," there is no argument over the consequences of growing older in American society, both physical and social.

One consequence is social. If there is one salient characteristic of American socity it is its worship of youth and its characteristics, such as freedom from responsibility, physical vigor, and potential. The characteristics that the aged often manifest are considered by many to be undesirable. As a result of growing older, many individuals resort to plastic surgery, hair dyes and transplants, skin creams, and a variety of other tactics and devices to repair the changes inflicted by time...and life.

A second consequence is physical. Unfortunately, the physical and biological changes that accompany increasing age are real and are generally in the direction of decline. Individuals in contemporary American society can expect several physiological declines to take place, the declines generally starting between the ages 20 to 25.

The Physiological Consequences of Aging

Biologists call physiological aging "senescence." Writing on senescence is difficult. This is because not only do individuals age at different rates but within the same individual different body parts may age at different rates. Thus, although aging is inevitable, senescence affects individuals and body parts within the same individual differently.

Biologists disagree about exactly when growth and development stop and senescence begins. As noted previously, a commonly quoted figure is that we spend the first 20 to 25 years growing and developing and the remainder of our life aging. What are the physiological consequences?

This question can best be answered by examining selected physiological variables of a 30-year-old man and by assuming each variable is functioning at 100 percent. The results of senescence can be seen by listing the percent of functioning or of tissue remaining in an average 75-year-old man. Some of the percentages are (see Crandall, 1980):

> brain weight (56 percent)
> blood flow to brain (80 percent)
> cardiac output at rest (70 percent)
> number of taste buds (36 percent)
> maximum oxygen uptake during exercise (40 percent)
> maximum work rate (70 percent)

These are only some of the declines. The list is unfortunately quite long. The good news is that for most of us the declines will not be noticeable since they are gradual. Also, although certain body organs, such as the kidneys, decline dramatically, most also have a reserve capacity. That is, the organ has the ability to decline more than 50 percent in its functioning and still perform adequately.

Scientists do not know why we age. There are, however, a variety of theories.

Theories on the Cause of Senescence

Throughout recorded history there have been numerous theories on why aging occurs. Although this has been the single most frequently researched topic in history, there are still only theories about why aging occurs and no miracle "fountain of youth" has as of yet been discovered. The lack of a single accepted reason for aging cannot be attributed to a lack of effort. Rather, it is because of the complexity of the issue. It is difficult for researchers to ascertain which changes are a result of a universal species-specific genetic aging process, which are the result of environmentally produced pathological condition, which are the result of life style, and which changes are the result of genetic background.

In contemporary American society we often confuse senescence, which is a natural, normal process all individuals will eventually go through if they live long enough, with certain pathological conditions, which are abnormal but which many (most?) individuals have come to accept as a normal consequence of aging. For example, cancer, heart disease, or tooth loss are so frequent in contemporary American society that individuals have come to tolerate and accept them as normal consequences of aging rather than as a diseased state often inflicted either by themselves (Roman philosopher Seneca said, "Man does not die, he kills himself") or by their environment. Most accept these diseases as trade-offs for industrialization and the "good life" without realizing that the "good life" can be had without the increased risks of heart disease, cancer, tooth loss, and a host of other diseases that are epidemic in our society. However, this book is not the place to talk about tobacco subsidies, poorly tested food additives, and the myriad of other factors that all contribute to the horrific health of Americans. Nor is it a good place to mention the common American attitude that "you can't do anything about it" or the belief that damaging the body is acceptable since by the time the consequences manifest themselves, the medical establishment will have developed the technology to repair the damage.

This book is the place to examine "normal" physiological indicators, such as blood pressure, of certain age groups and to then compare these indicators with those of runners in the same age group. However, before doing so it is necessary to examine senescence in more detail.

It is important to distinguish biological aging from other biological processes, such as cancer, and from other factors that may exacerbate the aging process, such as life style. Biological aging is universal. Cancer, however, is not universal. In fact, in some societies it is very rare. Aging is a natural condition resulting from genetic programming from "within" the organism. The organism is pre-programed for the change to take place and it is not caused by an outside condition. Cancer is caused by outside variables such as radiation or exposure to certain cancer-causing compounds.

Aging-related changes occur slowly rather than rapidly. As most of us know, a condition such as cancer can manifest and magnify itself with alarming speed. Aging-related changes have a deleterious impact on the body, resulting in a decline in the ability of the body to function. While cancer obviously falls into the category of deleterious change there are other factors which produce changes in the body, such as exercise, that may have a positive effect on the physiological functioning of the body.

Finally, aging is a unidirectional process (it cannot be reversed). With a condition such as cancer, it is becoming increasing possible to reverse or stop the process.

The next question that has to be asked is, why do human beings age? Although many theories have been proposed, there is no definitive answer. Generally, the theories have fallen into two categories, those meant to establish that the body is programmed to age, and those indicating a belief that environmental factors, such as radiation from the sun, cause aging to occur. Some of the more widely accepted and proposed theories are described briefly below.

The most popular hypothesis has been the "wear and tear" theory of senescence. This theory views the body as a machine and believes that the more it is used the sooner it will wear out. This theory is contradictory to those who believe in the value of exercise, since physical activity would be seen as increasing the rate of aging. Although there is not much evidence supporting this theory in certain body parts, such as the cardiovascular system, many contend that there is evidence to support the theory, especially for areas such as joints.

Changes in the level of hormones have also been as widely researched as the suspected cause of senescence. Hormones have been used to ameliorate some of the negative consequences of menopause. Hormonal therapy for menopause has, of course, been vigorously debated and even by its proponents it is portrayed only as a relief from the symptoms of aging, not from aging in and of itself. Variations of hormone therapy have been used for centuries. At one time the testicles of bulls were dried and then consumed as an alleged elixir of youth. The only known consequence of this "therapy" was to create many unhappy bulls. To date, hormones have not been found to retard the aging process; they may alleviate some of the negative symptoms of aging, although their use is not without controversy.

A theory that is currently in vogue is the autoimmunity theory. This theory states that as the body ages, more and more cell mutations occur. The mutations occur because of external factors such as radiation exposure or toxic chemicals. Our body responds to these cell mutations as "foreign bodies" and produce antibodies to destroy them. Thus, we end up destroying our own bodies.

Many believe that the body is programmed to age and eventually die. This theory has recently received a great deal of attention based on research that has shown that certain cells taken from young animals and placed in a culture divide about 50 times before dying. The same type of cells taken from an older animal will divide far fewer times. This and similar research appears to indicate that cells do have a finite number of times they can divide before they die. Before this research, it was widely believed that cells placed in a culture could divide indefinitely.

Another cause of aging that has been widely investigated recently deals with DNA. Current research indicates that our DNA may become damaged and hence send out the wrong instructions to cells. This in turn causes a variety of disorders which produced aging.

Most researchers now hold a dual theory of aging. While they adhere to one of the theories just discussed, they also recognize that a significant part of the aging process is caused by life style. For example, some researchers believe that as much as 50 percent of the aging process is caused by "hypokinetic" disease (*hypo* = below or deficient, + *kinetic* = motion) which refers to disease in an individual whose level of activity is insufficient to prevent it. This theory is in conflict with the "wear and tear" theory and is basically a "use it or lose it" theory (see Smith and Gillian, 1983).

The Consequences of Running on Aging

This section has two purposes. The first is to describe the physical consequences of aging that most Americans experience. The second is to describe the impact that running and the life style of runners have on the aging process. The material in this section will be presented in alphabetical order.

It should be noted that research on those over 40 is in its infancy when compared to the amount of research on other age groups. Thus research on older runners is difficult to obtain. Furthermore, a great deal of the research that does exist is flawed from a methodological perspective and thus of limited value.

Before starting this section the studies that will be frequently referred to need to be mentioned. Each of these studies examined one or more masters runners and will be mentioned in several of the following sections.

The first study examined Harold Chapman. At the time he was studied he was 71.7 years of age. When younger, Chapman had been an elite college middle-distance runner. After college Chapman did not engage in any physical training until age 67 when he resumed running. At age 70 he started competing and in his first masters race broke the record for his age group in the mile by 27 seconds (old 6:32, Chapman's 6:05). At the time of the study Chapman trained by running two to three miles a day at a seven minute pace. Chapman appears to have a remarkable genetic endowment. This can be seen in several of his physiological measurements, which will be discussed later, and because at the time of the study his mother was still physically active at 102 years of age (Dressendorfer, 1980).

The second study examined Wally Hayward. Hayward was 70 at the time the research on him was conducted. He is unique in that he has been running almost continually since 1926. He did reduce his workouts from 1954 to 1966 to once or twice a week because he had been declared a "professional" and could not compete in nonprofessional running events. When younger he was a world-class runner. For example, he placed tenth in the marathon in the 1952 Olympic Games (2:31:50). He also won the South African Comrades Marathon (54 miles) five times (1931, 1950, 1951, 1953, 1954). In training for the Comrades Marathon he recently ran 10–15 miles five days a week, 70 miles one day (yes, seventy), and then rested one day. His philosophy is to run further than the distance he will race one day a week to gain confidence. At the time of this writing he held the world's marathon record for his age group (3:06:24) (Maud et al., 1981).

The next runner is Dr. Paul E. Spangler. Spangler was 77 years old when he was examined; he held 14 world records for his age category and had another 14 pending. Spangler runs both sprints and distances races. Spangler did not start running until he was 67 years of age. At the time of the study he was running 7 to 10 miles a day (Webb et al., 1977). (At 84, Spangler completed a marathon in 4:53:35.)

Jack Wilmore and his associates (1974) examined four masters runners aged 71–74. The study provided only the initials of the men (DF, NJ, VS, and TR). At the time of the study DF held the world record for his age group in the 800 meter and 880 yard dash (3:15:0 and 3:27:5). He trained an average of 8–10 miles a week. NJ and VS held jointly the world record for the mile for their age group (6:55:0). NJ also held the world record in his age group for three miles, five kilometers, and ten kilometers. He ran an average of 30 miles per week. VS ran an average of 20 miles a week. TR held, at the time of the study, the world record for his age group in the two mile run (13:15:0).

Two studies were published on a group of champion American track athletes 40–75 years of age. The thoroughness of these studies on 25 masters athletes and the research design which separated the athletes into age groups (i.e., 40–49, 50–59, 60–69, and 70+) makes them important for our consideration (Pollock, 1974; Pollock et al., 1974).

The last study is one by G. H. Hartung and his associate E. J. Farge (1977) of the Baylor College of Medicine. They studied 48 healthy male runners 40–59 years of age (average age was 47). The men had a high socioeconomic profile in years of education, occupation, and income. Twenty-five of them had run a marathon within the last year.

Blood Pressure

Chapter 1, "Running and the Heart," examined blood pressure in some detail. It was pointed out there that generally blood pressure increases with increasing age. Given certain prevalent characteristics of the aging population this would be expected: an increase in obesity, cardiovascular disease, and salt intake. It was also noted in the chapter on the heart that blood pressure levels considered "high" for young individuals are considered "normal" for the aged. Thus, increases in blood pressure are accepted by many as a "normal," an apparently inevitable consequence of aging. Table I clearly shows that with increasing age blood pressure levels increase for most individuals.

Table I
Blood Pressure by Age and Sex

	Males		Females
Newborn		80/46	
5		100/67	
6	95/60		96/62
7–11	103/65		103/64
12–17	115/71		112/69
18–24	124/72		113/69
25–34	126/76		116/73
35–44	130/80		123/77
45–54	135/83		134/83
55–64	143/83		148/84
65–74	151/81		163/83
75–79	146/81		158/84
80–84	145/82		157/83

(Altman et al., 1974; Kohn, 1977)

It was pointed out in several of the studies in Chapter 1 that exercise programs have the ability to bring the blood pressure levels of hypertensive men to "normal levels." It would be interesting to know if masters runners can maintain blood pressure readings that are similar to those of healthy, younger individuals. The answer would help to provide information on whether it is sedentary living and life style, or aging that is responsible for the increase in blood pressure that generally accompanies increasing age.

There are several studies indicating that trained older athletes have blood pressure levels below those normally expected not only for their age category but also for young adults. (The average blood pressure for young adults is 120/80.)

The study on Wally Hayward, the 70-year-old, world-ranked marathoner who had been running for 52 years, found a blood pressure reading of 108/72. The studies on Harold Chapman and Paul Spangler found blood pressure readings of 121/70 and 120/70. Wilmore and his associates in their study of four master runners 70+ years of age found blood pressure readings of: DF 140/80, NJ 170/100 and VS 112/74 (TR's was not given). DF's blood pressure was normal for his age and VS's low. NJ's was high but the researchers noted that he was "quite apprehensive about the entire testing procedure" and thus this reading probably did not reflect his true blood pressure.

In 1975 the Toronto Rehabilitation Centre had a unique study opportunity when the World's Masters' Championships were held in Toronto.
There were 1,308 men and 77 women from many countries participating in
the events. The Centre examined 128 men and 7 women, who were
"average" contestants. The blood pressure readings for the contestants by sex
and age category were for men: < 40 = 124/79, 40–49 = 120/77,
50–59 = 127/77, 60–69 = 128/77, and 70–90 = 140/83. For women the
average blood pressure reading was 111/77 (Kavanagh and Shephard, 1977).
As is apparent from Table I, the readings for master runners were below
"average" for their age group.

The study by Hartung and Farge (1977) found similar results. The
average blood pressure of the 48 men they studied was 128/82.

Few studies exist on masters women runners. This is unfortunate since
although women have a lower incidence of high blood pressure up to
menopause, after menopause women are likely to have a blood pressure
reading higher than men. A study on ten masters female distance runners
did not mention blood pressure levels (Vaccaro et al., 1981b). A study of two
female masters swimmers 70 and 71 found blood pressure readings of 165/88
and 120/80; normal for this age is 159/85 (Vaccaro et al., 1981a). Unfortunately, this study is not one from which any conclusions can be drawn.

In summary, apparently blood pressure levels do not increase as a result
of senescence. Several examples of individuals with "below average" blood
pressure have just been noted. Rather, blood pressure appears to increase as
a result of diet, body composition (e.g., increasing obesity), life style, and
the consequences these have on the body in the form of arteriosclerosis or
"hardening of the arteries." The studies for men appear clear. Although not
many studies exist for women, the conclusion is probably justified for both
sexes.

Another question deals with the ability of older individuals to lower
their blood pressure levels through exercise rather than through drugs that
often have undesirable side-effects. In the chapter on the heart it was apparent that the blood pressure levels of younger men and women were readily alterable through training. The question is, are the blood pressure levels
of those 40+ years of age equally as alterable through exercise?

The answer appears to be yes, although not all programs have had
positive results. DeVries (1970) found that a six week program of exercise for
66 men aged 51–87 lowered both systolic and diastolic blood pressure (from
140/76 to 136/73). The exercise program consisted of one hour of
calisthenics, jogging/walking, and stretching three times a week. A similar
program for 23 women who ranged in age from 52 to 79 reported that three
months of vigorous exercise did not produce significant changes in blood
pressure (from 131/76 to 135/76) (Adams and deVries, 1973). However, a 20
week walking program for 16 sedentary men produced positive results. The
men were gradually introduced into the program and ended up training for
40 minutes a day four days a week. There were positive changes in
blood pressure (systolic blood pressure from 121 to 118; diastolic from 78 to
76) (Pollock et al., 1971). Tzankoff and his associates (1972) found that while

15 sedentary men who participated in an average of 2.3 "vigorous" 55 minute exercise sessions per week for six months (mostly paddleball and handball) did not lower their systolic blood pressure (pre- 121, post- 124), their diastolic blood pressure was significantly lowered (pre- 89, post- 77).

A five year study on two groups of men — one averaged 43 years of age at the start of the study and ran an average of 30 miles a week, and the other averaged 55 years of age at the start of the study and ran or cycled 30+ miles a week, both throughout the study — found either little change or a significant decrease in blood pressure over the course of the study. The group that averaged 43 years of age had an average blood pressure reading of 121/76 at the start of the study and 118/79 at the end of the study. The group that averaged 55 years of age had a reading 144/79 at the start of the study and 126/82 at the end of the study (Pollock et al., 1978).

Although the reduction in blood pressure in the above studies was not as dramatic as that seen in studies on younger individuals, it must be realized that the number of studies conducted to date on older individuals is small. The studies may not have yielded as positive results because the exercise programs were less intensive and shorter in duration than programs for younger individuals. Blood pressure levels of the aged can be lowered through exercise. The question that has not been answered is whether the training effect is lower in older individuals because of a difference in the intensity and duration of the programs, or because of the inability of the older individual to respond physiologically as rapidly or to the same extent.

Bones

The purpose of bones is well known. They are designed primarily to give runners periodic problems. Secondary reasons for their existence is to give the body shape and form, to provide protection for the internal organs, and to serve as a place for muscles to attach themselves. In most individuals bones reach their maximum size by age 20. The bones continue, however, to become more dense until about age 35–40. After age 35 women lose 0.75–1.00% of their bone mass per year. For men the bone mass loss does not start until about age 50–55 and the loss is about 0.4% a year (Smith, 1982; Smith, 1981a; 1981b; Smith, Sempos, and Purvis, 1981; Shephard, 1978; Smith, Reddan and Smith, 1981).

The loss of bone mass is called "osteoporosis." Although an abnormal and pathological condition, because of its prevalence among the aged osteoporosis has become an accepted, tolerated, and expected consequence of aging (see Oyster et al., 1984).

The consequences of osteoporosis are that the bones become weak and brittle. Thus, they break easier and heal slower. One other consequence is that the discs in the spine collapse, as does the cartilage between the discs. This causes individuals to "shrink" as they age. The "shrinking" is exacerbated because of poor muscle tone which often causes older individuals to stoop forward as the spine becomes bowed inward.

Can running prevent or delay osteoporosis? One way of answering this question would be to first examine the causes of osteoporosis. The causes are varied, but include a lack of physical activity, estrogens or androgens, or calcium. Other factors that may cause osteoporosis are bone trauma, or disorders in the endocrine system, digestive system, or bone marrow. In this book we are interested in only two of the causes, lack of physical activity and bone damage. Both will be examined below.

Something that physicians have recognized for decades is that prolonged bed rest produces a bone loss. Several studies have experimentally confirmed this observation. In one study three young men were subjected to 36 weeks of bed rest. The study found that the men experienced a 39 percent bone mineral loss. Another study of eight subjects who were restricted in activity found a 1.1 percent bone mineral loss per week of inactivity (see Smith, 1982). Thus, it appears that inactivity in the aged, especially over decades, not weeks, could have a profound effect on bone density.

It is believed that the bones respond, like other body parts, to stress. That is, they atrophy (decrease in size and ability to function through injury or disuse) or hypertrophy (increase in size and strength) according to usage. If muscle contractions stress the bones, it appears that the bones are more likely to hypertrophy. If there is little or no usage then there is atrophy or osteoporosis.

Hypertrophy of bones in the dominant arms of pitchers and tennis players has been confirmed in several studies (see Smith, 1982). What we need to examine is whether exercise can stop or reverse osteoporosis.

The answer appears to be yes. In one study a group of women, whose average age was 84, were studied for three years. The programs started with 30 women; 18 were in a nonexercise group and 12 were in an exercise group. The two groups of women were comparable in age, weight, and degree of mobility. The women in the exercise group were required to participate in an exercise class three times a week for 30 minutes each session. The exercises required little energy expenditure and could all be done while sitting in a chair. The exercises consisted of leg lifts, toe touches, arm lifts, and many other exercises designed specifically for this program and this age group.

After three years the results of the study were startling. The nonexercise group had a 3.6 percent bone mineral loss. The exercise group had a bone mineral gain of 2.29 percent (Smith, 1982). This indicated that stressing the bones through physical exercise increased the retention of bone minerals (see Smith, 1981b).

An elaboration of this study found similar results. In this study 80 women 69–95 were placed into four groups: control, exercise, drug (Vitamin D and calcium supplements), and drug/exercise. After three years it was found that the bone mineral content of the control group had decreased 3.29 percent. The exercise group had an increase of 2.29 percent, and the drug group an increase of 1.58 percent. The drug/exercise group had a decrease of .32 percent. This last finding was obviously not what would have been anticipated and the researchers noted that this group of women was older than the other groups and was less physically and mentally competent than the other groups. Thus, the drug/exercise combination needs further study before it is discarded. It may be the best mechanism of either maintaining or increasing bone density (Smith, Reddan, and Smith, 1981).

Very few studies have examined the bone mineral content of older long-distance runners. One such study examined 41 long-distance runners who ranged in age from 50 to 72 and found that the runners had 40 percent more bone mineral content than a comparison group of nonrunners (Lane et al., 1986).

The other question to be examined is, whether running produces mild bone trauma which increases osteoporosis. Unfortunately the answer to this question is not available. There is preliminary evidence indicating that the answer is no. In 1981 the *South African Medical Journal* published an article on Wally Hayward, the 70-year-old former Olympic marathon runner who as of 1986 held the world's marathon record for his age group (3:06:24 on a hilly course). Hayward has been running regularly for 52 years. The study was to determine the effects of almost 52 years of continuous, high-intensity training and competition. An examination of his muscular-skeletal history and system found no abnormalities. The study found an "excellent" skeletal system.

Cartilage

Cartilage is unique in that it does not have any nerves or blood vessels. Rather, it obtains its nutrients from the tissue surrounding it or by the synovial fluid in the joint. Cartilage acts as a buffer between where the bones come together in a joint; it also keeps the bones from rubbing against each other, which would be painful since bones, unlike cartilage, have an ample supply of nerves. Since cartilage is nurtured by the surrounding tissue, its health is determined, to a large extent, by the health of the surrounding tissue.

Increasing age has been found to bring about many changes in cartilage, some of which occur by age 20–30. Some of the changes are a cracking, fraying, or shredding of the surface of the cartilage. Also, increasing age brings about a progressive cell death and thus the depth of the cartilage is reduced. It is difficult to distinguish changes in cartilage produced by senescence from changes produced by trauma. In fact, many researchers do not believe that the changes brought about by aging are different from the changes brought about by osteoarthritis.

Although studies are limited, it does appear that both the strength and stiffness of cartilage decreases with increasing age (Adrian, 1981).

Studies on the impact of prolonged exercise on cartilage are mixed. It is believed that injuries to joints can exacerbate the "aging" of joints. For example, it has been found that males and blacks have a higher incidence of osteoarthritis than females and whites. It is believed that this is primarily because males and blacks are more involved in activities that are physically demanding, such as work or sports, and that in these activities the cartilage has a greater opportunity to be traumatized.

As was noted above, since cartilage does not have any blood vessels it relies on other sources such as the surrounding tissue for its nutrients. Thus, if aging affects the surrounding tissue the cartilage would most likely also be affected.

As most are aware, joints have a synovial fluid to help the cartilage on the ends of the bones in a joint to glide over each other. This fluid is produced by the synovial membrane, which lines the joint cavity. With increasing age there is a change in the chemical composition of the synovial fluid; this change in fluid is believed to decrease the strength of the cartilage (see Adrian, 1981; Balazs, 1977).

The impact of prolonged exercise on cartilage is unknown. In younger athletes exercise is believed to strengthen and increase the size of cartilage. This assumes, of course, that the joints and the cartilage are not injured. Whether an individual who has been exercising over a prolonged period can maintain the strength of the cartilage, or whether an older sedentary individual can have the same training effect on cartilage as a younger individual is unknown.

Cholesterol

Cholesterol was discussed in Chapter 1. Here it was mentioned that there is a positive correlation between cholesterol level and age. That is, with increasing age cholesterol levels generally increase. The table below shows the percentage of individuals by age and gender who have high cholesterol levels.

Table II

Percentage of Persons with High Serum Cholesterol by Age and Sex

Age	Females	Males
18–24	5.6	4.0
25–34	9.1	12.1
35–44	13.7	25.3
45–54	31.8	30.1
55–64	45.9	29.7
65–74	49.2	29.2

(U.S. Bureau of the Census, 1981)

As is clear from Table II, the percentage of the population with high cholesterol increases with increasing age. It is also apparent that from age 25 to 44 more men than women have high cholesterol. After age 44 women lose this edge, generally because of the consequences of menopause.

The coronary risk factor of high cholesterol has already been discussed. Suffice it to say here that the higher the cholesterol level the greater the risk of a coronary event (a heart attack or stroke, for example). Is the increase in cholesterol an inevitable consequence of aging or merely a reflection of factors such as diet and lack of exercise?

In comparison to the general population, several studies on runners have found that older runners have lower cholesterol levels than the general population. The average levels for the general population are shown below in Table III.

Table III

Cholesterol Levels

Age	Men	Women
0–12	194	197
13–19	197	198
20–29	227	224
30–39	242	230
40–49	246	215
50–59	254	272
60–69	259	265
70–79	258	275

(Sanadi, 1977)

Pollock (1974; Pollock et al., 1974) found that male runners 40–49 who ran an average of 40 miles a week had a total cholesterol level of 215.5. For those 50–59 who ran 42 miles a week the reading was 222. For the age group 60–69 who ran 29.7 miles a week the average reading was 209.8. And lastly, for those 70–75 who ran 20 miles a week the average reading was 230.7. Hartung and Farge (1977) found an average cholesterol level of 195. At age 70 Wally Hayward's total cholesterol reading was 247.

A study done by Wilmore and his associates (1974) on three endurance athletes 72–74 years of age found total cholesterol levels of 340 (8–10 miles per week), 215 (30 miles per week), and 137 (20 miles per week). Harold Chapman's level was 186, and Paul Spangler had a reading of 201.

A study on 13 male sprint and 13 male distance masters runners 40–78 years of age found low cholesterol levels. For example, the sprinters had a reading of 218.7 and the distance runners a reading of 203.0. It should be noted that the distance runners had weekly mileages of from 40 to 120 miles per week. The oldest athlete in this study was 78, ran from 150–200 kilometers per week, and had a cholesterol level of 178 (Barnard et al., 1979).

Unfortunately, as reported previously, studies on masters women runners are limited and data on cholesterol levels are lacking. Also, studies have not examined cholesterol for type: HDL, LDL, VLDL. However, the data that have been gathered indicate that runners generally have significantly lower total cholesterol levels than nonrunners of the same age. The data also indicate that masters nonrunners can lower their total cholesterol levels through running, especially if the exercise is combined with dietary modifications (see Shephard, 1978).

Fat

Fat has already been briefly discussed in other chapters. It has been mentioned that we need fat to survive, although a small amount is needed in comparison to what most people possess. Fat is especially important to long-distance runners since the longer an individual runs the more fat is utilized as a source of energy. An excess of fat increases the risk of a coronary event. In fact, for both men and women the greater the percentage of body fat the greater the likelihood of a heart attack or stroke.

What happens to the amount of body fat with increasing age? Generally it increases. Although studies have varied depending on the sample used, young men have been found to have body fat percentages ranging from 10 to 17. Elderly men have had ranges from 18 to 27. In contrast, young women have been found to have percentages ranging from 22 to 34 while for elderly women the figures are 29 to 38 (see Shephard, 1978; McArdle et al., 1981).

Does the amount of fat increase as an inevitable consequence of aging or because of factors such as inactivity and over-eating? Studies on aged athletes indicate that low body fat can be maintained even in advanced old age. Paul E. Spangler's body fat was 13.5 percent, and Harold Chapman's was 5.8 percent. The study on Wally Hayward reported that his body fat was 13.6 percent. In a study of 25 champion masters runners, Pollock and his associates (1974) found that body fat percentages were 11.2 percent for men 40–49 years of age, 10.9 for men 50–59, 11.3 for men 60–69, and 13.6 percent for men 70–75 years of age. A study of 26 male masters sprint and endurance athletes aged 40–78 found a relative fat content of 16.5 percent in the sprinters and 18 in the distance runners (Barnard et al., 1979).

Few studies have been done on older female runners. One study examined ten female long-distance runners whose mean age was 43.8 years of age. The study found that their body fat percentage was 18.3 percent, compared to 31.3 percent for sedentary women in the same age category (Vaccaro et al., 1981b). The oldest woman in the study was 49 and she had the lowest body fat content: 12.9 percent. A study of two female masters swimmers 70 and 71 found body fat reading of 20.3 and 26.8 percent. The average percentage for sedentary females in the same age category is 44.6 percent (Vaccaro et al., 1981a). A recent study on 38 female marathon runners whose mean age was 38 years, found an average body fat of 15.5

percent. These women were compared to a control group of the same age, whose average body fat was 27.8 percent (Upton et al., 1983).

Thus, the studies clearly demonstrate that the increase in body fat is mostly a product of a sedentary life style, not an inevitable consequence of aging. However, all the studies examined so far have been cross-sectional (they have only examined the subjects at one point in time). Thus, although Dr. Spangler has a body fat content of 13.5 percent at age 77, we do not know if or how much this value has changed. One study did examine 24 masters athletes over a ten year period to answer this question of inevitability. At the start of the study all the runners were training and competing at a high-intensity level. By the end of the study 11 were still training at the high-intensity level (high) while 13 had reduced training for a variety of reasons (low). At the start of the study the body fat contents for the high and low training groups were 11.6 and 14.3 percent. At the end of the study the body fat contents had increased to 13.6 and 16.3 percent. Both of the groups had experienced a significant increase in body fat. The researcher pointed out that while running had maintained cardiovascular efficiency, other aging changes, especially the loss of muscle mass in the upper part of the body, brought about a net increase in body fat. The researcher recommended a more "well-rounded" exercise program that would include exercises for the upper torso (see Legwold, 1982).

Heart

The proponents of running claim it has many benefits. The claim most frequently made has dealt with the positive benefit of exercise on the heart. In fact, one major reason many individuals run is to prevent heart disease, which is falsely believed by many to be an inevitable consequence of aging. What changes in the heart can the average individual expect to occur with aging? What impact will exercise have on the heart of the aging individual?

Resting Heart Rate

The resting heart rate varies by both age and sex. At birth the average heart rate of both males and females is approximately 130 beats per minute. The heart rate slows down throughout childhood and adolescence and by early adulthood the average resting heart rate is 75 for men and 78 for women. This changes little with increasing age (Bortz, 1982; Shephard, 1978). Table IV shows the resting heart rate for sex and age categories from birth to age 80 and over.

Generally, athletes have lower resting heart rates than nonathletes, often below 60 beats per minute. Lower heart rates are generally a sign of a healthy heart. The lower heart rate in athletes is simply an indication of an efficient heart, one that does not have to work as hard to perform the same function as the hearts of others. Can masters runners maintain low resting heart rates?

Table IV

Resting Heart Rate by Age and Sex

Age	Males	Females
1	116	122
10–19	85	90
20–29	76	78
30–39	75	78
40–49	76	78
50–59	75	77
60–69	74	76
70–79	75	75
80+	77	77

(Altman et al., 1974)

The answer appears to be yes. Wally Hayward's resting heart rate at age 70 was 52. Harold Chapman's at age 71 was 39 lying down and 57 standing up. Paul Spangler's at age 77 was 55. In a study of four masters runners 70 years of age and over the resting heart rates of three of the runners were reported. The heart rates were 48, 59, and 60 (Wilmore et al., 1974). In a study of 25 champion track athletes Pollock and his associates (1974) reported the following average heart rates: ages 40–49 = 48.1, 50–59 = 51.7, 60–69 = 46.8, and 70–75 = 57.8.

One five year study on two groups of men, one who averaged 43 years of age and the other who averaged 55 years of age at the start of the study, found that an exercise program may lower the resting heart rate of masters athletes. At the end of the study the younger group's resting heart rate dropped from 47 to 43 and the older group had dropped from 51 to 44 (Pollock et al., 1974). The average resting heart rate for the marathoners in Hartung and Farge's (1977) study was 59 beats per minute; for the non-marathoners it was 60 beats per minute.

Again, studies on women are limited. In a study on two masters women swimmers 70 years of age and over, the resting heart rates were 75 and 80 (Vaccaro et al., 1981a). A study by Upton and his associates (1983) on 38 women 31–50 years of age (mean age 38) who had run at least one marathon and who trained an average of 46 miles a week found an average resting heart rate of 55. A similar group of nonrunning women had an average resting heart rate of 78.

Maximum Heart Rate

This term deals with how many times the heart is capable of beating per minute. Generally, the more beats per minute a heart is capable of, the greater the athletic potential of the individual, although as we will see shortly another variable, stroke volume, is also important. Nonetheless, for equally trained individuals the one with the greatest maximum heart rate would probably have a physiological edge in competition.

Maximum heart rate declines with increasing age. The formula widely used to ascertain maximum heart rate is 220 minus the individual's age. Thus, a 20-year-old has a maximum heart rate of 200. A 60-year-old would have a maximum heart rate of 160. Why this decline occurs is not clearly understood. A widely believed explanation is that the amount of oxygen to the myocardium, or heart muscle, declines and thus the heart is not capable of working as hard or as fast. This explanation seemed logical since at high altitudes the maximum heart rate declines. However, since the administration of oxygen to aged individuals does not increase maximum heart rate, this explanation has not been widely accepted. A second explanation has dealt with the loss of elasticity of the heart wall. This means there is an increase of time required for the heart cycle to be completed (see Shephard 1978; 1981). Will exercise delay, or prevent the decline from taking place?

The answer to the "decline" part of this above question, appears to be yes. Wally Hayward at age 70 had a maximum heart rate of 165, or about 15 beats above what would be expected. When examined at age 77 Dr. Paul Spangler had a maximum heart rate of 160, or about 17 beats above what would be expected. The study on Harold Chapman at age 71 found a maximum heart rate of 154, or 11 beats above what would be expected. A study by Pollock (1974) on 25 runners between the ages of 40–49 confirmed the above results. He found that the maximum heart rates for the age groups 40–49, 50–59, 60–69, and 70–75 were: 177.8, 175, 163, and 166.3. In a study on four male masters athletes 70 and over Wilmore and his associates (1974) found maximum heart rates of 155 for a 71-year-old runner or about six beats above normal, 169 for a 72-year-old runner or 21 beats above normal, 166 for a 74-year-old runner or 20 beats above normal, and 174 for a 72-year-old runner or 30 beats above normal.

Studies on women are again lacking. The study on two swimmers 70 and over found maximum heart rates of 160 and 165, or about 10–15 beats above normal (Vaccaro et al., 1981a). A study of 10 women masters runners all 40 and over (average age 43.8) found a maximum heart rate of 190 in a 47-year-old woman who trained 50 miles a week, or 17 beats above normal, to 165 in a 42-year-old woman who trained 66 miles a week or about 13 beats below what would be expected (Vaccaro et al., 1981b).

In answer to the question, will training *prevent* the maximum heart rate from declining, the answer appears to be no. In a ten year study of 24 masters track champions, significant declines in maximum heart rate were found for both those runners who reduced the level and intensity of their training during the study (low-intensity) and for those runners who continued with the same level of training throughout the study (high-intensity). The high-intensity runners had a maximum heart rate of 177 at the start of the study. This dropped to 170 over the ten year study. The low-intensity runners started with a maximum heart rate of 170. This dropped to 163 by the end of the study (see Legwold, 1982).

A five year study by Pollock and his associates (1978) supports the conclusion that running can delay the decline in maximum heart rate, at least up to a certain age, but not stop it entirely. At the start of the study one group averaged 43 years of age and the other averaged 55 years of age. The maximum heart rate for the younger group was 173 beats per minute and for the older group, 169 beats per minute. After five years of training, at approximately the same level of intensity, the younger group had dropped to a maximum rate of 171, a 1 percent decline, but the older group had dropped to 160, a 5 percent decline. Thus, it seems apparent that runners can slow the decline in the maximum heart rate decline but not stop the decline.

Stroke Volume

The importance of maximum heart rate in exercise has already been mentioned. However, as is probably apparent to most runners, it is not just heart rate that is the important variable in athletic performance. A more important one is stroke volume. The stroke volume is the amount of blood pumped by the left ventricle with one beat of the heart. Research has found that the stroke volume of trained athletes is much greater than that of untrained individuals of the same age. For example, during strenuous exercise untrained young men may be able to pump 103 milliliters of blood per beat. In contrast, trained athletes have had outputs of up to 210 milliliters per beat (see Shaver, 1981). Thus, it can be seen that the heart of a trained athlete does not have to beat as fast to be as productive, if not more productive, as the heart of an untrained individual.

The consequences of aging on the stroke volume are minimal for light levels of work until old age. That is, older individuals are capable of maintaining the same stroke volume as younger individuals at light work loads. However, the stroke volume for demanding physical work is 10–20 percent less in the aged than in younger adults. The reason for this is not understood but it probably deals with the contractibility of the myocardium, or heart muscle (see Shephard, 1981; 1978; McArdle et al., 1981).

Will exercise prevent or delay the decrease in stroke volume in the aged? Studies to date are limited because few researchers have measured stroke volume in older subject's volume. Harold Chapman's was measured and it was 141 at age 71, a high measure, even for a much younger athlete.

Joints

Joints are obviously an area of injury for many young runners. Thus, if there are aging changes in joints that running may exaggerate, there is every reason for runners to be concerned.

A frequent condition of the aged is osteoarthritis (bone inflammation). According to Tonna (1977) it is not clear if osteoarthritis is an inevitable or merely a frequent consequence of aging. In fact, the histologic description of osteoarthritis conforms to that of the type of degenerative joint disease associated with normal aging (see Oyster et al., 1984). Osteoarthritis is a disease normally found first in joints that have the greatest use, such as the hip (see Rossman, 1977). Osteoarthritis is generally a relatively mild disease that occurs frequently in those 55 and over. Obviously obesity has the opportunity to magnify the severity and the progression of the disease. Exercise will often be painful in the afflicted joint, although exercise is not necessarily harmful and may loosen the joint (see Miller, 1976). Although more studies are needed, there is evidence that individuals who were runners in their youth have a lower incidence of osteoarthritis than nonrunners (see Lane et al., 1986).

Several studies have noted that with increasing age there is an increase in joint stiffness which results in the loss of mobility. This stiffness is usually a result of changes in the soft tissues such as muscles, tendons, and the joint capsule. Studies have found that exercise can easily reverse joint stiffness in both older men and women (see Chapman et al., 1972).

Joints do not necessarily deteriorate with years of running. At age 70 Wally Hayward was not found to have "degenerative changes in hip, knee, ankle, and foot joints." The authors concluded that "stable, well-aligned joints do not degenerate with years of competitive running" (Maud et al., 1981).

Additional studies have supported this finding. A study conducted in Finland examined the radiographic reports of 74 former runners. Each of the runners had won Finnish running championships and most had set Finnish or world records. The average age at examination was 55 and the average number of years of competitive running was 21. The runners were compared with 115 "normal" men. Osteoarthritis was found in 4 percent of the runners but in 8.7 percent of the nonrunners. The authors noted that the hip is designed for physical strain, such as running, and that individuals should not be worried about using it, even under heavy loads. The authors speculated that by running and placing pressure on the hip, the synovial fluid was forced into the cartilage thus providing nutrition and helping to maintain the joint (Puranen et al., 1974).

In 1981 the editor-in-chief of *The Physician and Sportsmedicine* wrote an editorial that summarized the results of research on sports and osteoarthritis. He said that there is a great deal of concern among runners about whether the repeated "microtrauma" or stress caused by years of exercise raises the likelihood of arthritis. After reviewing the literature he said that "dedicated runners and other athletes are not at a greater risk of developing osteoarthritis." He did point out, however, that joints that are injured, whether through exercise or an accident, are at a greater risk of becoming arthritic, and that the probability of arthritis increased with the severity of the joint trauma (Ryan, 1981).

Two additional studies have supported this conclusion. The first study, which examined 41 long-distance runners aged 50–72, concluded that running does not "predispose" runners to the "development of osteoarthritis" (Lane et al., 1986). The second was on 17 male runners aged 50–74 and concluded that "long-duration, high-mileage running need not be associated with premature degenerative joint disease in the low extremities" (Panush et al., 1986).

Ligaments

Ligaments are frequently injured in runners. As most are aware, ligaments are bands of fibrous tissue (tissue resembling fibers) that attach near the ends of bones where the bones meet to form joints. Ligaments hold the bones together and maintain joint stability. Certain ligaments allow the joints little mobility, such as the spine, while others are not as restrictive.

Ligaments have little elasticity; thus, a force that moves a joint farther than normal generally results in the ligaments becoming torn, stretched, or detached from the bone. A sprain, for example, is simply a stretched or torn ligament. If ligaments become detached from the bone it is called a rupture. Two areas where runners often damage ligaments are in their ankles and knees.

The strength and failure of aging ligaments have been studied, although not extensively. Most studies have found that with increasing age tendon strength decreases and failure rates increase (see Adrian, 1981), although some studies have shown the reverse. Although evidence is not conclusive, it appears that exercise throughout the life span increases ligament strength. Thus, an aged exercising individual has greater ligament strength than a nonexercising individual of the same age, although probably also a greater probability or likelihood of incurring a ligament injury.

Lungs

The lungs are an essential, though often neglected factor. The amount of oxygen the lungs are capable of inhaling and utilizing have a significant influence on performance. The studies on the aging lung indicate a decline in the ability of the lung to function with increasing age.

A frequently cited lung function is vital capacity. Vital capacity is simply the amount of air that can be expelled from the lungs after maximum inhalation. Men in their twenties have an average vital capacity of 5.20 liters. For women the measure is 4.17 liters. At age 60 the figures are 4.00 and 3.29, declines of 23 percent and 21 percent. As can be seen, there is a dramatic decline in vital capacity with increasing age.

Additionally, the amount of air left in the lungs, residual capacity, increases with increasing age. For men and women in their twenties, after exhalation 25 percent of the air remains in the lungs of men and 28 percent in women. For men and women in their sixties the figure is 40 percent for each.

It has also been found that the lungs decline in the ability to absorb oxygen with increasing age (Shaver, 1981; Reddan, 1981).

Another measure of the functional capacity of the lungs is the amount of air that can be inhaled or exhaled during a given period of time. The measure most commonly used is maximal exhalation. This is the amount of air exhaled during a given period of time, usually one minute. This is often called $V_E$max. Measures of $V_E$max can reach as high as 180 liters per minute in highly trained athletes. A five year study on two groups of men, the first averaging 43 years of age and the second, 55, at the start of the study, found that after maintaining approximately the same level of training for five years the younger group declined from 160 to 155 liters a minute (-3%) while the older group increased significantly from 148 to 160 ($+8\%$) (Pollock et al., 1978). This increase probably indicates the results of a more intensive training in the older group since most studies have found a slight decrease in $V_E$max with increasing age. For example, Pollock (1974) found the following figures for his study on American track champions, which indicated a gradual decline with increasing age: $40–49 = 150.9$, $50–59 = 139.9$, $60–69 = 140$, and $70–75 = 97.8$.

The question that naturally comes to mind is, are the declines a cause of senescence or of a sedentary life-style? The answer appears to be both. Although exercise may slow the aging process of the pulmonary system it will not stop the process.

Wally Hayward's vital capacity at age 70 was 4.73 liters and his residual capacity was 33.6 percent. Paul Spangler's vital capacity was 5.13 liters at age 77. Harold Chapman's vital capacity was 4.29. A study of masters athletes all in their seventies found vital capacities of 4.2, 3.7, 5.38, and 4.40. The residual capacity figures that were measured were 33.8 and 31.1 (Wilmore et al., 1974). A study of 25 masters athletes found the following vital capacity figures: $40–49 = 5.6$, $50–59 = 4.9$, $60–69 = 5.2$, and $70–75 = 4.4$ (Pollock, 1974).

Muscle

As most individuals are aware, the body has three types of muscle tissue. The first two types are also called "involuntary" since they are not consciously controlled. The first of these is smooth muscle, which forms the inner lining of the blood vessels, the digestive tract, as well as other organs. The second is cardiac muscle, which composes most of the heart. The third is skeletal muscle, of which there are more than 430 in the body. The skeletal muscle derives its name from the fact that it is attached to bone, thus providing stability to the skeletal system, and allowing movement.

As almost all runners are now aware, not all skeletal muscle is the same. Rather, it is composed of two distinct types of fibers that have been differentiated by both contractile and metabolic characteristics. These fibers are called fast- and slow-twitch.

The fast-twitch fibers are able to mobilize energy quickly for a contraction that is forceful. Thus, fast-twitch fibers are better suited for short, anaerobic type activities such as sprinting. The slow-twitch fibers take longer to activate, although they have a characteristic that allows them to maintain prolonged aerobic activity. Thus, the slow-twitch fibers are more suited for events such as distance running.

Although there can be large variations among individuals and even variations within different muscle groups in the same individual, about 45–55 percent of the muscle in sedentary individuals is composed of slow-twitch fibers. What is interesting is what happens to the skeletal muscles with increasing age.

The majority of the scientific literature claims that with increasing age the skeletal muscles decline in strength, size, elasticity, speed of response, ability to perform complex tasks, and endurance.

It is believed that the decline takes place largely from nonuse although it is also believed that some of the change is an inevitable consequence of aging.

What happens to the fast- and slow-twitch fibers with increasing age? Evidence indicates that the differences between the fibers diminish with increasing age, thus blurring the distinction between the two.

Data on whether athletes can change the composition of their muscle fibers are unresolved, but it appears to be that they cannot.

The last question that comes to mind deals with the impact of physical training on muscle: will it slow down or reverse the aging process on the skeletal muscle? First, it needs to be reiterated that much of the muscle loss takes place in old age is due to disuse. The percentage that is due to aging is unknown. It appears that strength losses are slow to occur, and in some studies do not occur until after the age of 60. For example, one study of 100 men who ranged in age from 22 to 62 who all did similar work in a machine shop found no differences in grip strength (see Shephard, 1978).

To best analyze if aging is inevitable we need to examine why the losses occur. Some studies have indicated that the number of muscle fibers decreases by as much as 25 percent in the aged, although the number of nerve fibers going to the muscles remain unchanged. One study by Moritani and deVries (1980) found that eight weeks of progressive strength training for young and old men produced similar gains in strength. However, the reasons for the gains were different. While the young men had significant muscle hypertrophy occur, which accounted for the change in strength, the muscle hypertrophy among the aged was insignificant. The increase in strength for the aged was achieved by a greater neural activation of the muscles. Thus, it appears that the aged, rather than relying on bulk, learned to use their existing muscles more efficiently.

Tendons

The structure of tendons is similar to that of ligaments; both are fibrous tissues that have little elasticity. Where both ends of ligaments are attached to bones, tendons are attached to muscles at one end and bone at the other. Thus, tendons serve to attach muscle to bone.

Generally, with increasing age it is believed that the strength of tendons decreases, although longitudinal studies are incomplete (Adrian, 1981). It is known that exercise strengthens tendons. Although more studies are needed before definitive conclusions can be drawn, it is believed that exercise will delay the weakening of tendons that occurs with increasing age. It is not known if the aged who exercise have stronger tendons because they are delaying senescence or if they are merely preventing the tendons from atrophying.

VO_2max

We have discussed VO_2max previously. Essentially it is the ability of the body to use oxygen. Obviously oxygen is important for aerobic exercise. The higher the VO_2max the better able is the individual to use oxygen and thus the greater the potential for athletic performance.

VO_2max declines dramatically with increasing age. Generally, the VO_2max reaches its peak between the ages of 18 and 25 (McArdle et al., 1982). After age 25 it declines at a rate of about 1 to 2 percent a year until by age 75 it is less than half its peak value (see Bortz, 1982; Kasch and Kulberg, 1981; Barnard et al., 1979; Astrand et al., 1973; Robinson et al., 1975). Is the decrease an inevitable consequence of aging or simply a result of deconditioning? What impact does exercise have on VO_2max in old age?

To answer the first question we need to examine individuals who have been involved in research programs for a significant period of time and who have had their VO_2max measured both when they were younger and when they had aged. There are several such studies.

One recent ten-year-long study on 24 masters track champions who were 50–82 years of age at the beginning of the study has helped to answer many of the above questions. When the study started, all the men were doing high-intensity training for competition. At the end of the study only about half of the men were still training at the same level of intensity. The researcher, Dr. Michael L. Pollock of the University of Wisconsin Medical School–Mount Sinai Medical Center, found that the VO_2max of the men in the 50–59 year age group decreased by 4.3 percent over the ten year period. The decreases for the 60–69 and 70 and over groups were 9 and 10.5 percent. Dr. Pollock noted that aging in this area could be delayed up until about age 55 to 60. After that, however, even training at the same level of intensity will not prevent significant declines in variables such as VO_2max.

Dr. Pollock's study did indicate that the higher the intensity of training the less the losses. For example, for the men who still maintained a high-intensity competition-oriented training their average VO_2max in 1971 was 54.2 and in 1981 it was 53.3, a loss of 2 percent. The men who still ran but did not have their previous high-intensity training had an average VO_2max in 1971 of 52.5. In 1981 it was 45.9, a loss of 13 percent (see Legwold, 1982).

In another study Pollock and his associates (1978) followed two groups of men for five years. At the start of the study the first group averaged 43 and the second, 55 years of age. The training of the men remained constant over the five year research period. The men who averaged 43 years of age at the start of the study declined in VO_{2max} from 59.6 to 57.2 (a drop of 4 percent). The men who averaged 55 declined from 52.9 to 50.0 (down 5.5 percent).

An earlier study by Pollock and his associates (1974) also found that a decline took place with increasing age. While this study, on 25 champion masters runners 40–75 years of age, found high VO_{2max} levels in comparison to sedentary groups of the same age, it also found a significant decline occurring with increasing age: 40–49 = 57.5, 50–59 = 54.4, 60–69 = 51.4, 70–75 = 40.0.

A study by Fred Kasch and Jeanne Kulberg (1981) of the Department of Physical Education at San Diego State University found similar results. They studied 15 men over a 15 year period. The researchers reported that although the frequency of exercise remained about the same over the 15 year study, 3.3 times per week, the duration and intensity decreased slightly, especially during the last five years. For example, during the last five years, average mileage decreased from 15 miles per week to 12 miles per week. The VO_{2max} levels at the start of the study when the average age of the men was 44.6, at 10 years when their average age was 55.2, and at 15 years when their average age was 60, were 44.6, 45.2, and 40.2.

The above study found that VO_{2max} increased slightly during the first ten years of the study but decreased 11 percent between the tenth to fifteenth years of the study. The most significant declines were found between the ages of 55 and 60. Although this decrease may seem significant the remaining VO_{2max} for these men is still 36 percent higher than that in sedentary men 60 and over (see Kasch and Kulberg, 1981). The authors did a separate analysis by eliminating four of the men who had significantly reduced their activity levels to see if this had an impact on VO_{2max} declines. It might be noted that one man had suffered a stroke, two had nonexercise-related injuries, and one was incapacitated by a myocardial infarction. By eliminating these four men, the study found that the VO_{2max} levels only declined 4 to 5 percent during the 15 year study. This decline was similar to what Pollock found, the major difference being that these men only trained at one-half to one-third the level in the Pollock study.

The authors concluded that older men can safely train at high aerobic levels and that it will retard the "usual" VO_{2max} declines by one-half or more.

The impact of literally a lifetime of high intensity running can be seen in the study of Wally Hayward at age 70. His VO_{2max} was 56.8. Harold Chapman's at age 71 was 57.3 after only four years of training, which is 36 percent higher than levels observed in nonathletic men 30 years of age, and 74 percent higher than what would be expected at his age. Paul Spangler's was 44.3 at age 77, a remarkable figure for someone his age. The four runners examined by Wilmore and his associates (1974) who were over 70 were found to have VO_{2max} levels of 37.6, 41.2, 43.1, and 47.2.

Two male ultramarathoners, one of whom was 45 and the other 49 years of age, were recently examined. The 49-year-old had a VO_2max of 65.1 and the 45-year-old, 63.7. Although VO_2max levels decline with increasing age, it was found that both of these men could use a greater percentage of their VO_2max than most younger runners. For example, the two used 85 percent of their VO_2max as compared to 75 percent in most younger long-distance runners. Thus, it is not just VO_2max that is the important variable, but the ability to use VO_2max. It may be that masters runners can compete with younger runners by their greater utilization of VO_2max (Costill and Winrow, 1970).

Another important question deals with the effect of training on VO_2max in older runners. One study found that VO_2max in most runners can be raised with training. A two year study of men whose average age was 47 years of age, and who engaged in 60 minutes of exercise three times a week, found that VO_2max increased from 32.6 to 39.9. A similar group that did not participate in exercise experienced a decrease from 33.8 to 32.7 (Kasch et al., 1973).

Studies at Indiana University have supported the above research. In a program that exercised sedentary men 44–66 years of age two times a week for six months found that their VO_2max levels increased by an average of 21.6 percent (Tzankoff et al., 1972).

Although VO_2max levels for masters women runners have not been studied as frequently as those of men, some studies do exist. In a study of ten elite women runners whose average age was 43.8 years, the mean VO_2max was 43.41. In sedentary women of the same age group, levels of 27.3 to 32.5 have been found. The highest value in this group was found in a 47-year-old woman who ran 65 miles a week. Her VO_2max level was 57 (Vaccaro et al., 1981b).

The study of two masters women swimmers 70 and over found VO_2max levels of 36.4 and 38.7. These values are double those normally found in women this age (Vaccaro et al., 1981a).

A study on 38 women marathoners whose average age was 38 and who ran an average of 46 miles a week found VO_2max average of 55.8. A similar group of sedentary counterparts had an average reading of 31.4 (Upton et al., 1983).

Several authors have noted that exercise can stop or greatly reduce the decline in VO_2max. They have also noted, however, that by age 60 to 70 the rate of decline becomes dramatic, even with continued exercise. In other words, exercise can stop or delay the decline of VO_2max up to a certain point. After a certain age, however, an inevitable decline starts to take place, although still at a slower rate than for those who do not exercise.

The Dangers of Running for Masters Runners

There are many myths about the older segment of the population. One myth, that was widespread for decades, dealt with the dangers of physical exercise. It was widely believed, by the directors of senior citizen centers as well as others, that if the aged engaged in any strenuous physical activity, within minutes they would be dead, dying, or injured. The myth stated that their hearts were too frail and their muscles too brittle to withstand any physical stress out of the ordinary.

For decades this belief kept most senior centers calm, serene repositories of card games, billiards, and crafts. Older Americans with a variety of diseases were told that "nothing" could be done to alleviate their conditions and that they should learn to live with the limitations imposed by their conditions. Others were told to go home and prepare to die.

Out of desperation many older Americans sought out nontraditional treatments, hoping for a cure. Many who were given no hope by the traditional medical establishment became vulnerable to the numerous con artists who preyed on the sense of desperation of those with chronic disorders.

Other older Americans decided to break with the sedentary life style that had been imposed on them, and which was often responsible for the pathological physical conditions from which they suffered. They decided that if exercise was beneficial for the young, it might also be beneficial for them. Many other individuals were "fed up" with the medical rhetoric that had controlled their life style for decades. Although most physicians were against exercise for the aged, many older Americans began to see that asking a pot-bellied, chain-smoking physician if they should exercise was a little absurd. They also realized that they lived in an ageist society in which their complaints were too often dismissed as whining or as nothing more than an attempt to obtain attention.

For example, when they complained that they had a pain in their left shoulder and were told that it was an inevitable consequence of aging and to learn to "live with it," many thought to themselves, "the other shoulder is just as old but it doesn't hurt at all." Or, when an aged patient mentioned a sexual problem they were told, "what can you expect at your age?" The more assertive older individuals replied, "a normal sex life!" The major point, that has already been made, is that we live in a society that discriminates against the aged. Physicians are not exempt from this. They are also not aware of the research that has been done on exercise and the aged. When asked about the aged and exercise they often responded from societal stereotypes rather than a base of scientific knowledge.

Older individuals who wanted to start a running program had to overcome another hurdle, namely societal disgust. Although tolerant of scantily dressed 20-year-old men and women runners, society has generally wanted to keep its older population somewhat under wraps. Only fairly recently has it become normal — and only in some places — to see a runner with wrinkled skin and liver spots running around the streets. Thus many of these early "older" runners, especially women, had to face a degree of scorn. Often their behavior was seen, by their offspring and spouses, not as exemplary, but rather as a source of embarrassment. The older segment of society was thus kept in its place by being told that exercise would cause a high incidence of deaths and injuries.

Running Injuries

There is little doubt that many aged runners are injured. Some exercise programs have reported that 50 percent of their aged participants become injured during a year. Because many of the older participants are overweight, have not exercised in decades, and often attempt to make up for decades of inactivity in a short span of time, a high injury rate is expected.

One study of runners at the World Masters' Championships in Toronto found that 57.2 percent of them had been injured within the last year. Middle distance runners had the highest rate of injury (68 percent), followed by sprinters (58 percent), and long-distance runners (54 percent). The injuries were often severe. For example, of those injured, 39.6 percent were forced to stop training for one week, 26.7 for one to four weeks, and 33.7 percent for four or more weeks (Kavanagh and Shephard, 1977).

In 1981 this author collected data on 103 men and 10 women 55 and over who were runners. Part of the study dealt with running-related injuries. The percent of men injured during the previous year was 50 percent. Only 20 percent of the women reported an injury. The figure for men is comparable with studies on younger runners. Although there was a tendency for the rate of injury to increase with increasing age, the trend was not statistically significant.

Distance as a cause of injury was also examined in the above study. After all, the aged are supposed to be frail and any distance running should produce a high injury rate. The study found that for those who ran 1 to 19 miles a week, 42 percent were injured at least once during the year. This increased to 54 percent for those who ran 20–29 miles a week but then dropped to 40 percent for those who ran 30–39 miles a week. For those who ran 40–49 miles and over 50 miles the injury rate increased to 70 percent.

The areas injured the most frequently were similar to those found in younger runners: the knee was first, followed by the achilles tendon, and then the heel.

Although many older runners were injured, the seriousness of their injuries was not great. In fact, usually the runners did not have to stop running for more than three days.

Another question that has been asked deals with racing and rate of injury. Racing would appear to be a natural source of injuries since racers often train and push at more intensive levels than nonracers. The study found that the rate of injury was almost exactly the same in racers and nonracers, indicating that racing can be a "safe" activity for most older individuals in terms of acute injuries.

Since many individuals started running to lose weight, the relationship between injury and weight was also examined. That is, it seems logical that the overweight runner would be at an increased risk of injury since the lower part of their bodies would be subject to more stress than in a lighter runner. Again, the study did not find that overweight runners had a higher rate of injury.

Was there a relationship between the rate of injury and the number of years of running? There are two opposite reasons for examining this question. First, many believe that running is harmful to the body. If this is true, we should find cumulative damage and a higher injury rate for chronic runners. Second, others believe that after jogging for several years runners learn to run correctly, become stronger, and more knowledgeable about preventing injuries.

Those who had been jogging for 19 or more years had an injury rate less than half that of those who had been running 18 years or less.

A recent study on 32 marathon runners over 60 years of age found similar results. The participants in the study were mostly highly educated males (31 out of 32). The average distance run per week was 37 miles and the average number of years running was 12. The injury rate during the previous year was 47 percent, with the most frequently injured areas being the knee, foot, and back. The profile of the average injured runner was someone who was 66 years of age, who ran 34 miles per week, and who had been running for nine years. The profile of the noninjured runner was someone who was 64 years of age, who ran 38 miles per week, and who had been running for 12 years. The researchers concluded that although the injury rate for these runners was "high," that it was similar to the injury rate of other younger runners who were running the same weekly mileage (Hogan and Cape, 1984).

In summary, it does *not* appear that the aged are predisposed to running-related injuries or that they suffer a higher rate of injuries than other age groups.

It appears, then, that properly trained, conditioned, and knowledgeable older runners will not suffer from an injury rate any greater than that of young runners. However, although they do not suffer from shin splints or sprained ankles, do they die more frequently than younger runners? Is running a safe sport for the aged?

Dangers of Running for the Aged

There is little doubt that masters runners will die, some while running. This does not necessarily mean that running is dangerous. After all, people die while eating, sleeping, making love, and watching television and few claim that these activities are dangerous. There are risks associated with many activities, and the risks often increase with increasing age. However, masters runners can lower the risks by having a thorough physical examination and by initially having their exercise monitored by a physician. There are many programs for masters runners where certain physiological variables, such as blood pressure and heart rate, are monitored in a laboratory or physician's office. If no problems occur, masters runners can learn to do their own physiological monitoring.

Masters runners, as should all runners, should also exercise only in the proper equipment, and environment. Allowing time for a proper warmup and cool down is also important. Most important, however, is to closely monitor the duration and intensity of the exercise. One primary source of injury for older runners is trying to make up for 50 years of sedentary living too rapidly.

There are several reasons older runners need to take special precautions when running. First, the ability of the body to regulate body temperature declines with increasing age. Thus, running in temperature extremes, either hot or cold, can be dangerous. Additionally, it takes the body longer to respond to increases or decreases in body temperature. Training at a level or in an environment that alters body temperature above normal limits may be dangerous.

Second, the vision and hearing senses of most older individuals decline with increasing age. This will mean that a potentially dangerous situation, such as a reckless, speeding car, may not be seen or heard until it is too late to avoid an accident.

Third, the reflexes of older individuals are not as fast as those of younger individuals. Although the decline is only a fraction of a second and not significant for most events, in a potentially life-threatening situation it may make the difference between life or death.

Fourth, older individuals do not heal as fast as younger individuals. Injuries that used to take a week to heal may now take two weeks. Some injuries may never completely heal. Because of this older runners need to take special precautions to reduce the risk of injury, such as a change in running surface, route, or in the duration and intensity of one's running.

In summary, running is safe for most older people if certain precautions are followed. This does not mean that even if the precautions are followed some individuals will not die while running. When an individual starts running he or she does not automatically receive a ten year warranty on his or her body. In other words, running does not guarantee immortality. Running, or other forms of exercise, will for most older Americans provide a slimmer, healthier, and more mentally alert individual.

For those not interested in running but who are interested in an active physical life, there are numerous organizations that will assist individuals over 40 in taking up and participating in sporting events such as swimming, diving, rowing, bicycling, softball, skiing, tennis, track and field. Through these organizations individuals can find instruction, companionship, and competition. A recent publication listed 22 organizations that will assist individuals 40 and over participate in sports (see Strovas, 1984).

Competitive Masters Running

Tables V and VI list two of the more popular running events for both men and women, the 10kilometer and the marathon, along with several age categories. The world record times are presented at the top of the table. The 1984 age group American record times are also presented, as is the percentage difference between this time and the world record time.

Table V
World Record Running Times for 10k
and United States Masters Records

| | MEN | | WOMEN | |
| | 10k Time | Percent Difference | 10k Time | Percent Difference |
Age				
World Record	27:22		31:35	
40–44	29:57	9.4	35:27	12.2
45–49	31:36	15.4	37:24	18.4
50–54	32:46	19.7	37:43	19.4
55–59	34:08	24.7	40:08	27.1
60–64	35:32	29.8	41:21	30.9
65–69	37:21	36.5	51:04	61.7
70+	43:59	60.7	54:58	74.0

Table VI

World Record Running Times for Marathon
and United States Masters Records

| | MEN | | WOMEN | |
| | Marathon Time | Percent Difference | Marathon Time | Percent Difference |
Age				
World Record	2:07:11		2:21:06	
40–44	2:15:15	6.3	2:46:43	18.2
45–49	2:21:32	11.3	2:54:34	24.4
50–54	2:25:51	14.7	2:52:02	23.7
55–59	2:36:43	23.2	3:14:46	21.9
60–64	2:46:45	31.1	3:15:30	38.6
65–69	2:52:45	35.2	4:01:30	71.2
70+	3:33:27	67.8	5:03:54	114.7

As is apparent, generally the percentage difference becomes larger with increasing age. This is for two reasons. The first and major reason is, of course, the effect of aging. We have seen the physiological declines that take place with increasing age, even in runners. Thus, a world class runner will not be able to maintain the same pace even with the same duration and intensity of training in his or her masters years. Because individuals age at different rates, the exact age when it will be impossible to improve one's time cannot be calculated. In 1974 at the age of 41, Jack Foster of New Zealand ran a marathon in 2:11:19, an incredible time even for a much younger individual (in 1982 at the age of 50 Foster ran a marathon in 2:20:28). Thus, Foster may not have peaked until his early forties. In 1982 at 44 years of age Joyce Smith of Great Britain ran a marathon in 2:29:43. Smith's time in the

1984 Olympics at age 44 was 2:32:48. In 1981 John Gilmour of Australia ran a 2:41:07 marathon at the age of 62.

The major point is simply that masters runners are still capable of turning in performances that are far better than 99 percent of all runners. Although senescence will not allow them to break world record times, it is primarily a reduction in the intensity and duration of training that is responsible for a decline in their times.

As masters runners spend more time training and receive better training advice, their times will come down dramatically, just as they did for women.

5
Injuries

Introduction

Injuries are a fact of life for runners. Most are of short duration, and cause little pain or incapacitation; others produce substantial and occasionally permanent damage. Most running injuries either require no special treatment or at most home medical care; some injuries are severe and require professional medical intervention, including surgery. Most running injuries are caused by running; others are caused by other factors and become apparent while running.

Simply because runners are injured is, of course, no reason to stop, or to not start, running. Most runners believe that the benefits gained from running far outweigh an occasional sprained ankle, blister, sore tendon, or pulled muscle. It must also be realized that injuries are not unique to running but are common in many sports.

Considering the amount of time runners are engaged in their sport, the number and seriousness of running-related injuries appears very low. It must be remembered that runners are engaged in an athletic activity for the entire time they are exercising. Runners who run for an hour a day are engaged in exercise for that entire time period. In contrast, tennis players who play tennis for an hour will spend a considerable part of the hour walking and standing still. The same is true of most other sports. That is, many sports involve short bursts of activity that are followed by an equal if not greater period of rest where the chance of an injury is substantially reduced. Additionally, runners generally do not engage in their sport on smooth, groomed surfaces. Rather, they are often on a surface that is uneven and filled with obstacles, which increases the likelihood of an injury, whether minor or major.

Thus, the nature of running makes injuries a fact of life for runners. The frequency of injuries is perhaps best demonstrated by the amount of literature on injuries available to runners. As pointed out in the introduction to this book, the themes of running books have gone through a number of stages, one of which has been the injury stage where both the prevention and cure of injuries have been stressed. Additionally, popular running magazines frequently have articles dealing with injuries, as well as a host of advertisements listing creams, orthopedic devices, and chemicals to alleviate runners' injuries.

This chapter of the book is divided into three sections. The first section will examine the frequency, severity, location, and cause of running injuries. The second section will detail some of the specific injuries and complaints induced by running. The third will examine the ultimate injury, death while running.

Frequency, Severity, Location, and Cause of Injuries

There have been relatively few "good" studies conducted on runners to determine the frequency, severity, location, and cause of running-related injuries. Furthermore, most of the studies that have been published have had severe methodological limitations, which has restricted their usefulness. Even some of the "better" studies still need to be read carefully so that the results are not incorrectly interpreted, the limitations of the data are noted, and incorrect extrapolations are not made.

The basic problem is that many of the studies examine only injured runners. While this type of study can be important and informative, naive researchers and readers often draw incorrect conclusions because they make faulty assumptions. One of the most frequent errors in studies that examine only injured runners is the attempt to generalize to all runners, or use faulty logic in drawing a conclusion. For example, one recent study by physicians who treated injured runners claimed that there was an inverse relationship between distance run per week and rate of injury. That is, as distance went up, the likelihood of injury went down. The authors based their conclusion on the fact that the vast majority of the injured runners they examined were "low mileage" runners, while they only saw a very small number of "high mileage" runners. The authors apparently assumed there were an equal number of low and high distance runners — an assumption that is probably not correct. By not knowing the number of low mileage and high mileage runners, we do not know if 10 percent of the low mileage runners and 90 percent of the high mileage runners were seeking medical treatment, or if the figures should be reversed.

Frequency of Injury

The first question we want to examine is, how frequently are runners injured?

There have been many articles on this subject, although, as noted previously, most of them have had severe methodological limitations. The articles have found that from 30 to 90 percent and more (see Glick and Katch, 1970) of runners are injured at least once a year. The discrepancy of figures is because the researchers have examined different types of runners, used different definitions of injury, and used different time frames.

For example, while some studies reported on elite, experienced runners who were averaging 75 to 100 miles a week, doing intervals and hill work, and running in weekly races, other studies concentrated on those running three miles four times a week, at a 12-minutes-a-mile pace.

Researchers have also defined the term "injury" very differently. One study noted that blisters were a "universal complaint" among the runners surveyed and thus did not categorize "blisters" as an injury in the analysis. Thus, this article could have listed an injury rate of 100 percent; however, by eliminating blisters as an injury the injury rate fell to less than 50 percent.

Additionally, most of the studies have used "self-report" rather than "medical examination" for the documentation of the injury. However, a novice runner is more likely to consider a sore muscle, the result of a progressively intensive training regime, to be a "pulled" muscle, and to thus consider himself to be "injured," while in contrast an elite runner may ignore a much more "serious" injury.

Lastly, the studies on the rate or frequency of injuries have differed because of the time frame used. Most of the studies use one year. That is, they ask the runner if he has been injured during the last year. However, some studies have simply asked, "Have you ever been injured?" Other studies have used a six month time frame.

Even given the above limitations, there have been several studies on frequency of injuries that are relevant and which will be examined. Two studies were conducted by *Runner's World* magazine on large random samples of its readers. The first study was published in 1977 and was based on four surveys, each with more than 1,000 participants. The study found that 60–70 percent of those surveyed claimed to have had at least one running-related injury during the last year.

In 1982 *Runner's World* published the results of a survey conducted for them by an independent research institute. Again, the subjects were the magazine's readers. This time 3,000 runners participated in the survey. Although the major purpose of the survey was to help compile information on running shoes, there were also a number of questions dealing with injuries. This survey found that 44 percent of the respondents said that they had had at least one running-related injury during the previous year.

A study conducted on runners in the 1980 Peachtree Road Race found that one year after the race 35 percent of the runners had been injured seriously enough to require a reduction in their weekly mileage as a minimum form of treatment (Koplan et al., 1982).

Severity of Injury

Many critics of running point, with some satisfaction, to the frequency of running-related injuries. However, if most of the injuries are relatively minor and do not permanently harm the runner, or contribute to a chronic debilitating condition, then surely the other benefits obtained from running, such as cardiovascular fitness, outweigh an occasional acute, minor running-related injury (see Sheehan, 1984a).

Table I
Injured Runners: Percent Reporting an Injury to a Specific Area

	Henderson 1977	James et al. 1978	Pagliano 1980*	Gudas 1980*	Clement 1981*	RW 1982	Gottlieb 1980	Lutter 1980	Hughes et al. 1985
Knee	25%	29%	30%	31%	41%	30%	30%	29%	17%
Achilles	18	11	6	7a	27b	10	6		7f
Shin	15	13		10		9	8		
Ankle	11		5	8		10	13		6
Heel	10						2		7
Arch	8	7	2	14c			4		
Calf	7						9		
Hip	7		3	5d	4	6	6	12	4g
Foot	6		**	22	20	7	5		13
Hamstring	6		2		4e		5		2
Back							3	9	0

* Rounded to nearest whole number
** Less than 1%
aAnd calf. bAnd lower leg. cAnd heel. dAnd groin. eAnd upper leg. fAnd calf. gAnd groin.

A survey on the severity of running-related injuries was published in the 1982 *Runner's World* annual shoe survey. Of the runners who reported being injured, the length the injury lasted was 5 percent for more than six months; 7 percent four to six months; 12–13 percent two to three months; 20 percent one to two months; 17–18 percent two to three weeks; and 9–10 percent one week or less. An additional 30 percent said that their injuries were still bothering them but did not note when they were injured. Of those injured, 64 percent said their injuries were severe enough to keep them from training.

Although this study is interesting, it leaves out a great deal of information on the severity of running injuries. A pulled muscle may be sore for two months but it may not prevent the individual from running or cause any permanent damage. Additionally, the study noted that 64 percent of the injured runners had injuries that prevented them from training, but it did not note the length of time these runners were prevented from training.

A study by Gottlieb and White (1980) provided information on the injuries of recreational runners. They found that as a response to their injuries, 12 percent of the injured runners did nothing, 32 percent decreased their mileage for about two weeks, and 40 percent did not run for about five weeks. The remainder had varied programs of recovery. Of the 91 injured runners, there was one each who required surgery, use of a brace, use of a crutch, and a cast. Additionally, 17 started using orthopedic devices.

Another study of 180 runners who sought medical help for running-related injuries reported that their injuries were treated as follows: rest 47 percent, orthopedic devices 46, reduced mileage 26, shoe change 19, steroid injection 17, antiinflammatory drug 14, and surgery 5 percent (James et al., 1978).

We can see from the above information that a substantial percentage of runners have injuries that keep them from training, that persist for a significant period of time, and that require professional medical attention.

Location of Injury

What are the most frequently injured areas? With recent advances in sportsmedicine and the increasing interest in running-related injuries, the classification of injuries has become more complex than in the past when the injured area would simply be designated as the "foot," or "knee." For example, Clement and his associates (1981) recently identified 19 running-related knee injuries, 20 running-related foot injuries, and 13 running-related lower leg injuries. As a result, runners have had to add a large number of new tongue-twisting words to their vocabularies.

Unfortunately, the majority of articles surveying runners have not kept pace with the advances made in the diagnosis and classification of running injuries. When listing injuries, most articles still report a general area such as the knee or the foot. They do not even specify if the injury was to a muscle, bone, ligament, tissue, or tendon. There have been a few exceptions (see Clement et al., 1981; Gudas, 1980; Lutter, 1980).

Table I presents the results of nine studies on injured runners. The table reports the location of the injuries as well as the percentage of injured runners reporting an injury to a specific area. Although not all of the researchers used the same categories, and the percentages vary, it appears that the knee is generally the "weak link." After the knee, there is relatively little consistency in the data, although the Achilles tendon, the shin, and the foot ranked as frequent sources of injury in more than one of the surveys.

Cause of Injury

A significant percentage of runners are injured on a yearly basis, with the knee frequently involved. Why are runners injured? The answer is in eight parts: anatomy, equipment, mileage, gender, training surface, age, training errors, and environment (see Larkins, 1984).

Anatomy

It is often a runner's own anatomy that produces an injury. While all individuals have anatomical "abnormalities," most abnormalities do not cause any problems in everyday life, or in other sports. However, when subjected to the repeated stress of running, then the abnormalities may produce an injury (Nilsson, 1982). The opportunity for anatomical factors to produce an injury can be seen by examining the stress running produces on the body. With every step runners have to absorb three to five times the weight of their body. The foot of a 150 pound runner will have to absorb 120 tons of force for every mile run (Drez, 1980). Thus, during running certain minor anatomical abnormalities have the opportunity to become magnified.

All of the following anatomical abnormalities, and others, have been found to produce running-related injuries: leg length discrepancy, pronation, genu valgum (knock-kneed condition), genu varum (bowleggedness), genu recurvatum (extension of the knee joint beyond normal limits), femoral neck anteversion (tipping forward), pes cavus (high arched feet), pes plantus (flatfootedness), and muscle insufficiency (especially hamstring, quadriceps, gastrocnemius, or soleus) (James et al., 1978; Klein, 1980; Clancy, 1980a; Lehman, 1984; Jackson and Gudas, 1982).

To ascertain if certain "anatomical abnormalities" were in fact a cause of runners' injuries, one study studied a college's long-distance runners for five years. After examining the runners and identifying their "abnormalities," the researchers were able to predict, with 75 percent accuracy, the runners who would be injured. The researchers noted that the best treatment for an athletic injury is its prevention. They speculated that if runners and coaches spent more time diagnosing the factors that would predispose an athlete to injury, and then took corrective measures, the athlete would be at a substantially reduced risk (Ross and Schuster, 1983).

Another study on injured runners found that those with anatomical abnormalities suffered injuries even though no change in training took place. This was because of chronic overloading of a weak area (Pinshaw et al., 1984).

Although anatomical abnormalities can cause injuries, how frequently they do so is not known. One study of runners who sought medical help for running-related injuries found that approximately 80 percent had anatomical abnormalities such as leg length discrepancy or pronation (Klein, 1980). Although the implication of the study was that anatomy was the cause of most of the diagnosed running-related injuries, the study did not note if the injuries of the runners were caused by their anatomical "problems." Additionally, the study did not specify the frequency with which these "abnormalities" are found in noninjured runners.

There is no doubt that anatomical abnormalities cause running-related injuries, although the extent to which they do is not known. Unfortunately, injuries caused by anatomical factors are often not treated correctly. Too often physicians treat the symptoms, such as tendonitis, rather than the cause. This means that after an injured runner has recovered from his injury and begins to increase his mileage, he will reach approximately the same level of training and the injury will return (see Lutter, 1980).

It has been reported that if treated correctly with more appropriate shoes, in-shoe orthoses (see Murphy, 1986), corrections for leg-length discrepancy, correction of training methods, the use of ice on the injured area, and or physiotherapy, the vast majority of injured runners are able to resume their preinjury distance within eight weeks. One study reported that proper diagnosis of anatomical abnormalities is especially important since a "cure" can be brought about before radical medical intervention is needed (e.g., drugs or surgery) (Pinshaw et al., 1984; see Sperryn and Restan, 1983).

Equipment

The characteristics of "good" and "bad" shoes have been frequently examined (see Gudas, 1980; James et al., 1978; Clement et al., 1981; Drez, 1980; Klein, 1982; Stamford, 1984). Suffice it to say that "Formosa flyers" will not offer the protection that most runners need (Burgess and Ryan, 1985). However, a major problem is not the design of running shoes but that many runners do not maintain their shoes. Very often runners allow their shoes to wear down, which creates an abnormal foot strike and overpronation which can cause a variety of injuries (see James et al., 1978).

Mileage

Almost all studies on running-related injuries have indicated that as the number of miles run per week increases so does the likelihood of an injury (Koplan et al., 1982; James et al, 1978).

Hughes and his associates (1985) studied runners in the Chicago Distance Classic and did not support the above conclusion. They reported that "sports runners" had a higher percentage of injuries than those classified as "long-distance," or "elite" runners. They reported that perhaps those running shorter distances were less physically prepared for the race, or were novice runners who incorrectly interpreted some of the discomfort produced by racing as being an indication of injury.

Gender

The chapter on women has a more detailed section on women and injury. As pointed out in that chapter, most studies have found that it does not appear that women suffer a higher rate of running-related injuries than men (Nilsson, 1982; Shively et al., 1981; Splain and Rolnick, 1984). It also appears that the sites of the injuries are almost identical for both sexes. In a study of 1,650 injured runners Clement and his associates (1981) found the following injury rate: knee, men 42 percent, women 41; lower leg, men 27 percent, women 29; foot, men 20, women 16; hip, men 4, women 6; lower back, men 3, women 4, and upper leg, men 4 percent, women 4. Similar findings were presented by Koplan and his associates (1982).

Although several studies have found that males and females are injured in the same areas in approximately the same frequency, one study noted that the type of injuries they incur are different, although the study did not specify if the bones, muscles, tendons, ligaments, or tissues in one gender versus another were stronger or weaker. The study also reported that injured men ran an average of 27 miles a week while injured women ran 19 miles a week. Based on this, and some other information, the study "suggested" that women under 30 years of age were "more susceptible" to running-related injuries than men. After age 30 the study found that the injury rates for men and women were equal (Clement et al., 1981; see James et al., 1978).

One recent study has noted a higher incidence of certain injuries to women. Hughes and his associates (1985) have reported that in their study of participants in the Chicago Distance Classic, women reported more orthopedic injuries than men, especially to the knee, the hip and the groin.

Training Surface

A number of studies have examined the consequence of running on certain surfaces. Generally, surfaces that are hard, have a camber (are convex), or that are slanted (up or down hills) produce more injuries (see Gudas, 1980; Smith, 1980). The "ideal" surface for staying injury-free, although probably not for training to win races, is one that is flat, smooth, and has some give to it (see Smith, 1980). Training on a hard surface may cause traumatic arthritis, especially in the second and third metatarsophalangeal joints; stress and or fatigue fractures may also occur in the metatarsals (Nilsson, 1982).

Age

Very few studies have examined the age of injured runners, and none has compared the injury rate of runners of different ages who run at the same level and intensity. The study on participants in the Chicago Distance Classic reported that those under 30 years of age had more orthopedic and dermatological injuries. Those over 30 years of age had an overall higher history of injuries to the foot, calf, and Achilles tendon (Hughes et al., 1985).

Based on runners as patients with running-related injuries, Clement and his associates (1981) found that most of their patients were in the 20- to 29-year-old age group. They had relatively few patients in the 10–19 or over 30 age groups. Gudas' (1980) findings were similar. Of the 224 injured runners he examined, there were very few under 20 or above 45. More studies are needed in this area before any definitive statements can be made.

Training Errors

Many injuries in runners are self-induced through training errors (Johnson, 1983; see McKenzie et al., 1985).

The most frequent training error is overtraining. Examples are high intensity training, racing without intervening rest days, a sudden increase in mileage and or intensity, hill training, interval training, and running on hard surfaces (Clancy, 1980a; James et al., 1978; Clement et al., 1981). One researcher found that 80 percent of all runners' injuries were caused by overtraining (Nilsson, 1982; see Stamford, 1983; Lehman, 1984).

There are several predictors of overtraining: sudden weight loss, an increase in the resting heart rate both before and after getting out of bed, little desire or motivation to train, insomnia, anorexia, chronic muscle soreness, a run-down feeling, a postworkout weight "significantly" lower than normal, an evening fluid intake "higher" than normal, going to bed later than normal, less sleep than normal, and depression. Since athletes are more susceptible to an illness or an injury during periods of overtraining, they should monitor themselves and reduce their level of training if they note the symptoms of overtraining (Stamford, 1983; *Physician and Sportsmedicine* 1983).

The results of overtraining are often seen in those who race or plan to race. One study on the entrants for a marathon found that 58 percent were injured while training for the race (Maughan and Miller, 1982). Two studies have found that not only training for racing, but racing itself is a frequent source of injury. This is because the training leading up to the race has left the runner in a weakened condition and often during the race the athlete runs more intensely. The first study found that during a marathon 18 percent of the runners approached a first aid station for a problem. During a half-marathon the figure was 4 percent (Nicholl and Williams, 1982a). The second study was also conducted on marathon runners and found that 17 percent reported being injured during the race (Maughan and Miller, 1982).

Another error many athletes make is waiting too long before reporting their injuries; this often increases the severity and healing time of the injury. One study on athletes seeking attention to their sports-related injuries found that more than half waited five days or longer after the injury before seeking medical attention. A study on athletes with stress fractures found that the average amount of time from the onset of symptoms to the receipt of medical care was 7.4 weeks (Taunton et al., 1981). The delay was often because the athletes had a high pain threshold or because they were accustomed to and tolerant of pain. Generally speaking, those who delayed seeking medical attention were those who had established high performance standards for themselves, and those who perceived their sport as a healthy way of life. Many others assumed that their injuries were a normal consequence of exercise, or did not want to believe that they were injured. Others simply did not want to be told to stop training (see Kent, 1982).

There is a danger, of course, in assuming that pain, swelling, or other symptoms result from a running-related injury. The danger is that the symptoms may be caused by another disorder that requires *immediate* medical attention. A study by Pfeiffer and Young (1980) reported the case of a jogger with a collapsed lung who continued to exercise for three weeks with distressing symptoms. Although in this case no dangerous complications resulted, the authors noted some of the life-threatening consequences that could have resulted from allowing this condition to go untreated.

The medical profession has recognized that runners constitute a unique group of patients who do not respond to traditional medical practices. The most important recognition is that runners do not, generally speaking, trust physicians, and that most runners will seek medical treatment only as a last resort. One recent study in a medical journal noted that of runners with an injury serious enough to keep them from running for seven to ten days, only one in 20 will seek medical attention (Brody, 1982).

Runners are suspicious of physicians mainly because physicians have the annoying habit of telling injured runners to temporarily stop running — an absurd prescription for most of them (see James et al., 1978; Krissoff and Ferris, 1979; Guten and Craviotto, 1985). Several physicians who treat runners have noted that telling a dedicated runner to rest will be unacceptable. It has been suggested that, whenever medically feasible, physicians should prescribe a reduced schedule of running, but an increase in other aerobic activities such as swimming or bicycling as "temporary" substitutes. More importantly, the articles have pointed out that physicians need to have understanding, patience, and the ability to speak the "runner's language." In evaluating the injury it is also important for the physician to not just treat the symptoms but to be able to determine what caused the injury (James et al., 1978; Clancy, 1978; Brody, 1982; Lutter, 1980; Clancy, 1980b).

Environment

This section will deal with five environmental conditions that may cause injuries: heat, cold, pollution, automobiles, and crime.

Heat Injuries. In August, 1979, 600 runners lined up at the starting line of a 10-mile race in Herndon, Virginia. The temperature was 88°F at the start of the race and 93°F by the time the race ended. During the race two runners became disoriented from heat stroke, wandered off the course and died. In 1977, 6,000 runners ran the Peachtree Race in Atlanta. Sixty runners were hospitalized for heat injuries, one for nine weeks with acute kidney failure. In the 1982 Sheffield Marathon, in England, 1 percent of the 2,289 participants were hospitalized with heat injuries. In 1978 1,300 runners ran a 10 kilometer race in Waterloo, Ontario. The temperature was 76°F. Fifteen runners were hospitalized for heat stroke (see Murphy, 1984). During the 1984 Olympics millions agonized during the women's marathon as one of the participants slowly weaved and staggered her way to the finish line.

In a recent Chicago Distance Classic, a 20-kilometer race, 3.2 percent of the participants claimed to have suffered from a heat illness; 18 percent indicated they had experienced one or more symptoms of heat illness (Hughes et al., 1985).

The list of medical reports on runners suffering from heat related injuries is growing, not only in this country but also others. Reports from South Africa, Australia, and Canada have noted the increase in heat-related injuries in runners. The most dangerous condition is, of course, heat stroke, which if not treated can result in permanent damage to the heart, brain, kidneys, and liver. It can also result in death.

The increase in the number of races in the summer months and in the number of novice runners has greatly increased the problem. Many runners do not know how to protect themselves from heat-injuries and there are reports of runners avoiding water both before and during distance races for fear of stomach distress. There are also reports of race officials at aid stations cautioning runners not to swallow water but only to rinse out their mouths. Furthermore, many race directors are ignorant of runners' needs and schedule races during the hottest time of the day, without water stations, or medical backup.

The human body is capable of functioning in a wide range of external temperatures. However, an increase or decrease of only 2°C in core body temperature can bring about significant physical and mental impairment. An increase of 5°C brings about death. Thus, it is important that core body temperature remain at a fairly constant level.

The hypothalamus controls the body temperature. Generally, the hypothalamus works very effectively. However, under extreme conditions, such as very high solar radiation (the sun), or metabolic heat production (through exercise), the hypothalamus may not be able to dissipate or lose enough body heat to prevent the internal temperature of the body from increasing to dangerous levels. The body can only tolerate an internal temperature of 41°C (105.8°F) for a short period of time before damage is done to internal organs such as the heart, brain, liver, or kidneys, or before death occurs.

During running most of the heat accumulation in the body is the result of metabolic heat, which is produced by the exercising muscles. In fact, the amount of heat produced by the muscles during exercise is as much as 20 times greater than when the muscles are at rest. A runner's heat production is between 1,000 and 1,500 kcal an hour from internal sources, and another 150 kcal an hour from external sources such as the sun. Every five minutes this can raise the core temperature of the body about 1°C. If the body did not dissipate the heat, within minutes the temperature of the body would increase to a dangerous and perhaps lethal level.

Fortunately the body is fairly efficient in dissipating heat. As the temperature of the body starts to rise, the hypothalamus starts the "cooling response," in which the veins in the skin are dilated. In fact, the blood flow to the skin increases from a rate of 5 percent during rest to 20 percent during maximum exercise. The body brings blood that has been warmed by the increasing core temperature of the body to the surface of the skin where the temperature is generally cooler and thus the blood is cooled. The cooled blood is then returned to the core of the body where it reduces the temperature of the internal organs while gathering more heat.

Sweating is another mechanism that helps to lower the temperature of the body. The evaporation of sweat from the skin brings about a cooling response. One liter of sweat can dissipate 580 kcals of heat per hour. However, since about 20 percent of the body's sweat drips from the body, the actual cooling effect is about 460 kcals per hour. During vigorous exercise the body can increase its sweating rate from one half liter per day, to between two and three liters per hour (McArdle et al., 1981).

There are a variety of factors that have an influence over the ability of the body to cool itself. Some of the major ones are external temperature, humidity, wind, and fluid replacement. The higher the external temperature and humidity the more difficult it is to dissipate heat. The greater the wind velocity the more quickly heat is dissipated.

Another important factor in the regulation of body temperature is fluid replacement. During the 1968 Olympic Marathon time trials the runners lost an average of 13.4 pounds. In exercise the body tries to compensate for fluid loss by decreasing the blood flow to the kidneys. As a result, during vigorous exercise urine production decreases by about 30 percent. Without fluid replacement the volume of blood drops which increases the amount of stress on the heart. Additionally, because of the decrease in body fluid blood pressure drops; to maintain blood pressure the body ceases sweating to preserve body fluids. This increases the internal temperature of the body.

It is very important for a runner to be "fully hydrated" before a run since a fully hydrated runner will have a lower body temperature while running than a runner who started running while dehydrated (see Sutton and Bar-Or, 1980). No matter how hard a runner tries, in a long race or run he will lose more fluid than he will be able to replace. While runners can lose two to three liters of fluid an hour in vigorous exercise, their stomachs can only empty 800ml an hour.

The decrease in body fluid results in a decrease in the volume of blood.

If there is not enough blood to maintain circulation the runner goes into shock. Fortunately, it appears that much of the fluid that is lost comes from the intracellular spaces rather than the blood plasma. Thus, runners can often tolerate body weight losses of 2 to 8 percent while running, without circulatory collapse (Costill, 1979).

Adequate fluid replacement does not guarantee that a heat injury will not occur. A study of runners who collapsed in a 10k race in Canada found that most of the runners had consumed fluids both before and during the race. The authors concluded that the temperature, humidity, and solar radiation made it impossible for some of the runners to dissipate enough heat to prevent heat injury (Hughson, Green, Houston et al., 1980).

Research has led to the following recommendations regarding fluid intake before, during and after a race (see Costill, 1979; see Nelson, 1985; Sherwood and Strong, 1985).

1. 10–30 minutes prior to the race 390–600ml of water should be consumed.

2. During the race the fluid intake should be frequent and in 100–250ml doses. This is because the more fluid, up to 600ml, the faster it leaves the stomach, which is what the runner desires since fluid in the stomach is not absorbed. The fluid needs to get into the intestines for absorption to take place.

3. The fluid should be cold, 40°F or 4°C, since cold fluids leave the stomach faster than warm fluids.

4. The fluid should contain a very low level of electrolytes, e.g., sodium, if any. Again this is for more rapid absorption.

5. The fluid should only contain a small amount of glucose, if any. Again, this has to do with rate of absorption.

Fluid intake during and after a race or run is very important. One indicator of an adequate fluid intake is the ability to urinate within one hour after running; if urination is not possible one hour after running then medical attention may be needed (Moore, 1983c).

Two recent studies on "water intoxication" has suggested that, though rare, there may be some exceptions to drinking large amounts of water before or during a race (Noakes, Goodwin et al., 1984). The first reported on four cases of water intoxication during ultramarathons (over seven hours). The second study was on two runners in the American Medical Joggers Association ultramarathon race in Chicago. Both developed water intoxication. Both recovered after medical intervention (Frizzell et al., 1986). Water intoxication occurs with excessive sodium losses from the body or an excessive consumption or retention of water (Frizzell et al., 1986). This is most likely to occur in ultramarathons, and in slower runners, who sweat less and have more time to consume large amounts of water.

Heat injury may also be caused or prevented by the minerals in the body. There are two very important minerals that help to regulate body temperature: sodium and potassium. For decades athletes have been gulping salt tablets, because of the belief that salt would help them to retain body fluids. According to the authors of *The Sportsmedicine Book* "Never...take salt tablets." Since more water than sodium is lost in exercise, the sodium level in the blood rises, which increases the risk of heat stroke. Since the sodium thickens the blood, the probability of blood clots increases. Blood clots increase the risk of a stroke, blindness, kidney failure, and death. Salt tablets also cause the stomach to retain water, which provides less fluid for sweating (see Weltman and Stamford, 1983c).

Most Americans consume more salt than they need. The average individual only needs about 200 milligrams per day, but consumes 8,000 to 20,000 milligrams. Although vigorous exercise may result in a salt loss of 1,500 milligrams (one liter of sweat contains 1,000–1,500 mg of sodium), most still take in this amount per day, even if on a salt restricted diet. A deficiency in salt may lead to fatigue and muscle cramps, but salt supplements should only be taken upon the advice of a physician.

Researchers disagree on the need to replace potassium. Potassium is lost in large quantities during exercise. During exercise potassium is released by the body and causes the veins to widen. This expansion allows an increased blood flow to the generally cooler surface of the skin. However, because potassium interferes with the contractibility of the heart it is eliminated from the blood stream in sweat and urine.

Some claim that potassium does not need to be replaced. They point out that potassium losses are small (about 85 mg in one pound of sweat – and a 150-pound male has 120 grams of potassium) and that the body conserves potassium when levels within the body are low. They also point out that even those who engage in heavy exercise are likely to consume far more potassium than they need in their diets. For example, one cup of orange juice has over 400 mg of potassium. These individuals do note, however, that there are several conditions under which a potassium deficiency may occur: vomiting and diarrhea, use of laxatives, use of diuretics, and consumption of certain foods such as licorice.

Others believe that runners need potassium supplements or diets rich in potassium.

With a heat injury the body temperature may increase to the level where the hypothalamus is damaged or cannot function. Additionally, with dehydration, blood volume declines and there is not enough blood to supply both the skin and the internal organs. When this occurs, the blood supply to the skin is decreased and the body temperature rises rapidly.

There are four common types of heat injury. The first is a heat cramp, which is the involuntary, unpredictable contraction of certain muscles. This is caused by fluid loss, generally through sweating, which causes an imbalance in certain body minerals that control muscle contractions.

The second type of heat injury is heat syncope (fainting). Several factors can cause this to occur, but the general explanation is that the blood volume has dropped which brings about a sudden drop in blood pressure resulting in dizziness or fainting (see Weltman and Stamford, 1983b).

The last two types of heat injury are far more dangerous. They are heat exhaustion and heat stroke. Heat exhaustion has been labeled a "mild" disorder, while heat stroke is "severe" (some call it a medical emergency) and has a 30 percent mortality rate (Richards, Richards, Schofield, and Sutton, 1979a; Whitworth and Wolfman, 1983). In heat exhaustion the clinical symptoms are fatigue, nausea, headache, thirst, a rectal temperature of $\leq$ 41°C, vasoconstriction (constriction of blood vessels), a pulse of 100–140 and active sweating. Additionally, the blood pressure reading is narrow with a severe orthostatic drop. The individual is usually conscious, although judgment may be impaired.

In heat stroke the clinical symptoms are disorientation, confused mental status, headache, vasodilation (dilation of blood vessels), dry skin (although active sweating may be present), a rectal temperature of $\geq$ 41C, a pulse of 120–180 and a blood pressure reading that has a wide range with a low diastolic. Heat stroke is especially dangerous since it often affects other organs such as the kidneys, heart, liver and brain. Thus, it is imperative to recognize and treat heat stroke victims immediately (see Kains et al., 1983; Hanson, 1979; Richards, Richards, Schofield, and Sutton, 1979a; Sherwood and Strong, 1985).

A recent symptom of heat injury not previously recognized is the sensation of "pins and needles" in the forearms (Noakes, 1982a).

Hanson and Zimmerman (1979) have noted that previously a lack of sweating was a clinical symptom used to distinguish heat exhaustion from heat stroke. However, they reported that they have noticed "active sweating" in all the cases of heat stroke they have examined.

It has also been reported that obtaining accurate temperatures on runners who have recently finished a race may be difficult. Oral temperatures may be affected by the runner having inhaled external air during the race. For example, after running on a cool day or after sucking ice the runner's mouth would generally be abnormally cool, perhaps not reflecting the temperature of the body. Even rectal temperatures may be misleading.

A recent study has confirmed that there are often significant differences between rectal and oral temperatures in runners. A study of 23 runners who finished the 14-mile Memorial Day race in Guam on a hot, humid, windless day were found to have oral temperatures 5.5°F below their rectal temperatures. One runner had an oral temperature of 94.6°F and a rectal temperature of 106°F, indicating hyperthermia. The author recommended that rectal temperature readings be used to determine the condition of runners (Rozycki, 1984a; see Rozycki, 1984b; Garbitelli, 1984).

Not only can some of the clinical symptoms, such as temperature, be difficult to obtain, but some of the more obvious symptoms may not be present or noticed by the runner. Of 22 heat injured runners in the 1979 Peachtree Road Race, nine said that they did not sense any of the common warning symptoms. Of those with warning symptoms, 12 noted that they became weak, tired, or dizzy (England et al., 1982).

While heat-related problems are an increasing source of concern, most runners do not collapse from heat injuries. The question of interest is, what *are* the characteristics of those who have heat-related injuries?.

The runner most likely to be affected by a heat injury, such as heat exhaustion or heat stroke, is the novice (Hughson, Green, Houston et al., 1980; Hanson and Zimmerman, 1979). This is so for eight reasons.

First, the novice runner generally lacks both the knowledge about running and the knowledge about his own body to either train or race in an intelligent manner. A Canadian study found that of 2,900 participants in a 10k race in 1978, 26 were hospitalized for heat injuries and all were novices to the 10k race (Hughson, Green, Houston et al., 1980; see Sutton, 1978; see Hughson and Sutton, 1978).

Second, many novice runners do not know about fluid replacement or hydration before running. They often avoid fluid intake before a race assuming that the extra weight will slow them down or that the water will produce stomach distress. Because novice runners lack basic knowledge and experience about running safely, Dr. George Sheehan (1982) has suggested that runners be "licensed to race": a "racer's license" would be required to enter a road race. To obtain the license the runner would have to pass a test dealing with running and racing knowledge.

Third, novice runners are also more likely to train during the coolest time of the day without realizing that most races are held during the hottest time of the day. During a race they forget to take the temperature difference into account by adjusting their pace.

Fourth, acclimatization to heat is very important for runners. The body is very capable of making rapid adjustments to heat, in fact, two weeks of progressively intensive training in hot weather will bring about heat acclimation: sweating response occurs much faster, an increased blood flow to the skin, double the nonacclimated sweating capacity, a more even distribution of sweating over the body surface for greater evaporation, and a lower salt content in the sweat. As heat acclimatization occurs less blood is shunted to the skin for cooling and can be sent to the heart and exercising muscles (McArdle et al., 1981; Smith, 1980). Novice runners are generally less conditioned than experienced runners, and studies have shown not only that less conditioned runners have less heat tolerance but that it also takes them longer to acclimate to the heat (see Sutton and Bar-Or, 1980).

Fifth, novice runners are less likely to recognize the "warning symptoms" of heat injury (e.g., dizziness, labored breathing, nausea, cold skin, either no or excessive sweating, headache, or muscle cramps) and thus will continue to run.

Sixth, novice runners may be "highly motivated" and trying to compete at a distance or at a pace they are not prepared for (Hanson and Zimmerman, 1979).

Seventh, novice runners are also more likely to get "caught up in the excitement of the race" and ignore water stations, their prerace pace rate, or heat-injury warning symptoms (see England et al., 1982). Additionally, novice runners probably do not have the conditioning to maintain a pace determined by excitement rather than conditioning.

Eighth, novice runners are also less likely to know the proper clothing to wear. Clothing that does not allow for evaporation of the moisture from the skin slows down the cooling response. A heavy synthetic sweat shirt does nothing but produce a very humid environment that reduces the amount of evaporation between the shirt and the skin. Obviously light colors reflect heat and dark colors absorb heat. On a hot day runners need loose fitting clothing that will allow the air to circulate around their skin and evaporate its moisture.

This does not mean that experienced runners are immune from any of the heat-related injuries described above (see Noakes, 1982a). They may be more highly motivated to win a race and thus ignore common safety rules and warning symptoms.

There are other risk factors that characterize both novice and experienced runners. It has been found, for example, that runners often run when they are ill or are recovering from an illness. They may be weak, and still replacing fluids from vomiting or diarrhea. Additionally, they may be taking medication which may distort heat-injury warning symptoms or mental judgment (see Sperryn, 1985). Studies have also associated two other variables with an increased risk of heat injury: age and obesity. Both the young and old, and the obese are more susceptible to heat injuries (see Sutton and Bar-Or, 1980).

Distance is also a major factor in heat injuries. Few heat problems occur in short races, even on hot days.

Another potential source of heat injuries is the use of a sunscreen during exercise. Runners are warned that the cumulative effects of the sun will cause premature aging of the skin and increase the likelihood of skin cancer. To prevent this, runners take preventative measures, such as using a sunscreen. Preliminary studies indicate that the use of a sunscreen during hot, dry weather results in a lower rate of sweat evaporation and a higher skin temperature. Using a sun screen during hot humid weather does not appear to increase skin temperature (Wells et al., 1984).

Race directors have also contributed to the risk. "Fun runs" have multiplied into the thousands and are now a part of most community summer events. These events are often put on as an afterthought by individuals with little or no knowledge of running. The courses to be run are not planned to include shaded areas or areas where local residents can be encouraged to spray the runners with water; consideration is often omitted of an out-and-back course design which allows for greater use of both spotters trained to notice warning signs and aid stations with two-way radio communications, or a course that will reduce the likelihood that runners who become disoriented will wander off and collapse without being noticed. Also, runners should be made aware of the temperature throughout the race by a wet bulb globe thermometer (WBGT), which takes into account ambient temperature, humidity, wind velocity, and radiant heat. Since in a race, such as a marathon, the temperature often changes significantly during the race, runners should be made aware of the current temperature by flags at aid stations. A red flag means that there is a high risk of heat injury (the WBGT is 23 to 28°C, or 73 to 82°F), an amber flag means moderate risk (WBGT is 18 to 23°C or 65 to 73 °F), a green means low risk (WBGT is below

18°C or 65°F), and a white flag means there is a risk of hypothermia (WBGT is below 10°C or 50°F) (see American College of Sports Medicine, 1984).

Additionally, water stations are often lacking, spaced too far apart, or without enough water for all the participants. Medical personnel are often absent. Even if present, they are often untrained to correctly treat the problems that runners are likely to experience. If present, there may not be enough medical personnel to handle the problems of the runners in an expedient manner. Formulas have been developed to help race directors predict the number of injured runners their race will have (Richards, Richards, and Whittaker, 1984).

It should be mentioned that although it is easy to criticize race directors, still most races today are far safer than "professional" races of only a few years ago. Until the 1976 Olympics, fluids were prohibited in the marathon until the 10k mark. In Boston in 1973 "international rules" prohibited runners from taking fluids from other than "official" sources; violators risked disqualification.

It has been suggested that race directors print instructions on the application form that detail the level of training the applicant should have achieved before entering the race, prerace nutrition, prerace fluid intake, suggested fluid intake during the race, warning symptoms of heat injury, anticipated temperature the day of the race, and what to do if they notice heat-injury symptoms in themselves or others. The form should also list the consequences of heat injuries. It has also been recommended that the form say that if certain conditions prevail on the day of the race, it will be rescheduled or delayed until safe conditions exist.

Providing information on the entry form dealing with who should and should not participate may help prevent problems. The 1982 Sheffield Marathon and half-marathon provided on the entry form the training levels that potential participants should have achieved before racing. One half of those who registered did not race. A follow-up study reported that 24 percent of the no-shows "decided that they were not fit enough" (Nicholl and Williams, 1982b). Additionally, taking precautionary measures such as those described in this section dramatically lowered the number of heat injuries in a 10k race in Waterloo, Ontario. In 1978, 1.3 percent of the runners suffered heat injuries. In 1979, on a similar day but after precautionary measures were taken, only .24 percent of the participants suffered heat injuries (Hughson et al., 1980; Hughson et al., 1983).

Race directors of the famous Sydney, Australia, "Sun City to Surf Run" have gone one step further by providing, prior to the run, seminars on running. The seminars included information on how to prevent and treat running-related medical injuries; the psychological aspects of running, including motivation; training, and diet. The seminars provided specific information about the training program necessary to safely complete the run, information about running in the race (e.g., such as not to run if you had been recently ill), and information about racing (e.g., listing the symptoms of heat injury, replacing fluids, and helping other runners) (Richards, Richards, Schofield, Ross, and Sutton, 1979; Kretsch et al., 1984). At registration all runners with medical problems are required to complete a medical information card that details medical problems and current medications. This card is carried during the race (Richards and Richards, 1984). The Boston Marathon has been providing a similar program for several years.

Heat injuries should not be treated lightly, and heat stroke *must* be treated by a physician since mortality is high (Sutton, 1979). Several articles have recommended that heat stroke patients stay in a hospital at least 24 hours (Hanson, 1979; Hart et al., 1980), although others believe hospitalization is not "absolutely" necessary (Noakes, 1982). Those who believe hospitalization is necessary believe that tests need to be conducted to ascertain if any damage has been done which needs immediate medical attention. They also believe that after a heat stroke the body may not be in control of the heat-regulation process for several hours. Thus, the runner may appear to have recovered, only to later lapse into a coma with a rising temperature. If help is not available the individual may again be in danger of permanent injury or death.

Although rapid treatment of heat stroke is essential, there is considerable disagreement on how to diagnose heat stroke and the most effective method of treatment (see Nash, 1985).

The victim needs to be moved immediately to a cool, shaded area. Many believe that rapid cooling — with wet towels packed with crushed ice placed around the neck, on the abdomen and groin, and under the armpits (axille) — then needs to take place (see Noakes, 1982). This widens the blood vessels in the skin which allows the cooling process to resume. Fluids are given intravenously since oral ingestion is too slow to do much immediate good. Fluid intake has to be closely monitored to prevent complications such as circulatory overload, and cerebral or pulmonary edema (Hanson and Zimmerman, 1979; Richards, Richards, Schofield, and Sutton, 1979a; see Boone, 1983).

Although in the past total immersion in cold water was a standard treatment, many medical authorities are now recommending that this not be done. There appear to be three reasons for this recommendation. First, the rapid immersion causes the blood vessels in the skin to initially contract (vasoconstriction), which impedes heat loss. Although vigorous massaging has been recommended to prevent vasoconstriction, evidence is lacking that it works. Second, suddenly placing an individual in cold water may cause cardiac arrhythmias (MacFarlane, 1983). Third, if other forms of resuscitation are necessary, especially forms that involve electric devices, they become difficult to institute. Fourth, a disoriented or confused individual may find the immersion threatening and struggle to get out of the cold water. This results in not only a patient management problem, but also in the generation of more body heat (see Richards, Richards, Schofield, and Sutton, 1979a; Khogali et al., 1983; Sherwood and Strong, 1985).

Runners who have had a heat stroke are more susceptible to another one. Studies indicate that individuals who have had a heat stroke are more susceptible to another one even two to five years after the first heat stroke. It is not known if this is because the ability to regulate body heat was permanently damaged by the first heat stroke, or if that individual has an inherent inability to regulate body temperature (see Caldroney, 1983; see Kilbourne et al., 1982).

Cold Injuries. Far less has been written about cold-related running injuries than heat-related running injuries. This is because fewer races are held in temperatures where cold-related injuries are likely to occur, and because runners often reduce their mileage during the winter months. Recently two deaths from running-induced hypothermia have been reported (Ledingham et al., 1982; Sutton, 1984a; see Sutton, 1983; 1984b), although hypothermia has been questioned as the cause of death in at least one of the cases (Maughan et al., 1982; Stansbie et al., 1982; Lloyd, 1983; Northcote and Ballantyne, 1983a; 1983b; see Sutton, 1978).

Although cold-related injuries have not received as much attention as heat-related injuries, they should not be taken lightly, as they can be damaging or fatal. This section examines the regulation of body temperature in a cold environment, specific cold-related running injuries, and ways to prevent cold-related injuries.

We have examined what happens to the body when the internal temperature continues to rise above 98.6°F (37°C). Obviously there are also consequences if the internal temperature drops below normal. With as much as a one degree drop in internal temperature the speech becomes slurred. A two degree drop brings about shivering and the fingers become numb and "lose their strength." When the body temperature drops three degrees a runner will become uncoordinated. A drop of four degrees brings about mental confusion and hallucinations. The muscles become rigid with a drop of nine degrees, and unconsciousness takes place when the drop is 14 degrees. Death occurs when the drop is 23 degrees (Mirkin and Hoffman, 1978).

As noted previously, the body is capable of adapting to a variety of external temperatures. When exposed to an environment that might lower the body's temperature, the body initially reduces the blood flow to the skin. This simply means that less blood will be exposed to the cooling external temperature, thus preserving body heat. Because of this, the skin will appear white. After the skin has cooled to about 59°F the body increases the blood supply to the skin, resulting in the skin's taking on a reddish color. Shivering will also occur; it is simply an involuntary contraction and relaxation of muscles, which produces a tremendous amount of heat.

There are two major cold-related injuries: hypothermia and frostbite. Hypothermia refers to a lowering of the body's temperature. As reported above, this can result in both physiological and psychological consequences. Individuals who have hypothermia need to be rapidly rewarmed. A warm bath, blankets, or the body heat of other individuals are some of the commonly used methods of rewarming. A time runners are most vulnerable to hypothermia is when they have stopped running because of factors such as exhaustion or injury.

Frostbite is the destruction of body tissue through freezing. It is exceptionally painful in the initial stages. Although exposed areas, such as the face, are the most likely to be frostbitten, covered areas are also susceptible. Often because of the exercise and the cold there is a reduced blood flow to the fingers, thus making them more susceptible to frostbite. Perhaps the most famous article on frostbite in a runner dealt with penile frostbite (Hershkowitz, 1977). Thus, both covered and uncovered areas have the potential of becoming frostbitten. Frostbite demands immediate attention. Rewarming the affected part in water about 108°F is a recommended treatment. The water should not be hotter than 108°F and the part should not be warmed and then rubbed with snow or ice, as was commonly believed in the past. Because the blood supply to the frostbitten area has often been permanently affected, the danger of gangrene or a lowered threshold for subsequent injury exists.

Frostbite can occur for unusual reasons. For example, a recent letter to *The Physician and Sportsmedicine* reported a case of frostbite caused by the use of metallic portable radio headphones (Nequin, 1985).

Two other cold-related injuries need to be briefly mentioned. The first are injuries caused by falling on snow or ice and injuries caused by running in snow covered areas where obstacles such as potholes are hidden, thus increasing the probability of an injury. The second concerns exercise-induced asthma. It has been found that cold weather may induce asthma in some individuals. In many cases the symptoms can be controlled with medication and the running can continue (see Burton, 1981).

Cold-related injuries are generally easily preventable. Runners should dress warmly and not run in dangerous circumstances, such as extremely cold temperatures or a cold temperature coupled with a strong wind. Runners should be careful about running too far away from shelter. A novice runner might run into a remote area, become exhausted, and have to walk. With the body not producing as much heat, the danger of hypothermia is present. The same rule applies to an experienced runner; an injury far from shelter may produce the same consequences. There are a number of books that have published charts and graphs that indicate "safe" running temperatures.

It is recommended that runners layer their clothing so that initially their clothing will keep them warm and then as they generate body heat and start sweating they can either take off or open up some of the layers to regulate body temperature. A runner who becomes sweat soaked, for example, will lose body heat 200 times faster than a runner who remains dry. Generally, clothing should not be discarded but tied around one's waist or kept in a back pack or other carrying device. The runner may feel warm initially, but as he or she tires and slows down, or if the temperature drops or the wind increases, the need for replacing the clothing for warmth may arise. To conserve body heat it is also recommended that runners wear mittens rather than gloves and that they wear a hat since the head gives off 40 percent of the heat of the body (see Weltman and Stamford, 1982).

Pollution. A major concern of many runners in urban areas is pollution. Although running is supposed to be a "healthful" activity, many find they are forced to run in areas heavily polluted with automobile exhaust and industrial fumes. People worry that by running they may be inhaling extensive amounts of poisons into their bodies. Exposure to carbon monoxide for instance will increase the risk of cardiovascular disease, emphysema, lung cancer, and chronic bronchitis (see Nicholson and Case, 1983; Hage, 1982).

Although this is an important concern, there has been very little research on the subject. In fact, it was not until the mid-1970s that research started to appear on the impact of pollution on athletes.

Studies indicate that runners are at a greater risk of being exposed to pollution than many other individuals. For example, runners are generally outdoors and have a faster and deeper respiration rate while running. This allows the pollutants to penetrate deeper into their lung tissues. The problem is exacerbated in that while running most runners switch from nasal to oral breathing, thus eliminating the filtering component of the nose (Hage, 1982).

Two recent studies have examined carbon monoxide levels in runners in urban environments. In the first study, with carbon monoxide levels greater than 7 parts per million, the breath of the runners showed an increase in carbon monoxide accumulation. The authors concluded, however, that running in low levels of carbon monoxide, 6.5 parts per million or less, at a submaximal level was safe (Honigman et al., 1982).

The second study found a threefold increase in carbon monoxide levels in runners who ran along a busy highway for 30 minutes. The researchers concluded that those who run in polluted urban areas are subject to carbon monoxide levels equivalent to one-half to one pack of cigarettes (Nicholson and Case, 1983; see Rogers, 1984a, Marwick, 1984).

Indoor pollution is becoming an increasing source of concern. The new indoor track surfaces are often composed of synthetic materials that emit vapors, either during the time it takes the surface to "cure" or continually, that can produce distress in athletes engaged in aerobic activity. One report on a facility under construction reported that athletes were coughing, wheezing, and short of breath due to toxic vapors given off by the track surface. The vapors were within federal standards, but high enough to cause distressing symptoms in the athletes. The author of the report noted that existing federal standards are inadequate for those performing aerobic activity (Larson, 1985).

Automobiles. Almost all runners have stories to tell about encounters with automobiles. The increase in the number of runners has led to a large number of runner deaths from "pedestrian accidents." In 1977 an issue of the *American Heart Journal* noted that during a past year 8,000 joggers were killed and over 100,000 injured by automobiles (Williams, 1983a). Although these figures were an exaggeration and represented *all* pedestrian deaths and injuries due to automobiles in 1977, joggers included, this is a growing problem.

One recent study looked at how many runners were killed during a given year by automobiles. The researchers used a newspaper clipping service to obtain data. They found 60 jogger-vehicle accidents in which 65 joggers were injured or killed. Of the 65 joggers, 30 were killed, the remaining 35 injured, 19 of them critically or seriously. Males represented 66 percent of those injured, and 50 percent of those injured were in the age category of 10 to 24. In 27 percent of the accidents the drivers were at fault. In 31 percent of the accidents both joggers and drivers were negligent, and in another 31 percent joggers were primarily responsible. In the remaining cases the responsibility could not be determined. In 53 percent of the accidents the runners were running with the traffic and either hit from behind or by a car crossing the center line. In 24 percent of the cases the runners were running against the traffic and again either hit by a vehicle crossing the center line or from a vehicle going against them. Thirteen percent of the accidents involved runners crossing intersections. The remainder occurred under other circumstances.

After studying the jogger-vehicle accidents the author made several recommendations for runners, most of which, plus others, are summarized below (see Williams, 1981a; 1981b):

1. Run where vehicles cannot go, or at least on roads with light traffic.

2. Do not run in the dark (either morning or night) where there are vehicles, or at least wear reflective devices.

3. Run against traffic (there are exceptions, such as a "blind curve").

4. Run on the road shoulder and not the road, and in single file.

5. Obey traffiic rules.

6. Stay alert to the drunk, the careless, the show-off, the malicious driver.

7. Be careful about running toward a rising or setting sun; driver visibility is often impaired.

8. Do not run in the rain where there are vehicles.

9. Pay attention in the winter when roads have been narrowed.

10. Do not use ear phones.

Crime. Besides having to run in a polluted environment infested with reckless, drunk drivers, runners must also contend with criminals. Although no firm figures are available, certainly the number of muggings and rapes of runners is substantial.

An "indication" of this can be seen in the response *Runner's World* magazine received to a request in the June, 1982, issue for runners to write to the magazine and relate their stories of harassment. According to the author who wrote the story on runner harassment, "letters poured in," with two-thirds of them from women. There were numerous stories about harassment that included both verbal and physical assaults. To lessen the probability of harassment or assault, the following guidelines are recommended (see Pietschmann, 1983; Rogers, 1984b; Merhar, 1984).

1. Run defensively. Plan a safe route. Avoid areas where a mugger or rapist could hide. Also, frequently survey the area to note potential risks. Mentally rehearse what to do if confronted with danger. Make the last part of your run, when you are tired, the safest. Be alert; look for and respond to suspicious behavior. Too often victims do not follow their "instincts" out of fear of being embarrassed.

2. Do not ignore or challenge automobiles — be aware of those that pose a threat and do not engage in any behavior that may provoke a driver.

3. Do not drift away mentally. Although the "runner's high" seems to have become a desired state, it may allow the runner to ignore danger. Listening to music or deep mental problem solving can have the same result.

4. Do not provoke others. Runners should ignore provocations such as verbal taunts or cat calls. Try to be invisible. Women runners should dress in a manner that will not attract attention.

5. Women should run in a group. It appears, so far, that more harassment is directed at women than men.

6. The potential for harassment, accidents, and assaults increases when it is dark; run only in well-lighted areas, and with running partners.

7. Carry identification when running. Hospitals need to know who you are.

8. Be prepared for harassment. Carry change so a telephone call can be made. Some even controversially suggest carrying tear gas or a weapon.

9. Do not let physical fitness be the basis for your security; it might permit potential dangerous signs to be ignored.

10. Always tell someone where you are going and when you will be back.

11. Do not provoke muggers by wearing anything they might want, such as jewelry.

One crime being reported more frequently is rape. About 27 percent of all the rape victims in the Golden Gate Park in San Francisco were joggers (Dunnett, 1981). There is, currently, a controversy over how women should react in rape situations. Some advocate that women fight back while others suggest a less aggressive reaction. The course of action will have to be decided upon by each woman. The best advice is, of course, not to become involved in a situation where rape can occur. This means to anticipate the potential danger of each situation and *not* assuming the attitude, "It can't happen to me."

Specific Injuries

While most runners are familiar with the common running injuries, such as shin splints, there are a number of other injuries about which less is known. This section will present information on some of them.

Urinary System

In describing the aftereffects of his record-shattering marathon in 1969 Derek Clayton noted that shortly after the race, he "was urinating quite large clots of blood...." While Clayton noted that it was "normal" for athletes to have blood in their urine, what he passed "in the next 48 hours was something unbelievable" (Clayton, 1979).

What Clayton experienced in establishing a world's record, that would last more than a decade, was far more dramatic than what most runners will ever experience. However, exercise-related hematuria (blood, or substance, in the urine) was first noted in the early 1900s (see Riess, 1979; Fassett, 1984) and has since been reported both in contact sports, such as football, hockey, boxing, rugby, and lacrosse, and in noncontact sports, such as baseball, cross-country, crew, and track (Alyeu and Parish, 1958; Fred and Natelson, 1977; Gardner, 1956). It has also been reported in military recruits undergoing basic military training (Schrier et al., 1970).

An article in the *Journal of the American Medical Association* in 1979 described exercise-related hematuria as a benign condition. The article was based on a study of 50 physicians who ran in the 1978 Boston Marathon. Of the 50 runners, all of whom had normal urine samples before the race, nine, or 18 percent, had blood in their urine after the race. In all of the affected runners the condition cleared by itself in two days. The authors of the article concluded that exercise-related hematuria is a "frequent, self-limited, and benign condition." Their report was written to alert physicians to the condition so that extensive testing to determine the origins of the blood would be reserved for cases in which the condition persisted beyond 48 hours (Siegel et al., 1979).

Not all physicians have agreed with the position that bloody urine can be ignored, even if the condition does not persist, and have recommended a more "traditional approach" which would include assuming a diseased condition until tests proved otherwise (see Anonymous, 1979b; Boileau et al., 1980; Whisnant, 1979; see Siegel, 1979; Kincaid-Smith, 1982; Votapka and Weigel, 1985).

Those adhering to the "traditional approach" do so because they believe that runners will assume that bloody urine is "normal" and thus not seek prompt medical attention and treatment for what may be a pathological condition that requires immediate medical intervention. Because of this, many physicians believe that bloody urine *is* a condition that requires prompt medical consideration. For those interested, Hoover and Cromie (1981) have described the medical examination and tests that should be made to distinguish between exercise-related hematuria, which does not need to be treated, and hematuria caused by other pathological conditions, which requires prompt medical intervention.

Although frequently reported in men, hematuria was not reported in women until recently (see Boileau et al., 1980; Fred, 1978). In a study of 383 runners who had just completed a marathon, hematuria was found in 22 percent of the women and 20 percent of the men (Boileau et al., 1980).

Exercise-related hematuria has not yet been reported in children (Hoover and Cromie, 1981).

Blood in the urine is "generally" not a normal condition. It can indicate a variety of diseases that cause bleeding in the urethra, bladder, ureters, or the kidneys. The list of diseases or conditions that can cause hematuria is quite extensive and includes infections, kidney stones, tumors, or cysts. The presence or absence of symptoms other than blood in the urine helps a physician determine the source of the condition. For example, kidney stones cause considerable pain, and infections often cause a burning sensation during urination.

What causes exercise-related hematuria? What can be done to prevent it? Does it cause any permanent damage? Although there is not one generally accepted theory as to the cause of exercise-related hematuria, there are several theories that have credibility. The first is the bladder trauma theory. There are two types of bladder trauma. The first is caused by an external source, such as the body contact found in football or hockey. The second is caused by internal structures such as the prostate gland in men. Since this is a book on running and there are no plausible external sources causing the hematuria, we will only examine the internal source.

Many researchers believe that exercise-related hematuria is caused by the bladder being traumatized by being bounced up and down on the bladder base or the prostate gland. Although each separate impact is not damaging, the cumulative effects of running produce minor trauma. Blacklock (1979; 1980) has reported bladder lesions in nine out of 17 long-distance runners with a history of hematuria. These lesions disappeared within a week (see Gilli et al., 1984).

Although the bladder trauma theory may account for some cases of hematuria, it is a limited theory since it does not explain why not all male runners experience hematuria or why male runners who experience it do not experience it every time they run. Additionally, if the bouncing of the bladder on the prostate is the source of the problem, this theory does not explain why women have exercise-related hematuria.

Because of the limitations of the above theories several other explanations have been set forth. They have dealt with diet, dehydration, distance, and age. Although some of these are promising for explaining some cases of hematuria, they have limitations in explaining all cases.

One theory has received support because it explains hematuria for both men and women: If the bladder is empty, it collapses and the walls rub against one another during exercise, causing minor irritation and bleeding.

Another widely-accepted theory of the cause of exercise-related hematuria deals with the impact of exercise on the blood flow to the kidneys. Essentially this theory notes that during exercise the blood flow to the kidneys is reduced by as much as 75 percent. This brings about a change in the vascular resistance in the kidneys which causes reversible damage to some of the minor blood vessels in the kidneys. The damage causes a small amount of bleeding.

The second question deals with ways to prevent the disorder. Although not universally accepted, some researchers who adhere to the bladder trauma theory, have suggested that runners should not run on an empty bladder. They believe that urine can act as a buffer and prevent bladder trauma. One writer has recommended drinking a liter of beer prior to running (Bassler, 1979a). However, others have suggested running on an empty bladder, claiming that the weight of the urine simply intensifies the pounding of the bladder on the bladder base. Evidence does not exist to support either position.

Does exercise-related hematuria cause permanent damage? Most of the studies have indicated that runners who have it do not have an increased incidence of kidney disease or failure (see Hoover and Cromie, 1981).

However, one recent study has suggested that male marathon runners may have a significantly higher incidence of kidney stones than normal. A study of male marathon runners in the 1977 New York City Marathon found that the participants had an incidence of kidney stones 4.5 times higher than what would be expected. Other diseases and conditions were well within or below normal limits. For example, high blood pressure and ulcer rates were found to be within normal limits, and diabetes mellitus and coronary heart disease rates were found to be far below normal levels. When asked about bloody, cloudy, smoky, or brown urine, 8 percent of the runners surveyed noted this condition after a workout, and 7 percent after a race. For those with kidney stones, 37 percent noted hematuria after a workout and 35 percent after a race. The authors speculated that the increase in kidney stone formation is caused by the temporary dehydration that occurs with running. They noted that several studies have reported a correlation between kidney stone formation and dehydration. The authors concluded that although the risks are small (19 men with kidney stones out of 1,893 surveyed) there is a real hazard associated with long-distance running, and that this demonstrates the importance of maintaining "a high fluid intake during long-distance running" (Milvy et al., 1978).

A more serious condition involving the urinary system is kidney failure. A recent study reported on ten cases of kidney failure in participants in the Comrades Marathon in South Africa (54 miles) over the last nine years. Almost all of the runners showed low fluid intake, vomiting and or diarrhea. Also, several of the men reported passing bloody urine at some point in the race. Four of them required dialysis. There appears to have been one case of chronic or permanent kidney damage (MacSearraigh et al., 1979).

Acute kidney failure also developed in a 32-year-old man who ran in the New York City Marathon in 1980. Upon examination after the marathon the man was found to have very abnormal biochemical findings. He required dialysis for two days. His urinalysis was abnormal for 22 days (Stewart and Posen, 1980).

Another condition described in the medical literature is "jogger's testicles" (Adno, 1984). The symptoms resemble prostatitis. The condition is apparently caused by unsupported testicles pulling on the "perineal floor and its structures" during running. A tight athletic supporter appears to resolve the condition.

Digestive System

The gastrointestinal track is a major source of concern for most runners, especially competitive runners. The concern is legitimate since running can speed up the evacuation of the bowels. Stories abound about runners having diarrhea during a race and simply having to "run through" the
episode, or of runners suddenly jumping behind trees or into ditches. A recent issue of a popular running magazine showed an elite marathon runner
suddenly bolting down an alley during a race, much to the amazement of
the other competitors.

Although runners have many "public rituals" before races there are
probably just as many "private rituals," many concerning their bowels.
Most of the rituals concern emptying the bowels, first to prevent embarrassment, second because bathrooms are hard to find at races, and third to get
rid of the extra weight. To prevent bowel problems many runners fast before
races, consuming only liquids. This may lead to carbohydrate depletion.
Others resort to enemas or laxatives, which only results in a loss of water and
an increased risk of dehydration.

According to an article in the *Journal of the American Medical Association*, "There is little doubt that running causes GI [gastrointestinal] disturbances." The article described the symptoms of two runners, abdominal
cramps and diarrhea. The runners noted that the symptoms increased after
an unusually vigorous exercise session, such as a race, or after a significant
increase in mileage. The symptoms generally decreased with conditioning
(Fogoros, 1980; see Sullivan et al., 1984).

A study of 707 participants in a marathon in Oregon reported some of
the following GI symptoms (Keeffe et al., 1984): the lower GI tract is
affected more than the upper; 37 percent had an urge to defecate during or
shortly after running; GI symptoms were reported more frequently by
women; the greater the running intensity, the more likely the runners were
to report diarrhea; young runners experienced GI symptoms more than
older runners; cramps, heartburn, nausea, and vomiting all increased in frequency with runs of greater intensity.

Although runners, and the physicians treating them, may assume that
GI disturbances are caused exclusively by running, there is some evidence
that food allergies may, in some cases, be the primary causal factor. Occasionally allergies by themselves may not cause significant GI distress in some
individuals, but when coupled with running will produce gastrointestinal
disturbances such as bloody diarrhea. The elimination of the foods to which
the runner is allergic will eliminate the gastrointestinal disturbances and
allow a resumption of running, at a more comfortable level. Although this
article alerted physicians to the catalytic effect of running on food allergies,
it also warned them that although the treatment of food allergies appears
simple and the results often dramatic, physicians must make certain of their
diagnosis. That is, treatment for food allergies may reduce the symptoms
but if the cause is not allergies, some other pathological condition is not being treated (Noakes, 1982b).

Exercise-induced hematuria is a well recognized consequence of running. Three studies have now also found that some runners bleed into the gut. The first study examined the stools of runners for blood, and found it in 8 percent of the samples. The researcher noted a number of factors that might cause the bleeding: hemorrhoids, ischemia of the gut, or damage to the intra-abdominal organs through repeated bouncing. The researcher said that while both the source and cause of the "oozing" of blood into the gut were a mystery, it may be a cause of runner anemia (Porter, 1983).

The second study on members of the American Medical Joggers Association who participated in the 1983 Boston Marathon found similar but slightly more dramatic results; 22 percent of the runners had gastrointestinal blood loss. The researchers found that younger runners and faster runners had the greatest amount of blood loss (McMahon et al., 1984; see Macrae et al., 1984; McMahon and Fisher, 1984).

The third study found that 87 percent of the runners surveyed had gastrointestinal blood loss. This study tried to make certain that the blood was not from factors such as aspirin use, bleeding gums, or other obvious sources. The researchers concluded that other factors were unlikely to be causing the blood loss and that running was the cause (Stewart et al., 1984).

The authors of the above article also speculated that this bleeding may cause "runner's anemia." They found that after racing many runners lost 3 ml of blood, with one runner who ran two long races in two days losing 43 ml of blood per day! In comparison, a woman's total blood loss in one menstrual cycle is 31 ml of blood (Solomon and Davis, 1983). The authors concluded that long-distance racing causes gastrointestinal bleeding, which may result in anemia (Stewart et al., 1984).

In an editorial response to the articles by McMahon and his colleagues and Steward and his colleagues, Buckman (1984) made the observation that it has not yet been investigated whether blood loss occurs during routine running, or only racing, and that the "pathophysiology of gastrointestinal bleeding during physical exertion" is unknown. Dr. Buckman continued by saying that when anemia or "clinically evident bleeding" is present, an examination for "GI abnormalities was warranted."

Although most articles have suggested that GI bleeding is not a severe problem, one recent article reported three "severe"cases of upper GI bleeding in runners, requiring blood transfusions in two cases (Papioannides et al., 1984).

Blood

Running, especially distance running, has the ability to bring about changes in what are considered normal blood chemistries.

The most frequently diagnosed blood disorder in runners is anemia (see Williamson, 1981; Colt and Heyman, 1984; Clark, 1985). Anemia is a deficiency of hemoglobin, a major portion of red blood cells. The major purpose of hemoglobin is to combine with oxygen in the lung and transport the oxygen to the body tissues. Iron is both a significant component of hemoglobin and essential for its production. In an anemic individual, because of a low hemoglobin count, there is not enough oxygen to meet the needs of the body; thus the individual feels tired and lethargic.

Anemia is not a disease but is the result of a disease or disorder. Anemia can be caused by factors such as loss of blood, an abnormally high destruction of red blood cells, a diet deficient in certain vitamins and minerals, iron absorption problems, or a decrease in red blood cell production (see Dorsen, 1985).

Although anemia is a serious condition, the cause of which may require prompt medical attention, it is now believed that there is a condition called "sports anemia," or "pseudoanemia," which if diagnosed does not need to be treated (see Dressendorfer et al., 1981; Williamson, 1981).

There are three explanations for sports anemia. First, researchers believe that it happens in runners because they have a larger total blood volume than nonrunners but their hemoglobin count remains unchanged, thus giving the impression of anemia. Another explanation is that through repeated foot contact many red blood cells are destroyed and thus the runner is more likely to have borderline anemia (see Eichner, 1985). A third explanation is that the body produces a borderline anemic state since it is the most desirable state for the rapid transportation of oxygen. Although common sense would suggest that the higher the hemoglobin count the greater the oxygen transportation ability, this is not true since the higher the hemoglobin count the thicker, and thus more difficult to pump, the blood becomes. Thus, the blood is kept in a state that allows for rapid transportation (see Bunch, 1980).

Although "sports anemia" may not require treatment, anemia is a serious disorder, that may be caused by life-threatening diseases or disorders that require prompt medical attention. Williamson (1981) has outlined the medical tests that should be performed to distinguish anemia from sports anemia.

Runners may be susceptible to anemia because of the bleeding mentioned previously, sweating, and diet. Many runners have restricted diets, which may cause an inadequate intake in iron, protein, or vitamin B_{12}, all of which are essential for red blood cell production and growth (see Jacobs and Wilson, 1984). A high fiber diet also decreases iron absorption by the GI tract (Colt and Heyman, 1984).

In addition to sports anemia, one recent medical report has appeared on aplastic anemia. Aplastic anemia is a very serious disease in which the bone marrow, which produces most of the blood, is affected. Individuals affected by the disease have, among other symptoms, frequent bleeding from both the mouth and nose and they bruise easily. The recent study on the runner with aplastic anemia reported that the anemia was caused by a practice of the runner. Before running he applied rubber cement over his blisters and then covered the blisters with tape. Rubber cement contains the chemical benzene which has been linked with aplastic anemia (Roodman et al., 1980). For further information see the section on injuries in Chapter Two.

Two recent studies have suggested that "sports anemia" is not caused by a deficiency in total body iron. Based on their research, and the many ways of measuring iron levels, the researchers concluded that there is no rational basis for iron supplementation in normal athletes (Magnusson 1984a; 1984b). It has also been suggested that in endurance athletes, the lower hemoglobin level is normal; the higher level in nonathletes is abnormal. For the time being, pending further studies, the average iron level of nonathletes is considered the norm (Arends, 1984).

Vision

Reports of damage to the eyes of athletes, especially in racket sports, has grown significantly in recent years. As would be expected, there have also been anecdotal articles concerning the impact of running on the eyes.

Several articles have suggested that running will literally jar the body apart. One of the alleged consequences of running was retinal detachment.

A study by the United States Retina Society membership found that this belief was unfounded. The study noted that on a yearly basis about one individual in 10,000 has a retinal detachment. This rate increases to four in 10,000 for those involved in traumatic sports such as boxing. The physicians who responded noted that collectively they had seen an average of 13,500 retinal detachments per year. Over the last five years of the 67,000 cases examined only 11 cases were attributed to running, or a rate of 1.6 per 10,000. Although this is a rate that is slightly higher than the national average, it is not statistically significant. The authors noted that individuals who have surgery for retinal detachment can often return to running after a relatively short period of recovery (Worthen, 1980).

Bone

As mentioned previously, running places tremendous stress on the body, especially on the load or weight-bearing structures such as the bones. With the increasing number of runners, and their increasingly intensive training schedules, the medical journals have been reporting injuries to bones more frequently.

A commonly reported injury has been stress fractures (see Fitch 1984), or cracks in bones. They are different from "complete fractures" where a bone has been completely separated into at least two parts. Stress fractures are extremely painful and will grow worse if training is not stopped to allow the bone time to heal (see Dugan and D'Ambrosia, 1983).

The cause of stress fractures is not completely clear. Some claim that they occur because of the stress of the foot-strike, while others believe that they are caused by the powerful action of muscles repeatedly pulling on the bones. Most agree that stress fractures are caused in large part by bones being subjected to more stress, either through muscular action or foot-strike, than they can accommodate. This can be clearly seen in the "classic pattern" leading to stress fractures: a new activity such as running, a significant increase in mileage, a change in running surface from soft to hard, new shoes which do not provide the appropriate amount of protection or which have not been broken in, old shoes which have lost their protection, an abnormal running style, or a return to running after a recent period of inactivity.

Basically, bones need time to adjust to the stress to which they are being subjected. It is known that when subjected to stress the skeleton can hypertrophy, or increase its strength in the stressed areas. Studies on ballet dancers, for example, have found that there is substantial hypertrophy in their big toes, a highly stressed area. A study of 20 male runners in a nine month marathon training program reported that the consistent runners had a significant increase in bone mineral content (Williams et al., 1984). Additionally, in individuals with osteoarthritis it has been found that if one side of a knee disintegrates the weight-bearing side that remains will hypertrophy. The same phenomenon occurs in runners. That is, the skeleton will hypertrophy in stressed areas. This is called remodeling. Essentially, the skeleton has the ability, within limits, to remodel itself to meet the stresses to which it is subjected (see Williams et al., 1984).

However, since cardiovascular fitness increases at a faster rate than bone remodeling, runners attain a cardiovascular fitness level that will allow them to run further or harder than their bones are capable of handling without a high probability of injury.

As noted above, stress fractures are very painful, and running simply increases the pain. Additionally, diagnosing a stress fracture can be very difficult, and several articles have noted that new stress fractures are especially difficult to diagnose using existing technology (see Daffner et al., 1982; Norfray et al., 1980; Norfray, 1980), although thermography and ultrasound-induced pain appear to be inexpensive, easy-to-perform tests that can detect stress fractures in the tibia and fibula with a high degree of success (Devereaux et al., 1984).

Stress fractures from running have been noted in the foot, the lower and upper leg bones, the pelvis and the back. The incidence of stress fractures generally decreases from the foot up. The metatarsals are seven times more likely to have a stress fracture than the bones in the lower leg, especially the tibia. The tibia is six times more likely to have a stress fracture than the femur (generally the femur neck) (Blatz 1981; also see Prescott, 1983; Abel, 1985; Julsrud, 1985; Spector et al., 1983).

Pelvic stress fractures have also been reported, especially in women (Prescott, 1983; Noakes, Smith et al., 1985). It is believed that the pelvic anatomy of women causes a foot-strike that transmits more stress to the pelvis.

Although stress fractures are increasing in frequency, with proper medical treatment, supervision, and rest they generally heal in four to six weeks, although some of the larger bones, such as the pelvis or femur, might need a longer period of time (see Pavlov et al., 1982).

Will running increase the likelihood of osteoarthritis? As noted in the section on joints in Chapter 4, "Running After 40," running does not appear to increase the incidence of osteoarthritis. However, injured areas, whether as a result of running or from other injuries, are more likely to develop osteoarthritis.

Recent studies have added support to this belief. The study involved 20 runners who sought medical treatment because of knee pain. Thirty percent (six of the 20) were found to have a "high incidence of degenerative changes" in their knees. The authors pointed out, however, that the majority (four out of six) with degenerative changes had been injured previously in the knee (most of the injuries were not running-related). Additionally, all of the runners with degenerative changes were bowlegged, which is a recognized causal factor of osteoarthritis (McDermott and Freyne, 1983).

Another study compared cross-country runners and swimmers from seven major Eastern colleges. The athletes had been at the colleges between 1930 and 1960. This study reported that the swimmers had a higher incidence of severe hip or knee pain: 2.4 to 2 percent. Additionally, to relieve the pain, 2.1 percent of the swimmers and .8 percent of the runners underwent surgery. The authors concluded that running at "moderate levels (25 miles per week) does not contribute to the development of osteoarthritis. They also said that the evidence "suggests" that there is no association between osteoarthritis and the number of years of running "heavy mileage" (Sohn and Micheli, 1985).

Two additional studies also support this conclusion. The first reported that running was associated with increased levels of bone mineral content, and also, that running does not predispose runners to osteoarthritis (Lane et al., 1986). The second concluded that for runners there is not an increased incidence of osteoarthritis, and that even high mileage running of long duration is not associated with "premature degenerative joint disease in the lower extremities" (Panush et al., 1986).

Back Problems

Back problems are a source of pain, discomfort, and incapacitation for many Americans. Although there have been numerous articles on running injuries, very few have mentioned back injuries (see Clark and Stanish, 1985). In Table I in this chapter, which reviewed eight studies on running injuries, only one study mentioned backs. This may be due to the fact that running does not produce a high incidence of back injuries or the fact that most of the studies were designed to ascertain injuries from only the foot to the hip.

One recent study noted the case histories of ten runners with herniated lumbar disks (Guten, 1981). The author stressed that the major cause of this injury was runners, not running! That is, runners brought on their injuries by "faulty approaches to training." The men in this study were treated with traction, steroid injections, and surgery. After treatment, only one of the men could not return to active athletic activity.

Another study on a runner who had developed a "very painful" back pain found that the pain was completely alleviated when a discrepancy in leg lengths was corrected (Blake and Fettig, 1983).

Another recent article in an Austrialian medical journal indicated that back surgery can be successful with runners and that the runner may return to running after surgery. The study reported on a runner who was forced to stop running because of a back injury. The study noted that the man had part of his spine immobilized with screws and cement and had since run 15,000 kilometers problem free (Graham, 1982).

Skin

Most runners are aware of the importance of the skin. It protects the delicate internal environment of the body.

Because the skin is the outermost barrier to the environment it is also the first to come into contact with objects and thus the most likely to be injured. Although no reliable figures exist on the percentage of runners who suffer from such problems, skin disorders and their management has been reported recently in *The Physician and Sportsmedicine*. Without listing all of the disorders, suffice it to say that runners suffer from fungal infections (e.g., athlete's foot), yeast infections, virus infections (e.g., herpes, warts), bacterial infections (e.g., boils), mites (e.g., scabies), friction disorders, abrasions from falling, or allergic reactions (see Stauffer, 1983). It is not known if runners suffer from a higher incidence of skin problems than nonrunners or athletes in other sports.

The most well known skin disorder is probably "jogger's nipples" (Levit, 1977). This is basically a friction disorder caused by the nipples rubbing against a shirt. The mesh nylon shirts of runners have increased the problem for some individuals. Band aids over the nipples, or petroleum jelly have been recommended to reduce the contact and friction.

Death: The Ultimate Injury

Most running injuries are temporary. Even permanent injuries are seldom incapacitating or life threatening. However, there is another type of "injury" that needs to be examined: death. There is a growing concern that running may precipitate this "ultimate" injury. The recent deaths of Jim Fixx, well-known author of two best-selling books on running, and of runners in New York City and Honolulu marathons, have created concern that runners may be at an increased risk of death, especially while running.

This appears to be a contradiction with what was presented in the chapter on the heart. There it was noted that running will reduce selected CHD risk factors. A natural conclusion, even though the evidence presented in the chapter on longevity did not support it, is that running will extend life expectancy. Few in contemporary society would expect the reverse. Three recent studies have addressed this contradiction.

The first study was by Koplan (1979). Koplan recognized that runners who die while running generally receive a disproportionate amount of publicity, and that running is often presumed to have precipitated the death. He realized, however, that individuals can be expected to die while engaged in a variety of activities, and that a certain number of individuals can be expected, by chance alone, to die while running. He estimated the number of runners who could be expected to die from cardiovascular disease by chance while running. Koplan's study was a statistical probability study that estimated the total number of runners, their cardiovascular risk factors, and the amount of time they spent running weekly. From mortality tables he computed the number that could be expected to die by chance while running. The resulting figures, based on four million runners, was from four to 104 per year. The lower figure was based on only the estimated time spent running being considered; the higher figure extended the time to a two hour post-exercise period.

In the second study, Thompson and his associates (1982) reported on 12 runners who died while running in Rhode Island between 1975 and 1980. The study concluded that the death rate during running was seven times higher than during sedentary activity. This seemed to support the belief that running precipitates coronary events. Additionally, based on the state's population and the estimated number of runners, the results indicated that the actual number of dead runners was seventeen times Koplan's estimate.

The third study was by Siscovick and his associates (1984). They completed a community-based study on men without known heart disease who experienced an out-of-hospital primary cardiac arrest as a result of suspected heart disease. They found that a disproportionate number of individuals had the cardiac event occur during exercise. However, the study also reported that overall those who exercised had only 40 percent the risk of having a primary cardiac arrest as sedentary individuals.

The Siscovick study appears to have resolved the apparent contradictions noted above by reporting that although those who exercised had a higher than normal rate of cardiac events while exercising, that overall their risk of a cardiac arrest was significantly lower than for nonexercisers. The debate is far from over, however, since the authors of the Siscovick study and others (Thompson and Mitchell, 1984) have pointed out the methodological limitations of this study.

While the debate continues, it would be beneficial to examine some of the characteristics of individuals who have died suddenly, from non-traumatic causes, during or shortly after running. Although many articles have been published on runners who died, the reports are scattered among a number of medical journals and over several years. Additionally, many described a unique individual. The review of all the articles which follows will allow for a comprehensive examination of the major causes of death as well as the common characteristics that might allow for the early identification of potential victims; a profile of high risk individuals could assist in preventing some deaths. This following review can also assist researchers in recognizing that both more, and more complete, information is needed on sudden death during running.

Collecting Research on Dead Runners

A computer search of *Index Medicus* was performed, covering the years 1975 through 1984. Articles listing individual characteristics of runners who suddenly died from nontraumatic causes during or shortly after running were obtained (Thompson et al., 1982; Bassler, 1984a; 1984b; Hilb, 1984; Ludmerer and Kissane 1984; Noakes and Rose 1984; Noakes et al., 1984; Parsons et al., 1984; Hanzlick and Stivers, 1983; Jackson et al., 1983; Whitworth and Wolfman, 1983; Ledingham et al., 1982: Virmani et al., 1982; Waller et al., 1981; Colt, 1980; Lynch, 1980; Waller and Roberts, 1980; Woodhouse et al., 1980; Noakes, Opie, Rose, and Kleynhans, 1979; Noakes, Rose, and Opie, 1979; Cantwell and Fletcher, 1978; Noakes et al., 1977; Opie, 1975a; 1975b). Because several authors wrote more than one article on the same dead runner(s), care was taken to exclude duplicate reports. Articles on dead runners that did not list individual characteristics, but rather provided a collective summary of characteristics, were not included (Thompson et al., 1979; Sugishita et al., 1983; Maron et al., 1980). An article on a runner who did not die suddenly during or shortly after running was not included (Green et al., 1976).

When available, the following information was recorded for each runner: age, sex, number of years of running, number of miles jogged per week before death, family history of coronary heart disease, cholesterol level, smoking status, blood pressure, participation in marathons, whether an autopsy was performed, extent of atherosclerosis, previous myocardial infarctions (diagnosed or not diagnosed), symptoms of CHD before death, cause of death, and whether death occurred while racing.*

The cause of death provided by the original author was used. High blood pressure (HBP) and elevated cholesterol were determined by Public Health Service standards. HBP was recorded if a reading before death showed systolic 160+ or diastolic 95+. Elevated cholesterol was recorded if a predeath reading was 260+ mg/100 ml (National Center for Health Statistics, 1984). The term coronary heart disease (CHD) is used for myocardial ischemia, coronary atherosclerosis, myocardial infarction, and coronary thrombosis. Rhythm disturbances are arrhythmia, dysrhythmia, and cardiac arrest.

Table II
Age and Cause of Death

Age	CHD	Rhythm	Unknown	Congenital	Other	Total	% of Total
1–19	1	0	3	1	1	6	7.2%
20–29	4	2	4	1	2	13	15.7%
30–39	12	2	2	0	0	16	19.3%
40–49	26	5	0	1	0	32	38.6%
50–59	12	1	0	0	0	13	15.7%
60–69	0	1	0	1	0	2	2.4%
70+	0	0	0	0	0	0	0
?	1	0	0	0	0	1	1.2%
Total	56	11	9	4	3	83	100%
% Total	67.5	13.3	10.8	4.8	3.6	100%	

Table II examines age and cause of death for 83 dead runners. Sex is not included since all the deceased were men. CHD was the cause of death for 56 of them (67.5 percent); rhythm disturbances accounted for 11 deaths (13.3 percent); nine (10.8 percent) died for unknown reasons; congenital factors accounted for four deaths (4.8 percent); three people (3.6 percent) died from "other" causes.

Table III presents information on selected conditions and characteristics of the dead runners by cause of death. This table is separated into three main categories by major causes of death: CHD variables, CHD risk variables, jogging history.

Several observations will be made from the available data about those who died from CHD, rhythm disturbances, unknown conditions, congenital disorders, and "other" causes. First, however, it is necessary to discuss the several limitations of this review.

The first concerns the cause of death. As mentioned, the cause of death provided by the original author(s) was used for this review; however, the cause of death in some articles was questioned in "letters to the editor" sections, with alternative causes of death generally offered. The cause provided in the original article was not changed because this was a "review" article, because the original author was in a better position to determine cause of death, and because cause of death has been and will continue to be a source of controversy in the medical profession; changing the cause would not necessarily make this review more accurate or resolve the controversy.

Determining the cause of death in several of the runners was difficult because of coexisting conditions. For example, several of them had CHD coupled with hypertrophic cardiomyopathy. Determining which caused the death may have been influenced by the perspective of the writer. Other coexisting conditions for those classified as dying from CHD or rhythm disturbances were heat stroke, nutritional deficiencies, and drug medication errors.

Table III

Selected Characteristics and Conditions of Those Dying from CHD, Rhythm Disturbances, and Unknown Causes

	CHD	Rhythm	Unknown
CHD Variables			
Severe Atherosclerosis	97.8%	27.3%	0
Warning Symptoms of CHD	52.4%	-	-
Prior MI (Diagnosed)	50.0%	-	-
Prior MI (Not Diagnosed)	65.5%	-	-
CHD Risk Factors			
Current Smoker	45.0%	0%	-
High Blood Pressure	51.3%	66.0%	66.7%
High Cholesterol	73.1%	0%	-
Family History of CHD	43.9%	0%	-
Jogging History			
Age Started Jogging			
0–19	2.4%	33.3%	25.0%
20–29	14.3%	33.3%	62.5%
30–39	31.0%	0%	12.5%
40–49	42.9%	33.3%	0%
50+	9.5%	0%	0%
Mean Weekly Mileage	30	66	11
0–9	19.4%	0	-
10–19	27.8	0	-
20–29	11.1%	25.0%	-
30–39	8.3%	0	-
40–49	16.7%	0	-
50+	16.7%	75.0%	-
Mean Number of Years Jogging	3	6	1.5
0–4	65.9%	33.3%	100%
5–9	17.1%	33.3%	0
10–14	9.8%	33.3%	0
15–19	2.4%	0	0
20+	4.9%	0	0
Completed Marathon	29%	90%	0

Another limitation associated with the cause of death is whether the reported "cause" was the "actual" cause or the result of a secondary condition. For example, it is believed that sudden death in athletes is generally caused by arrhythmia (Leon, 1985). However, the arrhythmia was often caused by a condition such as CHD. Whether arrhythmia or CHD is reported as the cause of death is a controversy in the medical profession that is beyond the scope and purpose of this book.

The second limitation of this review is that information on how representative these men are of dead runners or of runners in general is not available. In all probability marathoners are over-represented because of the debate that existed in the medical community during the 1970s on whether running a marathon provided immunity from CHD.

The third limitation is that many potentially important variables were either not reported or reported so infrequently that an analysis could not be performed to determine their significance. Height and weight are one such variable. Only three studies reported these variables. Thus, generally we do not know if the runners were lean or obese. Another potentially important variable that was not reported is personality type. Although the matter is difficult to empirically measure, especially after death, several authors mentioned that the dead men they studied were "compulsive runners" — typical "Type A" personalities. The running pace was generally not reported. Additionally, many important conditions were reported only for the time period shortly before death. Thus, the runner may have been reported to have been running 20 years and to have had a weekly mileage of 70 miles; however, the mileage for the first 19 years may have been 10 miles a week. There is also little information on dietary habits.

The data do permit several observations, which follow.

Cause of Death: CHD

First, 52 percent of the runners were known to have had warning symptoms of CHD such as shortness of breath, nausea, chest pain, and fainting. Most of the men ignored the symptoms, rationalizing them away as "unfitness" or some other condition that could be corrected through a more intensive training schedule. Among many of the men there appeared to be a denial of the possibility of the existence of heart disease. They literally tried to "run away" from their symptoms and disease. This is unfortunate, since running may have unmasked disease in previously asymptomatic men. An earlier diagnosis might have led to earlier treatment while the disease was perhaps more amenable to intervention. While exercise may reveal unknown disorders, it is also true that individuals with disease are at risk of suffering a fatal cardiac event, especially during exercise.

Several studies have reported that running has revealed diseases that have not been clinically diagnosed, such as aortic-valve stenosis (Waller et al., 1984), cardiac amyloidosis (Siegel et al., 1982), and CHD (Handler et al., 1982; Asay and Vieweg, 1981; Cantwell and Fletcher, 1969). While several of the dead runners sought medical advice about their symptoms, the advice was often ignored, especially if it dealt with a reduced training schedule.

The runners were not the only ones to ignore their symptoms; so did physicians. Often symptoms were ignored, or not considered to be important, because runners are supposed to be an elite group in terms of health. However, many are middle aged, or approaching middle age, and have multiple CHD risk factors. Physicians should be concerned when runners seek advice about new symptoms. However, even if symptoms are not ignored there is the possibility that a symptom will not be correctly diagnosed.

Maron and his associates (1980) found in their study of death in young athletes that of the seven who had their symptoms diagnosed, the correct diagnosis was made in only two cases.

Second, not only did many of the runners have symptoms, but 66 percent had evidence of a previous myocardial infarction that had not been clinically diagnosed (the runners who had a clinical history of myocardial infarctions are not included in the analysis of this item). Four of these men had ECGs within one year of their deaths. Three of the four had normal ECGs; one had an abnormal reading.

Third, the percentage with certain CHD risk factors far exceeds the percentage in the general male population over 20 years of age. For example, 45 percent of the dead runners smoked, in comparison to 35 percent of the general male population. While 51 percent of the dead runners had HBP, the figure for the general male population is 17 percent. The figures for high cholesterol are 73 percent for the runners and 17 for the general male population (National Center for Health Statistics, 1984).

The above paragraph indicates that although runners are often conceptualized as elite physical specimens, whose deaths are incomprehensible, it appears that many are at high risk in terms of CHD risk variables. In fact, they may have been running because of their high risk profile. Unfortunately, those who will benefit the most from exercise, because of their risk profile, are also often at the greatest risk of having a cardiac event.

Other studies have supported the observation that many runners are not the physical elite that they are often portrayed to be. Yamamoto and his associates (1983) found that the runners they examined were more obese and had more ECG abnormalities than nonrunners. Additionally, they found no differences in blood pressure, total cholesterol, and HDL-C between runners and nonrunners. In a study of 50 of the "best" runners in a San Diego running club it was reported that a "substantial" percentage had high blood pressure, elevated cholesterol levels, and increased body fat levels (Elrick, 1981).

However, a study by Hughes and his associates (1985) on runners in the Chicago Distance Classic indicates that the dead runners in this review may have a very different profile from runners in general. They reported that, for their sample, 4 percent were current smokers, 6.6 percent had HBP, and 0.8 percent had heart disease.

It appears that the CHD risk factors in this group of dead runners needed to be reduced either through an exercise schedule involving more duration and intensity, or through dietary modifications, smoking cessation, and perhaps medical intervention through drug therapy to correct high blood pressure and cholesterol.

Fourth, 97.8 percent had severe atherosclerosis (one or more coronary arteries blocked more than 75 percent by atherosclerosis). Since atherosclerosis begins early in life (Linder and DuRant, 1982) and since 83 percent of the runners started running at or after age 30, atherosclerosis had probably occurred in most of the men to a significant extent.

Fifth, 66 percent had been running for fewer than five years. It has been reported that it may take years for exercise to significantly reduce certain CHD risk factors (Fernhall et al., 1984).

Sixth, almost half did not jog far enough to achieve the 2000 and over kcal per week limit that has been speculated may be needed to achieve any type of protection from CHD. Paffenbarger and his associates (1978; 1984) have reported that CHD or risk of first heart attack is reduced among those who expend over 2000 kcal/week, although the expenditure did not have to be in sporting activity. Additionally, Siscovick and his associates (1982), in their study on primary cardiac arrest, reported that light and moderate leisure-time activity did not offer any protection; it was only high-intensity activity that afforded protection.

Seventh, all the reports to date are on men. This is probably because more men jog, and because men generally have more coronary risk factors, especially in the traditional runner who is under 50 years of age.

This does not mean that women are exempt from sudden death during exercise. There have been reports of women dying suddenly during exercise. For example, Sugishita and his associates (1983) studied 226 cases of sudden death during exertion, 20 percent of whom were women. For Maron and his associates (1980) the figure was 10 percent women.

Eighth, individuals are capable of intensive running and racing with advanced CHD. Thus, the ability to run, even without symptoms, does not indicate the absence of severe CHD.

Ninth, 29 percent of the runners had completed a marathon. This confirms the conclusion of a debate that existed in the medical community several years ago that involved marathon running and immunity from CHD. In the early 1970s letters appeared in several medical journals extolling the benefits of the marathoners' life style on the prevention of CHD (Bassler, 1978a; 1978b; 1977; 1975). The letters reported that no marathoner had yet been found to have died from CHD. This was debated for more than six years in medical journals, before substantial evidence was provided to discredit it (Noakes et al., 1979). This review reaffirms that marathoners are not immune from death due to CHD.

Tenth, prior to death 50 percent of the runners were reported to have suffered a clinically diagnosed myocardial infarction. They may have been running as a form of cardiac rehabilitation. Exercise is not a guarantee against the progression of heart disease. Even with an intensive exercise program, heart disease has been demonstrated to grow worse (Gamble and Froelicher, 1982).

Eleventh, 75 percent died racing. This same finding has been reported by others. For example, Sugishita and his associates (1983) reported that 62 percent of those they studied died during competition. Although they did not note the percentage, Maron and his associates (1980) reported a similar finding. Certainly mental stress coupled with anxiety and an increased level of physical exertion can place an individual with CHD at high risk of suffering a cardiac event.

Cause of Death: Rhythm Disturbances

First, two were racing at the time they died. Information was not provided on the others.

Second, although mileage was reported on only four men, it averaged 66 miles per week, more than double that of those who died from CHD. All the men, except one on whom information was not reported, were marathon runners, which also suggests high weekly mileage.

Third, 27 percent of the runners had severe atherosclerosis. Arrhythmia may occur without heart disease. According to Sugishita and his associates (1983), arrhythmia often disappears, to an extent, during exercise and then reappears during the postexercise period. This reappearance may induce sudden death. Other possible explanations are arrhythmia induced by severe exertion or exercise (Noakes and Opie, 1979b) the rise in serum catecholamines and free fatty acids, hyperkalemia induced by exercise, or heat disorders (Northcote and Ballantyne, 1984).

Fourth, 8 of the 11 deaths were reported by one physician (Bassler, 1984a; 1984b), who claimed that the rhythm disturbances were caused by a combination of low body fat, high mileage, and nutritional deficiencies. There was no empirical evidence provided to support this claim.

Cause of Death: Unknown

First, the men were generally low mileage runners (average distance per week was 11 miles) who were new to the sport (average time running 1.5 years).

Second, none of the men had severe CHD, and all were under 40. Although the number is small, this is a category on which we need more information. However, this may not be forthcoming. As has been noted, sudden, nonviolent, out-of-hospital deaths are generally not studied as thoroughly as other deaths (Sugishita et al., 1983). Coronary artery spasm has been offered as one possible explanation of sudden death in individuals with normal pathology findings (Thompson, 1982).

Cause of Death: Congenital Condition

The small number of reports makes any type of conclusion tentative at best. Although the number of reports in this review is small, other writers reporting on sudden death in athletes have reported a much higher percentage. This may be because they were examining a wider range of sports, which included more younger individuals in high school sports in whom congenital disorders were more likely to manifest themselves. Two of the four whose death was ascribed to a congenital condition had knowledge of their disorder. One individual had been advised to restrict his physical activity; he ignored the advice.

Cause of Death: Other

There is not enough information to draw any conclusions on runners in this category. The causes of death were: acute gastrointestinal hemorrhage, endocarditis, bronchopneumonia.

6
Psychological Aspects

Introduction

Runners are perceived of as being "different." Over this there is a great deal of agreement. There is less agreement, however, as to whether they are runners because of this difference, or whether they have been made different because of their running.

The first third of this chapter will examine studies on personalities — are athletes different from nonathletes in personality characteristics, and are runners different from other athletes or nonathletes in personality? The second section will examine the infamous "runners' high." Is it fact or fiction? The third will explore whether runners become addicted to running, and suffer withdrawal symptoms if they do not or cannot run.

Personality

For more than four decades researchers have been studying the personalities of athletes. The studies have generally been of two types. The first tried to ascertain if the personalities of athletes differed from those of nonathletes. Many claimed that this was an obvious fact since the personality of someone who chose to be a ballet dancer or sumo wrestler was obviously different from the personality of someone who selected a nonathletic way of life. However, others claimed that differences did not exist since athletics was only one part of a multifaceted life. Generally, these studies were designed to find out if a difference existed, not if personality differences were present prior to participation in athletics or if personality changes occurred as a result of participation in athletics.

The second type of study sought to ascertain if participation in athletics changed a participant's personality. These studies were generally designed to measure the impact of a vigorous exercise program or of participation in a sport on personality characteristics. Again, many claimed that there was an impact since an athlete had to become more disciplined and aggressive. In contrast, others believed that athletics were no more important in shaping personality than music lessons, or other nonathletic events.

First we shall briefly summarize the results of studies conducted to see if the personalities of athletes and nonathletes are different. This research is in three parts, the first indicating that differences exist, the second that no differences exist, and the third, which was designed to ascertain the impact of an exercise program or athletic activity on personality.

Personalities of Athletes vs. Nonathletes

For more than four decades researchers have been comparing the personalities of athletes and nonathletes. Researchers have been looking for the personality characteristics that compels one group to engage in a program of painful, sweaty, time-consuming exercise, and another group to be satisfied with a sedentary existence. The results are conflicting.

Part of the conflict is because researchers have often done very simple studies in a very complex area. Also, many studies have been unsophisticated methodologically. Additionally, the results have been conflicting because researchers have not tried to standardize studies by taking into consideration the impact of different sports, different calibers of athletes, different lengths of time in sports, different sexes, or different ages. As a result, a random assortment of studies exist on the personality characteristics of athletes of different sexes, ages, and calibers, in different sports. Even with these limitations a brief summary of the literature will be provided.

Studies Finding Differences in Personalities

The vast majority of studies have found differences between the personalities of athletes and nonathletes, with athletes faring better than nonathletes. This finding has been consistent with a prevalent belief in American society that participation in athletic events is valuable. This belief can be clearly seen in the physical education requirement of most elementary and secondary schools, and colleges and universities. Even today as many schools revise their academic program among growing criticisms of a lower level of educational quality, as evidenced by declining SAT scores and significantly lowered reading, math, and science scores, it is very seldom that physical education requirements are eliminated. This is in part to give coaches something to do during the "off season," but it is also because people appear to intuitively believe that physical education is "good for students."

One of the first "scientific" studies that supported this belief was done by Sperling (1942) who wanted to empirically test the widespread belief that "participation in athletics makes for more wholesome personalities." He found that athletes, in comparison to nonathletes, were more dominant and extroverted. He reported that based on the results of psychological tests, that the greater the athletic experience, the "more favorable [the] adjustment scores." Sperling concluded that "a more socially desirable degree of personality development accompanies a greater degree of experience in physical education activities" (see Carter and Shannon, 1940).

Although many studies took place between 1940 and 1949, most of them had one or more serious methodological limitations. Starting in the late 1940s researchers started to correct some of these limitations. One type of study that became very popular was to study the athlete in a particular sport.

One such study was conducted on weightlifters (Thune, 1949). Weightlifters at a local YMCA were compared to other YMCA participants. The weightlifters were found to be more introverted, and lacking in self-confidence. The weightlifters were more likely than other participants at the YMCA to believe that their sport had made them healthier. The author concluded that the weightlifters benefited from their sport, and that they had selected a sport that fit their type of personality.

A similar study was done in the early 1950s. This study was designed to find out if personality differences were contributing factors to the selection of elective college physical education classes. Male students in elective physical education classes in fencing, badminton, basketball, volleyball, boxing, and swimming were given a psychological test. Several personality differences were found. For example, fencers scored higher in feminine traits than the basketball players; badminton players were shown to be more extroverted than volleyball players; and volleyball players were more "emotionally unstable" than basketball players (Flanagan, 1951).

In 1954 a study was conducted at the University of Maryland to determine if "national athletic champions" had "normal" personalities. It found that athletes, who were in different sports, were more aggressive, had higher anxiety scores, and higher intellectual aspirations than nonathletes. Additionally, they were more self-assured and had emotions that lacked strict control. The researchers concluded that these characteristics appeared to be logical components of a champion athlete's personality. The researchers suggested that these personality characteristics made being a champion athlete a "matter of psychological necessity" (Johnson, Hutton, and Johnson, 1954).

Although most of the research was finding that personality differences existed, the methodological limitations still cast doubt on the conclusions. A 1958 study was designed to account for many of the confounding variables such as different sports, different age groups, different genders, or different caliber of athletes. While this study did not address all of the concerns noted above, it did examine the question of age, team vs. individual athletes, and caliber. The study found several differences between athletes and nonathletes, between athletes in different sports, between freshmen athletes and upperclass athletes, and between athletes of different caliber. Some of the differences were: upperclass athletes were significantly less anxious than lowerclass athletes and nonathletes; upperclass athletes and nonathletes were more dominant than lowerclass athletes and nonathletes; upperclass nonathletes were more socially responsible than lowerclass athletes and nonathletes; upperclass athletes in team sports had lower depression scores than upperclass athletes who participated in individual sports (Booth, 1958).

A study that appeared in *Research Quarterly* in 1964 found psychological differences in intelligence between athletes and nonathletes, but in a direction that was contrary to most published research. The study examined over 400 high school athletes (baseball, basketball, football, and swimming) and reported that the athletes had lower intelligence scores than nonathletes. Most of the athletes also displayed a higher hypochondriasis score, which means that they displayed an "abnormal" concern for physical symptoms, bodily functions, and bodily processes. The swimmers were the only athletic group to display a normal hypochondriasis score and the authors speculated that this was because swimming was the only sport that did not emphasize "hypochondriatic manifestations such as excessive taping" (Slusher, 1964).

For the first two decades the research in this area was almost exclusively on males. In 1967 a study was published which examined the personality traits of women on the 1964 United States Olympic Team. The study was designed to ascertain if there were any significant differences in the personality traits of women who participated in team sports versus those who participated in individual sports. The study found that there were significant differences. For example, athletes in individual sports were found to be more dominant, impulsive, and self-sufficient. These women also tended to dislike group situations and "procedural rules." Additional characteristics of the individual athletes were introversion, self-absorption, less inhibition, more radical thinking, artistic and creative interests, and "enjoying attention." The women athletes who were team athletes were not as self-absorbed or introverted as the athletes who participated in individual sports. These women were also self-reliant, and higher in sophistication than those in individual sports. The authors concluded that both groups were "more serious than average," expressed themselves freely, were more aggressive, brighter, and were somewhat "cool and aloof" (Peterson et al., 1967).

For almost two decades the researchers focused on high school and college age subjects. In 1969 a study on 60 adult males, whose average age was 38, found that those who engaged in vigorous physical activity three times a week had significantly different personality characteristics than a similar group of men who did not exercise. The major difference was that those who exercised were found to be more extroverted than those who did not exercise (Brunner, 1969).

An interesting study published in 1975 was designed to find out if those who participated in sporting activities that placed great psychological pressure on the individual were different in personality from the general public. The researchers studied sport parachutists, racing drivers, and football players. The parachutists had all made more than 1,000 jumps and were an elite group of competitors. The racing drivers were all world-class Grand Prix or top professional competitors. The football players were selected from three "outstanding" NFL teams.

The researcher recognized that the three sports were very different. Parachuting and road racing, for example, were individual sports, while football was a team sport. Also, parachuting and road racing required more precision and control than football. Additionally, racing drivers and football players engaged in the sport for a livelihood, while for the parachutists their sport was a recreational avocation.

The results demonstrated that the three groups were similar in several personal characteristics. For example, the men were all "exceptionally intelligent," "highly motivated," "toughminded," "exhibitionistic," enjoyed change, and had a strong "heterosexual need." Additionally, they all had "considerable leadership potential," and did not like to be told what to do.

There also were differences among the three. The parachutists and racing drivers, for example, had a higher need for independence and autonomy. They also tended to be more aggressive verbally and had little "need for close interpersonal relationships." As a result, their relationships with others often lacked depth. The football players were not as aggressive verbally, were more conservative, and were "less imaginative." They were also less independent.

A study by Dr. Paul M. Valliant and his associates (1981) examined several personality factors among nonathletes, athletes who were competitive (played against other organized teams), and athletes who were not competitive (engaged in sports but were not on a team and did not compete in organized competitive events). One clear difference in this study between both groups of athletes and the nonathletes was that the athletes were less imaginative. Also, the nonathletes scored lower on self-sufficiency than the athletes. Other differences were that noncompetitive athletes were more dominant than competitive athletes, and the competitive athletes were more dominant than the nonathletes. Women, both athletes and nonathletes, scored higher on the venturesome index than males. In terms of intelligence, the noncompetitive athletes scored significantly higher in intelligence than the nonathletes. For females, the athletes, both types, scored lower on intelligence than the nonathletes with the noncompetitive female athletes having the lowest scores.

In comparing the personalities of sailors of racing sloops with runners, Joesting (1981c) found several significant differences. Specifically, the runners scored significantly lower in depression and anxiety than the sailors.

Studies Finding No Differences in Personality

As can be seen, a number of studies found that the personalities of athletes are different from those of nonathletes. However, other studies have not found any significant differences between the personalities of athletes and nonathletes.

Sixteen personality factors of collegiate wrestlers were studied and it was found that there were no significant personality differences between different levels of wrestlers, other athletes, or the normal population (Kroll, 1967a).

A study by Kroll and his associate (1967b) was designed to ascertain if personality differences existed among advanced, intermediate, and novice karate participants and the general population. The hypothesis was that certain types of individuals were attracted to karate and that the effects of progressing through the hierarchical rankings would affect personality. The study concluded that the personalities of the participants did not change as they progressed through the rankings and that no differences could be found between the personalities of karate participants and the general population.

When college football players were compared with college men who had been football players in high school but not college, and nonathletes, no differences in personality were found (Berger and Littlefield, 1969).

Another study conducted on baseball and tennis players at Ohio State University found no significant differences between the baseball and tennis players. The study then further analyzed the difference between the personalities of high-ranked and low-ranked players in each sport; no differences were found (Singer, 1969).

Slight differences in personality were found in a study on weightlifters and bodybuilders. However, the study concluded that the two groups were very similar and that both were "normal in their personality profiles" (Darden, 1972).

Wendt and Patterson (1974) of Colorado State University found that no differences in personality existed between women athletes in individual and team sports.

Impact of Exercise Programs on Personality

Although many researchers believe that athletes have different personality traits from nonathletes, very few studies have been designed to ascertain if the differences exist because a certain type of individual is drawn to athletics, or if participation in athletics produces a certain type of personality.

Thirty-six men ages 60 to 79 were found to have personality changes occur as a result of a 14 week exercise program. The program had the men exercise three times a week for 25 to 50 minutes each session either in a program of walking and jogging or in cycling. While the cyclers did not experience any change in personality, the walkers/joggers became more self-sufficient and serious (Buccola and Stone, 1975).

A study conducted at Purdue University on 58 faculty and staff 21–61 years of age found that a physical fitness program brought about personality changes. The physical fitness program was four months in length and involved three 90-minute exercise sessions each week. The study found that significant changes in personality occurred during the exercise program. The participants became more "socially precise, persistent, and controlled" (Young and Ismail, 1976; see Ismail and Trachtman, 1973; Ismail and Young, 1977).

One study was conducted on women to examine the impact of an exercise program. The women, who averaged 44 years of age, participated in a 15 week walking and jogging program that met twice a week. Although subjective changes such as "feeling better" were noted, the researchers could not attribute the changes to the exercise program (Penny and Rust, 1980).

Personalities of Runners

One of the first studies conducted on runners was published in 1972. The researchers pointed out that while several studies had found that marathon runners had unique "anatomical and physiological characteristics," many individuals also had these same "anatomical and physiological prerequisites" but elected not to run marathons. The researchers reasoned that there must be another factor that predisposes individuals to run marathons. To find this "other" factor the researchers designed a study to ascertain if marathon runners had a "unique psychological profile."

The researchers collected psychological information on nine marathon runners. The psychological tests provided information to determine whether the marathon runners were introverted, neurotic, or anxious. The study found that the marathon runners scored within normal limits on all of the psychological factors measured except anxiety. On anxiety the runners scored lower than average (Morgan and Costill, 1972).

In 1977 the New York Academy of Sciences held a conference to examine scientific studies on the marathon. There were several studies presented on the psychological consequences of marathon running. One of the first was designed to replicate the above study by Morgan and Costill. Eleven world-class middle distance runners, eight world-class marathon runners, and eight "outstanding" college middle distance runners were examined. Psychological testing of all three groups found that they were very similar. All were below normal in tension, depression, fatigue and confusion, and above normal in vigor. The authors said that this personality profile should be "regarded as positive from a mental health standpoint" (Morgan and Pollock, 1977).

A second study presented at the conference was unique in that it examined 100 marathon runners. Most of the previous studies were limited in that their sample sizes were very small. The marathoners in this study were found to be more introverted and "sensing" (i.e., preferring to look at the "real" and concrete rather than the abstract) in comparison to the general population (Clitsome and Kostrubala, 1977).

A third study presented at the conference was on the personalities of sub-three-hour marathoners (Gontang et al., 1977). This study confirmed others in reporting that marathoners were introverted. It also found that they were persistent, hard-working individuals who worked well with tasks that were detailed and routine. Additionally, they were not found to be impulsive.

A study of the personalities of 48 middle aged men (average age, 47) who were runners and joggers found them to be more aloof, reserved, serious, imaginative, forthright, resourceful, and confident than the general population. The men were also more introverted and "socially clumsy" than normal (Hartung and Farge, 1977).

In 1981 a study was published on the differences between marathon runners and joggers. This study examined 30 male marathoners, and 38

male joggers who had not run a marathon. The study found that the two
groups were different on several personality scales. The marathoners had
personalities that were generally more reserved, intelligent, tender-minded,
imaginative, and self-sufficient. In contrast, the joggers were more happy-
go-lucky, apprehensive, and controlled. The authors concluded by saying
that the personality profile of the "marathoner is distinctly different from
that of the jogger." The authors said that they could not ascertain if the personalities were inherent or acquired (Valliant et al., 1981).

Another study also published in 1981 was on 46 individuals who ran in
the 100 mile Western States Endurance Run. This race is billed as the
"longest, most rugged race" in the United States. It involves an altitude gain
of 17,400 feet and a descent of 21,790 feet, along with temperatures ranging
from freezing to 100° F and above. The participants ranged from 18 to 70
years of age, with the average age being 33 years. The educational level was
high, with an average of 16 years of education. Twenty-six of the 46 participants finished the race within the allotted 24 hours. Based on personality
tests the authors concluded that "ultramarathon runners appear to be very
normal in personality." The authors pointed out, however, that those who
finished the race within the allotted time of 24 hours generally had more deviant scores than those who did not finish within 24 hours.

The deviant scores showed a high degree of "lack of social conformity,"
and of "emotional shallowness in relation to others, especially in the sexual
and affectional" areas. The authors observed that these personality
characteristics, of detachment from others, may allow the individual the
large amounts of time necessary to train for an ultramarathon. The authors
continued by mentioning that the elevated depression scores of the finishers
may indicate loneliness.

The authors concluded by saying that ultramarathoners are
"reasonably" well adjusted, but that their "fanatical devotion" to their sport
may predispose them to a psychological breakdown "when their physical
powers begin to wane" (Folkins and Wieselberg-Bell, 1981).

Freischlan (1981) investigated several psychosocial characteristics of
marathoners. First, ethnic background: Based on reports that certain ethnic
groups have a higher pain threshold than others, he examined a group of
marathoners. He found that the majority were of Northern European
ancestry, one of the ethnic groups reported to have a high pain threshold.

In 1982 a study was designed to find out if "average" marathon runners
differed in personality from college students. The researchers examined 348
marationers who ran the 1981 New York City Marathon (280 men whose
average age was 32 and who ran an average of 64 miles a week, and 68
women whose average age was 34 and who ran an average of 52 miles a
week). A psychological test called "Profile of Mood States" was administered. The results indicated several significant differences, namely that
marathon runners were less tense, fatigued, depressed and confused. Additionally, the marathoners were more "vigorous" than the nonrunners. The
authors concluded that the marathoners had very positive mood
characteristics. They pointed out that although their study did not demon-

strate that running in general, or marathon running in particular, produced the mood characteristics, they said that this study, coupled with several previous studies which found the same results, implied this conclusion (Gondola and Tuckman, 1982).

Several studies have indicated that individuals in solitary sports, such as running, are more introverted than individuals who participate in team sports, but one examination of 288 runners found that they were similar in extroversion to a group of adult industrial workers and women runners were found to be much more extroverted than male runners (Mikel, 1983).

Recently a study was conducted to ascertain if the personalities of competitive injured runners differed from those of noninjured runners. In terms of physical or training variables, the study found that injured runners ran more per week and were heavier and taller than noninjured runners. In terms of personality the injured runners were less "toughminded," and less "forthright," than the noninjured runners (Valliant, 1981).

Not all studies have found a difference between "committed runners" and the general population. A study on runners in the 1983 Dublin City Marathon did not find any significant differences between selected personality characteristics of marathoners and the general population (McLeavey et al., 1984).

Runner's High

It has been described by many runners: psychologically, as a feeling of euphoria, stimulation, creativity; physiologically, as a surge of unlimited energy, the feeling that in the last mile of a hard 16 mile training run you could easily leave behind Rob de Castella or Joan Benoit Samuelson.

Originally known as a physiological phenomenon called "second wind," the concept took on new meaning in the late 1960s when the psychedelic generation was at its height, and it became known as "spin out," referring to a temporary change in perception, personality, or mood.

Early research in this area tried to find if there were chemical compounds secreted within the body that allowed one person to exercise at a higher level of intensity or for a longer period of time than another. One group of compounds examined during this time were catecholamines, which are transmitter substances such as epinephrine (adrenaline) (see Howley et al., 1970).

It is known that when epinephrine is released into the blood stream, the body becomes prepared physiologically for the fight/flight response. When this response occurs the blood vessels in the skin contract, the blood flow to certain internal organs is diverted to the heart and arm and leg muscles, extra sugar is released from the liver, and the heart rate, blood pressure, and respiration all increase (see Cronan and Howley, 1974). To explain "second wind" or "spin out" it was hypothesized that the bodies of habitual exercisers developed a lower threshold level for their release. However, research did not always find that catecholamines increased with physical exercise.

Because of this, researchers began to look for other causes of the second wind or spin out.

In the early 1970s the discovery of opiate receptors in the brains of mammals gave new direction to the research (Pert and Snyder, 1973). Receptors are simply parts of a cell that certain compounds, such as opiates, join with, thus producing their effect. Since it was unlikely that the opiate receptors existed for compounds made from the opium poppy, a search began for naturally occurring opiates (see Goldstein, 1976). Researchers found that there was a pain-reducing chemical within the brain. This chemical was termed an "endorphin" (from *endo*, within, and *morphine*), which means a natural or body made analgesic or pain reducer.

There are several types of endorphins located in the brain or pituitary gland, all of which produce the effect of exogenous opiates (Pargman and Baker, 1980). The type most generally associated with the runner's high is the beta-endorphin. Beta-endorphins are a 30-amino acid sequence. It is not known at this time if the beta-endorphin is responsible for the runner's high, or if it is a 5-amino acid sequence found with the beta-endorphin called enkephalin (Pargman and Baker, 1980). Enkephalin is an opiate peptide (chain of amino acids) 20 to 50 times more powerful than exogenous opiates.

It was believed that beta-endorphins were responsible for reducing the pain that runners experienced, and for producing the runner's high. It was also speculated that beta-endorphins were responsible for causing addiction to running. It was reasoned that addiction occurred because through running the runner "shoots up" with beta-endorphins and then when the effect starts to wear off, and the runner experiences withdrawal symptoms, the runner must "shoot up" again by running.

Endorphins are produced not only in the brain but also by the pituitary gland and the adrenal glands. Chemically endorphins are similar, although many times more powerful, than opium. The release of endorphins also causes the release of other chemicals, such as cortisone. Cortisone helps the body utilize sugar for energy.

The discovery of opiate receptors and endorphins led to new research. One researcher noticed that the electrical stimulation of the brain produced a pain-relieving effect. This led to researchers hypothesizing that the electrical stimulation caused the release of endorphins which went to the opiate receptors and reduced pain.

To test this hypothesis six individuals, mostly cancer patients suffering from pain which could not be relieved with narcotic pain-reducing drugs, had electrodes surgically implanted in their brains through which an electrical current could be passed. Five of the six individuals reported that this provided total pain relief. For the sixth individual it provided partial relief.

To ascertain if the pain reduction was caused by endogenous opiates, such as endorphins, an opiate antagonistic (naloxone), which would nullify the effects of the opiate, was administered. If an endogenous opiate (endorphin) was causing the reduction in pain then the naloxone would eliminate the effects of the endorphins and cause the pain to return. With the administration of naloxone, all but one of the individuals reported the return of pain. The one individual who did not report the return of pain may have had an insufficient dosage.

The authors concluded that there is a neural system within the brain that used endogenous opiates to provide pain relief. The researchers then wanted to ascertain the extent of the pain relief. When they elicited acute pain with needle-pricks and heat/cold, the subjects reported normal pain sensation. In other words, the endorphins relieved chronic pain but not acute pain sensation (Hosobuchi et al., 1977).

Another study on clinical pain found similar results. This study sought to demonstrate that the brain is capable of releasing endogenous pain-reducing compounds, and that the pain-reducing compound is an endorphin. In this study 26 individuals who had surgery to remove impacted wisdom teeth were examined. The study sought to determine if a pain producing situation, such as dental surgery, would result in the body's producing a pain-reducing compound. If a compound was produced, the study then wanted to find out if it was an opiate. The results demonstrated that pain is an important activating mechanism in the release of a pain-reducing compound. It was then found that the injection of naloxone reversed the analgesic effects. This indicated that the chemical that reduced the pain was opiate in origin (Levine et al., 1978).

Researchers then started asking if there were other conditions under which endorphins might be released. One researcher suggested that the important variable for the reduction of endorphins was stress. To investigate this question the researchers studied physical activity, specifically treadmill running. The results showed that exercise significantly increased endorphins. The study further noted the analgesic effect of endorphins during exercise (Fraioli et al., 1980).

In 1980 the first linkage of endorphins with the runner's high was made in an article called "Running High: Enkephalin Indicted." Although no new empirical evidence was offered, the article did suggest the possiblity (Pargman and Baker, 1980).

In 1981 two studies on runners both found that running produces an elevation in beta-endorphin levels. The first study, published in the *Proceedings of the Society for Experimental Biology and Medicine*, found that 20 minutes of running produced a significant increase in beta-endorphin levels. The study found that men had a greater increase than women. The authors concluded that this may be responsible for the runner's high (Gambert et al., 1981). The second article, in the *New England Journal of Medicine*, studied seven women runners and simply noted that exercise stimulated the release of beta-endorphins (Carr et al., 1981). An editorial that appeared in response to the last study said there was still no "solid evidence" that beta-endorphins caused the runner's high (Appenzeller, 1981).

In 1982 evidence was published that endorphins were *not* responsible for the runner's high. In this study runners completed a psychological test called the "Profile of Mood States," before and after running. After running and completing the test runners were either injected with naloxone or sterile water and asked to take the test again. Thus, there were three testing periods: prerun, postrun, and postrun-injection. The postrun scores showed a significant reduction in anger/hostility and depression/dejection. If the postrun change was produced by endorphins, then naloxone would reverse the test results. However, the postrun injections did not produce any differences in the test scores. The authors concluded that the failure of naloxone to change mood "strongly suggests" that the changes in mood after running were not endorphin related (Markoff et al., 1982).

Another study indicated that while endorphins may not be causing the runner's high, there may still be a physiological explanation. It suggested that there may be two systems at work to relieve pain, one an opiate and the other a nonopiate. The researchers were aware of the placebo effect of pain reduction. (That is, it is well known that placebos are capable of reducing pain.) They wanted to find out if pain is reduced because it is a stressor that causes a release of opiates, and chose to study dental patients who had wisdom teeth removed. Two hours after the surgery, when pain should be severe, half the patients were given nothing and half, naloxone. Then each of these groups was further subdivided, with half of those who received nothing given a placebo and half no treatment. Both of the placebo groups experienced pain relief. Thus, the placebo produced a pain reduction even in the naloxone group, where the pain relief should have been blocked. This research demonstrated that pain relief was occurring from a compound other than an opiate (Gracely et al., 1983; see Herbert, 1983).

An additional empirical study published in 1984 has further confirmed that beta-endorphins do not play a role in the runner's high. In this study six women participated in an experiment requiring them to walk on a treadmill until exhaustion. At selected times during the test the women were asked to rate, on a 15-point scale, their level of exertion. All of the women completed the treadmill test twice. On one test the women were injected with a saline solution. On the second test the women were injected with naloxone. Additionally, several physiological measurements were made throughout the testing. The researchers hypothesized that if beta-endorphins did alleviate pain, the women injected with the saline solution would be able to exercise longer and with less perceived exertion than they would when injected with naloxone, which would block the effects of beta-endorphins. The results indicated that there were no differences in results between those injected with a saline solution and those injected with naloxone in terms of time to exhaustion, perceived exertion, and physiological measurements (McMurray et al., 1984).

The results of recent studies have led many to the conclusion that the runner's high does not exist (see Levin, 1982; 1983). One marathoner reported anecdotal observations that those who expect to experience a runner's high will be disappointed. He stated that rather than a high, beginning runners will find running "tough, tedious, tiring, and often painful." If there is a high, the writer continued, it is when the run is over and the next one does not have to be thought about for several hours. Runners run because of the secondary gains such as physical health and energy, the release of emotional tension, the spirit and excitement one feels at a race, and the fact that we live in a goal-oriented society where many goals are unattainable or ambiguous, and where running allows the individual to set and reach goals (see Partin, 1983; Allen, 1982; Straw, 1982; Smith, 1983).

Even though current researchers will have to search for another empirical cause of the runner's high, this does not necessarily mean that it does not exist. A study on 459 marathoners asked if they experienced a high when they ran. Forty-two percent of them said yes, generally between the 9- and 16-mile markers of a marathon. Eighteen percent of those reporting a high said it was a "trancelike" state, while the remainder said it was a feeling of "psychological well-being."

Addiction

One of the most apparent changes in running since, say, the fifties concerns duration and intensity. The emphasis in running has progressed from 10k races to marathons, with ultramarathons, triathlons, and ultra-triathlons currently become more popular.

For many, running has changed from a form of physical fitness or recreation to literally a vocation, or in many cases an unpaid occupation. The amount of training of many runners is far beyond what is necessary to maintain cardiovascular fitness, a certain body weight, or the other commonly given goals of running. Few individuals run or race for the t-shirts or cheap medals; but why do they run?

Many believe that it is addiction! Just as one can become addicted to drugs, some individuals believe that runners can become addicted to running. Just as drug addicts must keep increasing their intake of drugs to achieve satisfaction and prevent withdrawal, so runners must increase the intensity and duration of their running.

Defining Running Addiction

In his article "Negative Addiction in Runners" Morgan (1979b) said that there were three components of addiction. First, addicted runners believe that they "have" to run on a daily basis—in fact, that running is necessary to be able to function. Knowledge that a run will be missed because of an injury or other factor is enough to significantly disrupt the runner's functioning. Second, if an addicted runner is unable to run withdrawal symptoms will be experienced. These symptoms can be psychological, such as depression, anxiety, tension, irritability, guilt, or restlessness, or physiological, such as tics, insomnia, muscle soreness, changes in bowel functioning (such as constipation), or a loss of appetite.

Third, an addicted runner will continue to run even when there are medical, occupational, or social reasons not to run. For example, an injured runner will either try to run through the pain and discomfort, or take pain-killing medication. At work, urgent reports will wait until after the noon run. At home, domestic disputes will wait to be settled until after the evening workout. In summary, for addicted runners, running is their number one priority in life; running takes priority over the runner's health, job, family, and other interpersonal relationships (Morgan, 1979b).

Development of Running Addiction

The early stages of a running program are generally agonizing. The shortness of breath and aching muscles do little to convince runners that they will ever be running addicts. However, it must be remembered that individuals have to learn to enjoy many of their "addictions" or frequently repeated forms of behavior. For example, few individuals initially find smoking to be intrinsically pleasurable. It is only through peer pressure, perceived elevation of status and prestige, and acclimatization to the noxious fumes that allows the individual to continue smoking. Alcohol is another example where early experiences may be unpleasant but where addiction can ultimately occur. There are few who find the taste of most alcoholic drinks initially pleasurable, except perhaps the "fancy" sugared drinks that disguise the alcohol taste. Not only does the individual have to learn to enjoy the taste but also the consequences, such as altered perception, dizziness, behaviors that would be embarrassing when sober, and the morning after hangover.

Although running may initially not be pleasurable, if the individual is persistent, eventually what used to be an agonizing run will become an easy jog. As the runner makes significant improvements, there will be a feeling of accomplishment generated both from within and from others. It is natural for many runners to assume that if running three miles makes one feel good, running six miles should make one feel twice as good.

Percentage of Addicted Runners

Determining the percentage of addicted runners is at best a subjective assessment. Finding a random sample to study is one of the major problems. The percentage would probably be higher at a well-known marathon than at a 5k Fourth of July fun run in Middleville, U.S.A. Nonetheless, there have been studies that have tried to measure addiction or commitment to running.

One attempt to scientifically analyze addiction to running was presented in an article published in 1979. The article reported the results of a study that tested a scale to measure commitment to running. After determining that the scale did accurately measure the commitment, the authors then administered it to 250 male and 65 female runners whose mean age was 29 years. The study found that 32 percent of the males and 23 percent of the females said they were "very much" addicted to running; 53 percent of the males and 59 percent of the females said they were "somewhat" addicted to running; and 15 percent of the males and 18 percent of the females said they were not addicted to running. As can be seen, males were more likely to report they were significantly addicted to running than females. The authors reasoned that this may have been because the males had on the average been running longer than females (six years compared to two).

To further examine the differences between males and females the researchers looked at the differences in perceived addiction between runners who generally ran more than 40 minutes and those who generally ran less than 40 minutes. They examined the scores from the Commitment to Running Scale (12 = low commitment, 60 = high commitment). The average score for the over-40-minute male runners was 51, while for the over-40 females it was 48, a nonsignificant difference. The under-40-minute males had a score of 44 and the under-40 females had a score of 47, again a nonsignificant difference. The researchers did find that over-40-minute runners scored higher on the Commitment to Running scale than under-40 runners. Those who had high scores on the scale were also significantly more likely to perceive themselves as being addicted to running (Carmack and Martens, 1979).

In 1983 another study of addiction to running was published. It examined 419 marathon participants (320 males and 99 females) whose average age was 32 years. Eighty-two percent of the runners responded that they were "somewhat" addicted to running and 83 percent said that they experienced "discomfort" when a run was missed. Somewhat like the previous study, this study found that Commitment to Running scores did not differ significantly for males and females. This study found that those who had been running "seriously" for the longest period of time were more likely to perceive themselves as being addicted (Summers et al., 1983).

Negative Consequences

The negative addictive qualities of exercise were first seen by Dr. J. Crawford Little, a psychiatrist in northern England, who reported his observations in a 1969 article entitled "The Athlete's Neurosis — A Deprivation Crisis." Dr. Little reported on a group of neurotic males who had been referred to a psychiatric clinic. The neurotic athlete was defined as someone who "to the exclusion of other interest," overvalued "health and fitness." Dr. Little found that a threat to the individual's physical prowess such as an illness or injury, or even aging, could bring about a "neurotic episode." The author reported that men who "overvalued" their physical abilities were very vulnerable to a neurotic breakdown as they aged and thus became more susceptible to physical breakdowns and limitations.

Dr. Little said that until the episode which triggered the neurotic breakdown, the men had generally led lives "absent of neurotic markers." He said that this illness should not be treated lightly; it was rather, he cautioned, a "crippling" illness with severe consequences. Two examples mentioned were domestic problems and the inability to perform one's occupation which led to the loss of one's job and often prolonged unemployment.

In 1979 Dr. Little wrote a second article, "Neurotic Illness in Fitness Fanatics." In it he reported that athlete's neurosis was a very difficult disease to treat; it was exceptionally resistant to "psychological and physical therapies." This was because the men had "overvalued" physical fitness and as a result had almost exclusively derived their satisfaction in life from, and structured their lives around, fitness. Dr. Little saw the neurosis as being the reaction to an irretrievable loss, and that the men were experiencing a bereavement reaction. Dr. Little did say at the end of his article that he had not seen any runners with athlete's neurosis; however, most of his observations were made prior to the running boom.

As mentioned above, negative addiction can have serious consequences. Because of their addiction runners may be compelled to run on days when it is too hot or too cold, when the pollution index is too high, or when they are injured.

Although it is difficult to quantify many of the negative consequences of running addiction, a study of 459 marathoners did note some of the consequences (Summers et al., 1983). The researchers found that 36 percent of them reported negative consequences from running. Twenty percent said they had less time, 19 percent reported disruptions in their family life, 19 percent observed injury or soreness, 10 percent noted fatigue, and 7 percent said that running imposed a strain on interpersonal relationships. A further analysis of the data showed that young (14–20) single runners were most likely to report the negative consequences of injury/soreness or fatigue, and that the strain on interpersonal relationships was reported most frequently by married runners. Although Morgan (1979b) had observed that neglect of work was a major negative consequence of addicted runners, this study did not find this to be a problem.

One frequently seen consequence of addiction is "psychological burnout." Some of the psychological manifestations are that athletes are repulsed by former activities that brought them pleasure; they feel "locked into a routine"; they begin to believe that they are inadequate at their sport, which often elicits anger and a significant change in values and beliefs. Physiologically the athlete feels fatigued, and there are often weight changes. Feigley (1984) has described the susceptible personality and listed ways to prevent burnout.

In his analysis of negative addiction, Morgan (1979b) said that it is difficult to determine the amount of running necessary for addiction to occur—that is, to determine at what point the benefits of running become outweighed by the addiction and potential for self-injury or self-destruction. The major variable is not so much distance as perspective. If the runner is able to complete his or her other roles and responsibilities such as occupational, family, and social, then the runner is not addicted. If the runner cannot run and he or she does become incapacitated or limited in fulfilling other roles, then there is addiction.

There may be 20 mile a week runners who are addicted and 125 mile a week runners who are not addicted. Addiction cannot be determined merely by examining distance. If the runner controls his or her running there is no addiction; if running controls the runner, then there is addiction.

Positive Addiction

The positive benefits of running have been described in many publications. In examining the outcome of running one study used the Commitment to Running Scale (Carmack and Martens, 1979). They found that the positive consequences could be separated into five categories: physical health, psychological health, self-image, affiliation (interpersonal relationships and meeting other people), and achievement. The researchers found that the more committed the runners were the more they said they had gained from running. For example, 80 percent of the highly committed runners said they had benefited physically from their running. Only 68 percent of the low commitment runners said they had benefited physiologically from running. For the other categories the figures are: psychological health 85 percent and 58 percent, self-image 81 and 60, affiliation 84 and 52, and achievement 81 and 53 percent.

A study by Summers and his colleagues (1983) on 459 marathoners also reported on the positive consequences of running. As an outcome of running, 98 percent said that they were more fit, 96 said that running gave them a feeling of achievement, 90 said that it provided a challenge, 86 said that it made them feel better, and 86 percent said that running was enjoyable.

In analyzing the positive benefits in terms of the categories noted in the above study, the researcher noted that females saw more positive benefits than males.

7
Athletics and Longevity

Introduction

Allegations about the impact that participation in athletics will have on longevity have been made for centuries, and two contradictory viewpoints have emerged. The first claims that participation in athletics is detrimental to health and longevity; the second that it is beneficial. Each side has cited numerous examples to support its position.

The "beneficial" group have pointed to epidemiological studies indicating a lower rate of heart disease for those who exercise. In contrast, the "detrimental" group have pointed out numerous examples of healthy, physically fit athletes dying while exercising, of studies indicating that athletes have an abnormally high death rate from diseases such as cancer, and of reports that athletes are more likely to have Type A personalities, which predisposes them to a variety of pathological conditions.

Obviously the prevailing belief in contemporary American society is that participation in athletics is beneficial to health and longevity. Since the early 1960s this belief has become so prevalent that the number of Americans exercising has gone from 24 percent of the population in 1961, to 50 percent in 1980. Of the 237 million or so Americans (in 1986), it is estimated that as many as 40 million jog or run.

An assumption that most of those participating in athletics make is that physical exercise will lengthen their life span, although this is probably not the primary reason that they exercise. This assumption appears logical, especially since exercise is supposed to reduce the risk of heart disease, which is the primary cause of death in contemporary American society.

The assumption that athletic pursuits will increase life expectancy is one that has been examined scientifically for over 100 years. The major question this chapter will examine is, Do athletes or those who exercise live longer than nonathletes or those who do not exercise?

Longevity: The Misconceptions

As a society we take pride that every year life expectancy increases for Americans. This reflects our modern technology, level of medical care, and overall standard of living. It is widely quoted that in 1900 life expectancy in the United States was 48 years. By 1984 it had increased to 75 years, a 27-year gain in a short period of time.

These figures are correct and there is little that can be done to refute them. However, they need to be explained to have greater meaning.

In the past, the major causes of death in the United States were infectious diseases, such as diphtheria, smallpox, typhoid, whooping cough, influenza, tuberculosis, and measles. Additionally, the primary victims of death were infants, children, and adolescents. Obviously, today the reverse is true; the major causes of death in contemporary American society are from degenerative diseases, such as heart disease or cancer, and the primary victims are the aged.

Life expectancy figures are calculated in a simple way. The ages of all the people who have died in a society during the year under study are added together and the total is then divided by the total number that died. This results in the life expectancy figure for that society.

As is probably somewhat apparent, a society that has a high infant, child, and adolescent mortality rate would generally have a life expectancy lower than a society that had conquered these diseases. Americans are fortunate in having such a society. Diseases that used to kill thousands of children every year in U.S. society, and instilled fear and helplessness into the hearts of parents with young children, are now generally terms that mean little to most parents. Fortunately, diphtheria, smallpox, whooping cough, yellow fever, typhoid, scarlet fever, and a variety of other diseases are now largely footnotes in medical history textbooks.

However, in the past these diseases were devastating. The impact of these diseases can be seen by examining the past death rate of infants under one year of age and by then comparing it to the contemporary death rate. In the United States in 1865, 205 out of every 1,000 children born died during the first year of life. In 1940 the figure had been brought down to 47. In 1982 the figure was 11.5 (U.S. Bureau of the Census, 1970; 1986).

As can be readily seen, the medical sciences have made tremendous gains in lowering the infant death rate. However, perhaps the question that we need to ask is, In the past, if an individual survived infancy, childhood, and adolescence, what was his or her life expectancy in comparison to someone today? In other words, while recognizing that the medical sciences have made tremendous gains in the elimination of the diseases that decimated the young in the past, have the same gains been made for adults?

Many claim that they have. These individuals claim that improvements in nutrition, sanitation, medical care, and life style must certainly have increased adult life expectancy. Others, however, believe that little actual change has been made due to foods being stripped of their nutritional value and laced with salt, sugar, and harmful chemical additives. This, coupled with a largely sedentary life style, often in a polluted environment, interacts to produce a life expectancy that modern drugs and surgical techniques cannot significantly extend.

The infectious diseases that decimated early colonial America over and over again had an impact on lowering life expectancy. However, as Table I shows, although the gap between life expectancy at birth in 1850 and 1982 was 33 years for men and 38 years for women, the difference in the number of years of life remaining at ages 20, 40, 60, and 70 in 1850 and 1979 becomes progressively similar. This indicates that although the medical sciences have been able to make large strides in reducing mortality in the younger age categories, that the same reduction in mortality has not been achieved for the adult age categories.

Table I
Life Expectancy at Birth, and Number of Years of Life Remaining at Ages 20, 40, 60, and 70

	Birth		20		40		60		70	
	men	women	men	women	men	women	men	women	men	women
1850	38.3	40.5	40.1	40.2	27.9	29.8	15.6	17.0	10.2	11.2
1982	71.5	78.8	53.0	59.9	34.5	40.6	17.9	22.8	11.6	15.3
	33.2	38.3	12.9	19.7	6.6	10.8	2.3	5.8	1.4	4.1

(U.S. Bureau of the Census, 1970; 1986)

No criticism of the progress of medical sciences is implied. Contemporary Americans would find it difficult to conceptualize the fear that epidemics created in colonial America. The severity of these epidemics and an appreciation of medical progress, can be seen by examining the devastating results of a disease such as smallpox. In 1721, 14 percent of all Bostonians died as a result of a smallpox epidemic. In 1730, in another outbreak of the disease in Boston, 12.5 percent of the residents died. Smallpox also affected New York in 1730 and 7 percent of the city dwellers died. Other diseases, such as diphtheria, were just as lethal. In 1737 diphtheria killed 210 of the 1,200 residents of Hampton Falls. In 1736 one-half of the children in Haverhill, Massachusetts, died from "throat distemper," which was another name for diphtheria. Yellow fever killed 10 percent of the population of New York City in 1702 (Duffy, 1979).

The list could go on at some length. The major point is one that is well-known; namely, that medical researchers have done an excellent job in conquering many of the infectious diseases that were so devastating in the past. However, they have not yet made the same strides in conquering the degenerative diseases that are "epidemic" in contemporary American society.

It must be stated that part of the problem does not rest with the quality of medical research and care but with the complexity of the problem and with individuals who are intent on killing themselves through obesity, smoking, horrific nutritional habits, and an attitude that they cannot do anything to change or control their lives. Many of these individuals believe that behaviors or conditions that reduce life expectancy, such as smoking or obesity, will be compensated for through futuristic medical advances.

Now that we have examined some misconceptions about longevity, we should turn to the facts about it.

Longevity: The Facts

Since 1955 the Center for the Study of Aging and Human Development at Duke University has been conducting a series of longitudinal studies on the aged. As a result of their research they have been able to publish several articles and books on longevity (see Palmore, 1982; 1981; 1980; Busse and Maddox, 1985). Although there are still many unanswered questions, the researchers have found that there are several predictors of longevity, which can be divided into those over which individuals can exert control and those over which they cannot.

Longevity Factors That Can Be Controlled

Diet

The studies at Duke University have indicated that both "too much" and "too little" food reduces longevity. The studies also found that those who were under- or overweight had more illness than those close to their normal weight.

The researchers speculated that the lower longevity in the overweight individuals might be linked to lack of exercise.

It was noted that a high cholesterol intake has generally been associated with a high mortality rate. The Duke studies found the same trend, other than for persons who survived to old age, where cholesterol intake did not appear to influence the death rate.

Exercise

There have been many studies that have demonstrated that individuals who exercise live longer than those who do not exercise. The Duke research has again confirmed this finding. It may be, however, that those in better health are more capable of exercising.

Smoking

The strongest negative correlate of longevity that the Duke studies found was smoking. Smokers have a substantially lower life expectancy than nonsmokers. While smoking is unquestionably a major cause of death and disease, it is also likely that smokers are less health conscious than nonsmokers; this may contribute to their higher death rate.

Retirement and Work

In the past, it was widely believed that retired individuals had a much higher death rate than working individuals. It was also believed that retirement in and of itself brought about the increase in mortality. It is true that retired individuals have a higher death rate than working individuals of the same age. However, it must be realized that many people retire because of poor health. Studies have found that it is not retirement in and of itself that is responsible for the higher death rate of retirees, but preretirement factors, such as poor health (see Rowland, 1977).

Marital Status

Although there are some exceptions, generally speaking, married individuals have a lower mortality rate than unmarried individuals. Although it may be that marriage is beneficial for longevity, it may also mean that individuals who marry are more desirable in income and health, two correlates of longevity.

It has also been frequently noted that the death of a spouse increases the likelihood of death for the surviving spouse. This is often referred to as the "broken heart syndrome." Although several studies have supported this conclusion, there are several factors that must be considered before concluding that bereavement in and of itself produces the increased death rate. First, it may be that both the dead individual and the bereaved individual were in the same pathogenetic environment. That is, there may be something in the environment, such as a contagious disease, that resulted in the death of the first individual and is now affecting the second. Second, perhaps those in poor health have an increased likelihood to marry others in poor health. That is, individuals with certain undesirable characteristics, such as poor health, may have a limited pool from which to draw their mates.

Third, they may have shared an "unhealthy" or "high risk" life style. That is, they may have been heavy smokers and consumed large amounts of alcohol. Thus, the death of the surviving spouse is due to life style, not bereavement. Fourth, caring for a terminally ill spouse can be an emotionally draining and stressful experience. By the time the dying spouse dies the surviving spouse may be in a weakened physical condition, and thus more susceptible to illness and disease. The survivor then lacks the reserve capacity to fight off illness and disease and thus dies within six months of their spouse.

It should be mentioned that although the death rate of the recently bereaved is higher than expected, the time period for the higher death rate is of relatively short duration, generally under six months. It must also be mentioned that many individuals go through bereavement while their spouse is dying, and find the actual death to be a relief from stress and anxiety.

Sexual Activity

Sexual activity has been found to be an important variable in longevity for both men and women, although in different ways. For men it has been found that frequency of sexual intercourse is a strong predictor of longevity, with the more sexually active men having the greatest longevity. It is unknown if the longevity is a result of healthier men being more capable of sexual activity or from the physical stimulation and enhanced sense of self-worth that comes from the sexual activity.

Social Activity

Socially active individuals have a longer life expectancy than individuals who are less active. It is a reasonable explanation that individuals who are socially active are better able to maintain their mental and physical functioning than those who are inactive. It is also reasonable that those who are socially active are in better health. Thus, although social activity is a predictor of greater longevity, it may not be the activity in and of itself that is the contributing factor; rather, it may be that socially active individuals are in better health to begin with.

Socioeconomic Status

For men, socioeconomic status was an important predictor of longevity, with the men from the higher social classes having greater longevity. This probably represents a lifetime of better medical care, better nutrition, better housing, and occupations that are less physically hazardous. Although status was also an important predictor of longevity for women, the trend was not as strong as it was for men.

Satisfaction

Satisfaction with work was a strong predictor of longevity for men. Also, happiness for both men and women was also a strong predictor of longevity for both sexes.

Health

Although it is questionable if health belongs in the controllable or non-controllable section, it has been found that this is a strong correlate of longevity. Although this should not be surprising, what is surprising is that individuals' subjective ratings of their health have been found to be more important in predicting longevity than a physical rating. This appears to indicate that while actual physical condition is important in determining longevity, so is the way individuals react and adjust to their physical condition, with more accepting individuals having a greater longevity.

Longevity Factors That Cannot Be Controlled

Heredity

Unlike the other factors mentioned thus far, heredity is a variable that cannot be modified. Almost all studies have indicated that there is a strong correlation between the longevity of parents and that of their offspring. As a result, it has been widely believed that there was a genetic factor at work affecting longevity. However, the Duke research has contradicted this finding. The studies for individuals 60 and over found no correlation between the longevity of the parents and their offspring. The researchers at Duke concluded that the genetic influence on longevity is modifiable in one's later years by decades of environmental factors. The researchers noted that genetically inherited diseases, such as sickle cell anemia, appeared to take their toll at relatively early ages.

This conclusion is certainly encouraging for anyone with parents who died while in young adulthood or middle age. It indicates that after adolescence or young adulthood one's genes have little to do with life expectancy and that through life-style choices, individuals have the opportunity to extend their lives past those of their parents.

Gender

Women live longer than men. Part of the difference is due to biological factors. However, most of the difference is due to life style. Men smoke more and thus have a higher rate of cancer. They also drink more and are thus affected more by cirrhosis of the liver as well as accidents. Traditionally men have also held jobs that were more hazardous.

Race

Blacks have a higher mortality rate than whites, except beyond age 75. It is widely believed that most of the difference is attributable to socioeconomic status.

Intelligence

Researchers have found that those with higher levels of intelligence have greater life expectancy. There are several explanations that can account for this finding. The first is that higher intelligence scores are an indication of a better overall physical functioning. A second explanation is that individuals with higher intelligence levels are better able to solve problems and adapt to situations. A third explanation is that those with high intelligence levels also have a higher socioeconomic status.

Longevity: Athletes and Nonathletes Compared

As mentioned in the chapter on "Running and the Heart," exercise has not always been perceived of as being beneficial for health. Two early anatomists, Galen and Hippocrates, both believed that competing in sporting events would lead to an early death. Even by the twentieth century this belief was widely held. In 1911 Dr. Charles F. Stokes, the Surgeon General of the United States Navy, tried to discourage competitive athletic competition at the U.S. Naval Academy; he believed that it was "dangerous to one's health to excel at a sport" (see Montoye, 1974). One of Dr. Stokes' utterances that most readers of this book will find interesting is, "foot racing is not beneficial, but productive of serious harm" (*Medical Times*, 1912).

At the beginning of this chapter it was implied that a natural assumption would be that athletes live longer than nonathletes because of the benefit that exercise has on the heart. However, there are critics of exercise who believe that the heart is damaged through vigorous exercise. Other critics of exercise acknowledge the benefits of exercise on the heart but believe that other critical organs, such as the lungs, are damaged. If the critics of exercise are correct, then the damage done to the body through exercise may result in an early death.

There have been both proponents and critics of exercise for thousands of years. The questions that this section of the chapter will examine are hardly new. In the last 100 years many scientific studies have been conducted. In fact, scientific studies on the impact of exercise on longevity were started in the 1870s.

To date both the quantity and quality of the research on the relationship of participation in athletics to longevity is disappointing. The research is limited, and although a few excellent studies exist, most of the research is flawed methodologically. This section of the chapter will review in chronological order the literature on the relationship of participation in athletics and longevity.

Most of the early studies in this area examined the consequences of college athletics on longevity. The widespread belief was that irreparable physical damage occurred as a result of college athletics. It was believed that the physical damage ultimately shortened the life span of former college athletes because the lungs became much more susceptible to disease, such as tuberculosis, and that the heart, which became enlarged through exercise, became flabby and inefficient after the athlete stopped exercising.

One of the first "scientific" studies reporting the impact of exercise on life expectancy was published in 1873 by Dr. John E. Morgan, a distinguished English physician. Morgan's purpose in conducting the study was to ascertain if rowing physically damaged and produced early death in oarsmen. This study was important since it was widely believed in the 1870s that oarsmen generally did not live beyond 30 years of age. Morgan, a former oarsman, compared the longevity of men who had rowed for Oxford and Cambridge between 1829–1869 to life expectancy tables. Morgan found that the oarsmen lived about two years longer than the "average" Englishman (see Montoye, 1974). Morgan thus concluded that rowing was healthful, except for those who were in "poor health before commencing to row" or for those who "let themselves go in later life" (see Prout, 1972).

Morgan's study was interesting and may have temporarily laid to rest the concern over the negative effects of participation in athletics. However, Morgan's study was flawed methodologically. By comparing college educated men with "average" Englishmen Morgan made a significant error, which would be repeated many times in similar studies during the next 100 years. The error was that Morgan did not consider that college oarsmen would be expected to live longer than the "average" Englishman by virtue of their education, income, and social class. Thus, Morgan's study did not answer the question. Although oarsmen lived longer than the "average" Englishman, they may have had a shorter life expectancy than others who were nonathletes but similar in education, income, and social class. What was needed was a study that compared oarsmen with others who were similar in education, income, and social class: their nonathletic classmates.

The rumor of the harmful effects of vigorous physical exercise on longevity surfaced again in 1897 when three young British oarsmen died. Even though the first oarsman died from a ruptured appendix, the second from tuberculosis, and the third from an "overwhelming infection," the belief that rowing, and college athletics in general, was dangerous persisted (see Prout, 1972).

Because the controversy still existed in the early 1900s, another study was published in 1904. This study examined 123 men who had rowed for Harvard from 1852 to 1892. The study concluded that the oarsmen had a life expectancy that was 2.88 years greater than other insured individuals, and that the men were excellent insurance risks. Again, the study did not take into account that the oarsmen differed from insured men in general by virtue of their education, income, and social class (Meylan, 1904).

Starting in 1905 several of the studies began using a new way of analyzing life expectancy: noting the percentage of actual deaths to expected deaths. That is, the number of deaths that would normally be expected were ascertained from insurance tables for a certain group, such as college graduates. The number of expected deaths was then compared to the number of actual deaths. The result was a percentage. A figure of 100 percent meant that the number of actual deaths equaled the number of expected deaths. A figure greater than 100 percent meant that the number of actual deaths exceeded the number of expected deaths and a figure less meant that the number of actual deaths was less than the number of expected deaths.

In 1905 a study appeared on former Yale athletes using the above method (see Greenway and Hiscock, 1926). This study differed from previous studies in that it compared the athletes with both their classmates and insured men in general. The authors reported that the number of deaths for Yale athletes was only 49 percent that predicted by insurance tables. For Yale graduates in general the figure was 70 percent. Thus, the athletes had a significantly longer life expectancy than Yale graduates who were not athletes and insured men in general.

In 1906 another article appeared that tried to dispel the belief that participation in athletics was harmful. The article was written by Professor R. Tait McKenzie of the University of Pennsylvania who was responding to the concern that the "flower of American youth" was being sacrificed to the "molech [something demanding terrible sacrifice] of athleticism." McKenzie attempted to dispel the myth of premature death for athletes through an examination of the literature, especially Morgan's work.

In support of McKenzie's article, Dr. Sargent (1906) of Harvard wrote that the greatest cause of death in former athletes is the "immoral life many of them live after they have quit training."

However, the controversy still persisted. In 1911 Surgeon General Stokes of the U.S. Navy stated that "prolonged rigorous...physical exercise necessary to excellence in physical sports is believed to be dangerous in its after effects..." (Medical Times, 1912). Stokes then noted the medical records of midshipmen at the U.S. Naval Academy who had been athletes, concluding that as a result of participation in college athletics, athletes did not "render as many years of efficient service...as...his less athletic, but symmetrically developed classmates."

As a result of Dr. Stokes' statement a symposium on "The Effects of Athletics on Young Men" was published in 1912 in The Medical Times, a leading medical journal of the time. The journal asked medical men "occupying positions which make their word authoritative" to comment on the subject. The comments differed significantly, with many of the medical men agreeing with Dr. Stokes' statement. A minority of the authors either disagreed with Stokes or said that more research was needed before they could make a statement. A few of the writers asked for reform in college athletics.

One of those opposed to athletics was Dr. W. G. Anderson (1912) of Yale University who called the physiological changes that occurred as a result of vigorous exercise "abnormal developments." He stated that if athletes did not continue with exercise after college that they were predisposed to consumption (tuberculosis). This belief was echoed by Dr. Brown (1912) who felt that the "pulmonary expansion" developed during college athletics left athletes at a high risk of developing tuberculosis after becoming sedentary. However, Anderson concluded that while athletes were not "short-lived" their life expectancy was not due to athletics.

Many of the other participants in the symposium also believed that college athletics were harmful to longevity. Several of the physicians stated that the effects of vigorous exercise on the developing muscles and organs of children, adolescents, and young adults caused permanent damage (see Estes, 1912; Ross, 1912). The lungs and heart were major areas of concern. The critics of exercise spoke of the "dilation" of the heart which "terminates the usefulness of the youngster as an athlete." Several writers in the symposium said that if the athlete did not continue with the same level of training after college that muscular degeneration of the heart would take place, apparently at a much more rapid rate than for those who had not engaged in college athletics (see Brown, 1912; Clapp, 1912).

One of those who supported college athletics was Dr. Dudley Sargent from Harvard University. Dr. Sargent was critical of Dr. Stokes' statement and noted that it was not athletics which led to the shortened life span of former athletes from the Naval Academy but the methods the navy used to train naval officers. This sentiment was repeated by Dr. Stauffer, who said that the naval system where men "work and drill from dawn to dusk" was responsible for the increased death rate of the athletes.

Others were also critical of Dr. Stokes' statistics on naval midshipmen. Dr. George L. Meylan (1912), from Columbia University, examined the data and noted that although a significant number of former Naval Academy athletes had died, their mortality was only one-third that of other midshipmen and only one-sixth that of the general public.

The *Medical Times* symposium did not present any new scientific data or form any conclusions. More significantly, it did not note any of the methodological limitations in existing studies, nor did it make any recommendations for future studies.

In 1916 another study was published on the life expectancy of Yale athletes (Anderson, 1916). The author said, "The opinion prevails and recent articles in the medical and lay magazines have intensified the belief that athletes are now being pushed beyond the threshold of safety." To examine this, Anderson studied men who had lettered at Yale between 1855 and 1905. He found that of 808 men, 58 had died. However, the number of expected deaths was 125.9. The author found that 26 of the men had died from lung or heart disorders but noted that this was not greater than the death rate among nonathletes. He continued by saying that it could not be determined if the athletes had greater life expectancy because of their participation in athletics or if they were in athletics because they were a physically select group. He concluded by saying that while athletes have a greater than average life expectancy, their longevity may not be a result of athletics.

By the 1920s the question, far from resolved, became more complicated by the mass media's excessive publicity of the deaths of former college athletes. The general tone of these articles was that the deaths of former college athletes were produced by their participation in college athletics. Given the negative publicity athletics was receiving, some universities conducted their own studies to reassure their trustees and former athletes that college sports were safe.

One such study was published in the *Yale Alumni Magazine* in 1926. The authors of the article (Greenway and Hiscock, 1926) reported that an earlier study found that Yale athletes from the mid 1850s to 1904 had a favorable life expectancy in comparison to insured males in general. To ascertain if the trend continued the authors examined Yale athletes from 1904 to 1923.

By comparing the number of actual deaths to expected deaths, the figure for all Yale graduates was 84 percent. For Yale athletes it was 93 percent. Although this appeared to support the view of those who saw athletic participation as shortening longevity, a more detailed analysis found that the athletes had an excessive number of deaths due to war and accidents.

Removing these deaths from the total the figure for athletes became 44 percent. The authors went on to point out an important distinction between athletes and nonathletes. Namely, that in general the health and high level of physical fitness of athletes made them more likely to be drafted and thus killed in a time of war. Their athletic abilities also made them more likely candidates for death from accidents. This was because athletes were more likely than nonathletes to engage in water sports, mountain climbing, and other activities that placed them at greater risk of accidental death.

In 1927 a study appeared on professional cricket players. The author said that it was a common belief that athletes "exhaust" themselves and die "relatively young...from a weakened heart or phthisis" (tuberculosis). The author examined professional cricket players in England between 1888 to 1913 and found that they had a life expectancy substantially greater than men in the general population. The author also pointed out that cricket players were not an elite group in education, income, or social class, as were college athletes. Therefore, their longevity was more likely due to their sport rather than some other characteristic.

The results of an important set of studies were published in 1928, 1930, and 1932, by Louis Dublin, a statistician for the Metropolitan Life Insurance Company. All of Dublin's studies were based on extensive statistical data. Dublin's first article was based on 5,000 male athletes who graduated from several Eastern colleges between the late 1850s to 1905. His later articles were based on data gathered on 38,269 men who had graduated between 1870 to 1905 from eight Eastern colleges.

Dublin recognized that there was a great deal of misinformation about longevity and college athletes. Because of this, he said that every time a famous former college athlete died prematurely the death received extensive publicity, the magnitude of which reinforced the belief that college athletics were damaging to longevity.

Unlike previous researchers, Dublin was one of the first to recognize the "elite" status of the college male in terms of education, income, and social class and to realize that by comparing them with standard mortality tables the athletes would have a higher life expectancy.

One of the first results that Dublin reported, using the method of reporting the percentage of actual deaths to expected deaths, was the death rate by graduating class (e.g., prior to 1880, 1880–1889, 1890–1899, 1900–1905). He found that the figure for all graduating classes was 91.5 percent. The figures by graduating class were: prior to 1880 94.1 percent, 1880–1889 94.6 percent, 1890–1899 93.6 percent, 1900–1905 72.6 percent. The large gain in life expectancy after 1900 was probably caused by better screening for college entrance.

Dublin also reported differences in mortality by sport. For football players the percentage was 98. For oarsmen it was 94.1 and for trackmen, 91.8. It was also stated that for men who lettered in more than one sport the figure was 78.3 percent. Dublin was one of the first researchers to consider the possibility that not all athletic activities are equal in terms of their impact on longevity, a belief currently held by most researchers.

In Dublin's study there were several instances where former athletes experienced an excess in mortality over insured men in general. For example, in the graduating classes between 1890 and 1899, men who played baseball had an actual death percentage of 103.1, and two groups of oarsmen had percentages over 100; in 1890–1899, the percentage for oarsmen was 124 and in 1900–1905 the percentage was 113. For trackmen in the 1880–1889 graduating classes the percentage was 121.7.

When Dublin examined cause of death he found that athletes had a slightly higher death rate from heart disease. He said that the evidence "suggests" that exercise "may in a good many instances have deleterious effects on the heart."

Dublin observed that while overall former college athletes showed a "favorable mortality picture" he had expected to find more favorable results. He said that the athletes were the "cream of the cream of American manhood" and that "athletic activities in the earliest periods of loose supervision did considerable damage." He concluded that what was needed was a study comparing former college athletes with college men who did not engage in athletics.

In 1930 and 1932 Dublin published his second and third articles comparing the longevity of former college athletes with nonathletes. These articles were different from previous studies in that three groups of college men were compared: graduates, athletes, and honor men. He noted in his article that this type of comparison was necessary since college men were a select group physically, socially, and economically.

He found that at every age the athletes had a lower life expectancy figure than both the graduates and the honor men. The athletes did, however, have a life expectancy higher than American men in general. Table II below has the figures. There is also a column indicating life expectancy for men in 1982.

Table II
Life Expectancy of Select Groups of Men
at Certain Ages in 1932

Age	College Men			American	
	Graduates	Athletes	Honor	Men 1932	Men 1982*
32	37.59	37.25	39.48	36.03	41.9
42	29.44	28.92	31.07	27.66	32.7
52	21.43	20.85	22.79	19.79	24.0
62	14.48	14.09	15.56	13.06	16.5
72	8.81	8.41	9.50	7.91	11.6 (age 70)
82	4.56	4.24	4.98	4.41	7.0 (age 80)

(*Source: U.S. Bureau of the Census, 1986)

Dublin's study clearly indicated that athletes had a shorter life expectancy than both college graduates in general and college honor students.

A study on the life expectancy of army officers was published in 1931 (Reed, 1931). Army officers were a unique group to examine for two reasons. First, initially they were a physically elite group, and second, they were required to maintain a certain level of physical fitness throughout their service. Even with the occupational hazards of war and disease through being stationed in tropical countries, the study found that the officers had a life expectancy two years longer than white male civilians.

The above study also examined the impact of past participation in "strenuous" athletic activity, such as football, on the life expectancy of the officers. It was concluded that "it did not shorten the lives" of the men.

By 1937 more sophisticated devices were becoming available for learning the physiological influence of exercise on the human body. One study by Cooper and his associates (1937) used several devices to accurately obtain certain physiological measurements. Although drawing several conclusions that would be questioned today, the study was one of the first to report, using empirical physiological measurements, that "extreme physical effort in the trained athlete does not result in damage to the heart."

In 1939 another study was published, in the *British Medical Journal*, on 767 Cambridge and Oxford oarsmen who rowed between 1829 and 1928. The articles concluded that the life expectancy of oarsmen was slightly greater than insured males (Hartley and Llewellyn, 1939).

In 1944 a study of the mortality of men who had played in the Indiana basketball state finals from 1911 to 1935 was publicized. The belief was that basketball was the most "strenuous" of the high school sports and thus the one "most likely to result in permanent harm to the players." Although again flawed methodologically, the study showed that former basketball players had a lower death rate than insured males in general. This study confirmed a fact that other studies had indicated, namely that a disproportionate number of the athletes died from "external violence" such as war, accidents, or suicide.

By the 1950s studies on longevity and athletic participation were becoming more sophisticated methodologically. Researchers were beginning to realize that all athletes could not be lumped together. For example, the consequences of athletic participation on longevity for those on the golf team and those on the rowing team might be significantly different. Researchers were also starting to realize the importance of other factors, such as body type, and postcollege activity levels.

A study by Rook published in 1954 was similar to those of Dublin. He examined the records of men who had been at Cambridge between 1864 and 1900. He separated the men into three groups: athletes, intellectuals, and controls. Rook eliminated all men who had died as a result of war and accidents. He found that the athletes, up to 40 years of age, had a lower mortality rate. However, after age 40 the mortality rates of the three groups became similar. The average age at death was 67.97 for the athletes, 69.41 for the intellectuals, and 67.43 for the controls. These differences were not significant statistically.

Rook then compared the four sporting groups (track, cricketers, rowers, rugby football players). The men had a life expectancy that did not differ significantly (track 67.41, cricketers 68.13, rowers 67.08, rugby football players 68.84).

He then examined a variable that has received attention in recent years, namely physique. A limitation of this study was that the physiques of the men when they were in college were used in the analysis. The study found that men who had light physiques had an average age at death of 68.46 while those with heavy physiques died on the average at age 66.73. The difference in age at death between those with both light and heavy physiques and the control group did not differ statistically.

Rook also examined the likelihood of living to age 70 for the track men. He found that 57 percent of the sprinters, 56 percent of the distance men, and 34 percent of the hammer and weight men lived to age 70. He indicated that this was probably a result of differences in physique.

Rook was one of the first to examine cause of death and distinguish between the cause of death for athletes and nonathletes. Death from cardiovascular disease varied between the groups. For each group the percentage of death due to cardiovascular conditions were: track men 36.4 percent, cricketers 37.2, rowers 31.5, rugby players 42, intellectuals 39.9, and control group 41.5 percent. It was found that the athletes did not have a higher incidence of death from cardiovascular disease than nonathletes. In the control group 27.3 percent of the deaths from cardiovascular disease happened before the age of 65, 22.5 percent for the athletes. Between the ages of 65 and 75 the figure for athletes is 37.5 percent and for the controls 39.7. After age 75 the figure for athletes was 40 percent and for controls 33.

Both war and accidents as a cause of death differed for the athletes and for the nonathletes, even though the students examined were largely excluded from wars since the Boer Wars did not involve many men and only a few were under the age of 40 at the time of World War I. For every 1,000 men, 97.9 of the athletes died as a result of war or accidents. For the intellectuals the figure was 46.7, and for the control group the figure was 70.4.

Rook's study concluded that athletes did not die at an earlier age than nonathletes. It did find some indication that the intellectuals lived about a year and a half longer than the athletes, and that lightly built men had a greater probability for longer survival than heavily built men, but these differences were not statistically significant.

A study by Montoye and his associates (1956) on athletes and nonathletes at Michigan State University between 1855 and 1919 confirmed the findings of Rook. Montoye and his associates found that both college athletes and nonathletes lived about eight years longer than expected, which indicated the impact of education, income, and social class of college men during this time period, but the difference in the mean age at death for the athletes (73.86) and for the nonathletes (74.24) was not significant.

The Montoye study did point out some interesting differences between the two groups. For example, the athletes were much more likely to have been in the military, 66.4 percent compared to 55.8. The athletes were also more likely to drink, 77.6 percent to 66.5, and to smoke, 68.7 to 60.2.

In 1968 a question in the "Question and Answer" section of the *Journal of the American Medical Association* asked if the "demanding training program" that was required of rowing crews was damaging to the heart, especially when the men became older. This question was prompted by the rumor that all the members of the 1948 Harvard rowing crew had died of cardiac diseases (Moorstein, 1968).

Three individuals responded to the question.

The first individual was the Harvard University rowing team physician who responded that all 36 members of Harvard's 1948 rowing crew were still alive (Quigley, 1968).

The second individual answered that studies have indicated that oarsmen have a lower mortality rate than comparable groups, although the author noted that further studies were needed (Hein, 1968).

The third individual also noted that more studies were needed before conclusions could be drawn (Westura, 1968).

By the 1970s more studies were being published. One example was a study by Polednak and his associates (1970) on 2,631 undergraduate men who attended Harvard University between 1860 and 1912 and who had been measured anthropometrically as well as photographed. There were three groups examined: major athletes who had won a varsity letter, minor athletes who had not lettered, and nonathletes. The study found that generally the major athletes had the lowest life expectancy and the minor athletes the highest; the results were not statistically significant. The study reported that the major athletes were fatter, more muscular, and stockier than individuals in the other two groups. The minor athletes were close to the endomesomorphic physique of the major athletes, but not to the same extent. The study found that the causes of death for the three groups did not differ significantly (see also Polednak, 1972).

In 1972 a study was published in the *Journal of the American Medical Association* on the life expectancy of college oarsmen. The author stated that several sources had demonstrated that college athletes did not have a lower life expectancy than expected. The author then went on and said that to further explain this issue he had studied 172 graduates of Harvard and Yale who had been oarsmen between 1882 and 1902. The author then picked classmates at random with whom to compare the oarsmen.

The author found a significant difference in life expectancy between the oarsmen and the controls, with the oarsmen living longer. At Harvard the oarsmen lived an average of 67.79 years in comparison of 61.54 for the controls, a difference of 6.24 years. At Yale the figures were 67.91 and 61.56, a difference of 6.35 years.

The author did not have good data on the cause of death for the men and thus did not speculate about the importance of exercise in the prevention of heart disease. He concluded, however, that the probability was that the oarsmen continued to exercise after college and that they may have been more successful than their colleagues and that this may have accounted for their longevity. He admitted, however, that this would need further investigation (Prout, 1972).

In 1972 a study was published on Danish "athletic champions." The study was unique in that only Danish record-holders, or members of Danish national teams were included in the study. Also, the athletes examined were not exclusively college students; thus their death rate was more comparable to the general population. The study examined men born between 1880 and 1910. It found that up to age 50 the athletes had a death rate 39 percent lower than for the general male Danish population. After age 50, however, the death rate of the athletes was the same as the general population. The author mentioned that only 36 percent of the men in this study engaged in sports that required "unusual cardiovascular stress" (Schnohr, 1972).

In replying to the above article, Largey (1972) reported that he had examined *Who Was Who in America* and found that longevity was affected by the sport in which the athlete participated. Largey found that the mean age at death for certain sports differed significantly. For example, the mean age at death was 57.4 for football, 61.6 for boxing, 64.1 for baseball, and 71.3 for track and field. Schnohr (1972b) responded by saying that in his opinion the differences noted by Largey were primarily social class differences and unrelated to type of sport. Another author responded by noting that body type appeared to be the important variable, with the mesomorphic football players dying before the ectomorphic track and field men (Sheehan, 1972).

A study similar to the one above was published in 1974 except that this one dealt with champion Finnish skiers born between 1845 and 1910. The study found that the skiers lived an average of 2.8 years longer than men in the general population. In examining those who were still alive in 1955–57 it was found that out of the 90 survivors, 70 still skied every winter (Karvonen et al., 1974).

In 1974 Montoye published a follow-up study on the longevity of Michigan State University athletes. The study again found that former athletes were more likely to smoke and drink than were nonathletes. More of the athletes than the nonathletes participated in recreational sports and exercise after college. The study found that those who engaged in vigorous exercise after college had a lower death rate than those who engaged in moderate or mild exercise.

In 1977 a study appeared that examined the extent of participation in college athletics and mortality. The study was conducted on 628 athletes and 563 nonathletes who were students at Michigan State University and who had birth dates between 1855 and 1919. Athletes were defined as those who had been awarded varsity letters. Nonathletes who had birth dates similar to the athletes were then randomly selected. The study found that longevity did not differ between the two groups. It also found that the number of years the individual had engaged in college athletics did not appear to influence longevity (Olson et al., 1977).

A follow-up study on Michigan State University athletes was published in 1978 by Olson and his associates; the study found that the mean age at death for athletes was 68.31 while for nonathletes it was 70.17, a nonsignificant difference. The study also found that cause of death did not differ for the groups. Cancer was the cause of death for 18 percent of the athletes and 17 percent of the nonathletes. Cardiovascular disease killed 51 percent of the athletes and 50 percent of the nonathletes.

The above study is interesting in that it found that the cause of death did not differ between athletes and nonathletes. Several writers have suggested that athletes have a higher rate of death from cancer than nonathletes (see Schmidt, 1975). This study refutes that belief, although such a finding might logically be expected given the fact that participation in athletic activity has been reported to lower the risk for cardiovascular disease, the major cause of death in contemporary society.

Four recent studies on male Harvard alumni, by Paffenbarger and his associates (1978; 1983; 1984; 1986), have focused on the consequences of physical activity and its relationship to cardiovascular disease, heart attack, and high blood pressure. These studies are important since they are less concerned with amount of physical activity when the participant was in college but examine current level of physical activity.

In the first study it was found that those who did not expend more than 2,000 kilocalories per week in physical activity were at a 64 percent greater risk of heart attack than those who expended more than 2,000 kilocalories per week in exercise. This study found that former college athletes were at a lower risk *only* if they maintained "high" physical activity as alumni. Those who had not been athletic as students were at a lower risk of heart attack if they engaged in high physical activity in their middle years than former athletes who had low physical activity in middle age (Paffenbarger et al., 1978).

In the second study Paffenbarger and his associates (1983) found the same results in a study on high blood pressure. This study found that a background of college sports did not influence the probability of having high blood pressure. The important variable was present level of physical activity, with those not participating in "vigorous" exercise at a 35 percent greater risk of having high blood pressure than those engaging in physical activity. High blood pressure is the strongest clinical predictor of a potential coronary event.

The third study by Paffenbarger and his associates (1984), supported the earlier finding that participation in college athletics did not influence the death rate from cardiovascular disease. This replicated the finding that the important variable was postcollege physical activity level. Ex-athletes who became sedentary after college had the highest risk of dying from cardiovascular disease; noncollege athletes who remained sedentary after college had a slightly nonsignificant lower rate. Ex-athletes who remained physically active after college, and noncollege athletes who became physically active after college age had an almost identical low-risk chance of dying from cardiovascular disease. The authors went on and said that death from cardiovascular disease was statistically significantly less for individuals who expended 2,000 kilocalories or more per week in physical activity. They noted that consistency of exercise was important in maintaining cardiovascular health.

After completing their analysis of the data, the above researchers concluded that while a great deal of research demonstrated that sedentary individuals have shorter longevity than active individuals, few researchers were willing to claim that exercise extends longevity. They continued by saying that their results *implied* that longevity is greater in those who exercise, but that definitive statements are difficult to make because of the complexity of the subject being studied and the confounding variables that enter into the research design.

In the fourth study, after more data had been collected and analyzed, Paffenbarger and his associates (1986) were more optimistic about the effects of physical activity on life expectancy when they stated that over a lifetime "adequate" exercise could add one to two more years of life.

Another study, but one using physiological assessment rather than self-report, was done by Blair and his associates (1984). Over 6,000 men and women were examined over a 12 year period. All had normal blood pressure and no history of cardiovascular disease at the beginning of the study. The study was designed to study individuals over time and ascertain if there were significant differences in life style between those who maintained normal blood pressure and whose who developed high blood pressure. The study found that low-fit individuals had a risk of developing high blood pressure that was 1.52 times greater than the high-fit group. This held even when controlling for age, sex, body mass, and other possible confounding variables.

An editorial response to the above article said that "very suggestive evidence" was offered that exercise does protect individuals from developing high blood pressure (Kaplan, 1984). The writer then noted that some methodological problems in the study prevented him from making a stronger statement. He concluded by saying, "who knows, joggers may even live longer."

Although the majority of recent writing and research has emphasized the positive aspects of exercise on longevity, recently three negative aspects have received a great deal of publicity.

First, to enhance performance many athletes are using drugs that may have the cumulative effect of shortening life span. A recent report has suggested that a disproportionate number of former Soviet athletes are dying prematurely, allegedly as a result of training practices involving drugs (Rich, 1984). The death rate of Soviet athletes who competed since 1952 is 17.1 per thousand. This is high when compared to the U.S. rate of 4.5 and the British rate of 2.1. The major drugs suspected of causing the death are anabolic steroids (see Taylor, 1982). Some writers have suggested that further studies are needed before steroids can be implicated (Harries, 1985).

Second, runners are often in an "unfriendly" environment, which may shorten their lives. In addition to motor vehicles, criminals, and a polluted environment, runners must also contend with the possibility of heat stroke or frost bite. Simply by running, runners expose themselves to a number of potential dangers that may shorten life expectancy.

Third, runners may develop a life style that is dangerous. Through weight loss and reduction of body fat, high mileage, and a restricted diet, runners may alter certain body chemistries that produce arrhymthia and death (see Bassler, 1984a; 1984b).

In summary, although research and "common sense" indicate that athletic activity will lengthen life, the evidence is far from conclusive. A recent article by Dr. Bryant Stamford (1984) in *The Physician and Sportsmedicine* noted that there is currently "no conclusive scientific evidence" to support the belief that exercise lengthens the life span. As mentioned in the chapter on the heart, apparently certain forms of athletic activity, in the right duration and intensity, can have a significant influence on cardiac risk factors such as high blood pressure. Although the risk and rate of heart attacks may be lowered, life expectancy may not be significantly extended.

The current reason a more definitive statement cannot be forthcoming is that the studies are limited and dated and most are on athletes who had different nutrition, training, and life styles than athletes today. Additionally, most studies only considered the influence of college athletics on life expectancy and ignored postcollege activity levels. The last factor is that most were poorly designed from a scientific perspective; that is, they were flawed methodologically. As a result, the concerns that were expressed in the 1800s are still present: namely that vigorous exercise may be more harmful than beneficial. This can be seen every time a runner dies during the middle of a run or at the finish line: it is headline news. If fifty thousand overweight men die in their chairs while watching television, drinking beer, and eating popcorn it is an accepted statistic.

Overall the studies support the belief that athletes live longer than nonathletes. This would be logical simply because athletes are generally in better health. That is, due to the lack of health restrictions they have the option of exercising. Thus, to begin with they are an elite group. What is needed are long term (longitudinal) studies that compare different types of athletes to nonathletes and which take into account factors such as life style (especially nutrition), and postadolescent activity levels. Although these studies are difficult and expensive to conduct, it is only through studies of this type that any definitive answers will be obtained.

One important question has not yet been asked. Do athletes have a higher quality of life? To date, researchers have examined length of life rather than quality of life. Although "quality of life" is difficult to determine, one recent study suggests that for the aged running does produce a higher quality of life. This author (Crandall, 1982) conducted a study on 113 joggers 55 and over. This group had a diverse background and were certainly not elite in health. When reporting health problems, 24 percent listed arthritis, 10 percent hearing problems, 11 percent heart problems, 15 percent high blood pressure, and 20 percent poor vision. In addition there had been coronary by-pass operations as well as a variety of other physical problems among the runners. Thus, their past and present physical problems did not make them an "elite" group.

However, when comparing certain characteristics the joggers differed from others the same age. The table opposite shows the differences.

Table III
Characteristics of Joggers 55+ Years of Age
and the General Population 55+ Years of Age

	Joggers	Nonjoggers
Bed Days	1.27	12.9
Physician Visits	1.63	6.5
Hospital Days	9.13	11.6
% Hospitalized	7%	22.5%
% Overweight	30%	70–80%

As can be seen, during the last year the joggers had spent an average of only 1.27 days in bed compared to the nonjoggers who spent an average of 12.9 days. The number of physician visits and hospital days was also much smaller for the joggers than the nonjoggers. The number who were hospitalized was only one-third that of a similar group of nonjoggers and the percent who were overweight was less than half that of the nonjoggers.

Although hardly definitive, the above study suggests that those who exercise have a higher quality of life.

Bibliography

1. Running and the Heart

Adner, M.M., and Castelli, W.P., "Elevated high-density lipoprotein levels in marathon runners." *Journal of the American Medical Association* 243(6):534–536, 1980.

Anonymous, "Meeting defines, explores athlete's heart syndrome." *Physician and Sportsmedicine* 9(2):25, 1981.

Anonymous, "Marathons and coronary health." *Technology Review* 82(March–April):70–71, 1980.

Anonymous, "Cardiac patients run a good race." *Journal of the American Medical Association* 224(12):1580, 1973.

Arends, J., "Beer is anti-freeze." *Michigan Runner* 7(1):9, 1985.

Asay, R.W., and Vieweg, W.V.R., "Severe coronary atherosclerosis in a runner: An exception to the rule."*Journal of Cardiac Rehabilitation* 1(6):413–421, 1981.

Barker, L.F., "Discussion." *Southern Medical Journal* 13(7):488–490, 1920.

Barnes, L., "Jogging death autopsy runaround." *Physician and Sportsmedicine* 7(8):20–21, 1979.

Barry, A.J., Daly, J.W., Pruett, E.D.R., Steinmetz, J.R., Birkhead, N.C., and Rodahl, K., "Effects of physical training in patients who have had myocardial infarction." *American Journal of Cardiology* 17(1):1–8, 1966.

Bassler, T.J., "Hazards of restrictive diets." *Journal of the American Medical Association* 252(4):483, 1984a.

——————, "Cardiomythology." *Lancet* I(April 7):788–789, 1984b.

——————, "Death during jogging." *Journal of the American Medical Association* 249(6):730–731, 1983.

——————, "Running to death." *Chest* 81(6):772, 1982.

——————, "Letter to the editor." *New England Journal of Medicine* 302(1):57–58, 1980a.

——————, "Body build and mortality." *Journal of the American Medical Association* 244(13):1437, 1980b.

——————, "Regression of atheroma." *Western Journal of Medicine* 132(5):474–5, 1980c.

——————, "Rehabilitation through marathon running." *Western Journal of Medicine* 130(5):466, 1979a.

——————, "Heat stroke in a 'run for fun.'" *British Medical Journal* I(January 20):197, 1979b.

——————, "Statistics, marathoning, and CHD." *American Heart Journal* 96(4):560, 1978a.

——————, "More on immunity to atherosclerosis in marathon runners." *New England Journal of Medicine* 299(4):201, 1978b.

——————,"In defense of the hypothesis." *Physician and Sportsmedicine* 6(5):39–43, 1978c.

——————, "Marathon running and atherosclerotic plaques." *Annals of Internal Medicine* 88(1):134, 1978d.

————, "Marathon running and immunity to atherosclerosis." *Annals of the New York Academy of Sciences* 301(October): 579–592, 1977.

————, "Marathon vs. distance running." *New England Journal of Medicine* 294(2):114, 1976a.

————, "To the editor." *Annals of Internal Medicine* 85(3):389, 1976b

————, "Marathon vs. distance running." *New England Journal of Medicine* 294(2):114–115, 1976c.

————, "Is atheroma a reversible lesion?" *Atherosclerosis* 25:141, 1976d.

————, "Marathon running and immunity to heart disease." *Physician and Sportsmedicine* 3(4):77–80, 1975a.

————, "Life expectancy and marathon running." *American Journal of Cardiology* 36:410–411, 1975b.

————, "Life expectancy and marathon running." *American Journal of Cardiology* 36(September):410–411, 1975c.

————, "Coronary heart disease prevention." *Circulation* 49(March):594–595, 1974a.

————, "Prevention of coronary heart disease." *Journal of the American Medical Association* 228(5):365, 1974b.

————, "Marathoning." *Science* 183(January):256–257, 1974c.

————, "Prevention of CHD." *Lancet* I(June 1):1106–1107, 1974d.

————, "Prevention of heart-disease." *Lancet* I(April 6):626, 1974e.

————, "Long-distance runners." *Science* 182(October):113, 1973a.

————, "Cardiac rehabilitation." *Journal of the American Medical Association* 226(7):790, 1973b.

————, "Physician deaths." *Journal of the American Medical Association* 223(12):1391, 1973c.

————, "Letter to the editor." *Lancet* II(September 30):711–712, 1972a.

————, "Jogging deaths." *New England Journal of Medicine* 287(November 23):1100, 1972b.

————, "Letter to the editor." *Lancet* II(September 30): 711–712, 1972c.

————, and Cardello, F.P., "Fiber-feeding and atherosclerosis." *Journal of the American Medical Association* 235(17):1841–1842, 1976.

————, and ————, "Jogging and health." *Journal of the American Medical Association* 231(1):23, 1975.

————, and Scaff, J., "Impending heart-attacks." *Lancet* I(March 6):544–545, 1976.

————, and ————, "Letter to the editor." *New England Journal of Medicine* 292:(24):1302, 1975a.

————, and ————, "Marathon running after myocardial infarction." *Journal of the American Medical Association* 233(6):511, 1975b.

————, and ————, "Can I avoid a heart-attack?" *Lancet* I(May 4):863–864, 1974a.

————, and ————, "Mileage preferable to medication." *New England Journal of Medicine* 291(22):1192, 1974b.

Boyer, J.L., and Kasch, F.W., "Exercise therapy in hyperactive men." *Journal of the American Medical Association* 211(10):1668–71, 1970.

Brown, R., Davidson, L., McKeown, T., and Whitfield, A., "Coronary artery disease." *Lancet* II:1073, 1957.

Bruce, E.H., Frederick, R., Bruce, R.A., and Fisher, L.D., "Comparison of active participants and dropouts in CAPRI cardiopulmonary rehabilitation programs." *American Journal of Cardiology* 37(January):53–60, 1976.

Brunner, D., "Active exercise for coronary patients." *Rehabilitation Records* 9(September–October):29–31, 1968.

————, Manelis, G., Modan, M., and Levin, S., "Physical activity at work and the incidence of myocardial infarction, angina pectoris and death due to ischemic heart disease." *Journal of Chronic Disease* 27:217–233, 1974.

Caldwell, F., "Epidemiology takes its place on the sports medicine team." *Physician and Sportsmedicine* 13(3):135–140, 1985.

Cantwell, J.D., "To the editor." *Annals of Internal Medicine* 85(3):392, 1976.

_____, and Fletcher, G.F., "Sudden death and jogging." *Physician and Sportsmedicine* 6(3):94–98, 1978.

Cardello, F., "Letter." *New England Journal of Medicine* 294(2):115, 1976a.

_____, "Letter to the editor." *Annals of Internal Medicine* 85(3):392, 1976b.

Carruthers, M., Nixon, P., and Murray, A., "Safe sport." *Lancet* I(February 22):447, 1975.

Carson, P., "Activity after myocardial infarction." *British Medical Journal* 288(January 7):1–2, 1984.

Cassel, J., Heyden, S., Bartel, A.G., Kaplan, B.H., Tyroler, H.A., Cornoni, J.C., and Hames, C.G., "Occupation and physical activity and coronary heart disease." *Archives of Internal Medicine* 128(December):920–928, 1971.

Castelli, W.P., "Exercise and high-density lipoproteins." *Journal of the American Medical Association* 242(20):2217, 1979.

Clausen, J.P., Larsen, O.A., and Trap-Jensen, J., "Physical training in the management of coronary artery disease." *Circulation* 60(2):143–154, 1969.

Coe, W.S., "Cardiac work and the chair treatment of acute coronary thrombosis." *Annals of Internal Medicine* 40:42–48, 1954.

Colt, E., "Coronary-artery disease in marathon runners." *New England Journal of Medicine* 302(1):57, 1980.

Cooper, K.H., Pollock, M.L., Martin, R.P., White, S.R., Linnerud, A.C., and Jackson, A., "Physical fitness levels vs selected coronary risk factors." *Journal of the American Medical Association* 236(2):166–169, 1976.

Costill, D.L., Branam, G.E., Moore, J.C., Sparks, K., and Turner, C., "Effects of physical training in men with coronary heart disease." *Medicine and Science in Sports* 6(2):95–100, 1974.

_____, Pearson, D.R., and Fink, W.J., "Anabolic steroid use among athletes: changes in HDL-C levels." *Physician and Sportsmedicine* 12(6):113–117, 1984.

Council on Scientific Affairs, "Physician-supervised exercise programs in rehabilitation of patients with CHD." *Journal of the American Medical Association* 245(14):1463–1466, 1981.

Coverman, M.H., "Symptomatic coronary artery disease in a marathon runner." *Journal of the American Medical Association* 249(7):882, 1983.

Coyle, E.F., Martin, W.H., Ehsani, A.A., Hagberg, J.M., Bloomfield, S.A., Sinacore, D.R., and Holloszy, J.O., "Blood lactate threshold in some well-trained ischemic heart disease patients." *Journal of Applied Physiology* 54(1):18–23, 1983.

Crawford, D.W., and Blankenhorn, D.H., "Regression of atherosclerosis." *Annual Review of Medicine* 30:289–300, 1979.

Cunningham, D.A., and Rechnitzer, P.A., "Exercise prescription and the postcoronary patient." *Archives of Physical Medicine and Rehabilitation* 55(July):296–300, 1974.

Currens, J.H., and White, P.D., "Half a century of running: clinical, physiologic and autopsy findings in the case of Clarence DeMar ('Mr. Marathon')." *New England Journal of Medicine* 265(20):988–993, 1961.

Dayton, S., "Long-distance running and sudden death." *New England Journal of Medicine* 293(18):941, 1975.

DeBusk, R.F., Houston, N., Haskell, W., Fry, G., and Parker, M., "Exercise training soon after myocardial infarction." *American Journal of Cardiology* 44(7):1223–1229, 1979.

deCarvalho, A., "Hard running training and atherosclerosis: a radiological assessment." *Journal of Sports Medicine* 18:341–344, 1978.

Deftos, L.J., "Letter to the editor." *Annals of Internal Medicine* 85(3):390, 1976.

Dennis, C., "Which MI patient has second-event risk?" *Hospital Practice* 19(9):50–52, 1984.

Denolin, H., "Cardiac rehabilitation: an overview." In A. Raineri, J.J. Kellermann, and V. Rulli (eds.) *Selected Topics in Exercise Cardiology and Rehabilitation* (New York: Plenum Press, 1980), pp. 1–7.

DeSmet, J.M., Niset, G., Degre, G., and Primo, G., "Jogging after heart transplantation." *New England Journal of Medicine* 309(24):1521–1522, 1983.

Dock, W., "The evil sequelae of complete bed rest." *Journal of the American Medical Association* 125(16):1083–1085, 1944.

Dodek, A., "Mitral valve prolapse in a runner." *Canadian Journal of Applied Sport Science* 7(2):134–137, 1982.

Dressendorfer, R.H., Wade, C.E., Hornick, C., and Timmis, G.C., "High-density lipoprotein-cholesterol in marathon runners during a 20-day road race." *Journal of the American Medical Association* 247(12):1715–1717, 1982.

Defaux, B., Assmann, G., Schachten, H., "Acute cholesterol changes seen after severe exercise." *European Journal of Applied Physiology* 48:25–29, 1982.

Dunn, K., "Low-mileage runners had significant gains." *Physician and Sportsmedicine* 9(9):25, 1981.

Eckstein, R.W., "Effect of exercise and coronary artery narrowing on coronary collateral circulation." *Circulation Research* 5:230–235, 1957.

Eggertsen, S.C., and Berg., A.O., "Is it good practice to treat patients with uncomplicated myocardial infarction at home?" *Journal of the American Medical Association* 251(3):349–350, 1984.

Elrick, H., "Distance runners as models of optimal health." *Physician and Sportsmedicine* 9(1):64–68, 1981.

Epstein, F.H., "Reply." *Circulation* 49(March):595, 1974.

Epstein, L., Miller, G.J., Stitt, F.W., and Morris, J.N., "Vigorous exercise in leisure time, coronary risk-factors, and resting electrocardiogram in middle-aged male civil servants." *British Heart Journal* 38:403–409, 1976.

Erkelens, D.W., Albers, J.J., Hazzard, W.R., Frederick, R.C., and Bierman, E.L., "High-density lipoprotein-cholesterol in survivors of myocardial infarction." *Journal of the American Medical Association* 242(20):2185–2189, 1979.

Fardy, P.S., Doll, N., Taylor J., and Williams, M., "Monitoring cardiac patients: How much is enough." *Physician and Sportsmedicine* 10(6):146–152, 1982.

_____, Maresh, C.M., and Abbott, R.D., "A comparison of myocardial function in former athletes and non-athletes." *Medicine and Science in Sports* 8(1):26–30, 1976.

Farrell, P.A., Wilmore, J.H., and Coyle, E.F., "Exercise heart rate as a predictor of running performance." *Research Quarterly* 51(2):417–421, 1980.

Ferguson, R.J., Choquette, G., and Chaniotis, L., "Coronary arteriography and treadmill exercise capacity before and after 13 months of physical training." *Medicine and Science in Sports and Exercise* 5:67–68, 1973.

Fernhall, B., Manfredi, T.G., and Rierson, H., "Effects of 10 weeks of cardiac rehabilitation on blood clotting and risk factors." *Physician and Sportsmedicine* 12(2):85–96, 1984.

Fitzgerald, W., "Labile hypertension and jogging: new diagnostic tool or spurious discovery?" *British Medical Journal* 282(February 14):542–544, 1982.

Fletcher, G.F., "Cardiovascular response to exercise training." *Physician and Sportsmedicine* (5):83–87, 1977.

Fox, S.M., and Haskell, W.L., "Physical activity and the prevention of coronary heart disease." *Bulletin of New York Academy of Medicine* 44(8):950–967, 1968.

Froelicher, V., Battler, A., and McKirnan, M.D., "Physical activity and coronary heart disease." *Cardiology* 65:153–190, 1980.

Fu, F.H., "The effects of two modes of training on postmyocardial infarction patients." *Journal of Sports Medicine* 19:291–296, 1979.

Gamble, P., and Froelicher, V.F., "Can an exercise program worsen heart disease?" *Physician and Sportsmedicine* 10(5):69–77, 1982.

Ganda, O.P., "Letter to the editor." *Annals of Internal Medicine* 85(3):389–390, 1976.

Goldberg, L., and McMahon, M., "Relation of high-intensity exercise to recurrent rate of myocardial infarction and/or coronary death." *American Journal of Cardiology* 52(3):429, 1983.

Goldschlager, N., Cake, D., and Cohn, K., "Exercise-induced ventricular arrhythmias in patients with coronary artery disease." *American Journal of Cardiology* 31(April):434–440, 1973.

Gordon, J.N., and Fleiss, P.M., "To the editor." *Journal of the American Medical Association* 245(11):1120–1121, 1981.

Gordon, T., Castelli, W.P., Hjortland, M.C., Kannel, W.B., and Dawber, T.S., "High density lipoprotein as a protective factor against coronary heart disease." *American Journal of Medicine* 62(May):707–714, 1977.

Gottheiner, V., "Long-range strenuous sports training for cardiac reconditioning and rehabilitation." *American Journal of Cardiology* 22(September):426–435, 1968.

Green, L.H., "Letter to the editor." *Annals of Internal Medicine* 85(3):390, 1976.

_____, Cohen, S.I., and Kurland G., "Fatal myocardial infarction in marathon racing." *Annals of Internal Medicine* 84(6):704–706, 1976.

Gurewich, V., and Lapinska, I., "Symptomatic coronary artery disease in a marathon runner." *Journal of the American Medical Association* 249(7):881–882, 1983.

Gunby, P., "What causes sudden death in young athletes?" *Journal of the American Medical Association* 241(2):123–124, 1979.

Hagan, R.D., Smith, M.G., and Gettman, L.R., "High density lipoprotein cholesterol in relation to food consumption and running distance." *Preventive Medicine* 12(2):287–295, 1983.

Hage, P., "Exercise, HDL, clear postprandial fat." *Physician and Sportsmedicine* 11(6):35–36, 1983.

_____, "Exercise guildelines: which to believe?" *Physician and Sportsmedicine* 10(6):23, 1982.

_____, "Exercise value oversold, cardiac researcher says." *Physician and Sportsmedicine* 9(7):21, 1981.

Hall, J.A., Dixson, G.H., Barnard, R.J., and Pritikin, N., "Effects of diet and exercise on peripheral vascular disease." *Physician and Sportsmedicine* 10(5):90–101, 1982.

Handler, J.B., Asay, R.W., Warren, S.E., Shea, P.M., "Symptomatic coronary artery disease in a marathon runner." *Journal of the American Medical Association* 248(6):717–719, 1982.

Hanson, J., and Nedde, W.H., "Preliminary observations on physical training for hypertensive males." *Circulation Research* 26–27 (Supplement I):I-49–I-53, 1970.

Hardison, J.E., "Walking in the Peachtree Road Race." *Journal of the American Medical Association* 248(23):3153, 1982.

Harpur, J.E., Conner, W.T., Hamilton, M., Kellett, R.J., Galbraith, H.J.B., Murray, J.J., Swallow, J.H., and Rose, G.A., "Controlled trial of early mobilisation and discharge from hospital in uncomplicated myocardial infarction." *Lancet* II(December 18):1331–1334, 1971.

Harrison, T.R., "Abuse of rest as a therapeutic measure for patients with cardiovascular disease." *Journal of the American Medical Association* 125(16):1075–1077, 1944.

Hartung, G.H., "Jogging—the potential for prevention of heart disease." *Comprehensive Therapy* 6(9):28–32, 1980.

_____, "Physical activity and coronary heart disease risk—a review." *American Corrective Therapy Journal* 31(4):110–115, 1977.

_____, Farge, E.J., and Mitchell, R.F., "Effects of marathon running, jogging, and diet on coronary risk factors in middled-aged men." *Preventive Medicine* 10:316–323, 1981.

_____, Foreyt, J.P., Mitchell, R.E., Mitchell, J.G., Reeves, R.S., and Gotto, A.M., "Effect of alcohol intake on high-density lipoprotein cholesterol levels in runners and inactive men." *Journal of the American Medical Association* 249(6):747–750, 1983.

_____, _____, _____, Vlasek, I., and Gotto, A.M., "Relation of diet to high-density lipoprotein cholesterol in middle-aged marathon runners, joggers, and inactive men." *New England Journal of Medicine* 302(7):357–361, 1980.

_____, and Squires, W.G., "Exercise and HDL cholesterol in middle-aged men." *Physician and Sportsmedicine* 8(1):74–79, 1980.

Haskell, W.L., "Physical activity after myocardial infarction." *American Journal of Cardiology* 33(May 20):776–783, 1974.

_____, Camargo, C., Williams, P.T., Vranizan, K.M., Krauss, R.M., Lindgren, F.T., and Wood, P.D., "The effect of cessation and resumption of moderate alcohol intake on serum high-density lipoprotein subfractions." *New England Journal of Medicine* 310(13):805–810, 1984.

Havlik, R.J., "Understanding the decline in coronary heart disease mortality." *Journal of the American Medical Association* 247(11):1605–1606, 1982.

Hayes, M.J., Morris, G.K., and Hampton, J.R., "Comparison of mobilization after two and nine days in uncomplicated myocardial infarction." *British Medical Journal* II(July 6):10–13, 1974.

Hellerstein, H.K., "Exercise therapy in coronary disease." *Bulletin of the New York Academy of Medicine* 44(8):1028–1047, 1968.

Hennekens, C.H., Rosner, B., Jesse, M.J., Drolette, M.E., and Speizer, F.E., "A retrospective study of physical activity and coronary deaths." *International Journal of Epidemiology* 6(3):243–246, 1977.

Herold, K.C., and Herold, B.C., "Benefits and risks of exercise." *Journal of the American Medical Association* 249(21):2899, 1983.

Hypertension Detection and Follow-up Program Cooperative Group, "Five-year findings of hypertension detection and follow-up program." *Journal of the American Medical Association* 242(23):2562–2571, 1979.

Ibrahim, M.A., "In support of jogging." *American Journal of Public Health* 73(2):136–137, 1983.

Irvin, C.W., and Burgess, A.M., "The abuse of bed rest in the treatment of myocardial infarction." *New England Journal of Medicine* 243(13):486–489, 1950.

Jennett, S., Lamb, J.F., and Travis, P., "Sudden large periodic changes in heart rate in healthy young men after short periods of exercise." *British Medical Journal* 285(October 23):1154–1156, 1982.

Jennings, K., Reid, D.S., Hawkins, T., and Julian, D.J., "Role of exercise testing early after myocardial infarction in identifying candidates for coronary surgery." *British Medical Journal* 288(January 21):185–187, 1984.

Jokl, E., "A response to Dr. Friedman." *American Corrective Therapy Journal* 33(5):165–166, 1979.

Jones, R.J., "Mortality of joggers." *Journal of the American Medical Association* 247(18):2569, 1982.

Kahn, H.A., "The relationship of reported coronary heart disease mortality to physical activity of work." *American Journal of Public Health* 53(7):1058–1067, 1963.

Kallio, V., Hamalainen, H., Hakkila, J., and Luurila, O.J., "Reduction in sudden deaths by a multifactorial intervention programme after acute myocardial infarction." *Lancet* II(November 24):1091–1094, 1979.

Kannel, W.B., "Meaning of the downward trend in cardiovascular mortality." *Journal of the American Medical Association* 247(6):877–880, 1982a.

_____, "Exercise and sudden death." *Journal of the American Medical Association* 248(23):3143–3144, 1982b.

Karvonen, M.J., Rautaharju, P.M., Orma, E., Punsar, S., and Takkunen, J., "Heart disease and employment." *Journal of Occupational Medicine* 3(February):49–53, 1961.

Kasch, F.W., and Boyer, J.L., "Changes in maximum work capacity resulting from six months training in patients with ischemic heart disease." *Medicine and Science in Sports* 1(3):156–159, 1969.

_____, Phillips, W.H., Carter, J.E.L., and Boyer, J.L., "Cardiovascular changes in middle-aged men during two years of training." *Journal of Applied Physiology* 34(1):53–57, 1973.

Kaufman, S., Kaufman, B., Reynolds, D., Trayner, I., and Thompson G.R., "Effects of jogging on serum low density lipoprotein cholesterol." *Artery* 7(2):99–108, 1980.

Kavanagh, T., and Shephard, R.J., "Maximum exercise tests on 'postcoronary' patients." *Journal of Applied Physiology* 40(4):611–618, 1976.

_____, and _____, "Importance of physical activity in post-coronary rehabilitation." *American Journal of Physical Therapy* 52(6):304–313, 1973.

_____, _____, Chisholm, A.W., Qureshi, S., and Kennedy, J., "Prognostic indexes for patients with ischemic heart disease enrolled in an exercise-centered rehabilitation program." *American Journal of Cardiology* 44(December) 1230–1240, 1979.

_____, _____, Doney, H., and Pandit, V., "Intensive exercise in coronary rehabilitation." *Medicine and Science in Sports* 5(1):34–39, 1973.

_____, _____, and Pandit, V., "Marathon running after myocardial infarction." *Journal of the American Medical Association* 229(12):1602–1605, 1974.

_____, _____, _____, and Doney, H., "Exercise and hypnotherapy in the rehabilitation of the coronary patient." *Archives of Physical Medicine and Rehabilitation* 51(October):578–587, 1970.

Keren, G., and Shoenfeld, Y., "Sudden death and physical exertion." *Journal of Sports Medicine* 21:90–93, 1981.

Khosla, T., and Campbell, H., "Resting pulse rate in marathon runners." *British Medical Journal* 284(May 15):1444, 1982.

Koplan, J.P., "In reply." *Journal of the American Medical Association* 249(21):2889, 1983.

_____, "Cardiovascular deaths while running." *Journal of the American Medical Association* 242(23):2578–2579, 1979.

_____, Powell, K.E., Sikes, R.K., Shirley, R.W., and Campbell, C.C., "An epidemiologic study of the benefits and risks of running." *Journal of the American Medical Association* 248(23):3118–3121, 1982.

Kostrubala, T., "Letter." *Annals of Internal Medicine* 85(3):389, 1976.

Kueh, L.A., "Implications of athletes's bradycardia on lifespan." *Journal of Theoretical Biology* 88:279–286, 1981.

Lamers, H.J., Drost, W.S.J., Kroon, B.J.M., VanEs, L.A., Meilink-Hoedemaker, L.J., and Birkenhager, W.H., "Early mobilization after myocardial infarction: a controlled study." *British Medical Journal* I(February 3):257–259, 1973.

232   Bibliography

LaPorte, R.E., Brenes, G., Dearwater, S., Murphy, M.A., Cauley, J.A., Dietrick, R., and Robertson, R., "HDL cholesterol across a spectrum of physical activity from quadriplegia to marathon running." *Lancet I*(May 28):1212–1213, 1983.

Ledingham, I., MacVicar, S., Watt, I., Weston, G.A., "Early resuscitation after marathon collapse." *Lancet II*(November 13):1096–1097, 1982.

Lees, R.S., and Lees, A.M., "High-density lipoproteins and the risk of atherosclerosis." *New England Journal of Medicine* 306(25):1546–1547, 1982.

Lehtonen, A., and Viikari, J., "Letter to the editor." *New England Journal of Medicine* 302(1):57, 1980.

Leibel, B., Kobrin, I., and Ben-Ishay, D., "Exercise testing in assessment of hypertension." *British Medical Journal* 285(November27):1535–1536, 1982.

Levine, S.A., "The myth of strict bed rest in the treatment of heart disease." *American Heart Journal* 42:406–413, 1951.

_____, "Some harmful effects of recumbency in the treatment of heart disease." *Journal of the American Medical Association* 126(2):80–84, 1944.

_____, "The management of patients with heart disease." *Journal of the American Medical Association* 115(20):1715–1719, 1940.

_____, and Lown, B., "Armchair treatment of acute coronary thrombosis." *Journal of the American Medical Association* 148(16):1365–1369, 1952.

Levy, R.I., and Ward, G.W., "Hypertension control: A succeeding national effort." *Journal of the American Medical Association* 241(23):2546, 1979.

Lloyd, E., "Marathon medicine." *Lancet I*(January 1/8):69–70, 1983.

McIntosh, H.D., "Jogging: Thou shall not kill (thyself)." *Journal of the American Medical Association* 241(23):2547–2548, 1979.

_____, "Reply." *American Journal of Cardiology* 36(September):411, 1975.

McNamara, J.J., Molot, M.A., Stremple, J.F., and Cutting, R.T., "Coronary artery disease in combat casualties in Vietnam." *Journal of the American Medical Association* 216(7):1185–1187, 1971.

McNeer, J., Wagner, G.S., Ginsburg, P.B., Wallace, A.G., McCants, C.B., Conley, M.J., and Rosati, R.A., "Hospital discharge one week after acute myocardial infarction." *New England Journal of Medicine* 298(5):229–232, 1978.

Magder, S., Linnarsson, D., and Gullstrand, L., "The effects of swimming on patients with ischemic heart disease." *Circulation* 63(5):979–986, 1981.

Mallory, G.K., White, P.D., and Salcedo-Salgar, J., "The speed of healing of myocardial infarction." *American Heart Journal* 18(6):647–671, 1939.

Marlow, T., "Cardiovascular deaths while running." *Journal of the American Medical Association* 244(11):1194–1195, 1980.

Martin, R.P., Haskell, W.L., and Wood, P.D., "Blood chemistry and lipid profiles of elite distance runners." *Annals of the New York Academy of Sciences* 301(October):346–359, 1977.

Mattingly, T.W., "Paul Dudley White: The porpoise heart vs the athletic heart." *Journal of the American Medical Association* 236(2):185–187, 1976.

Mayou, R., Sleight, P., MacMahon, D., and Florencio, M.J., "Early rehabilitation after myocardial infarction." *Lancet II*(December 19):1399–1401, 1981.

Menotti, A., Puddu, V., Monti, M., and Fidanza, F., "Habitual physical activity and myocardial infarction." *Cardiologia* 54:119–128, 1969.

Milesis, C.A. "Effects of metered physical training on serum lipids of adult men." *Journal of Sports Medicine* 14:8–13, 1974.

_____, Pollock M.L., Bah, M.D., Ayres, J.J., Ward, A., and Linnerud, A.C., "Effects of different durations of physical training on cardio-respiratory function, body composition, and serum lipids." *Research Quarterly* 47(4):716–723, 1976.

Miller, B.F., and Keane, C.B., *Encyclopedia and Dictionary of Medicine, Nursing, and Allied Health*. Philadelphia: W. B. Saunders Co., 1978.

Miller, G.J., "High density lipoproteins and atherosclerosis." *Annual Review of Medicine* 31:97–108, 1980.

_____, and Miller, N.E., "Plasma-high-density-lipoprotein concentration and development of ischemic heart-disease." *Lancet* I(January 4):16–19, 1975.

Miller, S.S., *Symptoms: The Complete Home Medical Encyclopedia.* New York: Avon, 1976.

Milvy, P., "Statistics, marathoning and CHD." *American Heart Journal* 95(4):538–539, 1978a.

_____, "Reply." *American Heart Journal* 96(4):560–561, 1978b.

_____, "Statistical analysis of deaths from coronary heart disease anticipated in a cohort of marathon runners." *Annals of the New York Academy of Sciences* 301(October):620–626, 1977.

Montgomery, B.J., "High plasma insulin level a prime risk factor for heart disease." *Journal of the American Medical Association* 241(16):1665, 1979.

Montoye, H.J., Metzner, H.L., Keller, J.B., Johnson, B.C., and Epstein, F.H., "Habitual activity and blood pressure." *Medicine and Science in Sports* 4(4):175–181, 1972.

Morris, J.N., "Exercise, health, and medicine." *British Medical Journal* 286(May 21):1597–1598, 1983.

_____, "Occupation and coronary heart disease." *Archives of Internal Medicine* 104(December):903–907, 1959.

_____, Adams, C., Chave, S.P.W., Sirey, C., Epstein, L., and Sheehan, D.J., "Vigorous exercise in leisure-time and the incidence of coronary heart-disease." *Lancet* I(February 17):333–339, 1973.

_____, Chave, S.P.W., Adam, C., Sirey, C., Epstein L., and Sheehan, D.J., "Vigorous exercise in leisure-time and the incidence of coronary heart disease." *Lancet* I:1333–1339, 1973.

_____, Crawford, M.D., "Coronary heart disease and physical activity of work." *British Medical Journal* II(December 20):1485–1496, 1958.

_____, Heady, J., and Raffle, P.A.B., "Physique of London busmen." *Lancet* II(September 15):569–570, 1956.

_____, Heady, J.A., Raffle, P.A.B., Roberts, C.G., and Parks, J.W., "Coronary-heart disease and physical activity of work." *Lancet* II(Nov 21):1053–1120, 1953a.

_____, _____, _____, _____, and _____, "Coronary-heart disease and physical activity of work." *Lancet* II(November 28):1111–1120, 1953b.

_____, Kagan, A., Pattison, D.C., Gardner, M.J., and Raffle, P.A.B., "Incidence and prediction of ischemic heart-disease in London busmen." *Lancet* II(September 10):553–559, 1966.

_____, Pollard, R., Everitt, M.G., Chave, S.P.W., and Semmence, A.M., "Vigorous exercise in leisure-time: protection against coronary heart disease." *Lancet* II(December 6):1207–1210, 1980.

Moss, A.J., "Prediction and prevention of sudden cardiac death." *Annual Review of Medicine* 31:1–14, 1980.

Mueller, J. and Felts, J.H., "Letter to the editor." *Annals of Internal Medicine* 85(3):390, 1976.

National Exercise and Heart Disease Project, "Effects of a prescribed supervised exercise program on mortality and cardiovascular morbidity in patients after a myocardial infarction." *American Journal of Cardiology* 48(July):39–46, 1981.

Niset, G., Poortmans, J.R., Leclercq, R., Brasseur, M., DeSmet, J.M., and Primo, G., "Metabolic implications during a 20-km run after heart transplant." *International Journal of Sports Medicine* 6(6):340–343, 1985.

Noakes, T.D., Lionel, M.B., Opie, H., Rose, A.G., and Kleynhans, P.H.T., "Autopsy-proved coronary atherosclerosis in marathon runners." *New England Journal of Medicine* 301(2):86–89, 1979.

_____, and Opie, L.H., "Letter to the editor." *New England Journal of Medicine* 302(1):58, 1980.

_____, and _____, "Marathon running and the heart: The South African experience." *American Heart Journal* 98(5):669–671, 1979.

_____, and _____, "Marathon running and immunity to coronary atherosclerosis." *Atherosclerosis* 27:119–120, 1977.

_____, and _____, "Marathon runners and impending heart-attacks." *Lancet* I(May 8):1020, 1976.

_____, _____, and Beck, W., "Coronary heart disease in marathon runners." *Annals of the New York Academy of Sciences* 301(October):593–619, 1977.

_____, _____, and Rose, A.G., "Marathon running and immunity to coronary heart disease: fact versus fiction." *Clinics in Sports Medicine* 3(2):527–543, 1984.

_____, and Rose, A.G., "Exercise-related deaths in subjects with coexistent hypertropic cardiomyopathy and coronary artery disease." *South African Medical Journal* 66(4):183–187, 1984.

_____, _____, and Opie, L.H., "Hypertrophic cardiomyopathy associated with sudden death during marathon racing." *British Heart Journal* 41:624–627, 1979.

Nolewajka, A.J., Kostuk, W.J., Rechnitzer, P.A., and Cunningham, D.A., "Exercise and human collateralization: an angiographic and scintigraphic assessment." *Circulation* 60(1):114–121, 1979.

Northcote, R.J., and Ballantyne, D., "Sudden death in a marathon runner." *Lancet* I(February 19):417, 1983.

Olsen, Eric, "Fitness report from the morgue." *Runner* 4(8):57–63, 1982.

Opie, L.H., "Heart disease in marathon runners." *New England Journal of Medicine* 294(19):1067, 1976.

_____, "Sudden death and sport." *Lancet* I(February 1):263–266, 1975a.

_____, "Exercise, sport, and sudden death." *Lancet* I(May 17):1141–1142, 1975b.

_____, "Letter to the editor." *New England Journal of Medicine* 293(18):941–942, 1975c.

_____, Exercise training, the myocardium, and ischemic heart disease." *American Heart Journal* 88(5):539–541, 1974.

Orselli, R., "Letter to the editor." *Annals of Internal Medicine* 85(3):389, 1976.

Paffenbarger, R.S., "Paternal history of heart attack in marathoners." *New England Journal of Medicine* 302(1):56, 1980.

_____, and Hale, W.E., "Work activity and coronary heart mortality." *New England Journal of Medicine* 292(11):545–550, 1975.

_____, _____, Brand, R.J., Hyde, R.T. "Work-energy, personal characteristics, and fatal heart attack: A birth-cohort effect." *American Journal of Epidemiology* 105(3):200–213, 1977.

_____, Hyde, R.T., Wing, A.L., and Hsieh, C-C., "Physical activity, all-cause mortality, and longevity of college alumni." *New England Journal of Medicine* 314(10):605–613, 1986.

_____, _____, _____, and Steinmetz, C.H., "A natural history of athleticism and cardiovascular health." *Journal of the American Medical Association* 252(4):491–495, 1984.

_____, Laughlin, M.E., Gima, A.S., and Black, R.A., "Work activity of longshoremen as related to death from coronary heart disease and stroke." *New England Journal of Medicine* 282(20):1109–1113, 1970.

_____, Wing, A.L., and Hyde, R.T., "Physical activity as an index of heart attack risk in college alumni." *American Journal of Epidemiology* 108(3):161–175, 1978.

_____, Wolf, P.A., Notkin, J., and Thorne, M.C., "Chronic disease in former college students." *American Journal of Epidemiology* 83(3):314–328, 1966.

Pantano, J.A., and Oriel, R.J., "Prevalence and nature of cardiac arrhythmias in apparently normal well-trained runners." *American Heart Journal* 104(4):762–768, 1982.

Peters, R.K., Cady, L.D., Bischoff, D.P., Bernstein, L., and Pike, M.C., "Physical fitness and subsequent myocardial infarction in healthy workers." *Journal of the American Medical Association* 249(22):3052–3056, 1983.

Peterson, G.E., and Fahey, T.D., "HDL-C in five elite athletes using anabolic-androgenic steroids." *Physician and Sportsmedicine* 12(6):120–130, 1984.

Phibbs, B., *The Human Heart*. St. Louis: C.V. Mosby Company, 1971.

Philbrick, J.T., Horwitz, R.I., Feinstein, A.R., Langou, R.A., and Chandler, J.P., "The limited spectrum of patient studies in exercise test research." *Journal of the American Medical Association* 248(19):2467–2470, 1982.

Pickering, T.G., "Jogging, marathon running and the heart." *American Journal of Medicine* 66(5):717–719, 1979.

Pierach, C.A., "To the editor." *Journal of the American Medical Association* 249(7):882, 1983.

Pollock, M.L., Miller, H.S., Janeway, R., Linnerud, A.C., Robertson B., and Valentino, R., "Effects of walking on body composition and cardiovascular function of middle-aged men." *Journal of Applied Physiology* 30(1):126–130, 1971.

_____, Wilmore, J.H., and Fox, S.M., *Health and Fitness Through Physical Activity*. New York: John Wiley and Sons. 1978.

Pomrehn, P.R., Wallace, R.B., and Burmeister, L.F., "Ischemic heart disease mortality in Iowa Farmers." *Journal of the American Medical Association* 248(9):1073–1076, 1982.

Pratt, J.H., "Rest and exercise in the treatment of heart disease." *Southern Medical Journal* 13(7):481–488, 1920.

Raineri, A., Kellermann, J.J., and Rulli, V., *Selected Topics in Exercise Cardiology and Rehabilitation*. New York: Plenum. 1979.

Raskoff, W.J., Goldman, S., and Cohn, K., "The 'athletic' heart." *Journal of the American Medical Association* 236(2):158–162, 1976.

Rechnitzer, P.A. "Specific benefits of postcoronary exercise programs." *Geriatrics* 37(3):47–51, 1982.

_____, Cunningham, D.A., Andrew, G.M., Buck, C.W., Jones, N.L., Kavanagh, T., Oldridge, N.B., Parker, J.O., Shephard, R.J., Sutton, J.R., and Donner, A.P., "Relation of exercise to the recurrence rate of myocardial infarction in men." *American Journal of Cardiology* 51(January 1): 65–69, 1983.

_____, Pickard, H.A., Paivio, A.U., Yuhasz, M.S., and Cunningham, D., "Long-term follow-up study of survival and recurrence rates following myocardial infarction in exercising and control subjects." *Circulation* 45(April):853–857, 1972.

_____, Sangal, S., Cunningham, D.A., Andrew, G., Buck, C., Jones, N.L., Kavanagh, T., Parker, J.O., Shephard, R.J., and Yuhasz, M.S., "A controlled prospective study of the effects of endurance training on the recurrence rate of myocardial infarction." *American Journal of Epidemiology* 102(1):358–365, 1972.

Redwood, D.R., Rosing, D.R., and Epstein, S., "Circulatory and symptomatic effects of physical training in patients with coronary-artery disease and angina pectoris." *New England Journal of Medicine* 286(18):959–965, 1972.

Rennie, D., and Hollenberg, N., "Cardiomythology and marathons." *New England Journal of Medicine* 301(2):103–104, 1979.

Rigotti, N.A., Thomas, M.P.H., and Leaf, A., "Exercise and coronary heart disease." *Annual Review of Medicine: Selected Topics in the Clinical Sciences* 34:391–412, 1983.

Robertson, H.K., "Does life-long exercise protect against heart attack?" *British Medical Journal* 285(September 25):861, 1982.

Ross, R.S., "Early discharge after heart attacks and the efficient use of hospitals." *New England Journal of Medicine* 298(5):275–277, 1978.

Scaff, J.H., "Letter." *Annals of Internal Medicine* 85(3):391, 1976a.

_____, "Heart disease in marathon runners." *New England Journal of Medicine* 295(2):105, 1976b.

_____, and Bassler, T.J., "Imputs into coronary care." *Annals of Internal Medicine* 81(6):862, 1974.

Schaefer, O., "Vigorous exercise and coronary heart-disease." *Lancet* I(April 14):840, 1973.

Schnohr, P., "Longevity and causes of death in male athletic champions." *Lancet* I(December 18):1364–1366, 1971.

Schoenberger, J.A., "The downward trend in cardiovascular mortality: Challenge and opportunity for the practitioner." *Journal of the American Medical Association* 247(6):836, 1982.

Shaver, L.G., *Essentials of Exercise Physiology.* Minneapolis: Burgess, 1981.

Shaw, L.W. "Effects of a prescribed supervised exercise program on mortality and cardiovascular morbidity in patients after a myocardial infarction." *American Journal of Cardiology* 48(July):39–46, 1981.

Sheehan, G., "Letter to the editor." *Annals of Internal Medicine* 85(3):392, 1976.

Siegel, A.J., "Letter to the editor." *New England Journal of Medicine* 302(1):56, 1980.

_____, "The Bassler hypothesis: A eulogy." *Physician and Sportsmedicine* 6(5):37–39, 1978.

_____, Hennekens, C.H., Roner, B., and Karlson, L.K., "Paternal history of coronary-heart disease reported by marathoner runners." *New England Journal of Medicine* 301(2):90–91, 1979.

_____, and Milvy, P., "To the editor." *Journal of the American Medical Association* 244(11):1195, 1980.

Siscovick, D.S., Weiss, N.S., Fletcher, R.H., and Lasky, T., "The incidence of primary cardiac arrest during vigorous exercise." *New England Journal of Medicine* 311(14):874–877, 1984.

_____, _____, Hallstrom, A.P., Inui, T.S., and Peterson, D.R., "Physical activity and primary cardiac arrest." *Journal of the American Medical Association* 248(23):3113–3117, 1982.

Sivarajan, E.S., Bruce, R.A., Almes, M.J., Green, B., Belanger, L., Lindskog, B.D., Newton, K.M., and Mansfield, L.W., "In-hospital exercise after myocardial infarction does not improve treadmill performance." *New England Journal of Medicine* 305(7):357–362, 1981.

Stamler, J., "Prevalence and incidence of coronary heart disease." *Journal of Chronic Disease* 11:405, 1960.

Stevenson, J., Felek, V., and Rechnitzer, P., "Effect of exercise on coronary tree size in rats." *Circulation Research* 15:265–269, 1964.

Stokes, J., "Letter to the editor." *Annals of Internal Medicine* 85(3):393, 1976.

Storer, T.W., and Ruhling, R.O., "Essential hypertension and exercise." *Physician and Sportsmedicine* 9(6):59–66, 1981.

Streja, D., amd Mymin, D., "Moderate exercise and high-density lipoprotein-cholesterol: Observations during a cardiac rehabilitation program." *Journal of the American Medical Association* 242(20):2190–2192,, 1979.

Taylor, H.L., Klepetar, E., Keys, A., Parlin, W., Blackburn, H., and Puchner, T., "Death rates among physically active and sedentary employees of the railroad industry." *American Journal of Public Heath* 52(10):1697–1707, 1962.

Terjung, R.L., Baldwin, K.M., Cooksey, J., Samson, B., and Sutter, R.A., "Cardiovascular adaptation to twelve minutes of mild daily exercise in middle-aged sedentary men." *Journal of the American Geriatrics Society* 21(4):164–168, 1973.

Theroux, P., Waters, D.D., Halphen, C., Debaisieux, J.C., and Mizgala, H.F., "Prognostic value of exercise testing soon after myocardial infarction." *New England Journal of Medicine* 301(7):341–345, 1979.

Thom, T.J., and Kannel, W.B., "Downward trend in cardiovascular mortality." *Annual Review in Medicine* 32:427–434, 1981.

Thomas, G.S., Lee, P.R., Franks, P., Paffenbarger, R.S., *Exercise and Health.* Cambridge: Oelgeschlager, Gunn and Hain, 1961.

Thomas, T.R., and Etheridge, G.L., "The effect of track-and-field training on cardiovascular fitness." *Physician and Sportsmedicine* 9(2):49–51, 1981.

Thompson, P.D., "In reply." *Journal of the American Medical Association* 249(6):731, 1983.

_____, Funk, E.J., Carleton, R.A., and Sturner, W.Q., "Incidence of death during jogging in Rhode Island from 1975 through 1980." *Journal of the American Medical Association* 247(18):2535–2569, 1982.

_____, Lazarus, B., Cullinane, E., Henderson, L.O., Musliner, T., Eshleman, R., and Herbert, P.N., "Exercise, diet, or physical characteristics as determinants of HDL-levels in endurance athletes." *Atherosclerosis* 46:333–339, 1983.

_____, and Mitchell, J.H., "Exercise and sudden cardiac death." *New England Journal of Medicine* 311(14):914–915, 1984.

_____, Stern, M.P., Williams, P., Duncan, K., Haskell, W.L., and Wood, P.D., "Deaths during jogging or running." *Journal of the American Medical Association* 242(12):1265–1267, 1979.

Tieszen, R.L., "Letter to the editor." *Annals of Internal Medicine* 85(3):393, 1976.

Tzankoff, S.P., Robinson, S., Pyke, F.S., and Brawn, C.A., "Physiological adjustments to work in older men as affected by physical training." *Journal of Applied Physiology* 33(3):346–350, 1972.

Ullyot, J., *Running Free.* New York: G.P. Putnam's Sons, 1980.

U.S. Bureau of the Census, *Statistical Abstracts 1984.* Washington, D.C.: U.S. Government Printing Office, 1984.

U.S. Department of Health, Education, and Welfare, *Health United States: 1980.* Washington, D.C.: U.S. Government Printing Office, 1980.

U.S. Department of Health, Education, and Welfare, *Health United States: 1979.* Washington, D.C.: U.S. Government Printing Office, 1979.

Vaisrub, S., "Beware the lean and hungry look." *Journal of the American Medical Association* 242(18):1844, 1980a.

_____, "Exercise test after myocardial infarction." *Journal of the American Medical Association* 243(3):261, 1980b.

Vander, L., Franklin, B., and Rubenfire, M., "Cardiovascular complications of recreational physical activity." *Physician and Sportsmedicine* 10(6):89–96, 1982.

Virmani, R., Robinowitz, M., McAllister, H.A., "Nontraumatic death in joggers." *American Journal of Medicine* 72:874–882, 1982.

Waller, B.F., Csere, R.S., Baker, W.P., and Roberts, W.C., "Running to death." *Chest* 79(3):346–349, 1981.

_____, and Roberts, W.C., "Sudden death while running in conditioned runners aged 40 years and over." *American Journal of Cardiology* 45(June):1292–1300, 1980.

Walts, L.F., "To the editor." *Journal of the American Medical Association* 245(11):1120, 1980.

Wegner, N.K., "Early mobilization after myocardial infarction: Historical perspective and critical analysis." In A. Raineri, J.J. Kellermann, and V. Rulli (eds.) *Selected Topics in Exercise Cardiology and Rehabilitation*. (New York: Plenum, 1980), pp. 21–31.

Weltman, A., and Stamford, B., "Evaluating your risk for heart disease." *Physician and Sportsmedicine* 10(8):202, 1982a.

————, and ————, "Exercise and the cigarette smoker." *Physician and Sportsmedicine* 10(12):153, 1982b.

Wenger, A.K., Hellerstein, H.K., Blackburn H., and Castranova, S.J., "Uncomplicated myocardial infarction." *Journal of the American Medical Association* 224(4):511–514, 1973.

Wilcox, R.G., Bennett, T., Brown, A.M., MacDonald, I.A., "Is exercise good for high blood pressure?" *British Heart Journal* 285(September 18):767–769, 1982.

Willett, W., Hennekens, C.H., Siegel, A.J., Adner, M.M., and Castelli, W.P., "Alcohol consumption and high-density lipoprotein cholesterol in marathon runners." *New England Journal of Medicine* 303(20):1159–1160, 1980.

Williams, P.T., Wood, P.D., Haskell, W.L., and Vranizan, K., "The effects of running mileage and duration on plasma lipoprotein levels." *Journal of the American Medical Association* 247(19):2674–2679, 1982.

Wilmore, J.H., Royce, J., Girandola, R.N., Katch, F.I., and Katch, V.L., "Physiological alterations resulting from a 10-week program of jogging." *Medicine and Science in Sports* 2(1):7–14, 1970.

Wilson, P.K., Fardy, P.S., and Froelicher, V.F., *Cardiac Rehabilitation, Adult Fitness and Exercise Testing*. Lea and Febiger: Philadelphia, 1981.

Wood, P.D., Haskell, W., Klein, H., Lewis, S., Stern, M.P., and Farquhar, J.W., "The distribution of plasma lipoproteins in middle-aged male runners." *Metabolism* 25(11):1249–1257, 1976.

————, ————, Stern, M.P., Lewis, S., and Perry, C., "Plasma lipoprotein distributions in male and female runners." *Annals of the New York Academy of Sciences* 301(October):748–763, 1977.

Yamamoto, L., Yano, K., and Rhodes, G.G., "Characteristics of joggers among Japenese men in Hawaii." *American Journal of Public Health* 73(2):147–152, 1983.

Zeppilli, P., and Venerando, A., "Sudden death and physical exertion." *Journal of Sports Medicine* 21:299–300, 1981.

Zukel, W., "A short-term community study of the epidemiology of CHD." *American Journal of Public Health* 49:1630, 1959.

2. *Women and Running*

Albohm, M., "Does menstruation affect performance in sports?" *Physician and Sportsmedicine* 4(3):76–78, 1976.

Allsen, P.E., Parsons, P., and Bryce, G.R., "Effects of the menstrual cycle on maximum oxygen uptake." *Physician and Sportsmedicine* 5(7):53–55, 1977.

American College of Sports Medicine, "The female athlete in long-distance running." *Physician and Sportsmedicine* 8(1):135–136, 1980.

Andrews, V., "Women marathoners locked out." *The Runner* 1(11):46–49, 1979.

Anonymous, "Pregnant women advised to consider exercise risks." *Physician and Sportsmedicine* 10(2):27, 1982a.

Anonymous, "Add exercise to calcium in osteoporosis prevention." *Journal of the American Medical Association* 247(8):1106, 1982b.

Anonymous, "Running, jumping, and ... amenorrhoea." *Lancet* II(September 18):638–640, 1982c.

Anonymous, "Women say running helped pregnancy, labor." *Physician and Sportsmedicine* 9(3):24–25, 1981.

Anonymous, "The joy of running in regular cycles." *Science News* 118(1):6, 1980a.

Anonymous, "Fast lady." *Runner's World* 15(5):50–54, 1980b.

Anonymous, "Female athletes need good bras, MD reports." *Physician and Sportsmedicine* 5(8):15, 1977.

Astrand, P.O., Engstrom, L., and Eriksson, B.O., "Girl swimmers with special reference to respiratory and circulatory adaptations and gynecological and psychiatric aspects." *Acta Paediatrica Scandinavica* 147(Suppl):33–38, 1963.

Baker, E.R., Mathur, R.S., Kirk, R.F., and Williamson, H.O., "Female runners and secondary amenorrhea: correlation with age, parity, mileage, and plasma hormonal and sex-hormonal-binding globulin concentrations." *Fertility and Sterility* 36(2):183–187, 1981.

Ben-Rafael, Z., Blankstein, J., Sack, J., Lunenfeld, B., Oelsner, G., Serr, D.M., and Mashiach, S., "Menarche and puberty in daughters of amenorrheic women." *Journal of the American Medical Association* 250(23):3202–3204, 1983.

Besson, G., "Inner workings of the woman runner." *Runner's World* 14(1):62–67, 1979.

_____, "Anatomical, cardiorespiratory, and psychological aspects of running," in Runner's World (eds.), *The Complete Woman Runner* (Mountain View, CA: World Publications, 1978), pp. 125–39.

Bloomberg, R., "Menstruation alters perceived exertion." *Physician and Sportsmedicine* 8(6):29, 1980.

_____, "Coach says running affects menstruation." *Physician and Sportsmedicine* 5(9):15, 1977.

Bonen, A., Belcastro, A.N., Ling, W.Y., and Simpson, A.A., "Profiles of selected hormones during menstrual cycles of teenage athletes." *Journal of Applied Physiology* 50(3):545–551, 1981.

_____, Hayes, F.J., Watson-Wright, W., Sopper, M.M., Pierce, G.N., Low, M.P., and Graham, T.E., "Effects of menstrual cycle on metabolic responses to exercise." *Journal of Applied Physiology* 55(5):1506–1513, 1983.

Boston Women's Health Book Collective, *Our Bodies, Ourselves: A Book by and for Women*. New York: Simon and Schuster, 1973.

Boyden, T.W., Pamenter, R.W., Grosso, D., Stanforth, P., Rotkis, T., and Wilmore, J.H., "Prolactin responses, menstrual cycles, and body composition of women runners." *Journal of Clinical Endocrinology and Metabolism* 54(4):711–714, 1982.

Brooks, S.M., Sanborn, C.F., Albrecht, B.H., and Wagner, W.W., "Diet in athletic amenorrhoea." *Lancet* I(March 10):559–560, 1984.

Calabrese, L.H., Kirkendall, D.T., Floyd, M., Rapoport, S., Williams, G.W., Weiker, G.G., and Bergfeld, J.A., "Menstrual abnormalities, nutritional patterns, and body composition in female ballet dancers." *Physician and Sportsmedicine* 11(2):86–98, 1983.

Caldwell, F., "PMS symptoms are relieved by exercise." *Physician and Sportsmedicine* 12(5):23–24, 1984.

_____, "Title IX notwithstanding, girls expected to 'glow'." *Physician and Sportsmedicine* 11(6):40–41, 1983.

_____, "Menstrual irregularity in athletes: the unanswered question." *Physician and Sportsmedicine* 10(5):142, 1982.

Christensen, C.L., and Ruhling, R.O., "Physical characteristics of novice and experienced women marathon runners." *British Journal of Sports Medicine* 17(3):166–171, 1983.

Clement, D.B., and Asmundson, R.C., "Nutritional intake and hematological parameter in endurance runners." *Physician and Sportsmedicine* 10(3):37–43, 1982.

Cohen, J.L., Kim, C.S., May, P.B., and Ertel, N.H., "Exercise, body weight, and menstrual disorders in professional ballet dancers." *Physician and Sportsmedicine* 10(4):92–101, 1982.

Conniff, J.C.G., "James Nicholas: The orthopedic approach." *The Runner* 3(5):62–64, 1981.

Cooter, G.R., and Mowbray, K.W., "Effects of iron supplementation and activity on serum iron depletion and hemoglobin levels in female athletes." *Research Quarterly* 49(2):114–117, 1978.

Costill, D., and Higdon, H., "Hitting the gender wall." *The Runner* 2(1):60–65, 1979.

Crandall, R., *Gerontology: A Behavioral Science Approach*. Reading, Massachusetts: Addison-Wesley, 1980.

Cunningham, D.J., Stolwijk, J.A.J., and Wenger, C.B., "Comparative thermoregulatory responses of resting men and women." *Journal of Applied Physiology* 45(6):908–915, 1978.

Cureton, K.J., "Matching of male and female subjects using VO_2max." *Research Quarterly* 52(2):264–268, 1981.

_____, Hensley, L.D., and Tiburzi, A., "body fatness and performance differences between men and women." *Research Quarterly* 50(3):333–340, 1979.

Dale, E., Gerlach, D.H., Martin, D.E., and Alexander, C.R., "Physical fitness profiles and reproductive physiology of the female distance runner." *Physician and Sportsmedicine* 7(1):83–95, 1979a.

_____, _____, _____, and _____, "Physical fitness profiles and reproductive physiology of the female distance runner." *Physician and Sportsmedicine* 7(1):83–95, 1979b.

_____, _____, and Wilhite, A.L. "Menstrual dysfunction in distance runners." *Obstetrics and Gynecology* 54(1):47–53, 1979.

_____, and Goldberg, D.L., "Implications of nutrition in athletes' menstrual cycle irregularities." *Canadian Journal of Applied Sport Sciences* 7(2):74–78, 1982.

_____, Mullinax, K.M., and Bryan, D.H., "Exercise during pregnancy: Effects on the fetus." *Canadian Journal of Applied Sport Sciences* 7(2):98–103, 1982.

Daniels, J., Krahenbuhl, G., Foster, C., Gilbert, J., and Daniels, S., "Aerobic response of female distance runners to submaximal and maximal exercise." *Annals of the New York Academy of Sciences* 301(October):726–733, 1977.

deVries, H.A., *Physiology of Exercise for Physical Education and Athletics* (Third Edition). Dubuque, Iowa: Wm. C. Brown, 1980.

Diddle, A.W., "Athletic activity and menstruation." *Southern Medical Journal* 76(5):619–624, 1983.

Dixon, G., Eurman, P., Stern, B.E. Schwartz, B., and Rebar, R.W., "Hypothalamic function in amenorrheic runners." *Fertility and Sterility* 42(3):377–383, 1984.

Doolittle, T.L., and Engebretsen, J., "Performance variations during the menstrual cycle." *Journal of Sports Medicine* 12:54–57, 1972.

Dressendorfer, R.H., "Physical training during pregnancy and lactation." *Physician and Sportsmedicine* 6(2):74–80, 1978.

_____, and Goodlin, R.C., "Fetal heart rate response to maternal exercise testing." *Physician and Sportsmedicine* 8(11):91–94, 1980.

Drinkwater, B.L., Chesnut, C.H., and Bremner, W.J., "Bone mineral content of female athletes." *New England Journal of Medicine* 311(20):1320–1321, 1984.

_____, Kupprat, I.C., Denton, J.E., and Horrath, S.M., "Heath tolerance of female distance runners." *Annals of the New York Academy of Sciences* 301(October):777–792, 1977.

_____, Nilson, K., Chesnut, C.H., Bremner, W.J., Shainholtz, S., and Southworth, M.B., "Bone mineral content of amenorrheic and eumenorrheic athletes." *New England Journal of Medicine* 311(5):277–281, 1984.

Droel, C., "Pregnant but not barefoot." *The Runner* 4(6):6, 1982.

Dunn, K., "Toxic shock victims had less exercise, study says." *Physician and Sportsmedicine* 9(6):21–22, 1981.

Elliot, D.L., and Goldberg, L., "Weight lifting and amenorrhea." *Journal of the American Medical Association* 249(3):354, 1983.

Erdelyi, G.J., "Effects of exercise on the menstrual cycle." *Physician and Sportsmedicine* 4(3):79–81, 1976.

_____, "Gynecologic survey of female athletes." *Journal of Sports Medicine and Physicial Fitness* 2:174–179, 1962.

Estok, P.J., and Rudy, E.B., "Intensity of jogging: relationship with menstrual/reproductive variables." *Journal of Obstetric, Gynecologic and Neonatal Nursing* 13(6):390–395, 1984.

Evenson, L., "Exercise advised for oral contraceptive users." *Physician and Sportsmedicine* 10(3):27, 1982.

Falls, H.B., *Exercise Physiology.* New York: Academic, 1968.

Feicht, C.B., Johnson, T.S., Martin, B.J., Sparkes, K.E., and Wagner, W.W., "Secondary amenorrhoea in athletes." *Lancet* II(Nov. 25):1145–1146, 1978.

Ferris, E., "The myths surrounding women's participation in sport and exercise." *Journal of Sports Medicine* 19:309–311, 1979.

Fishman, J., "Fatness, puberty, and ovulation." *New England Journal of Medicine* 303(1):42–43, 1980.

Franklin, B.A., Lussier, L., and Buskirk, E.R., "Injury rates in women joggers." *Physician and Sportsmedicine* 7(3):105–112, 1979.

Frederickson, L.A., Puhl, J.L., and Runyan, W.S., "Effects of training on indices of iron status of young female cross-country runners." *Medicine and Science in Sports and Exercise* 15(4):271–276, 1983.

Frisch, R.E., "Reply." *Journal of the American Medical Association* 247(24):3312–3313, 1982.

_____, Gotz-Welbergen, A.V., McArthur, J.W., Albright, T., Witschi, J., Bullen, B., Birnholz, J., Reed, R.B., and Hermann, H., "Delayed menarche and amenorrhea of college athletes in relation to age of onset of training." *Journal of the American Medical Association* 246(14):1559–1563, 1981.

_____, and McArthur, J.W., "Menstrual cycles: fatness as a determinant of minimum weight for height necessary for their maintenance or onset." *Science* 185(4155):949–951, 1974.

_____, Wyshak, G., and Vincent, L., "Delayed menarche and amenorrhea in ballet dancers." *New England Journal of Medicine* 303(1):17–19, 1980.

Frye, A.J., and Kamon, E., "Responses to dry heat of men and women with similar aerobic capacities." *Journal of Applied Physiology* 50(1):65–70, 1981.

Galle, P.C. Freeman, E.W., Galle, M.G., Huggins, G.R., and Sondheimer, S.J., "Physiologic and psychologic profiles in a survey of women runners." *Fertility and Sterility* 39(5):633–639, 1983.

Garlick, M.A., and Bernauer, E.M., "Exercise during the menstrual cycle: variations in physiological baselines." *Research Quarterly* 39(3):533–542, 1968.

Garrick, J.G., and Requa, R.K., "Girls' sports injuries in high school athletics." *Journal of the American Medical Association* 239(21):2245–2248, 1978.

Gass, G.C., Camp, E.M., Watson, J., Eager, D., Wicks, L., and Ng, A., "Prolonged exercise in highly trained female endurance runners." *International Journal of Sports Medicine* 4(4):241–246, 1983.

Gehlsen, G., and Albohm, M., "Evaluation of sports bras." *Physician and Sportsmedicine* 8(10):89–96, 1980.

Gerber, E.W., Felshin, J., Berlin, P., and Wyrick, W., *The American Woman in Sport*. Reading, MA: Addison-Wesley, 1974.

Getchell, L.H., Kirkendall, D., and Robbins, G., "Prediction of maximal oxygen uptake in young adult women joggers." *Research Quarterly* 48(1):61–67, 1977.

Gillette, J., "When and where women are injured in sports." *Physician and Sportsmedicine* 3(5):61–63, 1975.

Gonzalez, E.R., "Premature bone loss found in some nonmenstruating sportswomen." *Journal of the American Medical Association* 248(5):513–514, 1982.

Gunby, P., "Increasing numbers of physical changes found in nation's runners." *Journal of the American Medical Association* 245(6):547–548, 1981.

_____, "What does exercise mean for the menstrual cycle." *Journal of the American Medical Association* 243(17):1699, 1980.

Guzman, C.A., and Caplan, R., "Cardiorespiratory response to exercise during pregnancy." *American Journal of Obstetrics and Gynecology* 108(4):600–605, 1970.

Hage, P., "Pregnant runners cite minor problems." *Physician and Sportsmedicine* 10(5):40, 1982.

_____, "Exercise and pregnancy compatible, MD says." *Physician and Sportsmedicine* 9(5):23–24, 1981.

Hale, R.W., Kosasa, T., Krieger, J., and Pepper, S., "A marathon: the immediate effect on female runners' luteinizing hormone, follicle-stimulating hormone, prolactin, testosterone, and cortisol levels." *American Journal of Obstetrics and Gynecology* 146(5):550–556, 1983.

Hauth, J.C., Gilstrap, L.C., and Widmer, K., "Fetal heart rate reactivity before and after maternal jogging during the third trimester." *American Journal of Obstetrics and Gynecology* 142(5):545–547, 1982.

Haycock, C.E., "The problem: Running for women over 50." *Physician and Sportsmedicine* 9(12):17, 1981.

_____, and Gillette, J.V., "Susceptibility of women athletes to injury: Myth vs. reality." *Journal of the American Medical Association* 236(2):163–165, 1976.

Heinonen, J., "The woman runner," in Runner's World (eds.), *The Complete Runner* (New York: Avon Books, 1974), pp. 89–93.

Henderson, J., "First-aid for the injured." *Runner's World* 12(7):32–37, 1977.

Higdon, H., "Running through pregnancy." *The Runner* 4(3):46–51, 1981.

Horner, M.R., "Vitamin supplements." *Running and Fitness* 16(4):6, 1984.

Howlett, T.A., Tomlin, S., Ngahfoong, L., Rees, L., Bullen, B.A., Skrinar, G.S., and McArthur, J.W., "Release of B endorphin and met-enkephalin during exercise in normal women: response to training." *British Medical Journal* 288(June 30):1950–1952, 1984.

Hunter, L.Y., and Torgan, C., "The bra controversy: Are sports bras a necessity?" *Physician and Sportsmedicine* 10(11):75–76, 1982.

Hutchinson, P.L., Cureton, K.J., and Sparling, P.B., "Metabolic and circulatory responses to running during pregnancy." *Physician and Sportsmedicine* 9(8):55–61, 1981.

Jarrett, J.C., and Spellacy, W.N., "Jogging during pregnancy: An improved outcome?" *Obstetrics and Gynecology* 61(6):705–709, 1983a.

_____, and _____, "Contraceptive practices of female runners." *Fertility and Sterility* 39(3):374–375, 1983b.

Jopke, T., "Pregnancy: A time to exercise judgment." *Physician and Sportsmedicine* 11(7):139–148, 1983.

Jurkowski, J.E., Jones, N.L., Walker, W.C., Younglai, E.V., and Sutton, J.R., "Ovarian hormonal response to exercise." *Journal of Applied Physiology* 44(1):109–114, 1978.

Kamon, E., Avellini, B., and Krajewski, J., "Physiological and biophysical limits to work in the heat for clothed men and women." *Journal of Applied Physiology* 44(6):918–925, 1978.

Keizer, H.A., Poortman, J., and Bunnik, G.S.J., "Influence of physical exercise on sex-hormone metabolism." *Journal of Applied Physiology* 48(5):765–769, 1980.

Kissin, R., (ed), "Runner's World update." *Runner's World* 15(11):11, 1980.

Klafs, C.E., and Lyon, M.J., *The Female Athlete: Conditioning, Competition, and Culture.* St. Louis MO: C.V. Mosby, 1973.

Klaus, E.J., "The athletic status of women," in E. Jokl and E. Simon (eds.), *International Research in Sport and Physical Education* (Springfield: C.C. Thomas, 1964), pp. 586–598.

Knowlton, R.G., Miles, D.S., Sawka, M.N., Critz, J.B., and Blackman, C., "Cardiorespiratory adaptations of females to cross-country training. " *Journal of Sports Medicine* 18:391–398, 1978.

Korcok, M., "Pregnant jogger: What a record!" *Journal of the American Medical Association* 246(3):201, 1981.

Kuscsik, N., "The history of women's participation in the marathon." *Annals of the New York Academy of Sciences* 301(October):862–876, 1977.

Larson, K.A., and Shannon, S.C., "Decreasing the incidence of osteoporosis-related injuries through diet and exercise." *Public Health Reports* 99(6):609–613, 1984.

Lewis, C.G., and Strickland, R.W., "A profile of the college female athlete." *Physician and Sportsmedicine* 11(3):153–156, 1983.

Lindberg, J.S., Fears, W.B., Hunt, M.M., Powell, M.R., Bull, D., and Wade, C.E., "Exercise-induced amenorrhea and bone density." *Annals of Internal Medicine* 101(5):647–648, 1984.

Loucks, A.B., and Horvath, S.M., "Athletic amenorrhea: a review." *Medicine and Science in Sports and Exercise* 17(1):56–72, 1985.

————, and ————, "Exercise-induced stress responses of amenorrheic and eumenorrheic runners." *Journal of Clinical Endocrinology and Metabolism* 59(6):1109–1120, 1984.

Lunn, J.A., "Sports bras for mature women." *Physician and Sportsmedicine* 11(2):16, 1983.

Lutter, J.M., "Mixed messages about osteoporosis in female athletes." *Physician and Sportsmedicine* 11(9):154–165, 1983a.

————, "Contraceptive practices of female runners." *Fertility and Sterility* 40(4):551, 1983b.

————, and Cushman, S., "Menstrual patterns in female runners." *Physician and Sportsmedicine* 10(9):60–72, 1982.

McArdle, W.D., Katch, F.I., Katch, V.L., *Exercise Physiology: Energy, Nutrition, and Human Performance.* Philadelphia: Lea and Febiger, 1981.

McArthur, J.W., "Endorphins and exercise in females: Possible connection with reproductive dysfunction." *Medicine and Science in Sports and Exercise* 17(1):82–88, 1985.

McConnell, T.R., and Sinning, W.E., "Exercise and temperature effects on human sperm production and testosterone levels." *Medicine and Science in Sports and Exercise* 16(1):51–5, 1984.

Malina, R.M., "Menarche in athletes: a synthesis and hypothesis." *Annals of Human Biology* 10(1):1–24, 1983.

————, "Delayed age of menarche of athletes." *Journal of the American Medical Association* 247(24):3312, 1982.

————, Harper, A.B., Avent, H.H., and Campbell, D.E., "Age at menarche in athletes and non-athletes." *Medicine and Science in Sports* 5(1):11–13, 1973.

————, Spirduso, W.W., Tate, C., and Baylor, A.M., "Age at menarche and selected menstrual characteristics in athletes at different competitive levels and in different sports." *Medicine and Science in Sports* 10(3):218–222, 1978.

Marcus, R., Cann, C., Madvig, P., Minkoff, J., Goddard, M., Bayer, M., Martin, M., Gaudiani, L., Haskell, W., and Genant, H., "Menstrual function and bone mass in elite woman distance runners." *Annals of Internal Medicine* 102(2):158–163, 1985.

Massicotte, D.R., Avon, G., and Corriveau, G., "Comparative effects of aerobic training on men and women." *Journal of Sports Medicine* 19:23–32, 1979.

Mathews, D.K., and Fox, E.L., *The Physiological Basis of Physical Education and Athletics* (Second Edition). Philadelphia: W. B. Saunders, 1976.

Miller, D.M., *Coaching the Female Athlete.* Philadelphia: Lea and Febiger, 1974.

Mirkin, G., "Iron deficiency and women." *Running and Fitness* 14(3):25, 1982.

Morehouse, L.E., and Miller, A.T., *Physiology of Exercise.* St. Louis: Mosby, 1976.

Morton, M.J., Paul, M.S., and Metcalfe, J., "Exercise during pregnancy." *Medical Clinics of North America* 69(1):97–108, 1985.

Nelson, R.C., Brooks, C.M., and Pike, N.L., "Biomechanical comparison of male and female distance runners." *Annals of the New York Academy of Sciences* 301(October):793–607, 1977.

Nickerson, H.J., and Tripp, A.D., "Iron deficiency in adolescent cross-country runners." *Physician and Sportsmedicine* 11(6):60–66, 1983.

Norval, J.D., "Running anorexia." *South African Medical Journal* 58(26):1024, 1980.

Novak, E.R., Jones, G.S., and Jones, H.W., *Novak's Textbook of Gynecology* (Eighth Edition). Baltimore: Williams and Wilkins, 1970.

O'Herlihy, C., "Jogging and the suppression of ovulation." *New England Journal of Medicine* 306(1):50–51, 1982.

Orselli, R.C., "Possible teratogenic hyperthermia and marathon running." *Journal of the American Medical Association* 243(4):332, 1980.

Pagliano, J., "Injury prevention," in Runner's World (eds.), *The Complete Woman Runner* (Mountain View, CA: World Publications, 1978), pp. 177–207.

Parr, R.B., Bachman, L.A., and Moss, R.A., "Iron deficiency in female athletes." *Physician and Sportsmedicine* 12(4):81–86, 1984.

Pate, R.R., Barnes, C., and Miller, W., "A matched physiological comparison of performance-matched female and male distance runners." *Research Quarterly* 56(3):245–50, 1985.

_____, Maguire, M., and VanWyk, J., "Dietary iron supplementation in women athletes." *Physician and Sportsmedicine* 7(9):81–86, 1979.

Paty, J.G., "Bone mineral content of female athletes." *New England Journal of Medicine* 311(20):1320, 1984.

Physician and Sportsmedicine, "Menstrual changes in athletes." *Physician and Sportsmedicine* 9(11):99–112, 1981.

Physician and Sportsmedicine, "Sports during pregnancy." *Physician and Sportsmedicine* 8(3):82–85, 1976.

Plowman, S., "Physiological characteristics of female athletes." *Research Quarterly* 46(December):349–362, 1974.

Pomerance, J.J., Gluck, L., and Lynch, V.A., "Physical fitness in pregnancy: Its effects on pregnancy outcome." *American Journal of Obstetrics and Gynecology* 119(7):867–876, 1974.

Powers, S.K., Hopkins, P., and Ragsdale, M.R., "Oxygen uptake and ventilatory responses to various stride lengths in trained women." *American Corrective Therapy Journal* 36(1):5–8, 1982.

_____, Riley, W., and Howley, E.T., "Comparison of fat metabolism between trained men and women during prolonged aerobic work." *Research Quarterly* 51(2):427–431, 1980.

Prior, J.C., Ho Yuen, B., Clement, P., Bowie, L., and Thomas, J., "Reversible luteal phase changes and infertility associated with marathon training." *Lancet* II(July 31):269–270, 1982.

Puhl, J.L., and Runyan, W.S., "Hematological variations during aerobic training of college women." *Research Quarterly* 51(3):533–541, 1980.

Rebar, R.W., and Cummings, D.C., "Reproductive function in women athletes." *Journal of the American Medical Association* 246(14):1590, 1981.

Rosen, L.W., McKeag, D.B., Hough, D.O., and Curley, V., "Pathogenic weight-control behavior in female athletes." *Physician and Sportsmedicine* 14(1):79–86, 1986.

Rosenzweig, S., "Body check: an update on amenorrhea in women runners." *The Runner* 5(3):12, 1982.

Rougier, G., and Linquette, Y., "Menstruation and physical exercise." *Presse Medicale* 70:1921, 1962.

Rudy, E.B., and Estok, P.J., "Intensity of jogging: its relationship to selected physical and psychosocial variables in women." *Western Journal of Nursing Research* 5(4):325–336, 1983.

Runyan, W.S., and Puhl, J., "Relationship between selected blood indices and competitive performance in college women cross-country runners." *Journal of Sports Medicine* 20:207–212, 1980.

Rush-Morrow, B., "Pregnant but not barefoot." *The Runner* 4(6):6, 1982.

Sanborn, C.F., Martin, B.J., and Wagner, W.W., "Is athletic amenorrhea specific to runners?" *American Journal of Obstetrics and Gynecology* 143(8):859–861, 1982.

Schaefer, C.F., "Possible teratogenic hyperthermia and marathon running." *Journal of the American Medical Association* 241(18):1892, 1979.

Schuster, K., "Equipment update: jogging bras hit the streets." *Physician and Sportsmedicine* 7(4):125–128, 1979.

Schwartz, B., Cumming, D.C., Riordan, E., Selye, M., Yen, S.S.C., and Rebar, R.W., "Exercise-associated amenorrhea: A distinct entity?" *American Journal of Obstetrics and Gynecology* 141(6):662–670, 1981.

Scott, E.C., and Johnston, F.E., "Critical fat, menarche, and the maintenance of menstrual cycles: a critical review." *Journal of Adolescent Health Care* 2(4):249–260, 1982.

Shangold, M.M., "How I manage exercise-related menstrual disturbances." *Physician and Sportsmedicine* 14(3):113–120, 1986.

————, "Causes, evaluation, and management of athletic oligo-amenorrhea." *Medical Clinics of North America* 69(1):83–97, 1985.

————, "Women's running." *Runner's World* 17(12):21, 1982a.

————, "Women's running." *Runner's World* 17(11):18, 1982b.

————, "Women's running." *Runner's World* 17(10):20, 1982c.

————, "Women's running." *Runner's World* 17(7):21, 1982d.

————, "Women's running." *Runner's World* 17(6):19, 1982e.

————, "Women's running." *Runner's World* 17(2):20, 1982f.

————, "Evaluating menstrual irregularity in athletes." *Physician and Sportsmedicine* 10(2):21–22, 1982g.

————, "Sports gynecology." *The Runner* 3(9):34–38, 1981a.

————, "The woman runner: Her body, her mind, her spirit." *Runner's World* 16(7):34–44, 88, 1981b.

————, "Sports and menstrual function." *Physician and Sportsmedicine* 8(8):66–69, 1980.

————, Freeman, R., Thysen, B., and Gatz, M., "The relationship between long-distance running, plasma progesterone, and luteal phase length." *Fertility and Sterility* 31(2):130–133, 1979.

————, Gatz, M.L., and Thysen, B., "Acute effects of exercise on plasma concentrations of prolactin and testosterone in recreational women runners." *Fertility and Sterility* 35(6):699–702, 1981.

_____, and Levine, H.S., "The effect of marathon training upon menstrual function." *American Journal of Obstetrics and Gynecology* 143(8):862–869, 1982.

Shapiro, Y., Pandolf, K.B., Avellini, B.A., Pimental, N.A., and Goldman, R.F., "Physiological responses of men and women to humid and dry heat." *Journal of Applied Physiology* 49(1):1–8, 1980.

Shaver, L.G., *Essentials of Exercise Physiology*. Minneapolis: Burgess, 1981.

Sheehan, G., "Iron in the fire." *Runner's World* 18(2):83, 1983.

Shively, R.A., Grana, W.A., and Ellis, D., "High school sports injuries." *Physician and Sportsmedicine* 9(8):46–50, 1981.

Shoenfeld, Y., Udassin, R., Shapiro, Y., Ohri, A., and Sohar E., "Age and sex differences in response to short exposure to extremely dry heat." *Journal of Applied Physiology* 44(1):1–4, 1978.

Skinner, M.S., "The story of one woman's pregnancy." *Runner's World* 13(11):56–57, 1978.

Skrinar, G.S., Ingram, S.P., and Pandolf, K.B., "Effect of endurance training on perceived exertion and stress hormones in women." *Perceptual and Motor Skills* 57:1239–1250, 1983.

Sparling, P.B., and Cureton, K. J., "Biological determinants of the sex difference in 12-minute run performance." *Medicine and Science in Sports and Exercise* 15(3):218–223, 1983.

Speroff, L., and Redwine, D.B., "Exercise and menstrual function." *Physician and Sportsmedicine* 8(5):218–223, 1980.

Stager, J.M., Ritchie-Flanagan, B., and Robertshaw, D., "Reversibility of amenorrhea in athletes." *New England Journal of Medicine* 310(1):51–52, 1984.

Stephenson, L.A., Kolka, M.A., and Wilkerson, J.E., "Perceived exertion and anaerobic threshold during the menstrual cycle." *Medicine and Science in Sports and Exercise* 14(3):218–222, 1982.

Ullyot, J., *Running Free*. New York: Putnam's Sons, 1980.

U.S. Bureau of the Census, *Statistical Abstracts of the United States: 1983*. Washington, D.C.: U.S. Government Printing Office, 1983.

VanDenbroucke, J.P., VanLaar, A., and Valkenburg, H.A., "Synergy between thinness and intensive sports activity in delaying menarche." *British Medical Journal* 284(June 26):1907–1908, 1982.

Warren, M.P., "The effects of exercise on pubertal progression and reproductive function in girls." *Journal of Clinical Endocrinology and Metabolism* 51(5):1150–1157, 1980.

Webb, J.L., Millan, D.L., and Stolz, C.J., "Gynecological survey of American female athletes competing at the Montreal Olympic games." *Journal of Sports Medicine* 19:405–412, 1979.

_____, and Proctor, A.J., "Anthropometric, training and menstrual differences of three groups of American collegiate female runners." *Journal of Sports Medicine* 23(2):201–209, 1983.

Wells, C.L., "Sexual differences in heat stress response." *Physician and Sportsmedicine* 5(9):79–91, 1977.

_____, Hecht, L.H., and Krahenbuhl, G.S., "Physical characteristics and oxygen utilization of male and female marathon runners." *Research Quarterly* 52(2):281–285, 1981.

_____, and Plowman, S.A., "Sexual differences in athletic performance: biological or behavioral?" *Physician and Sportsmedicine* 11(8):52–63, 1983.

Wentz, A.C., "Body weight and amenorrhea." *Obstetrics and Gynecology* 56(4):482–487, 1980.

Wheeler, G.D., Wall, S.R., Belcastro, A.N., and Cumming, D.C., "Reduced serum testosterone and prolactin levels in male distance runners." *Journal of the American Medical Association* 252(4):514–16, 1984.

Widmann, F.K., "Bone mineral content of female athletes." *New England Journal of Medicine* 311(20):1320, 1984.

Wilmore, J.H., and Brown, C.H., "Physiological profiles of women distance runners." *Medicine and Science in Sports* 6(3):178–181, 1974.

————, ————, and Davis, J.A., "Body physique and composition of the female distance runner." *Annals of the New York Academy of Sciences* 301 (October):764–776, 1977.

Wirth, V., Emmons, P., and Larson, D., "Running through pregnancy." *Runner's World* 13(11):55–59, 1978.

Zaharieva, E., "Olympic participation by women: effects on pregnancy and childbirth." *Journal of the American Medical Association* 221(9):992–995, 1972.

————, "Survey of sportswomen at the Tokyo Olympics." *Journal of Sports Medicine* 5:215–222, 1965.

Ziporyn, T., "Latest clue to exercise-induced amenorrhea." *Journal of the American Medical Association* 252(10):1258–1263, 1984.

3. *Young Athletes and Running*

American Academy of Pediatrics, "Climatic heat stress and the exercising child." *Physician and Sportsmedicine* 11(8):155–159, 1983.

————, "Risks in long-distance running for children." *Physician and Sportsmedicine* 10(8):82–86, 1982.

————, "Injuries to young athletes." *Physician and Sportsmedicine* 9(2):107–110, 1981a.

————, "Competitive sports for children of elementary age." *Physician and Sportsmedicine* 9(8):140–142, 1981b.

————, "Competitive athletics for children of elementary school age." *Pediatrics* 67(6):927–928, 1981c.

Andrew, G.M., Becklake, R., Guleria, J.S., and Bates, D.V., "Heart and lung functions in swimmers and nonathletes during growth." *Journal of Applied Physiology* 32(2):245–251, 1972.

Anonymous, "Physician urges caution for child marathoners." *Physician and Sportsmedicine* 10(6):26, 1982.

Astrand, P., "The child in sport and physical activity," in J.G. Albinson and G.M. Andrew (eds.), *Child in Sport and Physical Activity* (Baltimore: University Park, 1976), pp. 19–34.

Bailey, D.A., "The growing child and the need for physical activity." in J.G. Albinson and G.M. Andrew (eds.), *Child in Sport and Physical Activity* (Baltimore: University Park, 1976), pp. 81–96.

Barnes, L., "Running causes behavior changes in children." *Physician and Sportsmedicine* 9(8):23, 1981.

————, "Preadolescent training — how young is too young?" *Physician and Sportsmedicine* 7(10):114–119, 1979.

Bar-Or, O., "Climate and the exercising child — a review." *International Journal of Sports Medicine* 1:53–65, 1980.

————, Inbar, O., Rotshtein, A., and Zonder, H., "Voluntary hypohydration in 10 to 12 year old boys." *Journal of Applied Physiology* 48(1):104–108, 1980.

Berg, K., Sady, S.P., Beal, D., Savage, M., and Smith, J., "Developing an elementary school CHD prevention program." *Physician and Sportsmedicine* 11(10):99–105, 1983.

Blumenthal, S., Jesse, M.J., Hennekens, C.H., Klein, B.E., Ferrer, P.L., and Gourley, J.E., "Risk factors for coronary artery disease in children of affected families." *Journal of Pediatrics* 87(6):1187–1192, 1975.

Brown, C.H., Harrower, J.R., and Deeter, M.F. "The effects of cross-country running on pre-adolescent girls." *Medicine and Science in Sports* 4(1):1–5, 1972.

Brandt, E.N. and McGinnis, J.M., "National children and youth fitness study: Its contribution to our national objectives." *Public Health Reports* 100(1):497–499, 1985.

Burke, E.J., and Brush, F.C., "Physiological and anthropometric assessment of successful teenage female distance runners." *Research Quarterly* 50(2):180–187, 1979.

Burrington, J.D., "Exercise and children." *Comprehensive Therapy* 6(9):60–67, 1980.

Butts, N.K., "Physiological profiles of high school female cross country runners." *Research Quarterly* 53(1):8–14, 1982.

Cage, J.B., and Ivey, F.M., "Intercondylar fractures of the femur in an adolescent athlete." *Physician and Sportsmedicine* 11(6):115–118, 1983.

Caine, D.J., and Linder, K.J., "Growth plate injury: A threat to young distance runners." *Physician and Sportsmedicine* 12(4):118–124.

Chandy, T.A., and Grana, W.A., "Secondary school athletic injury in boys and girls." *Physician and Sportsmedicine* 13(3):106–111, 1985.

Chausow, S.A., Riner, W.F., and Boileau, R.A., "Metabolic and cardiovascular responses of children during prolonged physical activity." *Research Quarterly* 55(1):1–7, 1984.

Daniels, J., and Oldridge, N., "Changes in oxygen consumption of young boys during growth and running training." *Medicine and Science in Sports* 3(4):161–165, 1971.

Delmas, A., "Intense physical training among children and adolescents." *International Federation of Physical Education* 52(2):29–33, 1982.

Drash, A., "Atherosclerosis, cholesterol, and the pediatrician." *Journal of Pediatrics* 80(4):693–696, 1972.

Drinkwater, B.L., Kupprat, I.C., Denton, J.E., Crist, J.L., and Horvath, S.M., "Response of prepubertal girls and college women to work in the heat." *Journal of Applied Physiology* 43(6):1046–1053, 1977.

Duda, M., "Prepubescent strength training gains support." *Physician and Sportsmedicine* 14(2):157–161, 1986.

Dulberg, H.N., and Bennett, F.W., "Psychological changes in early adolescent males induced by systematic exercise." *American Corrective Therapy Journal* 34(5):142–146, 1980.

Ekblom, B., "Effect of physical training in adolescent boys." *Journal of Applied Physiology* 27(3):350–355, 1969.

Elovainio, R., and Sundberg, S., "A five-year follow-up study on cardiorespiratory function in adolescent elite endurance runners." *Acta Paediatrica Scandinavica* 72(3):351–356, 1983.

Feinstein, R.A., and Daniel W.A., "Anemia and 'anemia' in adolescents: Value in screening examinations for sports." *Physician and Sportsmedicine* 12(1):140–144, 1984.

Friedman, G., "A pediatrician looks at risk factors in atherosclerotic heart disease (abstract)." *Clinical Research* 20:250, 1972.

Garrick, J.G., "Sports medicine." *Pediatric Clinics of North America* 24(4):737–748, 1977.

Gilliam, T.B., Katch, V.L., Thorland, W., and Weltman, A., "Prevalence of coronary heart disease risk factors in active children, 7 to 12 years of age." *Medicine and Science in Sports* 9(1):21–25, 1977.

————, MacConnie, S.E., Geenen, D.L., Pels, A.E., and Freedson, P.S., "Exercise programs for children." *Physician and Sportsmedicine* 10(9):96–108, 1982.

Gunby, P., "What causes sudden death in young athletes?" *Journal of the American Medical Association* 241(2):123–124, 1979.

Hammer, A., Schwartzbach, A., and Paulev, P., "Children injured during physical education lessons." *Journal of Sports Medicine* 21:423–431, 1981.

Harvey, J.S., "Overuse syndromes in young athletes." *Pediatric Clinics of North America* 29(6):1369–1382, 1982.

Hatanpaa, M., and Hatanpaa, S., "Degenerative hip disease in adolescent athletes." *Medicine and Science in Sports* 8(2):77–80, 1976.

Haymes, E.M., Buskirk, E.R., Hodgson, J.L., Lundegren, H.M., and Nicholas, W.C., "Heat tolerance of exercising lean and heavy prepubertal girls." *Journal of Applied Physiology* 36(5):566–571, 1974.

_____, McCormick, R.J., and Buskirk, E.R., "Heat tolerance of exercising lean and obese prepubertal boys." *Journal of Applied Physiology* 39(3):457–461, 1975.

Hirsch, G.A., "The inside track." *The Runner* 5(2):4, 1982.

Kannel, W.B., and Dawber, T.R., "Atherosclerosis as a pediatric problem." *Journal of Pediatrics* 80(4):544–554, 1972.

Klein, K.K., "Developmental asymmetries and knee injury." *Physician and Sportsmedicine* 11(8):67–72, 1983.

Knochel, J.P., "Dog days and siriasis: How to kill a football player." *Journal of the American Medical Association* 233(6):513–515, 1975.

Kozar, B., and Lord, R.M., "Overuse injury in the young athlete: reasons for concern." *Physician and Sportsmedicine* 11(7):116–122, 1983.

Krahenbuhl, G.S., and Pangrazi R.P., "Characteristics associated with running performance in young boys." *Medicine and Science in Sports and Exercise* 15(6):486–490, 1983.

Larson, R.L., and McMahan, R.O., "The epiphyses and the childhood athlete." *Journal of the American Medical Association* 196(7):607–612, 1966.

Lauer, R.M., Connor, W.E., Leaverton, P.E., Reiter, M.A., and Clarke, W.R., "Coronary heart disease risk factors in school children: The Muscatine study." *Journal of Pediatrics* 86(5):697–706, 1975.

Legwold, G., "New verse, same chorus: Children aren't fit." *Physician and Sportsmedicine* 11(5):153–155, 1983a.

_____, "Adolescent athletes face emotional and physical abuse." *Physician and Sportsmedicine* 11(3):57–60, 1983b.

_____, "Preadolescents show dramatic strength gains." *Physician and Sportsmedicine* 11(10):25, 1983c.

_____, "Does lifting weights harm a prepubescent athlete?" *Physician and Sportsmedicine* 10(7):141–144, 1982.

Linder, C.W., and DuRant, R.H., "Exercise, serum lipids, and cardiovascular disease — risk factors in children." *Pediatric Clinics of North America* 29(6):1341–1354, 1982.

Lopez, R., and Pruett, D.M., "The child runner." *Journal of Physical Education, Recreation, and Dance* (April):78–81, 1982.

Luckstead, E.F., "Sudden death in sports." *Pediatric Clinics of North America* 29(6):1355–1362, 1982.

Macek, M., and Vavra, J., "F.I.M.S. position statement on training and competition in children." *Journal of Sports Medicine and Physical Fitness* 20(2):135–138, 1980.

McKenzie, D.C., Taunton, J.E., Clement, D.B., Smart, G.W., and McNicol, K.L., "Calcaneal epiphysitis in adolescent athletes." *Canadian Journal of Applied Sports Science* 6(3):123–125, 1981.

Malina, R.M., "Exercise as an influence upon growth." *Clinical Pediatrics* 8(1):16–26, 1969.

_____, Meleski, B.W., and Shoup, R.F., "Anthropometric, body composition, and maturity characteristics of selected school-age children." *Pediatric Clinics of North America* 29(6):1305–1324, 1982.

Maron, B.J., Roberts, W.C., McAllister, H.A., Rosing, D.R., and Epstein, S.E., "Sudden death in young athletes." *Circulation* 62(2):218–229, 1980.

Martens, R., "The uniqueness of the young athlete: Psychologic considerations." *American Journal of Sports Medicine* 8(5):382–385, 1980.

Moore, M., "When pediatric cardiology meets exercise physiology." *Physician and Sportsmedicine* 10(11):147–154, 1982a.

_____, "Prepubertal weight training called unproductive, dangerous." *Physician and Sportsmedicine* 10(1):126, 1982b.

Murase, Y., Kobayashi, K., Kamel, S., and Matsui, H., "Longitudinal study of aerobic power in superior junior athletes. " *Medicine and Science in Sports and Exercise* 13(3):180–184, 1981.

Murphy, P., "Youth sports coaches: Using hunches to fill a blank page." *Physician and Sportsmedicine* 13(4):136–142, 1985.

Murray, R.O., and Duncan, C., "Athletic activity in adolescence as an etiological factor in degenerative hip disease." *Journal of Bone and Joint Surgery* 53(3):406–419, 1971.

O'Connell, E., "Runner's World editorial." *Runner's World* 14(3):12, 1979.

Oka, M., and Hatanpaa, S., "Degenerative hip disease in adolescent athletes." *Medicine and Science in Sports* 8(2):77–80, 1976.

Pappas, A.M., "Epiphyseal injuries in sports." *Physician and Sportsmedicine* 11(6):140–148, 1983.

Percy, L.E., Dziuban, C.D., and Martin, J.B., "Analysis of effects of distance running on self-concepts of elementary students." *Perceptual and Motor Skills* 52(1):42, 1981.

Physician and Sportsmedicine, "Physical education for the elementary school child." *Physician and Sportsmedicine* 12(4):99–115, 1984.

_____, "Sports in Childhood." *Physician and Sportsmedicine* 10(8):52–60, 1982.

Rosegrant, S., "Boston sportsmedicine: Helping the young athlete." *Physician and Sportsmedicine* 9(10):105–107, 1981.

Rowland, T.W., and Hoontis, P.P., "Organizing road races for children: Special concerns." *Physician and Sportsmedicine* 13(3):126–132, 1985.

Ryan, A.J., "Defining age-groups in sports." *Physician and Sportsmedicine* 14(1):77, 1986.

_____, "Do children need physical education?" *Physician and Sportsmedicine* 12(4):41, 1984.

_____, "The very young athlete." *Physician and Sportsmedicine* 11(3):45, 1983.

_____, "Who's watching the children?" *Physician and Sportsmedicine* 10(8):49, 1982a.

_____, "The problem: Wrestling weight loss and growth." *Physician and Sportsmedicine* 10(8):48, 1982b.

Scientific Commission of the International Federation of Sportsmedicine, "Recommendations for physical activity and sports in children with heart disease." *The Journal of Sports Medicine and Physical Fitness* 22(4):401–406.

Shaffer, T.E., "The uniqueness of the young athlete." *American Journal of Sports Medicine* 8(5):370–371, 1980.

_____, "Doing what comes naturally." *Journal of the American Medical Association* 196(7):150, 1966.

Sheehan, G., "Children running? Why not?" *Physician and Sportsmedicine* 11(1):51, 1983a.

_____, "The parental effect on running." *Physician and Sportsmedicine* 11(2):51, 1983b.

Siegel, J.A., and Manfredi, T.G., "Effects of a ten-month fitness program on children." *Physician and Sportsmedicine* 12(5):91–97, 1984.

Speer, D.P., and Braun, J.K., "The biomechanical basis of growth plate injuries." *Physician and Sportsmedicine* 13(7):72–78, 1985.

Stackpole, J.W., and Murray, J.J., "School team physician." *Pediatric Clinics of North America* 29(6):1383–1398, 1982.

Stewart, K.J., and Gutin, B., "Effects of physical training on cardiorespiratory fitness in children." *Research Quarterly* 47(1):110–120, 1976.

Strong, W.B., "The uniqueness of the young athlete: medical considerations." *American Journal of Sports Medicine* 8(5):372–376, 1980.

_____, and Steed, D., "Cardiovascular evaluation of the young athlete." *Pediatric Clinics of North America* 29(6):1325–1341, 1982.

Sundberg, S., and Elovainio, R., "Cardiorespiratory function in competitive endurance runners aged 12–16 years compared with ordinary boys." *Acta Paediatrica Scandinavica* 71(6):987–992, 1982.

Thiene, G., Pennelli, N., and Rossi, L., "Cardiac conduction system abnormalities as a possible cause of sudden death in young athletes." *Human Pathology* 14(8):704–709, 1983.

Vaccaro, P., and Poffenbarger, A., "Resting and exercise respiratory function in young female child runners." *Journal of Sports Medicine* 22:102–107, 1982.

Wagner, J.A., Robinson, S., Tzankoff, S.P., and Marino, R.P., "Heat tolerance and acclimatization to work in the heat in relation to age." *Journal of Applied Physiology* 33(5):616–622, 1972.

Wilkins, K.E., "The uniqueness of the young athlete: musculoskeletal injuries." *American Journal of Sports Medicine* 8(5):377–382, 1980.

Wilmore, J.H., and McNamara, J.J., "Prevalence of coronary heart disease risk factors in boys, 8–12 years of age." *Journal of Pediatrics* 84(4):527–533, 1974.

4. Running After 40

Adams, G.M., and deVries, H.A., "Physiological effects of an exercise training regime upon women aged 52–79." *Journal of Gerontology* 28(1):50–55, 1973.

Adrian, M.J., "Flexibility in the aging adult," in E.L. Smith and R.C. Serfass (eds.), *Exercise and Aging: The Scientific Basis* (Hillside, N.J.: Enslow, 1981), pp. 45–58.

Altman, P.L., and Dittmer, D.S., *Biology Data Book* (Second Edition). Bethesda, MD: Federation of American Society for Experimental Biology, 1974.

Anonymous, "Seniors needn't go all out for fitness." *Journal of the American Medical Association* 246(3):202, 1981.

Astrand, I., Astrand, P.O., Hallback, I., and Kolbom, A., "Reduction in Maximal oxygen uptake with age." *Journal of Applied Physiology* 35(5):649–654, 1973.

Badenhop, D.T., Cleary, P.A., Schaal, S.F., Fox, E.L., and Bartels, R.L., "Physiological adjustments to higher- or lower-intensity exercise in elders." *Medicine and Science in Sports and Exercise* 15(6):496–502, 1983.

Bafitis, H., and Sargent, F., "Human physiological adaptability through the life sequence." *Journal of Gerontology* 32(4):402–410, 1977.

Balazs, E.A., "Intercellular matrix of connective tissue," in C.E. Finch and L. Hayflick (eds.), *The Handbook of the Biology of Aging* (New York: Van Nostrand Reinhold, 1977), pp. 222–240.

Barnard, R.J., Grimditch, G.K., and Wilmore, J.H., "Physiological characteristics of sprint and endurance masters runners." *Medicine and Science in Sports* 11(2):167–171, 1979.

Bortz, W.M., "Disuse and aging." *Journal of the American Medical Association* 248(10):1203–1208, 1982.

_____, "Effects of exercise on aging—effect of aging on exercise." *Journal of the American Geriatrics Society* 28(2):49–51, 1980.

Bruce, R.A., "Exercise, functional aerobic capacity, and aging—another viewpoint." *Medicine and Science in Sports and Exercise* 16(1):8–13, 1984.

Chapman, E.A., deVries, H.A., and Swezey, R., "Joint stiffness: Effects of exercise on young and old men." *Journal of Gerontology* 27(2):218–221, 1972.

Costill, D.L., and Winrow, E., "A comparison of two middle-aged ultramarathon runners." *Research Quarterly* 41(2):135–139, 1970.

Crandall, R.C., *Gerontology: A Behavioral Science Approach.* Reading, MA: Addison-Wesley, 1980.

Damon, A., Seltzer, C.C., Stoudt, H.W., and Bell, B., "Age and physique in healthy white veterans at Boston." *Journal of Gerontology* 27(2):202–208, 1972.

deVries, H.A., *Physiology of Exercise* (3rd Ed.). Dubuque, IA: Wm. C. Brown, 1980.

_____, "Physiological effects of an exercise training regimen upon men aged 52–88." *Journal of Gerontology* 25(4):325–336, 1970.

_____, and Adams, G.M., "Comparison of exercise responses in old and young men: I. The cardiac effort/total body effort relationship." *Journal of Gerontology* 27(3):344–348, 1972a.

_____, and _____, "Comparison of exercise responses in old and young men: II. Ventilatory mechanics." *Journal of Gerontology* 27(3):349–352, 1972b.

Dressendorfer, R.H., "Physiological profile of a masters runner." *Physician and Sportsmedicine* 8(8):49–52, 1980.

Drinkwater, B.L., Horvath, S.M., and Wells, C.L., "Aerobic power of females, ages 10–68." *Journal of Gerontology* 30(4):385–394. 1975.

Fitts, R.H., "Aging and skeletal muscles," in E.L. Smith and R.C. Serfass (eds.), *Exercise and Aging: The Scientific Basis* (Hillside, NJ: Enslow, 1981), pp. 31–44.

Gutmann, E., "Muscle," in C.E. Finch and L. Hayflick (eds.), *Handbook of The Biology of Aging* (New York: Van Nostrand Reinhold, 1977), pp. 445–469.

Hartung, G.H., and Farge, E.J., "Personality and physiological traits in middle-aged runners and joggers." *Journal of Gerontology* 32(5):541–548, 1977.

Heller, E.M., "Case report: 40 years of fitness." *Physician and Sportsmedicine.* 7(10):121–123, 1979.

Hogan, D.B., and Cape, R.D., "Marathoners over sixty years of age: Results of a survey." *American Geriatrics Society Journal* 32(2):121–123, 1984.

Kasch, F.W., "The effects of exercise on the aging process." *Physician and Sportsmedicine* 4(6):64–68, 1976.

_____, and Kulberg, J., "Physiological variables during 15 years of endurance exercise." *Scandinavian Journal of Sports Science* 3(2):59–62, 1981.

_____, Phillips, W.H., Carter, J.E.L., and Boyer, J.L., "Cardiovascular changes in middle-aged men during two years of training." *Journal of Applied Physiology* 34(1):53–57, 1973.

_____, and Wallace, J.P., "Physiological variables during 10 years of endurance exercise." *Medicine and Science in Sports* 8(1):5–8, 1976.

Kavanagh, T., and Shephard, R.J., "The effects of continued training on the aging process." *Annals of the New York Academy of Sciences* 301:656–670, 1977.

Kent, S., "Exercise and aging." *Geriatrics* 37(6):132–135, 1982.

Kohn, R.R., "Heart and cardiovascular system," in C.E. Finch and L. Hayflick (eds.), *Handbook of the Biology of Aging* (New York: Van Nostrand Reinhold, 1977), pp. 281–317.

Lane, N.E., Bloch, D.A., Jones, H.H., Marshall, W.H., Wood, P.D., and Fries, J.F., "Long-distance running, bone density, and osteoarthritis." *Journal of the American Medical Association* 255(9):1147–1151, 1986.

Legwold, G., "Masters competitors age little in ten years." *Physician and Sportsmedicine* 10(10):27, 1982.

McArdle, W.D., Katch, F.I., and Katch, V.L., *Exercise Physiology: Energy, Nutrition, and Human Performance*. Philadelphia: Lea and Febiger, 1981.

Matter, S., Stamford, B.A., and Weltman, A., "Age, diet, maximal aerobic capacity and serum lipids." *Journal of Gerontology* 35(4):532–536, 1980.

Maud, P.J., Pollock, M.L., Foster, C., Anholm, J.D., Guten, G., Al-Nouri, M., Hellman, C., and Schmidt, D.H., "Fifty years of training and competition in the marathon: Wally Hayward, age 70 – a physiological profile." *South African Medical Journal* (31 January):153–157, 1981.

Miller, S.S., (ed) *Symptoms: The Complete Home Medical Encyclopedia*. New York: Avon, 1976.

Montoye, H.J., and Lamphiear, D.E., "Grip arm strength in males and females, age 10–69." *Research Quarterly* 48(1):109–120, 1977.

Moritani, T., "Training adaptations in the muscles of older men," in E.C. Smith and R.C. Serfass (eds.), *Exercise and Aging: The Scientific Basis* (Hillside, NJ: Enslow, 1981), pp. 149–166.

———, and deVries, H.A., "Potential for gross muscle hypertrophy in older men." *Journal of Gerontology* 35(5):672–682, 1980.

Morse, C.E., and Smith, E.L., "Physical activity programming for the aged," in E.C. Smith and R.C. Serfass (eds.), *Exercise and Aging: The Scientific Basis* (Hillside, NJ: Enslow, 1981), pp. 109–120.

Munns, K., "Effects of exercise on the range of joint motion in elderly subjects," in E.C. Smith and R.C. Serfass (eds.), *Exercise and Aging: The Scientific Basis* (Hillside,NJ: Enslow, 1981), pp. 167–178.

Nagao, N., Arie, J., Inomoto, T., Imai, Y., and Sawada, Y., "Blood properties in middle-aged or older males with the habit of exercise running, especially fractions of serum cholesterols." *Journal of Human Ergology* 11:175–186, 1982.

Niinimaa, V., and Shephard, R.J., "Training and oxygen conductance in the elderly: I. The respiratory system." *Journal of Gerontology* 33(3):354–361, 1978.

Oyster, N., Morton, M., and Linnell, S., "Physical activity and osteoporosis in postmenopausal women." *Medicine and Science in Sports and Exercise* 16(1):44–50, 1984.

Panush, R.S., Schmidt, C., Caldwell, J.R., Edwards, N.L., Longley, S., Yonker, R., Webster, E., Nauman, J., Stork, J., and Pettersson, H., "Is running associated with degenerative joint disease?" *Journal of the American Medical Association* 255(9):1152–1154, 1986.

Parizkova, J., Eiselt, E., Sprynarova, S., and Wachtolova, M., "Body composition, aerobic capactiy, and density of muscle capillaries in young and old men." *Journal of Applied Physiology* 31(3):323–325, 1971.

Plowman, S.A., Drinkwater, B.L., and Horvath, S.M., "Age and aerobic power in women: a longitudinal study." *Journal of Gerontology* 34(4):512–520, 1979.

Pollock, M.L., "Physiological characteristics of older champion track athletes." *Research Quarterly* 45(4):363–373, 1974.

———, Miller, H.S., Janeway, R., Linnerud, A.C., Robertson, B., and Valentino, R., "Effects of walking on body composition and cardiovascular function of middle-aged men." *Journal of Applied Physiology* 30(1):126–130, 1971.

———, ———, and Ribisl, P.M. "Effects of fitness on aging." *Physician and Sportsmedicine* 6(8):45–49, 1978.

———, ———, and Wilmore, J., "Physiological characteristics of champion track athletes 40 to 75 years of age." *Journal of Gerontology* 29(6):645–649, 1974.

Puranen, J., Ala-Ketola, L., Peltokallio, P., and Saarela, J., "Running and primary osteoarthritis of the hip." *British Medical Journal* 2(May24):155–156, 1974.

Reddan, W.G., "Respiratory system and aging." in E.L. Smith and R.C. Serfass (eds.), *Exercise and Aging: The Scientific Basis* (Hillside, NJ: Enslow, 1981), pp. 89–108.

Robinson, S., Dill, D.B., Robinson, R.D., Tzankoff, S.P., and Wagner, J.A., "Physiological aging of champion runners." *Journal of Applied Physiology* 41(1):46–51, 1976.

————, ————, ————, ————, and ————, "Longitudinal studies of aging in 37 men." *Journal of Aplied Physiology* 38(2):263–267, 1975.

Rossman, I., "Anatomic and body composition changes with aging," in C.E. Finch and L. Hayflick (eds.) *The Handbook of the Biology of Aging* (New York: Van Nostrand Reinhold Company, 1977), pp. 189–240.

Ryan, A.J., "Exercise and arthritis: an encouraging report." *Physician and Sportsmedicine* 9(5):43, 1981.

Sager, K., "Exercises to activate seniors." *Physician and Sportsmedicine* 12(5):144–150, 1984.

————, "Senior fitness — for the health of it." *Physician and Sportsmedicine* 11(10):31–36, 1983.

Sanadi, D.R., "Metabolic changes and their significance in aging," in C.E. Finch and L. Hayflick (eds.), *Handbook of the Biology of Aging* (New York: Van Nostrand Reinhold, 1977), pp. 73–98.

Sato, I., Hasegawa, Y., Takahashi, N., Hirata, Y., Shimomura, K., and Hotta, K., "Age-related changes of cardiac control function in man: with special reference to heart rate control at rest and during exercise." *Journal of Gerontology* 36(5):564–572, 1981.

Shaver, L.G., *Essentials of Exercise Physiology.* Minneapolis: Brugess, 1981.

Shephard, R.J., "Cardiovascular limitations in the aged," in E.L. Smith and R.C. Serfass (eds.), *Exercise and Aging: The Scientific Basis* (Hillside, NJ: Enslow, 1981), pp. 19–30.

————, *Physical Activity and Aging.* Chicago: Year Book Medical Publishers, 1978.

Sidney, K.H., "Cardiovascular benefits of physical activity in the exercising aged," in E.L. Smith and R.C. Serfass (eds.), *Exercise and Aging: The Scientific Basis* (Hillside, NJ: Enslow, 1981), pp. 131–148.

————, and Shephard, R.J., "Maximum and submaximum exercise tests in men and women in the seventh, eighth, and ninth decades of life." *Journal of Applied Physiology* 43(2):280–287, 1977.

————, and ————, "Attitudes toward health and physical activity in the elderly: Effects of a physical training program." *Medicine and Science in Sports* 8(4):246–252, 1976.

Smith, E.L., "Exercise for prevention of osteoporosis: A review." *Physician and Sportsmedicine* 10(3):72–83, 1982.

————, "Age: The interaction of nature and nurture," in E.L. Smith and R.C. Serfass (eds.), *Exercise and Aging: The Scientific Basis* (Hillside, NJ: Enslow, 1981a), pp. 11–18.

————, "Bone changes in the exercising older adult," in E.L. Smith and R.C. Serfass (eds.), *Exercise and Aging: The Scientific Basis* (Hillside, NJ: Enslow, 1981b), pp. 179–186.

————, and Gilligan, C., "Physical activity prescription for the older adult." *Physician and Sportsmedicine* 11(8):91–101, 1983.

————, Reddan, W., and Smith, P.E., "Physical activity and calcium modalities for bone mineral increases in aged women." *Medicine and Science in Sports and Exercise* 13(1):60–64, 1981.

————, Sempos, C.T., and Purvis, R.W., "Bone mass and strength decline with age," in E.L. Smith and R.C. Serfass (eds.), *Exercise and Aging: The Scientific Basis* (Hillside, NJ: Enslow, 1981), pp. 59–88.

Stones, M.J., and Kozma, A., "Adult age trends in record running performances." *Experimental Aging Research* 6(5):407–416, 1980.

Strovas, J., "Seniors walk away from sedentary life." *Physician and Sportsmedicine* 12(4):144–152, 1984.

Suominen, H., Heikkinen, E., and Parkatti, T., "Effect of eight weeks' physical training on muscle and connective tissue of the m. Vastus lateralis in 69-year-old men and women." *Journal of Gerontology* 32(1):33–37, 1977.

Tomanek, R.J., Taunton, C.A., and Liskop, K.S., "Relationship between age, chronic exercise, and connective tissue of the heart." *Journal of Gerontology* 27(1):33–37, 1972.

Tonna, E.A., "Aging of skeletal-dental systems and supporting tissues," in C.E. Finch and L. Hayflick (eds.), *Handbook of the Biology of Aging* (New York: Van Nostrand Reinhold, 1977), pp. 470–495.

Tzankoff, S.P., Robinson, S., Pyke, F.S., and Brawn, C.A., "Physiological adjustments to work in older men as affected by physical training." *Journal of Applied Physiology* 33(3):346–350, 1972.

Upton, S.J., Hagan, R.D., Rosentswieg, J., and Gettman, L.R., "Comparison of the physiological profiles of middle-aged women distance runners and sedentary women." *Research Quarterly* 54(1):83–87, 1983.

U.S. Bureau of the Census, *Statistical Abstracts of the U.S.: 1981.* Washington, D.C.: U.S. Government Printing Office, 1981.

Vaccaro, P., Dummer, G., and Clarke, D., "Physiological characteristics of female masters swimmers." *Physician and Sportsmedicine* 9(12):75–78, 1981a.

_____, Morris, A.F., and Clarke, D.H., "Physiological characteristics of masters female distance runners." *Physician and Sportsmedicine* 9(7):105–108, 1981b.

Webb, J.L., Urner, S.C., and McDaniels, J., "Physiological characteristics of a champion runner: age 77." *Journal of Gerontology* 32(3):286–290, 1977.

Weisfeldt, M.L., "Aging of the cardiovascular system." *New England Journal of Medicine* 303(20):1172–1174, 1980.

Wilmore, J.H., Miller, H.L., and Pollock, M.L., "Body composition and physiological characteristics of active endurance athletes in their eighth decade of life." *Medicine and Science in Sports* 6(1):44–48, 1974.

Wright, T.W., Zauner, C.W., and Cade, R., "Cardiac output in male middle aged runners." *Journal of Sports Medicine* 22:17–21, 1982.

5. *Injuries*

Abel, M.S., "Jogger's fracture and other stress fractures of the lumbo-sacral spine." *Skeletal Radiology* 13:221–227, 1985.

Adno, J., "'Jogger's testicles' in marathon runners." *South African Medical Journal* 65(June 30):1036, 1984.

Alyea, E.P., and Parish, H.H., "Renal response to exercise — urinary findings." *Journal of the American Medical Association* 167:807, 1958.

American College of Sports Medicine, "Prevention of thermal injuries during distance running." *Physician and Sportsmedicine* 12(7):43–51, 1984a.

_____, "Prevention of thermal injuries during distance running: Position stand." *Medical Journal of Australia* (December 8/22):876–879, 1984b.

Andrews, J.R., "Overuse syndromes of the lower extremity." *Clinics in Sports Medicine* 2(1):137–148, 1983.

Anonymous, "Runners' enthusiasm causes most injuries." *Track and Field Journal* (13):49–50, 1982.

Anonymous, "No laughing matter: An 'allergy' exercise?" *Journal of the American Medical Association* 241(23):2474, 1979a.

Anonymous, "The haematuria of the long-distance runner." *British Medical Journal* II(July 21):159, 1979b.

Apple, D.F., "Knee pain in runners." *Southern Medical Journal* 72(11)1377–1379, 1979.

Arends, J., "Runners' anemia." *Michigan Runner* 6(11):2, 1984.

Asay, R.W., and Vieweg, W.V.R., "Severe coronary atherosclerosis in a runner: An exception to the rule?" *Journal of Cardiac Rehabilitation* (6):413–421, 1981.

Baer, S., and Shakespeare, D., "Stress fracture of the femoral neck in a marathon runner." *British Journal of Sports Medicine* 18(1):42–43, 1984.

Balaji, M.R., and DeWese, J.A., "Adductor canal outlet syndrome." *Journal of the American Medical Association* 245(2):167–170, 1981.

Barach, J., "Physiologic and pathological effects of severe exertion (the marathon race) on the circulatory and renal systems." *Archives of Internal Medicine* 5:382, 1910.

Bassler, T.J., "Hazards of restrictive diets." *Journal of the American Medical Association* 252(4):483, 1984a.

_____, "Cardiomythology." *Lancet* I(April 7):788–789, 1984b.

_____, "Coronary-artery disease in marathon runners." *New England Journal of Medicine* 302:57–8, 1980.

_____, "Beer as prevention for runner's haematuria." *British Medical Journal* II(November 17):1293, 1979a.

_____, "Heat stroke in a 'run for fun.'" *British Medical Journal* I(January 20):197, 1979b.

_____, "Heatstroke in a 'run for fun.'" *British Medical Journal* I(September 1):547, 1979c.

_____, "In defense of the hypothesis." *Physician and Sportsmedicine* 6(May):39–43, 1978a.

_____, "More on immunity to atherosclerosis in marathon runners." *New England Journal of Medicine* 299:201, 1978b.

_____, "Marathon running and immunity to atherosclerosis." *Annals of the New York Academy of Sciences* 301(October):579–592, 1977.

_____, "Marathon running and immunity to heart disease." *Physician and Sportsmedicine* 3(April):77–80, 1975.

Berman, D.L., "Etiology and management of hallux valgus in athletes." *Physician and Sportsmedicine* 10(8):103–107, 1982.

Blacklock, N.J., "Bladder trauma from jogging." *American Heart Journal* 99(6):813–814, 1980.

_____, "Bladder trauma in the long distance runner." *American Journal of Sports Medicine* 7(4):239, 1979.

Blake, R.L., and Fettig, M.H., "Chronic low back pain in a long-distance runner." *Journal of the American Podiatry Association* 73(11):598–601, 1983.

Blatz, D.J., "Bilateral femoral and tibial shaft stress fracture in a runner." *American Journal of Sports Medicine* 9(5):322–325, 1981.

Boileau, M., Fuchs, E., Barry, J.M., and Hodges, C.V., "Stress hematuria: athletic pseudonephritis in marathoners." *Urology* 15(5):471–474, 1980.

Boone, W.B., "Management of heatstroke." *Journal of the American Medical Association* 249(2):194, 1983.

Brody, D.M., "Techniques in the evaluation and treatment of the injured runner." *Orthopedic Clinics of North America* 13(3):541–558, 1982.

Buckman, M.T., "Gastrointestinal bleeding in long-distance runners." *Annals of Internal Medicine* 101(1):127–128, 1984.

Bunch, T.W., "Blood test abnormalities in runners." *Mayo Clinic Proceedings* 55(2):113–117, 1980.

Burgess, I., and Ryan, M.D., "Bilateral fatigue fractures of the distal fibulae caused by a change of running shoes." *Medical Journal of Australia* 143(7):304–305, 1985.

Burton, R.M., "Exercise-induced asthma in cold weather." *Physician and Sportsmedicine* 9(9):131–132, 1981.

Butler, J.E., Brown, S.L., and McConnell, G.G., "Subtrochanteric stress fractures in runners." *American Journal of Sports Medicine* 10(4):228–232, 1982.

Caldroney, R.D., "Risk factors in heatstroke." *Journal of the American Medical Association* 249(2):193, 1983.

Campbell, G., and Warnekros, W., "A tarsal stress fracture in a long-distance runner." *Journal of the American Podiatry Association* 73(10):532–535, 1983.

Cantwell, J.D., and Fletcher, G.F., "Sudden death and jogging." *Physician and Sportsmedicine* 6(3):94–98, 1978.

_____, and _____, "Cardiac complications while jogging." *Journal of the American Medical Association* 210:130–131, 1969.

Clancy, W.G., "Runners' injuries." *American Journal of Sports Medicine* 8(2):137–144, 1980a.

_____, "Runners' injuries." *AJSM* 8(4):287–289, 1980b.

_____, "Editorial comment." *AJSM* 6(2):49–50, 1978.

Clark, A., and Stanish, W.D., "An unusual cause of back pain in a young athlete." *American Journal of Sports Medicine* 13(1):51–54, 1985.

Clark, N., "Increasing dietary iron." *Physician and Sportsmedicine* 13(1):131–132, 1985.

Clayton, D., "Antwerp, 1969." *Runner's World* 14(5):71–72, 1979.

Clement, D.B., Taunton, J.E., Smart, G.W., and McNicol, K.L., "A survey of overuse running injuries." *Physician and Sportsmedicine* 9(5):47–58, 1981.

Cohen, I.J., "Unexpected gain from jogging." *Lancet* II(July 19):154, 1980.

Colt, E., "Coronary-artery disease in marathon runners." *New England Journal of Medicine* 302:57, 1980.

_____, and Heyman, B., "Low ferritin levels in runners." *Journal of Sports Medicine and Practice* 24:13–17, 1984.

Colt, E.W.D., and Spyropoulos, E., "Running and stress fractures." *British Medical Journal* II(September 22):706, 1979.

Costill, D.L., *A Scientific Approach to Distance Running.* Los Altos, CA: Track and Field News, 1979.

Cushing, D., "Are joggers on the road to osteoarthritis?" *Physician and Sportsmedicine* 7(9):19–20, 1979.

Daffner, R.H., Martinez, S., and Gehweiler, J.A., "Stress fractures in runners." *Journal of the American Medical Association* 247(7):1039–1041, 1982.

Dancaster, C.P., and Whereat, S.J., "Renal function in marathon runners." *South African Medical Journal* 45:547–551, 1971.

Detmer, D.E., "Chronic leg pain." *American Journal of Sports Medicine* 8(2):141–144, 1980.

Devereaux, M.D., Parr, G.R., Lachmann, S.M., Page-Thomas, P., and Hazleman, B.L., "The diagnosis of stress fracture in athletes." *Journal of the American Medical Association* 252(4):531–533, 1984.

Dorsen, P.J., "Runner's anemia or 'I wonder where the blood went.'" *Minnesota Medicine* 68(10):768–769, 1985.

Dressendorfer, R.H., Wade, C.E., and Amsterdam, E.A., "Development of pseudoanemia in marathon racing during a 20-day road race." *Journal of the American Medical Association* 246(11):1215–1218, 1981.

Drez, D., "Running footware." *American Journal of Sports Medicine* 8(2):140–141, 1980.

Dugan, R.C., and D'Ambrosia, R., "Fibular stress fractures in runners." *Journal of Family Practice* 17(3):415–418, 1983.

Dunn, K., "A tenuous partnership: Novice runners and distance races." *Physician and Sportsmedicine* 8(11):109–111, 1980.

_____, "Contusions may cause runner's hematuria." *Physician and Sportsmedicine* 7(10):20–21, 1979.

Dunnett, W., "The rape threat." *Runner's World* 16(6):52–55, 1981.

Eggold, J.F., "Orthotics in the prevention of runners' overuse injuries." *Physician and Sportsmedicine* 9(3):125–131, 1981.

Eichner, E.R., "Runner's macrocytosis: a clue to footstrike hemolysis." *American Journal of Medicine* 78(2):321–325, 1985.

Ellis, F.R., and Campbell, I.T., "Fatal heat stroke in a long distance runner." *British Medical Journal* 287(November 19):1548–1549, 1983.

Elrick, H., "Distance runners as models of optimal health." *Physician and Sportsmedicine* 9(January):64–68, 1981.

England, A.C., Fraser, D.W., Hightower, A.W., Tirinnanzi, R., Greenberg, D.J., Powell, K.E., Slovis, C.M., and Varsha, A., "Preventing severe heat injury in runners: Suggestions from the 1979 Peachtree Road Race experience." *Annals of Internal Medicine* 97(2):196–201, 1982.

Falsetti, H.L., Burke, E.R., Feld, R.D., Frederick, E.C., and Ratering, C., "Hematological variations after endurance running with hard- and soft-soled running shoes." *Physician and Sportsmedicine* 11(8):118–127, 1983.

Fassett, R., "Exercise haematuria." *Australian Family Physician* 13(7):518–519, 1984.

Fernhall, B., Manfredi, T.G., and Rierson, H., "Effects of ten weeks of cardiac rehabilitation on blood clotting and risk factors." *Physician and Sportsmedicine* 12(February):85–98, 1984.

Ferstle, J., "Noel D. Nequin: Crusading for road-race safety." *Physician and Sportsmedicine* 10(2):133–136, 1982.

Fitch, K.D., "Stress fractures of the lower limbs in runners." *Australian Family Physician* 13(7):511–515, 1984.

Fogoros, R.N., "Runner's trots: Gastrointestinal disturbances in runners." *Journal of the American Medical Association* 243(17):1743–1744, 1980.

Fred, H.L., "More on the grossly bloody urine of runners." *Archives of Internal Medicine* 138:1610–1611, 1978.

_____, and Natelson, E.A., "Grossly bloody urine of runners." *Southern Medical Journal* 70(12):1394–1396, 1977.

French, J.K., and Frengley, P.A., "Hypoglycaemia-induced seizures following a marathon." *New Zealand Medical Journal* 96(May 25):407, 1983.

Frizzell, R.T., Lang, G.H., Lowance, D.C., and Lathan, S.R., "Hyponatremia and ultramarathon running." *Journal of the American Medical Association* 255(6):772–774, 1986.

Gamble, P., and Froelicher, V.F., "Can an exercise program worsen heart disease?" *Physician and Sportsmedicine* 10(May):69–77, 1982.

Garbitelli, B., "Oral or rectal?" *Physician and Sportsmedicine* 12(10):10–15, 1984.

Gardner, K.D., "Athletic pseudonephritis — alteration of urine sediment by athletic competition." *Journal of the American Medical Association* 161:1613, 1956.

Gilli, P., DePaoli, E., Tataranni, G., and Farinelli, A., "Exercise-induced urinary abnormalities in long-distance runners." *International Journal of Sports Medicine* 5(5):237–240, 1984.

Glick, J.M., and Katch, V.L., "Musculoskeletal injuries in jogging." *Archives of Physical Medicine and Rehabilitation* 51(3):123–126, 1970.

Godshall, R.W., Hansen, C.A., and Rising, D.C., "Stress fractures through the distal femoral epiphysis in athletes: A previously unreported entity." *American Journal of Sports Medicine* 9(2):114–116, 1981.

Goldsmith, H.J., "Acute renal failure after a marathon run." *Lancet* I(February 4):278–279, 1984.

Gottlieb, G., and White, J.R., "Responses of recreational runners to their injuries." *Physician and Sportsmedicine* 8(3):145–149, 1980.

Graham, C.E., "Painless jogging for 15000km after a lumbosacral stabilisation with screws and cement." *Medical Journal of Australia* (May 1):389, 1982.

Grana, W.A., and Coniglione, T.C., "Knee disorders in runners." *Physician and Sportsmedicine* 13(5):127–133, 1985.

Green, L.H., Cohen, S.I., and Kurland, G., "Fatal myocardial infarction in marathon racing." *Annals of Internal Medicine* 84:704–706, 1976.

Gudas, C.J., "Patterns of lower-extremity injury in 224 runners." *Comprehensive Therapy* 6(9):50–59, 1980.

Guten, G., "Herniated lumbar disk associated with running." *American Journal of Sports Medicine* 9(3):155–159, 1981.

_____, and Craviotto, D., "Bone scan changes in a marathon runner." *Wisconsin Medical Journal* 84(8):11–12, 1985.

Hage, P., "Air pollution: Adverse effects on athletic performance." *Physician and Sportsmedicine* 10(3):126–132, 1982.

Hagerman, F.C., Hikida, R.S., Staron, R.S., Sherman, W.M., and Costill, D.L., "Muscle damage in marathon runners." *Physician and Sportsmedicine* 12(11):39–48, 1984.

Hajek, M.E., and Noble, H.B., "Stress fracture of the femoral neck in joggers." *American Journal of Sports Medicine* 10(2):112–116, 1982.

Handler, J.B., Asay, R.W., Warren, S.E., and Shea, P.M., "Symptomatic coronary artery disease in a marathon runner." *Journal of the American Medical Association* 248:717–719, 1982.

Hanson, P.G., "Heat injury in runners." *Physician and Sportsmedicine* 7(6):91–96, 1979.

_____, and Zimmerman, S.W., "Exertional heatstroke in novice runners." *Journal of the American Medical Association* 242(2):154–157, 1979.

Hanzlick, R.L., and Stivers, R.R., "Sudden death due to anomalous right coronary artery in a 26-year-old runner." *American Journal of Forensic Medical Pathology* 4(3):265–268, 1983.

Hart, L.E., Egier, B.P., Shimizu, A.G., Tandan, P.J., and Sutton, J.R., "Exertional heat stroke: The runner's nemesis." *Canadian Medical Journal* 122(May 24):1144–1150, 1980.

Heide, T., "The haematuria of the long-distance runner." *British Medical Journal* II(September 1):547, 1979.

Hershkowitz, M., "Penile frostbite, an unforeseen hazard of jogging." *New England Journal of Medicine* 296(January 20):178, 1977.

Hilb, J.A., "Sudden death of a runner." *Journal of the Kentucky Medical Association* 82(1):9–12, 1984.

Honigman, B., Cromer, R., Kurt, T.L., "Carbon monoxide levels in athletes during exercise in an urban environment." *Journal of the Air Pollution Control Association* 32(1):77–79, 1982.

Hooper, P.L., "Exercise-related hematuria." *Journal of the American Medical Association* 241(18):1892–1893, 1979.

Hoover, D.L., and Cromie, W.J., "Theory and management of exercise-related hematuria." *Physician and Sportsmedicine* 9(11):91–95, 1981.

Hughes, J.H., "Unusual intra-abdominal bleeding." *Annals of Emergency Medicine* 9(12):647–648, 1980.

Hughes, W.A., Noble, H.B., and Porter, M., "Distance race injuries: An analysis of runners' perceptions." *Physician and Sportsmedicine* 13(11):43–58, 1985.

Hughson, R.L., "Long-distance running in the heat." *Canadian Medical Journal* 123(October 4):607–608, 1980.

_____, Green, H.J., Houston, M.E., Thompson, J.A., MacLean D.R., and

Sutton, J.R., "Heat injuries in Canadian mass participation runs." *Canadian Medical Journal* 122(May 24):1141–1144, 1980.

————, Staudt, L.A., and Mackie, J.M., "Monitoring road racing in the heat." *Physician and Sportsmedicine* 11(5):94–105, 1983.

————, and Sutton, J.R., "Heat stroke in a 'run for fun.'" *British Medical Journal* II(October 21)1158, 1978.

Hunter, L.Y., "Stress fracture of the tarsal navicular." *American Journal of Sports Medicine* 9(4):217–219, 1981.

Jackson, M.A., and Gudas, C.J., "Peroneus longus tendinitis: A possible biomechanical etiology." *Journal of Foot Surgery* 21(4):344–348, 1982.

Jackson, R.T., Beaglehole, R., and Sharpe, N., "Sudden death in runners." *New Zealand Medical Journal* 96:289–292, 1983.

Jacobs, M.B., and Wilson, W., "Iron deficiency anemia in a vegetarian runner." *Journal of the American Medical Association* 252(4):481–482, 1984.

James, S.L., Bates, B.T., and Osternig, L.R., "Injuries to runners." *American Journal of Sports Medicine* 6(2):40–50, 1978.

Johnson, R., "Common running injuries of the leg and foot." *Minnesota Medicine* 66(7):441–444, 1983.

Jones, B.H., "Overuse injuries of the lower extremities associated with marching, jogging, and running: A review." *Military Medicine* 148(10):783–787, 1983.

Julsrud, M.E., "Bilateral stress fracture in a long-distance runner." *Journal of the American Podiatric Medical Association* 75(7):385–389, 1985.

Juniper, C.P., "Exercise-induced asthma." *British Medical Journal* (February 23):565, 1980.

Kains, J.P., DeWit, S., Close, P., Melot, C., Nagler, J., VanRooy, P., "Exertional heat stress disease." *Acta Clinica Belgica* 38(5):315–323, 1983.

Kannel, W.B., "Exercise and sudden death." *Journal of the American Medical Association* 248:3143–3144, 1982.

Keeffe, E.B., Lowe, D.K., Gross, J.R., and Wayne, R., "Gastrointestinal symptoms of marathon runners." *Western Journal of Medicine* 141(4):481–484, 1984.

Kent, F., "Athletes wait too long to report injuries." *Physician and Sportsmedicine* 10(4):127–129, 1982.

Khogali, M., Gumaa, K., and Mustafa, M.K.Y., "Fatal heat stroke in a long distance runner." *British Medical Journal* 287(November 19):1549, 1983.

Khoury, M., Kirks, D., Martinez, S., and Apple, J., "Bilaterial avulsion fractures of the anterior superior iliac spines in sprinters." *Skeletal Radiology* 13:65–67, 1985.

Kilbourne, E.M., "Risk factors in heatstroke." *Journal of the American Medical Association* 249(2):194, 1983.

————, Choi, K., Jones, T.S., and Thacker, S.B., "Risk factors for heatstroke." *Journal of the American Medical Association* 247(24):3332–3336, 1982.

Kincaid-Smith, P., "Haematuria and exercise-related haematuria." *British Medical Journal* 285(December 4):1595–1596, 1982.

Klein, K.K., "The shoes: Runners beware." *American Corrective Therapy Journal* 36(4):103–104, 1982.

————, "Evaluation of running injuries." *Physician and Sportsmedicine* 8(2):141–143, 1980.

Koplan, J.P., "Cardiovascular deaths while running." *Journal of the American Medical Association* 242:2578–2579, 1979.

————, Powell, K.E., Sikes, R.K., Shirley, R.W., and Campbell, C.C., "An epidemiologic study of the benefits and risks of running." *Journal of the American Medical Association* 248(23):3118–3121, 1982.

Krebs, P.S., Scully, B.C., and Zinkgraf, S.A., "The acute and prolonged effects of marathon running on 20 blood parameters." *Physician and Sportsmedicine* 11(4):66–73, 1983.

Kretsch, A., Grogan, R., Duras, P., Allen, F., Sumner, J., and Gillam, I., "1980 Mel bourne marathon study." *Medical Journal of Australia* 141(12–13):809–14, 1984.

Krissoff, W.B., and Ferris, W.D., "Runners' injuries." *Physician and Sportsmedicine* 7(12):55–64, 1979.

Kummant, I., "Peachtree heat injury lawsuit dismissed." *Physician and Sportsmedicine* 9(9):26, 1981.

Kuusi, T., Kostiainen, E., Vartiainen, E., Pitkanen, L., Ehnholm C., Korhonen, H.J., Nissinen, A., and Puska, P., "Acute effects of marathon running on levels of serum lipoproteins and androgenic hormones in healthy males." *Metabolism* 33(6):527–531, 1984.

Landry, M., Zebas, C.J., "Biomechanical principles in common running injuries." *Journal of the American Podiatric Medical Association* 75(1):48–52, 1985.

Lane, N.E., Bloch, D.A., Jones, H.H., Marshall, W.H., Wood, P.D., and Fries, J.F., "Long-distance running, bone density, and osteoarthritis." *Journal of the American Medical Association* 255(9):1147–1151, 1986.

Larkins, P.A., "Evaluating runners' injuries." *Australian Family Physician* 13(7):503–506, 1984.

Larson, D.C., "Toxic vapor exposure and aerobic exercise." *Physician and Sportsmedicine* 13(1):76–80, 1985.

Lathan, S.R., and Cantwell, J.D., "A run for the record: Studies on a trans-American ultramarathoner." *Journal of the American Medical Association* 245(4):367–368, 1981.

Latshaw, R.F., Kantner, T.R., Kalenak, A., Baum, S., and Corcoran, J.J., "A pelvic stress fracture in a female jogger." *American Journal of Sports Medicine* 9(1):54–56, 1981.

Ledingham, I., MacVicar, S., Watt, I., and Weston, G.A., "Early resuscitation after marathon collapse." *Lancet* II(November 13):1096–1097, 1982.

Legwold, G., "Are we running from the truth about the risks and benefits of exercise?" *Physician and Sportsmedicine* 13(5):136–148, 1985.

Lehman, W.L., "Overuse syndromes in runners." *American Journal of Family Practice* 29(1):157–161, 1984.

Levine, J., "Chrondromalacia patellae." *Physician and Sportsmedicine* 7(8):41–9, 1979.

Leon, A.S., "Physical activity levels and coronary heart disease." *Medical Clinics of North America* 69(1):3–20, 1985.

Levit, F., "Jogger's nipple." *New England Journal of Medicine* 297(20):1127, 1977.

Lindenberg, G., Pinshaw, R., and Noakes, T.D., "Lliotibial band friction syndrome in runners." *Physician and Sportsmedicine* 12(5):118–130, 1984.

Linder, C.W., and DuRant, R.H., "Exercise, serum lipids, and cardiovascular disease – risk factors in children." *Pediatric Clinics of North America* 29(6):1341–1354, 1982.

Lloyd, E., "Marathon medicine." *Lancet* I(January 8):69–70, 1983.

Lombardo, S.J., and Benson, D.W., "Stress fractures of the femur in runners." *American Journal of Sports Medicine* 10(4):219–227, 1982.

Ludmerer, K.M., and Kissane, J.M., eds., "Sudden death in a 47-year-old marathon runner." *American Journal of Medicine* 76(March):517–526, 1984.

Lutter, L., "Injuries in the runner and jogger." *Minnesota Medical Journal* 63(1):45–51, 1980.

Lynch, P., "Soldiers, sport, and sudden death." *Lancet* I(June 7):1235–1237, 1980.

McClendon, I., "Honolulu Marathon clinics stress safety, not winning." *Physician and Sportsmedicine* 10(5):153–156, 1982.

McDermott, M., and Freyne, P., "Osteoarthrosis in runners with knee pain." *British Journal of Sports Medicine* 17(2):84–87, 1983.

MacFarlane, P., "Recognizing and treating heat stroke and exhaustion in the road runner." *Canadian Nurse* 79(4):21–23, 1983.

McKenzie, D.C., Clement, D.B., and Taunton, J.E., "Running shoes, orthotics, and injuries." *Sports Medicine* 2:334–347, 1985.

McMahon, L.F., and Fisher, R.L., "Gastrointestinal blood loss in runners." *Annals of Internal Medicine* 101(6):875, 1984.

————, Ryan, M.J., Larson, D., and Fisher, R.L., "Occult gastrointestinal blood loss in marathon runners." *Annals of Internal Medicine* 100(6):846–847, 1984.

Macrae, F., St. John, D.J.B., and Caligiore, P., "Gastrointestinal blood loss in runners." *Annals of Internal Medicine* 101(6):875, 1984.

MacSearraigh, E.T.M., Kallmeyer, J.D., and Schiff, H.B., "Acute renal failure in marathon runners." *Nephron* 24(5):236–240, 1979.

Magnusson, B., Hallberg, L., Rossander, L., and Swolin B., "Iron metabolism and 'sports anemia': A study of several iron parameters in elite runners with differences in iron status.'" *Acta Medica Scandinavica* 216(2):149–155, 1984a.

————, ————, ————, and ————, "Iron metabolism and 'sports anemia': A hematological comparison of elite runners and control subjects." *Acta Medica Scandinavica* 216(2):157–164, 1984b.

Mangi, R., Jokl, P., and Dayton, O.W., *The Runner's Complete Medical Guide.* New York: Summit Books, 1979.

Maron, B.J., Roberts, W.C., McAllister, H.A., Rosing, D.R., and Epstein, S.D., "Sudden death in young athletes." *Circulation* 62:218–229, 1980.

Marwick, C., "Olympic athletes may face extra challenge – pollution." *Journal of the American Medical Association* 251(19):2495–2497, 1984.

Massey, E.W., "Effort headache in runners." *Headache* 22(3):99–100, 1982.

Maughan, R.J., Light, I.M., Whiting, P.H., and Miller, J.D.B., "Hypothermia, hyperkalaemia, and marathon running." *Lancet* (December 11):1336, 1982.

————, and Miller, J.D.B., "Popular marathons: Forecasting casualties." *British Medical Journal* 285(December 11):1736, 1982.

Medhat, M.A., "Knee injuries: damage from running and related sports." *Journal of the Kansas Medical Society* 84(7):379–383, 1983.

————, Redford, J.B., "Knee injuries." *Journal of the Kansas Medical Society* 84(7):379–383, 1983.

Merhar, G., "Safety on the run." *Running and Fitness* 16(5):8–10, 1984.

Milvy, P., "Statistical analysis of deaths from coronary heart disease anticipated in a cohort of marathon runners." *Annals of the New York Academy of Sciences* 301(October):620–626, 1977.

————, Colt, E., and Thornton, J., "A high incidence of urolithiasis in male marathon runners." *Journal of Sports Medicine* 21(3):295–298, 1981.

Mirkin, G., and Hoffman, M., *Sportsmedicine Book.* Boston: Little, Brown, 1978.

Moore, M., "Pelvic stress fractures more common in women." *Physician and Sportsmedicine* 11(5):25–26, 1983a.

————, "Runners' training excesses cause injury." *Physician and Sportsmedicine* 11(6):31, 1983b.

————, "Boston Marathon medical coverage: The road racer's safety net." *Physician and Sportsmedicine* 11(6):168–178, 1983c.

————, "What are we learning from road races." *Physician and Sportsmedicine* 10(8):151–157, 1982.

Morris, A.F., "Sleep disturbances in athletes." *Physician and Sportsmedicine* 10(9):75–85, 1982.

Morton, A.R., Hahn, A.G., and Fitch, K.D., "Continuous and intermittent running in the provocation of asthma." *Annals of Allergy* 48(February):123–129, 1982.

Murphy, P., "Orthoses: Not the sole solution for running ailments." *Physician and Sportsmedicine* 14(2):164–169, 1986.

————, "Olympic marathon fury heats up." *Physician and Sportsmedicine* 12(10):161–163, 1984.

Nash, H.L., "Treating thermal injury: Disagreement heats up." *Physician and Sportsmedicine* 13(7):134–144, 1985.

National Center for Health Statistics, *Health United States: 1984.* Hyattsville, Maryland: National Center for Health Statistics, DHHS publication no. (PHS)85-1232, 1984.

Nelson, R.A., "Preventing and treating dehydration." *Physician and Sportsmedicine* 13(3):176–177, 1985.

Nequin, N.D., "Frostbitten by earphones." *Physician and Sportsmedicine* 13(3):16, 1985.

Nicholl, J.P., and Williams, B.T., "Popular marathons: Forecasting casualties." *British Medical Journal* 285(November 20):1464–1465, 1982a.

_____, and _____, "Medical problems before and after a popular marathon." *British Medical Journal* 285(November 20):1465–1466, 1982b.

Nichols, T.W., "Bicycle-seat hematuria." *New England Journal of Medicine* 311(October 25):1128, 1984.

Nicholson, J.P., and Case, D.B., "Carboxyhemoglobin levels in New York City runners." *Physician and Sportsmedicine* 11(3):135–138, 1983.

Nilsson, S., "Jogging injuries." *Scandinavian Journal of Social Medicine*, Supplement 29:171–178, 1982.

Noakes, T.D., "Heatstroke during the 1981 National Cross-Country running championships. " *South African Medical Journal* 59(January 30):145, 1982a.

_____, "Food allergies in the runner." *Journal of the American Medical Association* 247(10):1406, 1982b.

_____, "Muscle injuries in sport." *South African Medical Journal* 56(1):6, 1979.

_____, Goodwin, N., Rayner, B.L., Branken, T., and Taylor R.K.N., "Water intoxication: A possible complication during endurance exercise." *Medicine and Science in Sports and Exercise* 17(3):370–375, 1985.

_____, and Opie, L.H., "Heatstroke in a 'run for fun.'" *British Medical Journal* II(July 7):52, 1979a.

_____, and _____, "Marathon running and the heart: The South African experience." *American Heart Journal* 98:669–671, 1979b.

_____, _____, and Beck, W., "Coronary heart disease in marathon runners." *Annals of the New York Academy of Sciences* 301:593–619, 1977.

_____, _____, and Rose, A.G., "Marathon running and immunity to coronary heart disease: Fact versus fiction," *Clinics in Sports Medicine* 3:527–543, 1984.

_____, _____, _____, and Kleynhans, H.T., "Autopsy-proved coronary atherosclerosis in marathon runners." *New England Journal of Medicine* 301(2):86–89, 1979.

_____, and Rose, A.G., "Exercise-related deaths in subjects with coexistent hypertrophic cardiomyopathy and coronary artery disease." *South African Medical Journal* 66:183–187, 1984.

_____, _____, and Opie, L.H., "Hypertrophic cardiomyopathy associated with sudden death during marathon racing." *British Heart Journal* 41:624–627, 1979.

_____, Smith, J.A., Lindenberg, G., and Wills, C.E., "Pelvic stress fractures in long distance runners." *American Journal of Sports Medicine* 13(2):120–123, 1985.

Noble, H.B., Hajek, M.R., and Porter, M., "Diagnosis and treatment of Iliotibial band tightness in runners." *Physician and Sportsmedicine* 10(4):67–74, 1982.

Norfray, J.F., "Diagnosis of stress fracture." *Journal of the American Medical Association* 244(13):1436, 1980.

_____, Schlachter, L., Kernahan, W.T., Arenson, D.J., Smith, S.D., Roth, I.E., and Schlefman, B.S., "Early confirmation of stress fractures in joggers." *Journal of the American Medical Association* 243(16):1647–1649, 1980.

Northcote, R.J., and Ballantyne, D., "Reducing the prevalence of exercise related cardiac deaths." *British Journal of Sports Medicine* 18(4):288–292, 1984.

————, and ————, "Sudden death in a marathon runner." *Lancet* I(February 19):417, 1983a.

————, and ————, "Sudden cardiac death in sport." *British Medical Journal* 287:1357–1359, 1983b.

Northway, M., "The ordeal of Steve Heidenreich." *Runner's World* 16(1):49–50, 1981.

Ogden, J.A., McCarthy, S.M., and Jokl, P., "The painful bipartite patella." *Journal of Pediatric Orthopedics* 2(3):263–269, 1982.

Opie, L.H., "Long-distance running and sudden death." *New England Journal of Medicine* 293:941–942, 1975a.

————, "Sudden death and sport." *Lancet* I(February 7):263–264, 1975b.

Paffenbarger, R.S., Hyde, R.T., Wing, A.L., and Steinmetz, C.H., "A natural history of athleticism and cardiovascular health." *Journal of the American Medical Association* 252:491–495, 1984.

————, Wing, A.L., and Hyde, R.T., "Physical activity as an index of heart attack risk in college alumni." *American Journal of Epidemiology* 108:161–175, 1978.

Panush, R.S., Schmidt, C., Caldwell, J.R., Edwards, N.L., Longley, S., Yonker, R., Webster, E., Nauman, J., Stork, J., and Pettersson, H., "Is running associated with degenerative joint disease?" *Journal of the American Medical Association* 255(9):1152–1154, 1986.

Papaionnides, D., Giotis, C., Karaginnis, N., and Voudouris, C., "Acute upper gastrointestinal hemorrhage in long-distance runners." *Annals of Internal Medicine* 101(5):719, 1984.

Parrotte, D.M., "Risk factors in heatstroke." *Journal of the American Medical Association* 249(2):193, 1983.

Parsons, M.A., Anderson, P.B., and Williams, B.T., "An 'unavoidable' death in a people's marathon." *British Journal of Sports Medicine* 18(1):38–39, 1984.

Pavlov, H., Nelson, T.L., Warren, R.F., Torg, J.S., and Burstein, A.H., "Stress fractures of the pubic ramus." *Journal of Bone and Joint Surgery* 64-A(7):1020–1025, 1982.

Pepys, M.B., and Hind, C.R.K., "Diagnosis of chest pain in marathon runners." *Lancet* I(February 4):278, 1984.

Percy, E.C., and Gamble, F.O., "An epiphyseal stress fracture of the foot and shin splints in an anomalous calf muscle in a runner." *British Journal of Sports Medicine* 14(2 & 3):110–113, 1980.

Pfeiffer, R.P., and Young, T.R., "Case report: Spontaneous pneumothorax in a jogger." *Physician and Sportsmedicine* 8(12):65–67, 1980.

Physician and Sportsmedicine, "Overtraining of athletes." *Physician and Sportsmedicine* 11(6):93–110, 1983.

Pietschmann, D., "Harassment on the run." *Runner's World* 18(2):26–30, 64–68, 1983.

Pinshaw, R., Atlas, V., and Noakes, T.D., "The nature and response to therapy of 196 consecutive injuries seen at a runner's clinic." *South African Medical Journal* 65(8):291–298, 1984.

Piterman, L., "The hazards of jogging and running." *Australian Family Physician* 11(12):943–948, 1982.

Porter, A.M.W., "Do some marathon runners bleed into the gut?" *British Medical Journal* 287(November 12):1427, 1983.

Porter, K., "Benoit: From hospital bed to victory stand in 17 days." *Physician and Sportsmedicine* 12(10):167–170, 1984.

Prescott, L., "Pelvic stress fractures more common in women." *Physician and Sportsmedicine* 11(5):25–26, 1983.

Richards, R., and Richards, D., "Exertion-induced heat exhaustion and other medical aspects of the City-to-Surf fun runs, 1978–1984." 141(12–13):799–805, 1984.

_____, _____, and Schofield, P.J., "Biochemical and haematological changes in Sydney's 'The Sun City-to-Surf' fun runners." *Medical Journal of Australia* 2(9):449–553, 1979.

_____, _____, _____, and Sutton, J.R., "Management of heat exhaustion in Sydney's 'The Sun City-to-Surf' fun runners." *Medical Journal of Australia* 2(9):457–461, 1979a.

_____, _____, _____, and _____, "Reducing the hazards in Sydney's 'The Sun City-to-Surf' runs, 1971 to 1979." *Medical Journal of Australia* 2(9):453–457, 1979b.

_____, _____, _____, Ross, V., and Sutton, J.R., "Organization of the Sun City-to-Surf Fun Run, Sydney, 1979." *Medical Journal of Australia* 2(9):470–474, 1979.

_____, _____, and Whittaker, R., "Method of predicting the number of casualties in the Sydney City-to-Surf fun runs." *Medical Journal of Australia* 141(12–13):805–808, 1984.

Riess, R.W., "Athletic hematuria and related phenomena. " *Journal of Sports Medicine* 19:381–387, 1979.

Rigotti, N.A., Thomas, G.S., and Leaf, A., "Exercise and coronary heart disease." *Annual Review of Medicine* 34:391–412, 1983.

Roberts, J.A., "Loss of form in young athletes due to viral infection." *British Medical Journal* I(February 2):357–358, 1985.

Robinson, C.R., "Jogging in Tasmania." *New England Journal of Medicine* 285(22):1267, 1971.

Rogers, C.C., "Of magic, miracles, and exercise myths." *Physician and Sportsmedicine* 13(5):156–166, 1985.

_____, "The Los Angeles Olympic Games: Effects of pollution unclear." *Physician and Sportsmedicine* 12(5):172–183, 1984a.

_____, "Fitness may be a woman's best defense." *Physician and Sportsmedicine* 12(10):146–156, 1984b.

Roodman, G.D., Reese, E.P., and Cardamone, J.M., "Aplastic anemia associated with rubber cement used by a marathon runner." *Archives of Internal Medicine* 140(May):703, 1980.

Ross, C.F., and Schuster, R.O., "A preliminary report on predicting injuries in distance runners." *Journal of the American Podiatry Association* 73(5):275–277, 1983.

Rozycki, T.J., "Oral and rectal temperatures in runners." *Physician and Sportsmedicine* 12(6):105–108, 1984a.

_____, "Reply." *Physician and Sportsmedicine* 12(10):15, 1984b.

Sadat, M., Kutty, M.S., and Corea, J.R., "Deep vein thrombosis in a jogger." *American Journal of Sports Medicine* 12(2):169, 1984.

Schaffer, C.F., "Possible teratogenic hyperthermia and marathon running." *Journal of the American Medical Association* 241(18):1892, 1979.

Schrier, R.W., Hano, J., and Keller, H.I., "Renal, metabolic, and circulatory responses to heat and exercise: Studies in military recruits during summer training, with implications for acute renal failure." *Annals of Internal Medicine* 73:213, 1970.

Sheehan, G., "Diary of an injured runner." *Physician and Sportsmedicine* 12(11):37, 1984a.

_____, "When should the race end?" *Physician and Sportsmedicine* 12(10):41, 1984b.

_____, "Licensed to race." *Physician and Sportsmedicine* 10(8):41, 1982.

Sherwood, B.K., and Strong, W.B., "Heat stress in athletes." *Journal of the Medical Association of Georgia* 74(7):478–480, 1985.

Shields, C.L., "Achilles tendon injuries and disabling conditions." *Physician and Sportsmedicine* 10(12):77–84, 1982.

Shively, R. A., Grana, W.A., and Ellis, D., "High school sports injuries." *Physician and Sportsmedicine* 9(8):46–50, 1981.

Shyne, K., "Runners who know limits avoid serious injuries." *Physician and Sportsmedicine* 11(1):26, 1983.

Siegel, A.J., "Reply." *Journal of the American Medical Association* 242(15):1610, 1979.

————, French, W.J., and Roberts, W.C., "Spontaneous exercise testing: Running as an early unmasker of underlying cardiac amyloidosis." *Archives of Internal Medicine* 142:345, 1982.

————, Hennekens, C.H., Solomon, H.S., and VanBoeckel, B., "Exercise-related hematuria: Findings in a group of marathon runners." *Journal of the American Medical Association* 241(4):391–392, 1979.

Siscovick, D.S., Weiss, N.S., Fletcher, R.H., and Lasky, T., "The incidence of primary cardiac arrest during vigorous exercise." *New England Journal of Medicine* 311(14):874–877, 1984.

————, ————, Hallstrom, A.P., Inui, T.S., and Peterson, D.R., "Physical activity and primary cardiac arrest." *Journal of the American Medical Association* 248:3113–3117, 1982.

Smart, G.W., Taunton, J.E., and Clement, D.B., "Achilles tendon disorders in runners — a review." *Medicine and Science in Sports* 12(4):231–243, 1980.

Smith, W.B., "Environmental factors in running." *American Journal of Sports Medicine* 8(2):138–140, 1980.

Sohn, R.S., and Micheli, L.J., "The effect of running on the pathogenesis of osteoarthritis of the hips and knees." *Clinical Orthopaedics and Related Research* 198(September):106–109, 1985.

Solomon, E.P., and Davis, W.P., *Human Anatomy and Physiology.* New York: Saunders College Publishing, 1983.

Spector, F.C., Karlin, J.M., DeValentine, S., Scurran, B.L., and Silvani, S.L., "Spinal fracture of the distal tibia: An unusual stress fracture." *Journal of Foot Surgery* 22(4):358–361, 1983.

Sperryn, P.N., "Medical problems in marathons." *Australian Family Physician* 14(9):903–904, 1985.

————, and Restan, L., "Podiatry and the sports physician — an evaluation of orthoses." *British Journal of Sports Medicine* 17(4):129–134, 1983.

Stamford, B., "A 'stitch' in the side." *Physician and Sportsmedicine* 13(5):187, 1985.

————, "Choosing shoes for your sport." *Physician and Sportsmedicine* 12(10)):191, 1984.

————, "Avoiding and recovering from overtraining." *Physician and Sportsmedicine* 11(10):180, 1983.

Stansbie, D., Tomlinson, K., Putman, J.M., and Walters, E.G., "Hypothermia, hyperkalaemia, and marathon running." *Lancet* (December 11):1336, 1982.

Stauffer, L.W., "Skin disorders in athletes: Identification and management." *Physician and Sportsmedicine* 11(3):101–119, 1983.

Stewart, J.G., Ahlquist, D.A., McGill, D.B., Ilstrup, D.M., Schwartz, S., and Owen, R.A., "Gastrointestinal blood loss and anemia in runners." *Annals of Internal Medicine* 100(6):843–845, 1984.

Stewart, P.J., and Posen, G.A., "Case report: Acute renal failure following a marathon." *Physician and Sportsmedicine* 8(4):61–63, 1980.

Stirt, J.A., "Jogging your way through CPR." *Journal of the American Medical Association* 249(14):1827, 1983.

Subotnick, S.I., "The flat foot." *Physician and Sportsmedicine* 9(8):85–88, 1981.

Sugishita, Y., Matsuda, M., Iida, K., Koshinaga, J., and Ueno, M., "Sudden cardiac death at exertion." *Japanese Circulation Journal* 47:562–572, 1983.

Sullivan, S.N., "The effect of running on the gastrointestinal tract." *Journal of Clinical Gastroenterology* 6(5):461–465, 1984.

————, "The gastrointestinal symptoms of running." *New England Journal of Medicine* 304(15):915, 1981.

————, Champion, M.C., Christofides, N.D., Adrian, T.E., and Bloom, S.R., "Gastrointestinal regulatory peptide responses in long-distance runners." *Physician and Sportsmedicine* 12(7):77–82, 1984.

Sutker, A.N., Jackson, D.W., and Pagliano, J.W., "Lliotibial band syndrome in distance runners." *Physician and Sportsmedicine* 9(10):69–73, 1981.

Sutton, J.R., "Fun runs, safe runs." *Physician and Sportsmedicine* 12(7):38–40, 1984a.

————, "Not so fun run." *Medical Journal of Australia* 141(12–13):782–783, 1984b.

————, "The chilliness of a long-distance runner." *Lancet* I(March 12):600, 1983.

————, "Heatstroke from running." *Journal of the American Medical Association* 243(19):1896, 1980.

————, "43°C in fun runners!" *Medical Journal of Australia* 2(9)):463–464, 1979.

————, "Community jogging vs arduous racing." *New England Journal of Medicine* 286(17):951, 1978.

————, and Bar-Or, O., "Thermal illness in fun running." *American Heart Journal* 100(6):778–781, 1980.

Taunton, J.E., Clement, D.B., and McNicol, K., "Plantar fasciitis in runners." *Canadian Journal of Applied Sport Science* 7(1):41–44, 1982.

————, ————, and Webber, D., "Lower extremity stress fractures in athletes." *Physician and Sportsmedicine* 9(1):77–86, 1981.

Tehranzadeh, J., Kurth, L.A., Elyaderani, M.K., and Bowers, K.D., "Combined pelvic stress fracture and avulsion of the adductor longus in a middle-distance runner." *American Journal of Sports Medicine* 10(2):108–111, 1982.

Temple, C., "Hazards of jogging and marathon running." *British Journal of Hospital Medicine* 17(March):237–240, 1983.

Thompson, P.D., "Cardiovascular hazards of physical activity." *Exercise and Sport Sciences Review* 10:208–235, 1982.

————, Funk, E.J., Carleton, R.A., and Sturner, W.Q., "Incidence of death during jogging in Rhode Island from 1975 through 1980." *Journal of the American Medical Association* 247(18):2535–2538, 1982.

————, and Mitchell, J.H., "Exercise and sudden cardiac death." *New England Journal of Medicine* 311(14):914–915, 1984.

————, Stern, M.P., Williams, P., Duncan, K., Haskell, W.L., and Wood, P.D., "Death during jogging or running: A study of 18 cases." *Journal of the American Medical Association* 242(12):1265–1267, 1979.

Travis, S.P.L., "Dehydration in marathon runners." *Lancet* II(July 18):155, 1981.

————, and Templer, M.L., "Carboloading and dehydration." *Lancet* II(June 20):1370–1371, 1981.

U.S. Bureau of the Census, *Statistical Abstracts of the United States.* Washington, D.C.: United States Government Printing Office, 1985.

Valliant, P.M., "Injury and personality traits in non-competitive runners." *Journal of Sports Medicine* 20:341–346, 1980.

Virmani, R., Robinowitz, M., and McAllister, H.A., "Nontraumatic death in joggers." *American Journal of Medicine* 72(June):874–882, 1982.
Votapka, T., and Weigel, J.W., "Runner's hematuria." *Kansas Medicine*
86(4):117–118, 1985.
Wade, C.E., Dressendorfer, R.H., O'Brien, J.C., and Claybaugh, J.R., "Overnight
basal urinary findings during a 500km race over 20 days." *Journal of Sports
Medicine* 22:371–375, 1982.
Waller, B.F., Csere, R.S., Baker, W.P., and Roberts, W.C., "Structure—function
correlations in cardiovascular and pulmonary diseases (CPC)." *Chest*
79(3):346–349, 1981.
_____, George, K.T., Olson, J.F., and King, A.D., "Severe aortic-valve stenosis
unmasked by amateur running." *Catheterization and Cardiovascular Diagnosis*
10:233–236, 1984.
_____, and Roberts, W.C., "Sudden death while running in conditioned runners
aged 40 years or over." *American Journal of Cardiology* 45:1292–1300, 1980.
Warhol, M.J., Siegel, A.J., Evans, W.J., and Silverman, L.M., "Skeletal muscle injury and repair in marathon runners after competition." *American Journal of
Pathology* 118(2):331–339, 1985.
Wells, T.D., Jessup, G.T., and Langlotz, K.S., "Effects of sunscreen use during exercise in the heat." *Physician and Sportsmedicine* 12(6):132–142, 1984.
Weltman, A., and Stamford, B., "Beware when exercising in the heat." *Physician
and Sportsmedicine* 11(5):171, 1983a.
_____, and _____, "How to recognize and treat heat disorders." *Physician and
Sportsmedicine* 11(6):201, 1983b.
_____, and _____, "Coping with heat stress in preseason football." *Physician
and Sportsmedicine* 11(8):179, 1983c.
_____, and _____, "Exercising safely in winter." *Physician and Sportsmedicine*
10(1):130, 1982.
Whisnant, J.D., "Exercise-related hematuria." *Journal of the American Medical
Association* 242(15):1610, 1979.
Whiting, P.H., Maughan, R.J., MIller, J.D.B., and Leiper, J.D., "Popular
marathons: Forecasting casualties." *British Medical Journal* 286:395, 1983.
Whitworth, J.A.G., and Wolfman, M.J., "Fatal heat stroke in a long distance run-
ner." *British Medical Journal* 287(October 1):948, 1983.
Williams, A.F., "When motor vehicles hit joggers: An analysis of 60 cases." *Public
Health Reports* 96(5):448–451, 1981a.
_____, "Making the runner safe from the hazards of the road." *Runner's World*
16(8):40–42, 1981b.
Williams, J.A., Wagner, J., Wasnich, R., and Heilbrun, L., "The effect of long-
distance running upon appendicular bone mineral content." *Medicine and
Science in Sports and Exercise* 16(3):223–227, 1984.
Williamson, M.R., "Anemia in runners and other athletes." *Physician and Sports-
medicine* 9(6):73–76, 1981.
Wishnitzer, R., Vorst, E., and Berrebi, A., "Bone marrow iron depression in com-
petitive distance runners." *International Journal of Sports Medicine* 4:27–30,
1983.
Woodhouse, S.P., Anderson, K.R., and Mulheron, D.J., "Sudden death of a young
man during a sponsored jogging event." *New Zealand Medical Journal*
91(June 25):454–456, 1980.
Worthen, D.M., "Retinal detachment and jogging." *Ophthalmic Surgery*
11(4):253–255, 1980.
Yamamoto, L., Yano, K., and Rhodes, G.G., "Characteristics of joggers among
Japenese men in Hawaii." *American Journal of Public Health* 73:147–152,
1983.

6. Psychological Aspects

Aamodt, M.G., Alexander, C.J., and Kimbrough, W.W., "Personality characteristics of college athletes and non-athletes and baseball, football, and track team members." *Perceptual and Motor Skills* 55:327–330, 1982.

Akil, H., Mayer, D.J., and Liebeskind, J.C., "Antagonism of stimulation-producing analgesia by naloxone, a narcotic antagonist." *Science* 191(March 5): 961–962, 1976.

Allen, M.E., "The runner's calm." *Journal of the American Medical Association* 248(23):3094, 1982.

Anshel, M.H., "Effects of sexual activity on athletic performance." *Physician and Sportsmedicine* 9(8):65–68, 1981.

Anthrop, J., and Allison, M.T., "Role conflict and the high school female athlete." *Research Quarterly* 54(2):104–111, 1983.

Appenzeller, O., "What makes us run?" *New England Journal of Medicine* 305(10)578–580, 1981.

Baekeland, F., "Exercise deprivation." *Archives of General Psychiatry* 22(April):365–369, 1970.

Banister, E.W., and Griffiths, J., "Blood levels of adrenergic amines during exercise." *Journal of Applied Physiology* 33(5):674–676, 1972.

Berger, B.G., and Mackenzie, M.M., "A case of a woman jogger: A psychodynamic analysis." *Journal of Sport Behavior* 3(1):3–16, 1980.

Berger, R.A., and Littlefield, D.H., "Comparison between football athletes and nonathletes on personality." *Research Quarterly* 40(4):663–665, 1969.

Bloom, F., Segal, D., Ling, N., and Guillemin, R., "Endorphins: Profound behavioral effects in rats suggest new etiological factors in mental illness." *Science* 194(November 5):630–632, 1976.

Booth, E.G., "Personality traits of athletes as measured by the MMPI." *Research Quarterly* 29(1):127–138, 1958.

Bortz, W., "The runner's high." *Runner's World* 17(4):58–59, 88, 1982.

Brennan, J., and Long, J.V.F., "A running therapy." *Journal of Psychedelic Drugs* 11(3):243–245, 1979.

Brennan, M.A., "Comparison of female dancers, gymnasts, athletes, and untrained subjects on selected characteristics." *Perceptual and Motor Skills* 51:252, 1980.

Browman, C.P., "Physical activity as a therapy for psychopathology: A reappraisal." *Journal of Sports Medicine* 21:192–197, 1981.

Brown, E.Y., Morrow, J.R., and Livingston, S.M., "Self-concept changes in women as a result of running." *Journal of Sport Psychology* 4:354–363, 1982.

Brunner, B.C., "Personality and motivating factors influencing adult participation in physical activity." *Research Quarterly* 40(3):464–469, 1969.

Buccola, V.A., and Stone, W.J., "Effects of jogging and cycling programs on physiological and personality variables in aged men." *Research Quarterly* 46(2):134–139, 1975.

Buchsbaum, M.S., Davis, G.C., and Bunney, W.E., "Naloxone alters pain perception and somatosensory evoked potential in normal subjects." *Nature* 270(December 15):620–622, 1977.

Callen, K.E., "Mental and emotional aspects of long-distance running." *Psychosomatics* 24(2):133–151, 1983.

Carmack, M., and Martens R., "Measuring commitment to running: A survey of runner's attitudes and mental status." *Journal of Sport Psychology* 1:25–42, 1979.

Carr, D.B., Bergland, R., Hamilton, A., Blume, H., Kasting, N., Arnold, M., Martin, J.B., and Rosenblatt, M., "Endotoxin-stimulated opioid peptide secretion: Two secretory pools and feedback control in vivo." *Science* 217(August 27):845–848, 1982.

_____, Bullen, B.A., Skrinar, G.S., Arnold, M.A., Rosenblatt, M., Beitins, I.Z., Martin, J.B., and McArthur, J.W., "Physical conditioning facilitates the exercise-induced secretion of beta-endorphin and beta-lipotropins in women." *New England Journal of Medicine* 305(10):560–563, 1981.

Carter, G.C., and Shannon, J.R., "Adjustment and personality traits of athletes and non-athletes." *School Review* 48(2):127–130, 1940.

Chung, S., and Dickenson, A., "Pain, enkephalin and acupuncture." *Nature* 283(January 17):243–244, 1980.

Clitsome, T., and Kostrubala, T., "A psychological study of 100 marathoners using the Myers-Briggs type indicator and demographic data." *Annals of the New York Academy of Sciences* 301(October):1010–1019, 1977.

Cronan, T.L., and Howley, E.T., "The effect of training on epinephrine and norepinephrine excretion." *Medicine and Science in Sports* 6(2):122–125, 1974.

Darden, E., "Sixteen personality factor profiles of competitive bodybuilders and weightlifters." *Research Quarterly* 43(2):142–147, 1972.

deVries, H.A., "Tranquilizer effect of exercise: A critical review." *Physician and Sportsmedicine* 9(11):47–55, 1981.

Driscoll, R., "Anxiety reduction using physical exertion and positive images." *Psychological Record* 26:87–94, 1976.

Feigley, D.A., "Psychological burnout in high-level athletes." *Physician and Sportsmedicine* 12(10):109–119, 1984.

Flanagan, L., "A study of some personality traits of different physical activity groups." *Research Quarterly* 22:312–323, 1951.

Folkins, C., "Effects of physical training on mood." *Journal of Clinical Psychology* 32(2):385–388, 1976.

_____, Lynch, S., and Gardner, M., "Psychological fitness as a function of physical fitness." *Archives of Physical Medicine and Rehabilitation* 53:503–8, 1972.

_____, and Sime, W.E., "Physical fitness training and mental health." *American Psychologist* 36(4):373–389, 1981.

_____, and Wieselberg-Bell, N., "A personality profile of ultramarathon runners: A little deviance may go a long way." *Journal of Sport Behavior* 4(3):119–127, 1981.

Fraioli, F., Moretti, C., Paolucci, D., Alicicco, E., Crescenzi, F., and Fortunio, G., "Physical exercise stimulates marked concomitant release of B-endorphin and adrenocorticotropic hormone (ACTH) in peripheral blood in man." *Experientia* 36:987–989, 1980.

Francis, K.T., and Carter, R., "Psychological characteristics of joggers." *Journal of Sports Medicine* 22(3):386–391, 1982.

Freischlag, J., "Selected psycho-social characteristics of marathoners." *International Journal of Sports Psychology* 12:282–288, 1981.

Gambert, S.R., Garthwaite, T.L., Pontzer, C.H., Cook, E.E., Tristani, F.E., Duthie, E.H., Martinson, D.R., Hagen, T.C., and McCarty, D.J., "Running elevates plasma b-endorphin immunoreactivity and ACTH in untrained human subjects." *Proceedings of the Society for Experimental Biology and Medicine* 168:1–4, 1981.

Goldstein, A., "Opioid peptides (Endorphins) in pituitary and brain." *Science* 193(September 17):1081–1086, 1976.

Gondola, J.C., and Tuckman, B.W., "Extent of training and mood enhancement in women runners." *Perceptual and Motor Skills* 57:333–334, 1983.

_____, and _____, "Psychological mood state in average marathon runners." *Perceptual and Motor Skills.* 55:1295–1300, 1982.

Gontang, A., Clitsome, T., and Kostrubala, T., "A psychological study of 50 sub-3-hour marathoners." *Annals of the New York Academy of Sciences* 301(October):1020–1027, 1977.

Gracely, R.H., Dubner, R., Wolskee, P.J., and Deeter, W.R., "Placebo and nalox-one can alter post-surgical pain by separate mechanisms." *Nature* 306(November 17):264–265, 1983.

Greist, J.H., Klein, M.H., Eischens, R.R., Faris, J., Gurman, A.S., and Morgan, W.P., "Running as treatment for depression." *Comprehensive Psychiatry* 20(1):41–54, 1979.

Grevert, P., and Goldstein, A., "Endorphins: Naloxone fails to alter experimental pain or mood in humans." *Science* 199(March 10):1093–1095, 1978.

Guillemin, R., Vargo, T., Rossier, J., Minick, S., Ling, N., Rivier, C., Vale, W., and Bloom, F., "B-Endorphin and adrenocorticotropin are secreted concomitantly by the pituitary gland." *Science* 197(September 30):1367–1369, 1977.

Guyot, G.W., Fairchild, L., and Hill, M., "Physical fitness and embedded figures test performance of elementary school children." *Perceptual Motor Skills* 50:411–414, 1980.

Hage, P., "Exercise 'dropout profile' aids program compliance." *Physician and Sportsmedicine* 9(12):27, 1981.

Hammer, W.M., and Wilmore, J., "An exploratory investigation in personality measures and physiological alterations during a 10-week jogging program." *Journal of Sports Medicine* 13:238–245, 1973.

Harris, M.B., "Runners' perceptions of the benefits of running." *Perceptual and Motor Skills* 52:153–154, 1981a.

———, "Women runners' views of running." *Perceptual and Motor Skills* 53:395–402, 1981b.

Hartley, L.H., Mason, J.W., Hogan, R.P., Jones, L.G., Kotchen, T.A., Mougey, E.H., Wherry, F.E., Pennington, L.L., and Ricketts, P.T., "Multiple hormonal responses to graded exercise in relation to physical training." *Journal of Applied Physiology* 33(5):602–606, 1972.

Hartung, G.H., and Farge, E.J., "Personality and physiological traits in middle-aged runners and joggers." *Journal of Gerontology* 32(5):541–548, 1977.

Hawkins, D.B., and Gruber, J.J., "Little league baseball and players' self-esteem." *Perceptual and Motor Skills* 55:1335–1340, 1982.

Henry, F., "Personality differences in athletes and physical education and aviation students." *Psychological Bulletin* 38:745, 1941.

Herbert, W., "Placebo: Killing pain without opiates." *Science News* 124(December 3):359, 1983.

———, "Melancholy genes." *Science News* 123(February 13):108–109, 1982.

Hosobuchi, Y., Adams, J.E., and Linchitz, R., "Pain relief by electrical stimulation of the central gray matter in humans and its reversal by naloxone." *Science* 197(July 8):183–186, 1977.

House, J.D., "Perception of voluntary control of cardiac function in distance runners and non-runners." *Perceptual and Motor Skills* 57:25–26, 1983.

Howley, E.T., "The effects of different intensities of exercise on the excretion of epinephrine and norepinephrine." *Medicine and Science in Sports* 8(4):219–222, 1976.

———, Skinner, J.S., Mendez, J., and Buskirk, E.R., "Effect of different intensities of exercise on catecholamine excretion." *Medicine and Science in Sports* 2(4):193–196, 1970.

Hughes, J., Smith, T.W., Kosterlitz, H.W., Fothergill, L.A., Morgan, B.A., and Morris, H.R., "Identification of two related pentapeptides from the brain with potent opiate agonist activity." *Nature* 258(December 18):577–579, 1975.

Hunt, D.H., "A cross-racial comparison of personality traits between athletes and nonathletes." *Research Quarterly* 40:704–707, 1969.

Ismail, A.H., and Trachtman, L.E., "Jogging the imagination." *Psychology Today* 6(March):79–82, 1973.

_____, and Young, R.J., "Effect of chronic exercise on the personality of adults."
    Annals of the New York Academy of Sciences 301(October):958–969, 1977.

Jette, M.., "Habitual exercisers: A blood serum and personality profile." *Journal of
    Sports Medicine* 3(1):12–17, 1975.

Joesting, J., "Affective changes before, during and after a 50-mile run." *Perceptual
    and Motor Skills* 52:162, 1981a.

_____, "Running and depression." *Perceptual and Motor Skills* 52:442, 1981b.

_____, "Comparison of personalities of athletes who sail with those who run."
    Perceptual and Motor Skills 52:514, 1981c.

_____, "Comparison of students who exercise with those who do not." *Perceptual
    and Motor Skills* 53:426, 1981d.

Johnsgard, K., Ogilvie, B., and Merritt, K., "The stress seekers: A psychological
    study of sports parachutists, racing drivers, and football players." *Journal of
    Sports Medicine* 15(2):158–169, 1975.

Johnson, W.R., Hutton, D.C., and Johnson, G.B., "Personality traits of some cham-
    pionship athletes as measured by two projective tests: Rorschach and H-T-P."
    Research Quarterly 25:484–485, 1954.

Jones, R.D., and Weinhouse, S., "Running as self therapy." *Journal of Sports
    Medicine* 19:397–404, 1979.

Jorgenson, C.B., and Jorgenson, D.E., "Effect of running on perception of self and
    others." *Perceptual and Motor Skills* 48:242, 1979.

Kangilaski, J., "B-endorphin levels lower in arthritis patients." *Journal of the
    American Medical Association* 246(3):203, 1981.

Kolata, G.B., "New drugs and the brain." *Science* 205(August 24):774–776, 1979.

Kotchen, T.A., Hartley, L.H., Rice, T.W., Mougey, E.H., Jones, L.G., and Mason,
    J.W., "Renin, norepinephrine, and epinephrine responses to graded exercise."
    Journal of Applied Physiology 31(2):178–184, 1971.

Kroll, W., "Sixteen personality factor profiles of collegiate wrestlers." *Research
    Quarterly* 38(1):49–57, 1967a.

_____, "Discriminant function and hierarchial grouping analysis of karate par-
    ticipants' personality profiles." *Research Quarterly* 38(3):405–411, 1967b.

_____, and Petersen, K.H., "Personality factor profiles of collegiate football
    teams." *Research Quarterly* 36(4):433–440, 1965.

Lakie, W.L., "Personality characteristics of certain groups of intercollegiate
    athletes." *Research Quarterly* 33(4):566–573, 1962.

Lampert, A., Nirenberg, M., and Klee, W., "Tolerance and dependence evoked by
    an endogenous opiate peptide." *Proceedings of the National Academy of Science
    USA* 73(9):3165–3167, 1976.

LaPlace, J.P., "Personality and its relationship to success in professional baseball."
    Research Quarterly 25(2):313–319, 1954.

Ledwidge, B., "Run for your mind: Aerobic exercise as a means of alleviating anxiety
    and depression." *Canadian Journal of Behavioral Science Review*
    12(2):126–140, 1980.

Levin, D.C., "In reply." *Journal of the American Medical Association* 249(1):21,
    1983.

_____, "The runner's high: Fact or fiction?" *Journal of the American Medical
    Association* 248(1):24, 1982.

Levine, J.D., Gordon, N.C., Jones, R.T., and Fields, H.L., "The narcotic an-
    tagonist naloxone enhances clinical pain." *Nature* 272(April 27):827–828, 1978.

Lewis, J.W., Cannon, J.T., and Liebeskind, J.C., "Opioid and nonopioid
    mechanisms of stress analgesia." *Science* 208(May 9):623–625, 1980.

_____, Tordoff, M.G., Sherman, J.E., and Liebeskind, J.C., "Adrenal medullary
    enkephalin-like peptides may mediate opioid stress analgesia." *Science*
    217(August 6):557–559, 1982.

Little, J.C., "Neurotic illness in fitness fanatics." *Psychiatric Annals* 9(3):48–56, 1979.

_____, "The athlete's neurosis—a deprivation crisis." *Acta Psychiatrica Scandinavica* 45:187–197, 1969.

Lion, L.S., "Psychological effects of jogging: A preliminary study." *Perceptual and Motor Skills* 47:1215–1218, 1978.

McKelvie, S.J., and Huband, D.E., "Locus of control and anxiety in college athletes and non-athletes." *Perceptual and Motor Skills* 50:819–822, 1980.

McLeavey, B.C., Corkery, M.B., and Cronin, T.E., "The marathon runner: Profile of health or vulnerable personality." *Irish Medical Journal* 77(2):37–39, 1984.

MacLennan, A.J., Drugan, R.C., Hyson, R.L., Maier, S.F., Madden, J., and Barchas, J.D., "Corticosterone: A critical factor in an opioid form of stress-induced analgesia." *Science* 215(March 19):1530–1532, 1982.

McMurray, R.G., Sheps, D.S., and Guinan, D.M., "Effects of naloxone on maximal stress testing in females." *Journal of Applied Physiology* 56(2):436–440, 1984.

Markoff, R.A., Ryan, P., and Young, T., "Endorphins and mood changes in long-distance running." *Medicine and Science in Sports and Exercise* 14(1):11–15, 1982.

Martin, J., "In activity therapy, patients literally move toward mental health." *Physician and Sportsmedicine* 5(7):85–89, 1977.

Marx, J.L., "Neurobiology: Researchers high on endogenous opiates." *Science* 193(September 24):1227–1229, 1976.

_____, "Opiate receptors: Implications and applications." *Science* 189(August 29):708–710, 1975.

Miczek, K.A., Thompson, M.L., and Shuster, L., "Opiod-like analgesia in defeated mice." *Science* 215(March 19):1520–1522, 1982.

Mikel, K.V., "Extraversion in adult runners." *Perceptual and Motor Skills* 57:143–146, 1983.

Moore, M., "Endorphins and exercise: A puzzling relationship." *Physician and Sportsmedicine* 10(2):111–114, 1982.

Morgan, W.P., "The trait psychology controversy." *Research Quarterly* 51(1):50–76, 1980.

_____, "Negative addiction in runners." *Physician and Sportsmedicine* 7(2):57–70, 1979.

_____, "The mind of the marathoner." *Psychology Today* 12(April):38–49, 1978.

_____, "Selected psychological considerations in sport." *Research Quarterly* 45(4):375–390, 1974.

_____, "Physical working capacity in depressed and nondepressed psychiatric females: A preliminary study." *American Corrective Therapy Journal* 24(1):14–16, 1970.

_____, and Costill, D.L., "Psychological characteristics of the marathon runner." *Journal of Sports Medicine and Physical Fitness* 12:42–46, 1972.

_____, and Horstman, D.H., "Psychometric correlates of pain perception." *Perceptual and Motor Skills* 471:27–29, 1978.

_____, and Pollock, M.L., "Psychologic characterization of the elite distance runner." *Annals of the New York Academy of Sciences* 301(October):382–403, 1977.

_____, Roberts, J.A., Brand, F.R., and Feinerman, A.D., "Psychological effect of chronic physical activity." *Medicine and Science in Sports* 2(4):213–217, 1970.

_____, _____, and Feinerman, A.D., "Psychologic effect of acute physical activity." *Archives of Physical Medicine and Rehabilitation* 52(September):422–425, 1971.

Morley, J.E., "Food peptides." *Journal of the American Medical Society* 247(17):2379–2380, 1982.

Muller, B., and Armstrong, H.E., "A further note on the 'running treatment' for anxiety." *Psychotherapy: Theory, Research, and Practice* 12(4):385–387, 1975.

Naughton, J., Bruhn, J.G., and Lategola, M.T., "Effects of physical training on physiologic and behavioral characteristics of cardiac patients." *Archives of Physical Medicine and Rehabilitation* 49:131–137, 1968.

Orava, S., "About the strains caused by a marathon race to fitness joggers." *Journal of Sports Medicine* 17:49–57, 1977.

Orwin, A., "Treatment of a situational phobia — a case for running." *British Journal of Psychiatry* 125:95–98. 1974.

_____, "The running treatment: A preliminary communication on a new use for an old therapy (physical activity) in the agoraphobic syndrome." *British Journal of Psychiatry* 122:175–179, 1973.

Pargman, D., and Baker, M.C., "Running high: Enkephalin indicated." *Journal of Drug Issues* 10(3):341–349, 1980.

Partin, C., "Runner's high." *Journal of the American Medical Association* 249(1):21, 1983.

Penny, G.D., and Rust, J.O., "Effect of a walking-jogging program on personality characteristics of middle-aged females." *Journal of Sports Medicine* 20:221–226, 1980.

Percy, L.E., Dziuban, C.D., and Martin, J.B., "Analysis of effects of distance running on self-concepts of elementary students." *Perceptual and Motor Skills* 52:42, 1981.

Pert, C.B., and Snyder, S.H., "Opiate receptors: Demonstration in nervous tissue." *Science* 179(March 9):1011–1013, 1973.

Peterson, S.L., Weber, J.C., and Trousdale, W.W., "Personality traits of women in team sports vs. women in individual sports." *Research Quarterly* 38(4):686–690, 1967.

Ransford, C.P., "A role for amines in the antidepressant effect of exercise: A review." *Medicine and Science in Sports and Exercise* 14(1):1–10, 1982.

Rasch, P.J., and O'Connell, E.R., "TPS scores of experienced karate students." *Research Quarterly* 34(1):108–119, 1963.

Rheingold, H., "Endorphins: An emotional story." *Esquire* 99(May):140–141, 1983.

Riddle, P.K., "Attitudes, beliefs, behavioral intentions, and behaviors of women and men toward regular jogging." *Research Quarterly* 51(4):663–674, 1980.

Robbins, J.M., and Joseph, P., "Commitment to running: Implications for the family and work." *Sociological Symposium* 30(Spring):87–108, 1980.

Rossier, J., French, E.D., Rivier, C., Ling, N., Guillemin, R., and Bloom, F.E., "Foot-shock induced stress increases B-endorphin in blood but not brain." *Nature* 270(December 15):618–620, 1977.

Roth, E., "Running to lift the spirits." *American Education* 17(May):30, 1981.

Sachs, M.L., and Pargman, D., "Running addiction: A depth interview examination." *Journal of Sports Behavior* 2:143–155, 1979.

Sage, G.H., and Loudermilk, S., "The female athlete and role conflict." *Research Quarterly* 50(1):88–96, 1979.

Schendel, J., "Psychological differences between athletes and nonparticipants in athletics at three educational levels." *Research Quarterly* 36(1):52–67, 1965.

Sharp, M.W., and Reilley, R.R., "The relationship of aerobic physical fitness to selected personality traits." *Journal of Clinical Psychology* 31:428–430, 1975.

Sheehan, G., "The 'runner's high.'" *Physician and Sportsmedicine* 12(1):39, 1984.

_____, "The best therapy." *Physician and Sportsmedicine* 11(7):43, 1983.

Singer, R.N., "Personality differences between and within baseball and tennis players." *Research Quarterly* 40(3):582–588, 1969.

Skrinar, G.S., and Ingram, S.P., "Effect of endurance training on perceived exertion and stress hormones in women." *Perceptual and Motor Skills* 57:1239–1250, 1983.

Slusher, H.S., "Personality and intelligence characteristics of selected high school athletes and nonathletes." *Research Quarterly* 35(4):539–545, 1964.

Smith, L.R., "Joggers, runners, and racers." *Journal of the American Medical Association* 249(17):2329, 1983.

Snyder, E.E., and Spreitzer, E., "Socialization comparisons of adolescent female athletes and musicians." *Research Quarterly* 49(3):342–349, 1978.

Snyder, S.H., "The opiate receptor and morphine-like peptides in the brain." *American Journal of Psychiatry* 135(6):645–652, 1978.

_____, "Opiate receptors and internal opiates." *Scientific American* 236(3):44–56, 1977.

Sperling, A.P., "The relationship between personality adjustment and achievement in physical education activities." *Research Quarterly* 13:351–363, 1942.

Straw, W.E., "Runner's 'hi.'" *Journal of the American Medical Association* 248(23):3094–3095, 1982.

Steinberg, S., "Endorphins: New types and sweet links." *Science News* 124(August 22):136, 1983.

Summers, J.J., Machin, V.J., and Sargent, G.I., "Psychosocial factors related to marathon running." *Journal of Sports Psychology* 5:314–331, 1983.

Thaxton, L., "Physiological and psychological effects of short-term exercise addiction on habitual runners." *Journal of Sport Psychology* 4:73–80, 1982.

Thirer, J., and O'Donnell, L.A., "Female intercollegiate athletes' trait-anxiety level and performance in a game." *Perceptual and Motor Skills* 50:18, 1980.

Thune, J.B., "Personality of weightlifters." *Research Quarterly* 20:296–306, 1949.

Tu, J., and Rothstein, A.L., "Improvement of jogging performance through application of personality specific motivational techniques." *Research Quarterly* 50(1):97–103, 1979.

Valliant, P.M., "Personality and injury in competitive runners." *Perceptual and Motor Skills* 53:251–253, 1981.

_____, "Injury and personality traits in non-competitive runners." *Journal of Sports Medicine* 20:341–346, 1980.

_____, Bennie, F.A.B., and Valiant, J.J., "Do marathoners differ from joggers in personality profile: A sports psychology approach." *Journal of Sports Medicine* 21:62–67, 1981.

_____, Simpson-Housley, P., and McKelvie, S.J., "Personality in athletic and non-athletic college groups." *Perceptual and Motor Skills* 52:963–966, 1981.

Volavka, J., Mallya, A., Baig, S., and Perez-Cruet, J., "Naloxone in chronic schizophrenia." *Science* 196(June 10):1227–1228, 1977.

Wagemaker, H., and Goldstein, L., "The runner's high." *Journal of Sports Medicine* 20(2):227–229, 1980.

Watkins, L.R., and Mayer, D.J., "Organization of endogenous opiate and nonopiate pain control systems." *Science* 216(June 11):1185–1192, 1982.

Watson, S.J., Khachaturian, H., Akil, H., Coy, D.H., and Goldstein, A., "Comparison of the distribution of dynorphin systems and enkephalin systems in the brain." *Science* 218(December 10):1134–1136, 1982.

Wei, E., and Loh, H., "Physical dependence on opiate-like peptides." *Science* 193(February 2):1262–1263, 1976.

Weinstein, W.S., and Meyers, A.W., "Running as treatment for depression: Is it worth it?" *Journal of Sport Psychology* 5:288–301, 1983.

Weltman, A., and Stamford, B., "Psychological effects of exercise." *Physician and Sportsmedicine* 11(1):175, 1983.

Wendt, D.T., and Patterson, T.W., "Personality characteristics of women in intercollegiate competition." *Perceptual and Motor Skills* 38:861–862, 1974.

Wilson, V.E., Berger, B.G., and Bird, E.I., "Effects of running and of an exercise class on anxiety." *Perceptual and Motor Skills* 53:472–474, 1981.

_____, Morley, N.C., and Bird, E.I., "Mood profiles of marathon runners, joggers and non-exercisers." *Perceptual and Motor Skills* 50:117–118, 1980.

Wood, D.T., "The relationship between anxiety state and acute physical activity." *American Corrective Therapy Journal* 31(May–June):67–69, 1977.

Worringham, C.J., and Messick, D.M., "Social facilitation of running: An unobtrusive study." *Journal of Social Psychology* 121:23–29, 1983.

Young, M.L., and Cohen, D.A., "Self-concept and injuries among female high school basketball players." *Journal of Sports Medicine* 21:55–61, 1981.

Young, R.J., and Ismail, A.H., "Personality differences of adult men before and after a physical fitness program." *Research Quarterly* 47(3):513–519, 1976.

Ziegler, S.G., Klinzing, J., and Williamson, K., "The effects of two stress management training programs on cardiorespiratory efficiency." *Journal of Sport Psychology* 4:280–289, 1982.

Zindler-Wernet, P., and Bailey, J.T., "Coping with stress through an 'on-site' running program for Stanford ICU nurses." *Journal of Nursing Education* 19(6):34–37, 1980.

7. *Athletics and Longevity*

Anderson, W.G., "Further studies in the longevity of Yale athletes." *Mind and Body: A Monthly Journal Devoted to Physical Education* 23(Dec.):374–378, 1916.

_____, "Some observations on mortality among Yale students." *Medical Times* 40(February):32–34, 1912.

Babbitt, J.A., "Physical dangers in football and other sports." *Medical Times* 40(February):36–37, 1912.

Bassler, T.J., "Hazards of restrictive diets." *Journal of the American Medical Association* 252(4):483, 1984a.

_____, "Cardiomythology." *Lancet* I(April 7):788–789, 1984b.

_____, "Letter to editor." *Lancet* II(September 30):711–712, 1972.

Blair, S.N., Goodyear, N.N., Gibbons, L.W., and Cooper, K.H., "Physical fitness and incidence of hypertension in healthy normotensive men and women." *Journal of the American Medical Association* 252(4):487–490, 1984.

Bowler, J.W., "Cure for athletic ills." *Medical Times* 40(March):61–62, 1912.

Brown, K.S., "A critique of several epidemiological studies of physical activity and its relationship to aging, health, and mortality." *Annals of the New York Academy of Sciences* 301:703–719, 1977.

Brown, L., "Athletic exercise must be continued." *Medical Times* 40(February):38–39, 1912.

Busse, E.W., and Maddox, G.L., *The Duke Longitudinal Studies of Normal Aging.* New York: Springer, 1985.

Clapp, R.G., "The effects of athletics on participants." *Medical Times* 40(March):64–65, 1912.

Cooper, E.L., O'Sullivan, J., and Hughes, E., "Athletics and the heart: An electrocardiographic and radiological study of the response of the healthy and diseased heart to exercise." *Medical Journal of Australia* I(16):569–579, 1937.

Crandall, R., "A study on joggers 55+ years of age." Paper presented at the Western Gerontological Society Meeting in San Diego, CA, 1982.

Dublin, L.I., "College honor men live longer." *Statistical Bulletin of the Metropolitan Life Insurance Company* 13:5–7, 1932.

_____, "College-bred men are found to live longer than others." *New York Times* July 20, 1930.

_____, "Longevity of college athletes." *Harpers* 157(July):229–238, 1928.

Duffy, J., *Epidemics in Colonial America*. Baton Rouge: Louisiana State University Press, 1979.

Estes, W.L., "A radical change is needed." *Medical Times* 40(February):35–36, 1912.

Fardy, P.S., "Cardiovascular function in former athletes." *Physician and Sportsmedicine* 6(8):35–40, 1978.

Greenway, J.C., and Hiscock, I.V., "Mortality among Yale athletes." *Yale Alumni Weekly* 35(June):1086–1088, 1926.

Gwathmey, J.A., "Our system of physical training wrong." *Medical Times* 40(February):37–38, 1912.

Harries, M., "Deaths of athletes." *British Medical Journal* 290(March 2):656, 1985.

Hartley, P.H.S., and Llewellyn, G.F., "The longevity of oarsmen: A study of those who rowed in the Oxford and Cambridge boat race from 1829 to 1928." *British Medical Journal* I(April 1):657–662, 1939.

Hein, F.V., "Life expectancy of Ivy League rowing crews." *Journal of the American Medical Association* 205(9):106, 1968.

Hill, A.B., "Cricket and its relation to the duration of life." *Lancet* II(October 29):949–950, 1927.

Kaplan, N.M., "Joggers may live longer...." *Journal of the American Medical Association* 252(4):528, 1984.

Karpovich, P.V., "Longevity and athletics." *Research Quarterly* 12(May 12):451–455, 1941.

Karvonen, M.J., "Endurance sports, longevity, and health." *Annals of the New York Academy of Sciences* 301(October):653–655, 1977.

_____, Klemola, H., Virkajarvi, J., and Kekkonen, A., "Longevity of endurance skiers." *Medicine and Science in Sports* 6(1):49–51, 1974.

Khosi, T., "Longevity of athletes." *Lancet* II(December 16):1318, 1972.

Lampert, W.A., "No after effects among 1,100 men." *Medical Times* 40(February):38, 1912.

Largey, G., "Athletic activity and longevity." *Lancet* II(August 5):286, 1972.

McKenzie, R.T., "Athletes do not die prematurely from cardiac disease." *Medical Times* 40(March):67, 1912.

_____, "Relation of athletics to longevity." *Medical Examiner and General Practioner* 16(July):195–198, 1906.

McPherson, B.D., "Former professional athletes." *Physician and Sportsmedicine* 6(8):52–59, 1978.

Medical Times, "The effects of athletics on young men." *Medical Times* 40(February):32–38, 1912.

Metropolitan Life Insurance Company, "Longevity of major league baseball players." *Statistical Bulletin* (April):2–4, 1975.

Meylan, G.L., "The effects of athletics in later life." *Medical Times* 40(March): 63–64, 1912.

_____, "Discussion." *Medical Examiner and General Practioner* 16(July):198–199, 1906.

_____, "Harvard University oarsmen." *Harvard Graduates Magazine* 9(March):362–367, 543, 1904.

Montoye, H.J., "Health and longevity of former athletes." in W.R. Johnson and E.R. Buskirk (eds.), *Science and Medicine of Exercise and Sport* (second edition) (New York: Harper and Row, 1974), pp. 366–376.

_____,, Van Huss, W.D., and Nevai, J.W., "Longevity and morbidity of college athletes: A seven-year follow-up study." *Journal of Sports Medicine and Physical Fitness* 2(3):133–140, 1962.

_____, _____, Olson, H., Hudec, A., and Mahoney, E., "Study of the longevity and morbidity of college athletes." *Journal of the American Medical Association* 162:1132–1134, 1956.

Moorstein, B.E., "Life expectancy of Ivy League rowing crews." *Journal of the American Medical Association* 205(9):106, 1968.

Naismith, J., "The aftereffects of athletics." *Medical Times* 40(March):65–66, 1912.

Olson, H.W., Montoye, H.J., Sprague, H., Stephens, K., Van Huss, W.D., "The longevity and morbidity of college athletes." *Physician and Sportsmedicine* 6(8):62–65, 1978.

_____, Teitelbaum, H., Van Huss, W.D., and Montoye, H.J., "Years of sports participation and mortality in college athletes." *Journal of Sports Medicine* 17:321–326, 1977.

Paffenbarger, R.S., Hyde, R.T., Wing, A.L., and Hsieh, C.C., "Physical activity, all-cause mortality, and longevity of college alumni." *New England Journal of Medicine* 314(10):605–613, 1986.

_____, _____, _____, and Steinmetz, C.H., "A natural history of athleticism and cardiovascular health." *Journal of the American Medical Association* 252(4):491–495, 1984.

_____, Wing, A.L., Hyde, R.T., and Jung, D.L., "Physical activity and incidence of hypertension in college alumni." *American Journal of Epidemiology* 117(3):245–257, 1983.

_____, _____, and _____, "Physical activity as an index of heart attack risk in college alumni." *American Journal of Epidemiology* 108(3):161–175, 1978.

Palmore, E.B., "Predictors of the longevity differences.: A 25-year follow-up." *Gerontologist* 22(6):513–518, 1982.

_____, *Social Patterns in Normal Aging: Findings from the Duke Longitudinal Study.* Durham, NC: Duke University Press, 1981.

_____, "Predictors of longevity." in S.G. Haynes and M. Feinleib (eds.), *Epidemiology of Aging* (Washington, D.C.: U.S. Government Printing Office, 1980), pp. 57–64.

Phillips, P.C., "Athletics a benefit to the participants." *Medical Times* 40(February):36, 1912.

Polednak, A.P., "College athletics, body size, and cancer mortality." *Cancer* 38(7):382–387, 1976.

_____, "Previous health and longevity of male athletes." *Lancet* II(September 30):711, 1972a.

_____, "Longevity and cause of death among Harvard College athletes and their classmates." *Geriatrics* 27(October):53–64, 1972b.

_____, "Mortality from renal diseases among former college athletes." *Annals of Internal Medicine* 77:919–922, 1972c.

_____, "Longevity and cardiovascular mortality among former college athletes." *Circulation* 66(October):649–654, 1972d.

_____, and Damon, A., "College athletics, longevity, and cause of death." *Human Biology* 42(1):34–46, 1970.

Pomeroy, W.C., and White, P.D., "Coronary heart disease in former football players." *Journal of the American Medical Association* 167:711–714, 1958.

Prout, C., "Life expectancy of college oarsmen." *Journal of the American Medical Association* 220(13):1709–1711, 1972.

Quigley, T.B., "Life expectancy of Ivy League rowing crews." *Journal of the American Medical Association* 205(9):106, 1968.

Raycroft, J.E., "The aftereffects of competitive athletics." *Medical Times* 40(March):66, 1912.

Reed, D.B., "The aggregate aftereffects generally good." *Medical Times* 40(February):37, 1912.

Reed, L.J., "Longevity of army officers in relation to physical fitness." *Military Surgeon* 69(4):379–385, 1931.

Rich, V., "Mortality of Soviet athletes." *Nature* 311(Oct. 4):402–403, 1984.

Richardson, M.H., "No observation of permanent injuries." *Medical Times* 40(February):38, 1912.

Robinson, S., Dill, D.B., Robinson, R.D., Tzankoff, S.P., and Wagner, J.A., "Physiological aging of champion runners." *Journal of Applied Physiology* 41(1):46–51, 1976.

Rook, A., "An investigation inot the longevity of Cambridge sportsmen." *British Medical Journal* I(April 3):773–777, 1954.

Rose, C.L., and Cohen, M.L. "Relative importance of physical activity for longevity." *Annals of the New York Academy of Sciences* 301:671–701, 1977.

Ross, G.G., "Athletics have deleterious effect." *Medical Times* 40(February):38, 1912.

Rowland, K.F., "Environmental events predicting death for the elderly." *Psychological Bulletin* 84(2):349–352, 1977.

Sargent, D.A., "The results of athletics on college students." *Medical Times* 40(February):34–35, 1912.

_____, "Discussion." *Medical Examiner and General Practioner* 16(July):198–199, 1906.

Schmid, L., "Malignant tumours as causes of death of former athletes." *Journal of Sports Medicine* 15:117–124, 1975.

Schnohr, P., "Athletic activity and longevity." *Lancet* II(September 16):605, 1972.

_____, "Longevity and causes of death in male athletic champions." *Lancet* II(December 18):1364–1366, 1971.

Sharpe, A.H., "Football safe for physically qualified men." *Medical Times* 40(February):35, 1912.

Sheehan, G.A., "Longevity of athletes." *American Heart Journal* 86(September):425–426, 1973.

_____, "Athletic activity and longevity." *Lancet* II(November 4):974, 1972.

Shock, N., "Physical activity and the rate of aging." in A.P. Polednak (ed.), *The Longevity of Athletes* (Springfield, Ill: Charles C. Thomas, 1979), pp. 5–13.

Stamford, B., "Exercise and longevity." *Physician and Sportsmedicine* 12(6):209, 1984.

Stauffer, N.P., "The naval system at fault." *Medical Times* 40(March):67, 1912.

Stengel, A., "The immediate and remote effects of athletics upon the heart and circulation." *American Journal of the Medical Sciences* 79(November):544–553, 1899.

Taylor, W.N., *Anabolic Steroids and the Athlete.* Jefferson, NC: McFarland, 1982.

U.S. Bureau of the Census, *Statistical Abstracts of the United States: 1986.* Washington, D.C.: U.S. Government Printing Office, 1986.

_____, *Statistical Abstracts of the United States: 1982*–1983. Washington, D.C.: U.S. Government Printing Office, 1984.

_____, *Historical Abstracts of the United States, Colonial Times to 1970.* Washington, D.C.: U.S. Government Printing Office, 1970.

Wakefield, M.C., "A study of mortality among the men who have played in the Indiana high school state final basketball tournaments." *Research Quarterly* 15(March):2–11, 1944.

Westura, E.E., "Life expectancy of Ivy League rowing crews." *Journal of the American Medical Association* 205(9):106, 1968.

Wyeth, J.A., "Other forms of exercise preferable." *Medical Times* 40(February):38, 1912.

Yamaji, K., and Shephard, R.J., "Longevity and causes of death of athletes." *Journal of Human Ergology* 6(1):15–27, 1977.

Index

281